T0317489

SUCCESSFUL INVESTING IS A PROCESS

Since 1996, Bloomberg Press has published books for financial professionals on investing, economics, and policy affecting investors. Titles are written by leading practitioners and authorities, and have been translated into more than 20 languages.

The Bloomberg Financial Series provides both core reference knowledge and actionable information for financial professionals. The books are written by experts familiar with the work flows, challenges, and demands of investment professionals who trade the markets, manage money, and analyze investments in their capacity of growing and protecting wealth, hedging risk, and generating revenue.

For a list of available titles, please visit our web site at www.wiley.com/go/bloombergpress.

SUCCESSFUL INVESTING IS A PROCESS

Structuring Efficient Portfolios for Outperformance

Jacques Lussier

BLOOMBERG PRESS
An Imprint of
WILEY

Copyright © 2013 by Jacques Lussier

All rights reserved. No part of this work covered by the copyright herein may be reproduced or used in any form or by any means—graphic, electronic or mechanical—without the prior written permission of the publisher. Any request for photocopying, recording, taping or information storage and retrieval systems of any part of this book shall be directed in writing to The Canadian Copyright Licensing Agency (Access Copyright). For an Access Copyright license, visit www.accesscopyright.ca or call toll free 1-800-893-5777. For more information about Wiley products visit www.wiley.com.

Care has been taken to trace ownership of copyright material contained in this book. The publisher will gladly receive any information that will enable them to rectify any reference or credit line in subsequent editions.

The material in this publication is provided for information purposes only. Laws, regulations, and procedures are constantly changing, and the examples given are intended to be general guidelines only. This book is sold with the understanding that neither the author nor the publisher is engaged in rendering professional advice. It is strongly recommended that legal, accounting, tax, financial, insurance, and other advice or assistance be obtained before acting on any information contained in this book. If such advice or other assistance is required, the personal services of a competent professional should be sought.

Library and Archives Canada Cataloguing in Publication Data

Lussier, Jacques
    Successful investing is a process : structuring efficient portfolios
for outperformance / Jacques Lussier.

Includes bibliographical references and index.
Issued also in electronic formats.
ISBN 978-1-118-45990-4

        1. Investments. 2. Portfolio management. 3. Finance, Personal.
I. Title.
HG4521.L8627 2013   332.6   C2012-906769-5

ISBN 978-1-118-46478-6 (eBk); 978-1-118-46479-3 (eBk);
978-1-118-46480-9 (eBk)

John Wiley & Sons Canada, Ltd.
6045 Freemont Blvd.
Mississauga, Ontario
L5R 4J3

Printed in Canada
1 2 3 4 5 FP 17 16 15 14 13

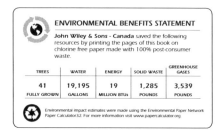

ENVIRONMENTAL BENEFITS STATEMENT

John Wiley & Sons - Canada saved the following resources by printing the pages of this book on chlorine free paper made with 100% post-consumer waste.

TREES	WATER	ENERGY	SOLID WASTE	GREENHOUSE GASES
41	19,195	19	1,285	3,539
FULLY GROWN	GALLONS	MILLION BTUs	POUNDS	POUNDS

Environmental impact estimates were made using the Environmental Paper Network Paper Calculator 3.2. For more information visit www.papercalculator.org

Contents

PART II: UNDERSTANDING THE DYNAMICS OF PORTFOLIO ALLOCATION AND ASSET PRICING   51

PART III: THE COMPONENTS OF AN EFFICIENT PORTFOLIO-ASSEMBLY PROCESS   113

Acknowledgments

I always say *Successful Investing Is a Process* is the one book I wish I could have read a long time ago, although even with the intent, I doubt it could have been written prior to 2007. So much relevant research has been completed in the last decade. Sadly, it also took the hard lessons learned from a financial crisis of unprecedented proportion in our generation to allow me to question some of my prior beliefs and thus enable and motivate me to write it over a period of more than two years. This book is not about the financial crisis, but the crisis did trigger my interest in questioning the value and nature of services provided by our industry with the hope that some changes may occur over time. It will not happen overnight.

Like most books, it is rarely completed without the help and encouragement of colleagues, friends and other professionals. I must first thank Hugues Langlois, a former colleague and brilliant young individual currently completing his Ph.D. at McGill University, for helping me identify the most relevant academic articles, review the integrity of the content and execute some of the empirical analyses that were required. His name appears often throughout the book. I must also thank Sofiane Tafat for coding a series of Matlab programs during numerous evenings and weekends over a period of eight months.

As I was completing the manuscript in 2012, I was also lucky enough to have it evaluated by a number of industry veterans. Among them, Charley Ellis, Nassim Taleb, Rob Arnott, Yves Choueifaty, Vinay Pande, Bruce Grantier, Arun Murhalidar, as well as several academicians. Some of these reviewers also provided me with as much as ten pages of detailed comments, which I was generally able to integrate into the book. Most of all, I considered it significant that they usually agreed with the general philosophy of the book.

I must not forget to thank Karen Milner at Wiley and Stephen Isaacs at Bloomberg Press for believing in this project. I probably had already completed eighty percent of its content before I initially submitted the book for publication in early 2012. I must also thank other individuals at Wiley that were involved in the editing and marketing: Elizabeth McCurdy, Lucas Wilk and Erika Zupko. Going through this process made me realize how much work is involved after the initial unedited manuscript is submitted. I was truly impressed with the depth of their work.

Finally, a sincere thank you to my wife Sandra, who has very little interest in the world of portfolio management, but nevertheless diligently corrected the manuscript two times prior to submission and allowed me the 1800 hours invested in this project during evenings, weekends and often, vacations. I hope she understands that I hope to complete at least two other book projects!

Preface

In principle, active management creates value for all investors. The financial analysis process that supports proper active management helps promote greater capital-allocation efficiency in our economy and improve long-term returns for all. However, the obsession of many investors with short-term performance has triggered, in recent decades, the development of an entirely new industry of managers and researchers who are dedicated to outperforming the market consistently over short horizons, although most have failed. Financial management has become a complex battle among experts, and even physicists and mathematicians have been put to the task. Strangely enough, the more experts there are, the less likely we are to outperform our reference markets once fees have been paid. This is because the marginal benefit of this expertise has certainly declined, while its cost has risen. As Benjamin Graham, the academician and well-known proponent of value investment, stipulated in 1976: "I am no longer an advocate of elaborate techniques of security analysis in order to find superior value opportunities . . . in light of the enormous amount of research being carried on, I doubt whether in most cases such extensive efforts will generate sufficiently superior selections to justify their cost [1]." If these were his thoughts 35 years ago, what would he say now?

Forecasting the performance of financial assets and markets is not easy. We can find many managers who will attest to having outperformed their reference markets, but how do we know that their past successes can be repeated, or that their success was appropriately measured? How many accomplished managers have achieved success by chance and not by design, or even have achieved success without truly understanding why? Much of the evidence over the past 40 years says that:

- there are strong conceptual arguments against consistent and significant outperformance by a great majority of fund managers and financial advisors (especially when adjusted for fees);
- many investors do not have the resources to do proper due diligence on fund managers and/or do not understand the qualities they should be looking for in a manager; and
- conflicts of interest, marketing prerogatives and our own psychological biases are making it difficult to exercise objective judgment when selecting and recommending managers. For example, what if a manager that should be considered for an

investment mandate underperformed for the last three years? Is he likely to be rec-ommended by advisors? Is he less likely to be selected than managers who recently outperformed?

I have worked 10 years as an academician, and more than 18 years in the financial industry. In my career, I have met with approximately 1,000 traditional and hedge fund managers, and have been involved in almost all areas of research that are relevant to investors today. Some managers should never have existed, a majority of them are good but unremarkable and a few are incredibly sophisticated (but, does sophis-tication guarantee superior performance?) and/or have good investment processes. However, once you have met with the representatives of dozens of management firms in one particular area of expertise, who declare that they offer a unique expertise and process (although their "uniqueness" argument sometimes seems very familiar), you start asking yourself: How many of these organizations are truly exceptional? How many have a unique investment philosophy and process, and a relative advantage that can lead to a strong probability of outperformance? I could possibly name 20 organi-zations that I believe to be truly unique, but many investors do not have access to these organizations. So what are investors supposed to do? There has got to be a more reliable and less costly investment approach.

One of the few benefits of experiencing a financial crisis of unprecedented scope (at least for our generation) is that all market players, even professionals, should learn from it. As the 2007 to 2008 credit/subprime/housing/structured product crises pro-gressed, I reflected on what we are doing wrong as an industry. I came up with three observations. First, the average investor, whether individual or institutional, is not provided with a strong and coherent investment philosophy. In 2009, I read an invest-ment book written by one of the most well-known financial gurus, someone whom is often seen on American television and covered in magazines and newspapers. The book was full of details and generalities, so many details that I wondered what an investor would actually do with all this information. What those hundreds of pages never offered was a simple investment philosophy that investors could use to build a strong and confident strategic process.

Second, there is the issue of fees. The financial and advisory industries need inves-tors to believe that investing is complex, and that there is significant value added in the advisory services being provided to investors. If it were simple, or perceived as simple, investors would be unwilling to pay high advisory fees. Investing is in fact complex (even for "professionals"), but the advice given to investors is often the same every-where. Let's first consider individual investors. They are usually being offered about six portfolio allocations to choose from, each one for a different investment risk profile. Some firms may offer target date funds, funds where the asset allocation (i.e., the mix between less risky and more risky assets) is modified over time (it gets more conserva-tive). Some will also offer guarantees, but guarantees are never cheap. There are several investment concepts, but in the end, they all seek to offer portfolios adapted to the economic and psychological profile of an investor and his goals. These may be good concepts, but even if we accept the argument that investing is complex, paying a high price to get similar advice and execution from most providers makes no sense. I often say that fees on financial products are not high because the products are complex, but that the products are complex because the fees are high. I could spend many pages just explaining this statement.

These comments can also be extended to institutional investors. The management concepts sold to these investors have evolved in the last two decades, but most advisory firms were offering similar concepts at any point in time. Investors were advised to incorporate alternative investments in the late 1990s and early 2000s (real estate, hedge funds, private equity, etc.). The focus moved to portfolio concepts that are structured around the separation of Beta and Alpha components, or Beta with an Alpha overlay, and then, as pension plans faced larger deficit funding, to liability-driven and performance-seeking portfolios, etc. Furthermore, investing in private and public infrastructure through debt or equity is now recommended to most investors. All of these initiatives had the consequence of supporting significant advisory/consulting fees, although, as indicated, the asset-management concepts offered to investors are not significantly differentiated among most advisors.

Third, most investors are impatient. We want to generate high returns over short horizons. Some will succeed, but most will fail. The business of getting richer faster through active management does not usually offer good odds to some investors. However, if we cannot significantly increase the odds of outperforming others over a short investment horizon, we can certainly increase those odds significantly in the medium to long term.

This book is not about using extremely complex models. Playing the investment game this way will put you head to head with firms that have access to significant resources and infrastructure. Furthermore, these firms may not even outperform their reference market. Just consider what happened to the Citadel investment group in 2008, one of the premier investment companies in the world, with vast financial resources that allowed it to hire the best talent and design/purchase the most elaborate systems. Citadel is a great organization, but their flagship fund still lost nearly 55%. As I indicated, strangely enough, the more smart people there are, the less likely it is that a group of smart people can outperform other smart people, and the more expensive smart management gets. Smart people do not work for cheap, and sometimes the so-called value added by smart people is at the expense of some hidden risks.

This book is about identifying the structural qualities/characteristics required within portfolio allocation processes to reliably increase the likelihood of excess performance. It is about learning from more than half a century of theoretical and empirical literature, and about learning from our experiences as practitioners. It is about providing statistically reliable odds of adding 1.5% to 2.0% of performance (perhaps more), on average, per year over a period of 10 years without privileged information. We seek to exploit the inefficiencies of traditional benchmarks, to introduce efficient portfolio management and rebalancing methodologies, to exploit the behavioral biases of investors and of corporate management, to build portfolios whose structure is coherent with liability-driven investment (LDI) concerns, to maximize the benefits of efficient tax planning (if required) and to effectively use the concept of diversification, whose potential is far greater than what is usually achieved in most investment programs (because diversification is not well understood). As we progress through each chapter of this book, we will realize that our objective is not so much to outperform the market, but to let the market underperform—a subtle but relevant nuance. Furthermore, this book will help you understand that the financial benefits of what is often marketed to investors as financial expertise can generally be explained through the implicit qualities that may be present in replicable investment processes.

This is why it is so important to understand the relevant qualities within portfolio-allocation processes that lead to excess performance. It will help segregate performances that result from real expertise (which is normally rare) from performances that are attributed to circumstantial or policy-management aspects. It will also help design efficient and less costly portfolio solutions. Thus, what is at stake is not only risk-adjusted expected performance, but the ability to manage, with a high level of statistical efficiency, assets of $100 billion with less than 20 front-office and research individuals.

Much of what I will present has been covered in financial literature (all references are specified), but has not, to my knowledge, been assembled nor integrated into a coherent global investment approach. I have also incorporated new research in several chapters when the existing literature is incomplete. Finally, the approach is not regime dependent nor is it client specific. An investment process adapts itself to the economic and financial regime (even in a low-interest-rate environment), not the other way around. An investment process should also apply similarly to the investment products offered to small retail, high-net-worth and institutional investors. Different constraints, financial means and objectives do not imply a different portfolio-management process. Service providers should not differentiate between smaller investors and larger investors on the basis of the quality of the financial products and the depth of the portfolio-management expertise being offered. However, larger investors should benefit from more adapted (less standardized) and less costly investment solutions. Therefore, this book is specifically designed for either institutional investors seeking to improve the efficiency of their investment programs, or for asset managers interested in designing more efficient global investment platforms for individual investors. It is also appropriate for sophisticated individual investors.

The book is divided into four parts and eleven chapters. Part I seeks to demystify the fund management industry and the belief that superior performance can only be obtained with superior analytical abilities. Chapter 1 makes the traditional argument that investing is a negative-sum game (after all fees) for the universe of investors, but also that it is likely to remain a negative-sum game even for specific subsets of investors (for example, mutual fund managers versus other institutional investors). Furthermore, the likelihood of outperforming the market may have declined over the past 30 years, as management fees and excessive portfolio turnover have increased. Chapter 2 illustrates that excess performance by asset managers is not proof of expertise, that successful managers may attribute their success to the wrong reasons (an argument that will be further developed in Chapter 6) and finally that some managers maintain systematic biases that explain much of their performance. Therefore, some investors could replicate those biases at a low cost. Finally, Chapter 3 discusses the inefficiency and instability of capitalization-based equity indices.

Part II introduces the four dimensions of the investment process, as well as basic notions and concepts about asset valuation and forecasting that are helpful in supporting the remainder of the book. For example, Chapter 4 emphasizes the importance of understanding that portfolio structural characteristics lead to more efficient diversification. It makes the argument that many idiosyncrasies of the financial world can be explained, at least in part, by a proper understanding of volatility and diversification. For example, why some studies support the existence of a risk premium in commodities while others do not, why low-volatility portfolios outperform in the long run, why equal-weight portfolios often perform very well, why hedge fund portfolios could appear attractive in the long run, even if there is no Alpha creation, etc. Finally, Chapter 5 explains why it is difficult to make explicit return forecasts and that investors should put more emphasis on predictive factors that can be explained by cognitive biases, since those variables are more likely to show persistence.

Part III explains how we can build portfolio components and asset-allocation processes that are statistically likely to outperform. It also discusses how taxation influences the asset allocation and asset location decision (for individual investors only). Thus, Part III introduces the core components of the proposed approach. Chapter 6 implicitly makes the argument that an equity portfolio is more likely to outperform if its assembly process incorporates specific structural characteristics/qualities. It also makes the argument that the portfolios of many successful managers may incorporate these characteristics, whether they are aware of it or not. Thus, if we have a proper understanding of these characteristics, we can build a range of efficient portfolios without relying on the expertise of traditional managers. Chapter 8 makes similar arguments, but for commodities, currencies and alternative investments. It also makes the argument that the performance of several asset classes, such as commodities and private equity, are exaggerated because of design flaws in the indices used to report their performance in several studies. The same may be true of hedge funds. Chapter 7 illustrates different methodologies, from simple to more sophisticated, that can be used to improve the efficiency of the asset-allocation process. It compares and explains the sources of the expected excess performance. All of these chapters provide detailed examples of implementation. Part III also incorporates a chapter on taxation (Chapter 9). Among the many topics covered, three are of significant importance. First, postponing/avoiding taxation may not be in the best interest of investors if it impedes the rebalancing process. Second, the tax harvesting of capital losses may not be as profitable as indicated by a number of studies. Third, equity portfolios can be built to be both structurally and tax efficient.

Finally Part IV integrates all of these notions into a coherent framework. It also illustrates the powerful impact on risk, return and matching to liabilities of applying the integrated portfolio-management philosophy discussed in this book. Chapter 10 describes how to build portfolios that are structurally coherent with LDI concerns. It explains that many of the concepts discussed in Chapters 6, 7 and 8 will lead to the design of portfolios that implicitly improve liability matching. Finally, Chapter 11 is a case study that incorporates many of the recommendations presented in this book. It shows that a well-designed investment process can significantly and reliably enhance performance and reduce risk. Furthermore, the book provides the foundations that can be used to build more performing processes.

However, it is important to recognize that most of the recommendations in this book are based on learning from the evidence already available, and that significant efforts are made to link the literature from different areas of finance. We have access to decades of relevant financial literature, and an even longer period of empirical observations. We have more than enough knowledge and experience to draw appropriate and relevant conclusions about the investment process. We simply have not been paying enough attention to the existing evidence.

Note

1. Graham, Benjamin (1976), "A conversation with Benjamin Graham," *Financial Analysts Journal* 32(5), 20–23.

Introduction

Investing has always been a challenge. It is only possible to understand the relevant "science" behind the investment structuring process once we understand that investing is also an art. Artwork takes different shapes and forms, and we can often appreciate different renditions of the same subject. Fortunately, the same is true of investing. There is more than one way to design a successful investment process, and, like artwork, it takes patience to fully appreciate and build its value.

However, investors in general have never been so confused and have never encountered the kind of challenges we face today: low interest rates in a dismal political, fiscal, economic, demographic and social environment. All this is occurring in the most competitive business environment we have ever known. We live in a world of sometimes negative real (inflation adjusted) returns and of unprecedented circumstances. Therefore, we do not have an appropriate frame of reference to truly evaluate risk and to anticipate the nature of the next economic cycle. Defined benefit pension funds are facing huge deficits, and some are considering locking in those deficits at very low rates, while others are searching for all sorts of investment alternatives to improve their situation. At the same time, it seems that they are timid about making appropriate changes, and these changes do not necessarily involve taking more risk, but taking the right risks at a reasonable cost. Small investors are faced with exactly the same difficulties, but simply on a different scale.

There are at least two other reasons why investors are so confused. The first reason is benchmarking with a short look-back horizon. The obsession with benchmarking as well as ill-conceived accounting (for corporate investors) and regulatory rules are increasingly polluting the investment process. For example, plan sponsors know their performance will be monitored and compared every quarter against their peer group, whether the comparison is truly fair or not, since the specific structure of liabilities of each investor is rarely considered in this comparison. Furthermore, under the US Department of Labor's Employee Retirement Income Security Act (ERISA), they have fiduciary responsibilities and can be made liable if prudent investment rules are not applied. But who establishes the standards of prudent investment rules? In theory, the standard is utterly process oriented [1]. Nevertheless, to deflect responsibility, and because of unfamiliarity with the investment process, plan sponsors will retain the services of one or several portfolio managers. However, because selecting the right managers is also a responsibility that many plan sponsors do not want to take on alone, consultants will be hired with the implicit understanding that hiring a consultant is in itself indicative of prudence and diligence. Since the consultant does not want to be made liable, it is unlikely that he or she will advise courses of action that are significantly different from the standard approach. Therefore, this entire process ensures that not much will really change, or that changes will occur very slowly.

It may also be that managers and consultants lack, on average, the proper conviction or understanding that is required to convince plan sponsors and other investors to implement a coherent and distinctive long-term approach. A five- to ten-year track record on everything related to investing is only required when we are dealing with intangible expertise and experience, since we cannot have confidence in any specific expertise without proven discipline. And the passage of time is the only way we can possibly attest to the discipline or expertise of a manager. However, a well-thought-out process does not require the discipline of a manager, but simply the discipline of the investor. It is the responsibility of the investor to remain disciplined. Furthermore, investing is not a series of 100-meter races, but a marathon. There is more and more evidence that the fastest marathon times are set by runners who pace themselves to keep the same speed during the entire race. Ethiopia's Belayneh Dinsamo held the world marathon record of 2:06:50 for 10 long years. He set the record by running nearly exact splits of 4:50 per mile for the entire 26 miles, even if the running conditions were different at every mile (flat, upward or downward sloping roads, head or back wind, lower or higher altitude, etc.). We could argue that an average runner could also improve his or her own personal time using this approach. The same may be true of successful investing. The best performance may be achieved, on average, by those who use strategies or processes designed to maintain a more stable risk exposure. Yet, when investors allocate to any asset class or target a fixed 60/40 or 40/60 allocation, they are allowing market conditions to dictate how much total risk they are taking at any point in time. Traditional benchmarking does not allow the investor to maintain a stable portfolio risk structure.

However, the other reason why investors are so confused is that the relevant factors leading to a return/risk-efficient portfolio management process have never been well explained to them. How can we expect investors to confidently stay the course under those circumstances? Investors' education is key, but then we still need to communicate a confident investment philosophy, and to support it with strong evidence. Does the average industry expert understand the most important dimensions of investing? I think not. What do we know about the importance or relevance of expertise and experience in asset management, or about the type of expertise that is truly needed? Whenever a manager is attempting to sell his or her services to an investor, the presentation will incorporate a page that explains how many years of experience the portfolio management team has. It will say something like, "Our portfolio management team has a combined 225 years [or any other number] of portfolio management experience." Is it relevant experience? Do these managers understand the true reasons for their successes (or failures)? Some do. Many do not. This book offers the arguments that an investor needs to manage distinctively and more efficiently. It answers many of the questions that are puzzling investors. Among them:

- Should we index, be active or passive and why?
- Can we identify the best managers?
- Even if we can, do we need them?
- Are traditional benchmarks efficient?
- What can we reasonably forecast?
- What aspects or qualities are truly required in an investment process?
- Is it the same for equities, commodities, currencies, hedge funds, asset allocation, etc.?
- How many asset classes or risk premiums are enough?
- Do we need alternative investments?
- How do we structure a portfolio and maintain its balance?
- Do we truly understand the impact of taxation on the allocation process (for individuals)?
- What is this concept of Beta and Alpha, and would we really need Alpha if we had a better Beta?
- How much risk can we really afford to take, and how do we answer this question?
- What are the risks we should be worried about?
- How do we incorporate liabilities into this analysis?
- Can we create a global portfolio assembly and allocation process that incorporates all of these concerns?

This is a fairly long list of questions, but having reflected for two years about what is relevant and what is not, what works and what does not and what is sustainable and what is not, I have never been so comfortable with my convictions. When I look at asset managers, I no longer think in terms of their expertise and experience, or their so-called forecasting abilities, but in terms of whether or not the investment process offers the necessary underlying structural qualities that can lead to outperformance. By the end of this book, most investors will have a much clearer understanding of investment dynamics, and will be able to assemble the right components to build an efficient and appropriate portfolio that is resilient to almost any context.

Note

1. Monks, Robert A.G. and Nell Minow (2011), *Corporate Governance*, John Wiley & Sons, Inc.

PART I

The Active Management Business

CHAPTER 1

The Economics of Active Management

Active management is at best a zero-sum game. It means that, collectively, we cannot beat the market, since the collectivity of all investors is the market. Therefore, as a single investor among many, we can only beat the market at the expense of someone else. It becomes a negative-sum game once we incorporate the fees required by active managers, and other costs imposed by active management, such as trading and administration. The more money we collectively pour into expensive active management, the more likely we are to collectively get poorer.

Imagine a group of four individuals, each wanting to share an apple pie. We could agree initially that each individual deserves a slice of equal size (i.e., a form of neutral indexed position), but one individual wants a bigger serving. He can only do so at the expense of someone else. The pie will not get bigger simply because he wants to have more of it.

In order to have a chance to get a bigger slice of the pie, our individual must be willing to risk losing a portion of his slice, and find at least one other individual who is willing to do the same thing. These two individuals will play heads or tails. Whoever wins the coin toss gets a bigger portion, and the loser gets a smaller portion. The same goes for active management. It is at best a zero-sum game.

Now let's assume these two individuals want to increase their chances of winning a bigger slice, and each hires an expert at tossing coins. They will pay these experts by giving them a portion of their slice. Since our two betting individuals have to share their two slices of the pie with others, the portions left for these two individuals are smaller than two full slices. Much like active management, the presence of a new player and his or her fees have transformed this situation into a negative-sum game, and to be a winner, you have to win in the coin toss a portion of the pie that is bigger than the one you are giving to your coin-tossing expert.

How much of their returns are investors giving to the financial industry? No one really knows for sure, but according to John C. Bogle, founder and retired CEO of The Vanguard Group, the wealth transfer in the United States in 2004 from investors to investment bankers, brokers, mutual funds, pension management, hedge funds, personal advisors, etc. is estimated at $350 billion (excluding investment services of banks and insurances companies) [1]. This represents nearly 3% of all US GDP a year! Some intermediation is obviously essential, but if we consider the management fees that actively managed products require, the costs related to excessive trading activity and the significant distribution costs of many financial products, it could be shown that unnecessary intermediation is reducing the wealth of all investors (or is transferring this wealth to a small select group) by 15% in present value terms, possibly more. Excessive intermediation could even become a drag on the overall economy. As investors, we have to make better decisions than just betting on which active manager will be the next winner, and whether or not there is such a thing as a reliable coin-tossing expert. Furthermore, investors cannot necessarily rely on advisors for that purpose, because advisors are often biased in favor of offering the most recent winners, and thus are not always objective or often knowledgeable enough to make an informed recommendation. There are obviously exceptions, but this is often true.

Therefore, the purpose of this first chapter is not to determine if we can identify managers or strategies that can outperform the market. It is simply to make the argument that more than half, perhaps two-thirds, of assets being managed will underperform whatever the asset category or investment horizon. Finally, although the discussions in Chapter 1 are sometimes supported by the finance literature related to individual investors, who often pay significantly higher management fees than institutional investors, the investment principles that are presented, the questions that are raised and the implications of our assumptions are relevant to both individual and institutional investors.

Understanding Active Management

Active management is a complex issue. We want to believe that our financial advisor can identify skilled managers, or that we are skilled managers. We buy actively managed products because we hope the management fees that are being paid to investment professionals will help us outperform the market and our peers. However, before we even address the particularities of active managers' performances and skills, we have to realize that active management is globally a negative-sum game. It basically means that even before we have hired a manager, our likelihood of outperforming the market by investing in an actively managed product is almost always much less than 50%. Why is that?

First, we live in a world where the market value of all assets within a financial market is simply the sum of the market value of all single securities in that market. For example, the market value of the large-capitalization (large-cap for short) equity segment in the United States is equal to the sum of the market value of every single security in that particular segment (i.e., Exxon, IBM, Johnson & Johnson, etc.). This is true of all financial markets, whether they are categorized according to asset classes (equities and fixed income), size (large capitalization, small capitalization, etc.), sectors (financial, industrial, etc.), style (growth, value) or country (United States, Canada, etc.). Second, all of these securities have to be owned directly or indirectly by investors at any moment in time, whether these investors are institutions such as pension funds and endowment funds, corporations such as life insurance companies, hedge funds, mutual funds, individuals or even governments or government-related entities. Even central banks are investors. Investors as a group collectively own the market. What is the implication of this for active management?

To illustrate, we will use a simple example. We will assume an equity market is only comprised of the securities of two companies, X and Y. However, the conclusion would be the same if there were 1,000 or 10,000 securities. The first company, X, has a market value of $600 million, while the second company, Y, has a market value of $400 million. Thus, the entire value of the market is $1 billion. Consequently, X accounts for 60% of the value of the entire market, and Y the other 40%. Now, let's assume the returns on the shares of each company are respectively 30% and 0% during the following year. What will be the weight of each company in the market?

After one year, X is worth $780 million, while Y is still worth $400 million. The market value of both companies, and thus of the entire market, is now $1,18 billion (+18%), and their respective market weights are now 66.1% (780/1,180) and 33.9% (400/1,180). This is illustrated in Table 1.1.

In this example, the entire value of the market is initially $1,000 million, while it is $1,18 billion one period later. The performance of the market was 18%. Who owns this market? As we already indicated, it is owned by all investors, either directly or indirectly (through products such as mutual funds).

Let's assume that among all investors, some investors are passive investors who are indexed to this market. This means they are not betting on which security (X or Y) will perform better. They are perfectly content to invest in each company according to the same proportion as in the overall market. Their initial investment was $300 million, or 30% of the entire market. What was the performance of these passive investors? It was 18% before fees, the same as the market. If passive investors realized an 18% return, what was the aggregate performance of all active investors that owned the other $700 million in securities, or 70% of this market? It had to be 18% in aggregate before fees for all active investors, or the same as passive investors. It cannot be otherwise. Once we have removed the assets of all indexed investors who received a performance equivalent to the market, what we have left are the collective assets of all active investors who must share a performance equal to the market. It is that simple.

TABLE 1.1 The Structure of a Hypothetical Equity Market

	Initial Market Value M$	Initial Market Weight (%)	Performance (%)	New Market Value M$	New Market Weights (%)
X	600	60	30	780	66.1
Y	400	40	0	400	33.9
Index	1,000	100	18	1,180	100

Of course, some active managers will outperform the market, but if the aggregate performance of active managers is the same as that of the market, some will have to underperform. To simplify further, let's assume there are only two active investors, each with an initial investment of $350 million. If an active manager realizes a performance of 21%, or 3% above the market because he had a 70% allocation to X and 30% to Y (70% × 30% + 30% × 0% = 21%), the other active manager has to have a performance of 15%, or 3% below the market, and he must have had a 50% allocation to X and 50% to Y (50% × 30% + 50% × 0% = 15%). Again, it cannot be otherwise since the positions held by all investors are equal to the total positions available in the market, and the sum of the aggregate performance of all active and passive managers alike cannot be more than the performance of the market. It must be equal.

Now, let's imagine there are thousands of active managers out there. Since the sum of their aggregate performance cannot be more than that of the market, we can safely assume that investors and managers that represent 50% of all money invested actively in a market will underperform that market, and investors and managers that represent 50% of all money invested actively in a market will outperform that market. It cannot be otherwise. Therefore, we have shown that active management is, at most, a zero-sum game. It simply redistributes existing wealth among investors, whether individual or institutional.

When I mention that active management is a negative-sum game and not a zero-sum game, it is because of fees: management fees, advisory fees, trading fees, etc. In aggregate, active and passive managers alike will not realize the performance of the market because they both pay fees, although fees for active management can be significantly higher. In the previous example, if the average of all fees paid by investors is 1.0%, the aggregate performance of all investors net of fees will only be 17.0%. The performance drain could be slightly less, since investors could recuperate part of this wealth transfer through their ownership of the financial sector, but it could only amount to a small fraction of the drain. Thus, the greater the fees paid to advisors, the lower the probability that investors can match or outperform the market.

To illustrate further, let's assume an investor has a choice between two products to invest in the US large-capitalization equity market. One product, which is indexed to the market, is relatively cheap. The total expenses related to this product are 0.2% yearly. The second product, an actively managed product, is more expensive. Its total expenses are 1.0% per year. Thus, in order for this investor to achieve a higher performance with the actively managed product, the active manager must outperform the indexed product by about 0.8% per year (assuming the index product is an accurate representation of the market), and this must be done in a world where all active investors in aggregate will do no better than the market return before fees. If 0.8% in fees per year does not seem so important, maybe you should consider their impact on a 10-year horizon using some assumptions about market returns. Table 1.2 shows the cumulative excess performance (above the market) required from an active manager over 10 years to outperform an indexed product when the difference in management fees is as specified, and when the gross market return is either 0%, 2.5%, 5%, 7.5% or 10% yearly.

TABLE 1.2 Impact of Fees on Cumulative Performance (%)

Management Process	Performance	Scenario				
		#1	#2	#3	#4	#5
	Yearly Gross Performance	0.0	2.5	5.0	7.5	10.0
Passive (0.2% fees)	Cumulative Performance (10 Years)	−2.0	25.5	59.8	102.3	154.7
Active (1.0% fees)	Cumulative Performance (10 Years)	−9.6	16.1	48.0	87.7	136.7
Cumulative Performance Spread		7.6	9.5	11.8	14.6	18.0

The example illustrates that the impact of fees on performance is not independent of market returns. The greater the market performance, the greater the cumulative excess performance required from an active manager to match the performance of a cheap index alternative, because investors not only pay fees on their initial capital, but also on their return. At a low 5% average annual return, the manager must outperform a cheap index product by 11.8% over 10 years. At 7.5% average annual market return, he must outperform by 14.6%. This requires a lot of confidence in your active manager, and what we have indicated about active management being a zero-sum game before fees is true for any investment horizon, one year, five years, ten years, etc. How likely is it that an active manager can outperform the market adjusted for fees over a long period of time, such as 10 years? It all depends on two factors. First, what is the level of fees, and second, what is the usual range of performance for all active managers against the market. For example, if all managers were requiring 1% yearly fees, we need to have some managers that outperform the market by at least 1% yearly on average (before fees) to be able to calculate a positive probability of outperforming the market. If not, the probability is nil.

Several studies have looked at this issue from different angles. I will initially reference only one study and come back with more evidence later. Rice and Strotman (2007) published very pertinent research about the fund-management industry [2]. Their research analyzed the performance profile of 1,596 mutual funds in 17 submarket segments over a 10-year time frame ending on December 31, 2006. The authors used the range of performance (before fees) observed for all managers against their respective markets over this period to estimate the likely probability of any manager outperforming the market in the next 10 years. The study shows that about two-thirds of managers in their entire data set have performances that range between −2.14% and +2.14% compared to their respective markets. Based on this information, Table 1.3 presents the approximate probability that the average manager can outperform the market after fees.

TABLE 1.3 Fees and Probability of Outperformance (%)

Total Yearly Fees	Probability of Outperforming the Market
0.5	41
1.0	32
1.5	24

Source: Rice and Strotman (2007).

We can conclude that an investor paying annual fees of 1.0% would have less than one chance out of three of outperforming the market, and two out of three of underperforming. This is an approximate estimate that relies on assumptions about the range of performance of active managers, and does not adjust for the particular portfolio structure of an investor, or for the style of a manager. Although institutional investors are likely to pay even less than 1.0% fees on most equity products (although significantly more on hedge funds), their likelihood of outperforming the market still remains well below 50%. Therefore, it is difficult to argue against the fact that fees reduce your probability of outperforming the market to less than 50%, and that higher fees will reduce your probability even more.

Evidence on the Relative Performance of Active Managers

The statement that active management is a negative-sum game is based on all active managers in aggregate. However, asset managers may cater to specific investors (retail, high-net-worth, institutional, etc.), and some large institutional investors have their own internal management teams. Therefore, if active management is globally a negative-sum game, it could, in theory, be a positive-sum game for a specific group of investors (such as mutual fund investors), but this could only happen at the expense of other groups of investors. More specifically, it could happen if, for example, mutual fund managers were not only better than the other active managers out there, but also good enough to compensate for their own fees.

However, I doubt very much that this could be the case in aggregate for the larger, more efficient capital markets. There is much evidence that supports a contrary view. Let's start with the common-sense arguments with a specific look at mutual funds. First, in the United States, institutional investors, defined as pension funds, insurance companies, banks, foundations and investment companies (that manage mutual funds), owned 37.2% of all equities in 1980, while the number grew to 61.2% by 2005. During the same period, the share of equities owned by mutual funds grew from 2.3% to 23.8%, and then reached a peak of about 29% prior to the 2008 liquidity crisis [3]. Therefore, in this active-management game, institutional investors who can afford the best expertise are playing against other institutional investors who can also afford the best expertise on a large scale. Furthermore, mutual funds are no longer a small player, but a very large component of the market. It becomes more and more difficult to assume that as a group they could be expected to consistently outperform other groups of investors, at least in the US market and other developed markets, since they have become such a significant segment of the entire market themselves. But do not forget, they must not only outperform other groups of investors, but also outperform enough to cover excess costs (compared to a cheap alternative) related to their own products.

In 2006, researchers completed a study on the issue of mutual fund fees around the world [4]. It covered 46,799 funds (86% of the total as of 2002) in 18 countries. The study compared total annual expense ratios for all funds (balanced, equity, bonds and money market). These observations are presented in Table 1.4.

TABLE 1.4 Fees Around the World (%)

Country	Total Annual Expense Ratio
Australia	1.60
Canada	2.68
France	1.13
Germany	1.22
Switzerland	1.42
United Kingdom	1.32
United States	1.42

Source: Khorona, Servaes and Tufano (2006).

Individual investors in the US and in several other countries benefit from a lower level of fees while Canada has among the highest fees. It seems, according to the authors, that the more concentrated a banking system is in each country, the higher the fees are. Canada has, in fact, one of the most concentrated banking systems in the world. Thus, even if we assumed that, in Canada, mutual fund managers as a group were better than other active managers, considering the much higher level of fees they require, they would have to be significantly better than US managers on average.

This study was obviously the subject of criticism in Canada. Some have argued that the methodology of the study overestimates the fees paid in Canada and underestimates those paid in the United States. However, even if we agree with the precise arguments that were raised against this study, they would only justify a fraction of the difference in fees between the two countries.

Furthermore, while competition among institutional managers has become fiercer, management expense ratios (MERs) have gone up in the United States since 1980, from an average of 0.96% to an average of 1.56% in the mid-2000s (although competition from low-cost alternatives is now improving this matter) [5]. Why? In an industry that has grown so much in size, the investors should have expected some economies of scale. Instead, the industry has delivered more specialized and complex products that have considerably added to the confusion of investors. However, fund-management expenses are not the only factors detracting from performance. A 2009 study by Kopcke and Vitagliano [6] looked at the fees of the 100 largest domestic equity funds that are used within defined contribution plans (US 401(k) plans). The horizon of the study was short, but it provides an interesting look at total expenses including costs related to trading within the industry. From the information within their study, we can determine the weighted average MER, sales load fees and trading-related costs for the 100 funds. Remember that 401(k) plans are usually employer-sponsored plans, and thus investors within these plans should benefit from lower MER than the average mutual fund investor. These funds had weighted average MER, sales load and costs related to trading of 0.51%, 0.11% and 0.67% respectively.

Costs related to trading, an item that is usually invisible to the average investor, are significant, and can, in some cases, be even greater than the MER.

The study also showed the average annual turnover of securities within these funds to be around 48%, and only 30% if turnover is weighted by the size of the fund. Bigger funds have much lower trading volume. The average turnover level in this study is not entirely consistent with other estimates for the overall industry, but there is little doubt that the turnover is significant. The 2009 Investment Company Institute Factbook [7] shows a weighted average annual turnover rate for the industry of 58% from 1974 to 2008. The level was 58% as well in 2008, but much closer to 30% in the 1970s. Although Maginn and Tuttle (2010) [8] estimate the range of turnover for equity value managers to be between 20% and 80%, they also estimate the range for growth managers to be between 80% and several hundred percent. By comparison, many indexed equity products have turnover rates in the 6% to 10% range. A higher turnover means more trading and market impact costs, but also more tax impact costs related to the early recognition of capital gains. According to John C. Bogle, the turnover in US large-cap equity funds may have reduced the after-tax return of investors by 1.3% yearly between 1983 and 2003. When compounded over many years, this is incredibly significant.

So the common-sense argument is that institutional investors are all trying to outperform one another with their own experts, that many products have fairly significant management fees and that the level of trading required by active management imposes significant trading costs. Under these circumstances, outperforming a passive benchmark in the long run appears to be improbable for a majority of active managers. This common-sense argument should be convincing enough, but for those who are skeptical, there are many studies on the issue. In the interest of time and space, I will concentrate on a few. However, I can already indicate that after more than 35 years of research, going back 60 years in time, the main conclusion that these studies have reached is not ambiguous: active managers in aggregate underperform indexed products after fees.

Chen, Hong, Huang and Kubik (2004) looked at the performance of mutual funds according to size. [9] Their study on 3,439 funds over the period 1962 to 1999 concluded that the average fund underperformed its risk-adjusted benchmark by 0.96% annually. Furthermore, the underperformance was 1.4% adjusted for fund size, indicating that bigger funds underperformed even more. They also found that the typical fund has a gross performance net of market return of about 0%. In their study, funds were categorized into five distinct group sizes. All groups underperformed after fees. These conclusions do not only apply to the US markets. For example, Table 1.5 presents the scorecard of US, Canadian and Australian mutual funds for a five-year period ending in 2010.

It is probably no coincidence that Canada has the lowest scorecard and among the highest mutual fund fees in the world. We could cite other studies, but they all point to the same general conclusion: a one to one tradeoff, on average over time, between performance and expenses (i.e., more fees equal less return).

TABLE 1.5 Percentage of Funds Outperforming their Benchmark (2006–2010)

Category of Funds	United States	Canada	Australia
Domestic Large CAP	38	3	30
Domestic Small/Mid-Cap	37 Small–22 Mid	29	71 Small
International	18	12	26
Global	40	15	–
Fixed Income	30	–	18

Source: SPIVA Scorecard Year-End 2010 for US, Canada and Australia.

Relevance of Funds' Performance Measures

The issue being raised is not the accuracy of the performance measures of funds, but of their usefulness to the investment-decision process. We will address three types of performance measures: performance against other funds, fund rating systems and performance against benchmark indices.

One methodology often used to evaluate managers is to rank them against their peers for horizons such as one, two, three, five and even ten years. For example, is my manager a first-quartile manager (better than 75% of managers), a median manager (better than 50% of managers), etc.? I never gave much thought to this ranking approach until I realized that the mutual fund industry, like most industries, has a high degree of concentration. For example, in 2008, the largest 10 sponsors of mutual funds in the United States controlled 53% of all assets in that group. Also, in 2007, a study by Rohleder, Scholz and Wilkens was completed on the issue of survivorship bias of US domestic equity funds. [10] We can conclude from this study, which covered most of the industry, that the largest 50% of funds accounted for more than 99% of the assets of US domestic equity funds.

Although I will not specifically address the issue of mutual fund survivorship, extensive literature has demonstrated that an industry-wide performance bias is created by the tendency to close or merge funds that performed poorly, causing their track record to be removed from the existing universe of funds. [11] Thus, if we do not take into account the performance of these funds, the surviving funds paint an inaccurate picture of the performance of the industry. This would be equivalent to an investor earning a 10% return on 90% of his allocation, and a negative 20% return on 10% of his allocation, stating that if we ignored the allocation on which he lost money, he had a 10% return!

Furthermore, we know that smaller funds have a wider range of return around their benchmark, since larger funds are more likely to maintain a more prudent investment policy. They are more likely to protect their asset base and reputation, while small funds are more likely to take more aggressive active investment positions. They do not have the marketing budgets of large funds, and their managers know they have to outperform large funds to attract new capital. Thus, it is likely that we will find a greater number of smaller funds than large funds whose performances are below and above the median of managers, if even by chance, and also because there are more small funds than large funds.

Under such circumstances, quartile rankings have a lesser meaning. If smaller funds have a wider range of performance and are greater in number, we could expect that smaller funds (many of them unknown to most investors) accounting for much less than 50% of all assets would dominate the first two quartiles in the long run. This is reinforced by Bogle's argument that excessive size can, and probably will, kill any possibility of investment excellence. [12] Furthermore, the industry is not stable enough to make such performance measures useful. According to the Rohleder, Scholz and Wilkens study, there were 1,167 mutual funds in the United States in 1993. In December 2006, there were 7,600 funds, but 3,330 funds had closed during this period. The average life of a fund was 71 months. Finally, only 658 funds were operational for the entire period, but they were the biggest, with 52.5% of all assets by the end of the period. What is the true significance of a first- or second-quartile ranking when this measure is applied to an unstable population of funds, and when chance may account for the excess performance of many managers in the short term? The situation has not improved in later years. Thirty percent of large-capitalization managers operating in 2006 were no longer operating by the end of 2009.

Another rating approach is the scoring system. Better-known systems are Morningstar and Lipper Leaders. Although these systems are designed to rank the historical performance of funds on the basis of different risk-adjusted methodologies, investors have been relying on these systems to allocate their investments to mutual funds. The authors of an Ecole des Hautes Etudes Commerciales du Nord (EDHEC) paper on this issue [13] referenced different studies showing that funds benefiting from high ratings receive a substantial portion of new inflows [14]. However, as I will start to explain in Chapter 2, past performances in mutual funds are only an indicator of future performance in very specific circumstances. Furthermore, other studies [15] have shown that a significant percentage of funds have performance attributes that are not consistent with their stated objectives. If these funds are classified within these scoring systems according to their stated objectives, these rankings may not be relevant or useful, since the benchmarks may not be appropriate to the investment approach or policy of the managers.

This observation was confirmed by my own experience. In the early 2000s, I was involved in a process to select a fairly large number of external fund managers in the equity space for an institutional client. One of the first steps in the selection process was to eliminate from our potential pool of asset managers any fund whose historical performance was "statistically" inconsistent with its declared mandate. We found this to be an issue with a significant percentage of funds—as many as 30%.

Finally, the last approach is a comparison against a benchmark index. So far in this Chapter, I was careful to discuss the issue of fund performance against that of the market (and not the index), simply because most indices are not truly representative of the market. They are only an approximation of the market. Thus, some fund managers that are benchmarked against a specific index may be able to select their portfolio positions for a universe of securities, which is wider than that of the index itself. Theoretically, this should help these managers outperform their reference benchmark by offering them a wider playing field than what they are measured against. However, that may not be enough.

Closing Remarks

The likelihood of a manager outperforming the market is less than 50% in most markets. This is not a forecast, but a logical consequence of market structure. Of course, there may be exceptions. Financial markets in some countries or some specific segment of financial markets (such as emerging or growth markets) may be less efficient than our domestic markets, and professional expertise may be more valuable in these cases, since it may be possible to extract value at the expense of other groups of investors. Other factors may also create inefficiencies, such as the fact that many investors have motivations that are not driven by a profit-maximization objective, or that investors may be subject to investment constraints. For example, several investors or categories of investors may have their investment process constrained by guidelines, which may keep them from owning an indexed position even if they wanted to. Regulations may keep many institutional investors from investing in different types of securities, such as lesser-quality bonds. Large investors may not bother to invest in market segments that offer too little liquidity, or that would force them to maintain very small allocations compared to the size of their portfolio. Others may restrict themselves from investing in industries linked to pollution or health hazards. Finally, some investors do not buy and sell securities for the purpose of maximizing their expected investment performance or outperforming the market. Many are more concerned with matching their liability requirements, while others, like central banks, trade for the purpose of economic and financial market stability. This is all true, but the fact remains that a large majority of studies have not found evidence of outperformance by fund managers when properly adjusted for risks, despite all the circumstances listed above, which should, in fact, help these managers outperform.

Furthermore, most individual investors have a day job. Most cannot handle the complexity of investing, given the time they can reasonably allocate to this process. Institutional investors may, in theory, have greater resources that can be devoted to choosing the right managers, but individual investors face a more difficult task because marketing considerations may dominate even more the fund recommendations they will receive. Fund management companies may advertise products that outperformed significantly in the recent past. If an investment company has 20 funds on its platform, it is likely that some of them have done well recently, even if by chance. They may even close the funds that have not performed well to get rid of an embarrassing track record. According to John C. Bogle:

> Sixty years ago, the mutual fund industry placed its emphasis on fund management as a profession—the trusteeship of others people's money. Today, there is much evidence that salesmanship has superseded trusteeship as the industry's prime focus [16].

To support this view, Bogle mentions the numerous changes that have occurred since 1945, which I relate with some of my own interpretation. During this period the mutual fund industry has grown from 68 funds to now close to 8,000. The growing number of funds and the growth of assets have transformed the industry into the biggest shareholder in the United States. The industry has multiplied the number of specialty funds, and one may wonder if this is really to the benefit of investors. Funds were managed then by investment committees, which have gradually been replaced by a system of star managers. This may have contributed to a threefold increase in turnover (stars may be less patient, or feel that they have more to prove than investment committees) and thus to a decline in the investment horizon. The turnover is so large that we may ask if the average fund manager out there acts as an investor or a speculator. Furthermore, the industry has turned from a profession to a business with a different incentive structure. Investment firms are being acquired like any other business, and the buyer is seeking an after-tax return on his investment. The price paid is based on the revenue stream and the quality of the client base. This may explain why fees have increased so significantly, since this is now more than ever a profit-maximizing business. The "profit maximizing" objective of the financial industry may be in conflict with the interest of investors. For example, the industry, which delivered 89% of the indexed returns to individual investors from 1945 to 1965, delivered only 79% from 1983 to 2003. This number confirms the assertion that unnecessary intermediation may reduce the wealth of investors by at least 10% to 15%. However, individual investors are not the only group to have experienced higher fees. For example, it has been reported that pension funds in 2008 were paying 50% higher fees on their total assets than five years prior [17]. Chasing performance and paying higher fees has probably contributed to the pension fund debacle. Therefore, we can certainly conclude that investment management remains a negative-sum game, but also that the game has turned more negative, at least until recently. Greater sophistication has not rewarded individual and institutional investors, and both groups of investors have taken notice. Nevertheless, this entire discussion was not about specific active managers, but about the asset management industry. Thus, we have to ask the question: Are there good active managers that can outperform the markets after fees, and can we identify them?

Notes

1. Bogle, John C. (2005), "The relentless rules of humble arithmetic" in "Bold thinking on investment management," *The Financial Analysts Journal 60th Anniversary Anthology*, CFA Institute, 127–144.
2. Rice, Matthew, and Geoff Strotman (2007), "The next chapter in the active vs. passive management debate," DiMeo Schneider & Associates, L.L.C.
3. Brancato, Carolyn Kay and Stephan Rabimov (2007), "The 2007 Institutional Investment Report", The Conference Board of Canada.
4. Khorona, Ajay, Henri Servaes, and Peter Tufano (2006), "Mutual funds fees around the world," Working Paper, Georgia Institute of Technology, London Business School, Harvard Business School.
5. Arnott, Robert D., Jason C. Hsu, and John C. West (2008), *The Fundamental Index: A Better Way to Invest*, John Wiley & Sons, Inc., p. 184.
6. Kopcke, Richard W., and Francis M. Vitagliano (2009), "Fees and trading costs of equity mutual funds in 401(k) plans and potential savings from ETFs and commingled trusts," Center for Retirement Research at Boston College.
7. Investment Company Institute, "2009 Investment Company Factbook—A review of trends and activity in the investment company industry," 49th Edition.
8. Maginn, John L., Donald L. Tuttle and Dennis W. McLeavey (2010), *Managing Investment Portfolios: A Dynamic Process*, John Wiley & Sons, Inc., Chapter 7.
9. Chen, Joseph, Harrison Hong, Ming Huang, and Jeffrey D. Kubik (2004), "Does fund size erode mutual fund performance? The role of liquidity and organization," *American Economic Review* 96(5), 1216–2302.
10. Rohleder, Martin, Hendrik Scholz, and Marco Wilkens (2007), "Survivorship bias and mutual fund performance: Relevance, significance, and methodological differences," Ingolstadt School of Management; Catholic University of Eichstaett-Ingostadt.
11. Carhart, Mark M., Jennifer N. Carpenter, Anthony W. Lynch, and David K. Musto (2002), "Mutual fund survivorship," *The Review of Financial Studies* 15(5), 1439–1463.
12. Bogle, John C. (2000), *Common Sense on Mutual Funds: New Imperatives for the Intelligent Investor*, John Wiley & Sons, Inc., 99–100.
13. Amenc, Noel, and Véronique Le Sourd (2007), "Rating the ratings—A critical analysis of fund rating systems," EDHEC-Risk Institute.
14. Del, Guercio, and Paula A. Tkac (2001), "Star Power: The effect of Morningstar ratings in mutual fund flows," Working Paper no. 2001–15, Federal Reserve Bank of Atlanta; Adkisson, J.A., and Don R. Fraser (2003), "Realigning the Stars: The Reaction of Investors and Fund Managers to Changes in the Morningstar Rating Methodology for Mutual Funds," Texas A&M University, working paper.
15. DiBartolomeo, Dan, and Erik Witkowski (1997), "Mutual fund misclassification: Evidence based on style analysis," *Financial Analysts Journal* 53(5), 32–43; Kim, Moon, Ravi Shukla, and Michael Tomas (2000), "Mutual fund

objective misclassification," *Journal of Economics and Business* 52(4), 309–323; Jin, Xue-jun, and Xia-Ian Yang (2004), "Empirical study on mutual fund objective classification," *Journal of Zhejiang University Science* 5(5), 533–538.

16. Bogle, John C. (2005), "The mutual fund industry 60 years later: For better or worse" in "Bold thinking on investment management," *The Financial Analysts Journal 60th Anniversary Anthology*, CFA Institute, 37–49.

17. Inderst, Georg (2009), "Pension fund investment in infrastructure," OECD Working Paper on Insurance and Private Pensions, No. 32.

CHAPTER 2

What Factors Drive Performance?

In early 2010, I came across the following statement in a blog discussing exchange-traded funds (ETFs):

> Anyone who is willing to settle for the guaranteed mediocrity provided by ETFs is just too lazy to understand that there are many mutual fund managers out there who consistently and significantly outperform their benchmark indices.

As I will illustrate in this book, this belief is what will allow other patient and process-oriented investors to outperform those who are constantly searching for the best managers and latest winners. I have met with the managers of more than 1,000 hedge fund and mutual fund organizations in my career, and although there are many well-structured organizations with good analytical talent, I still would not expect their funds to outperform consistently.

Thus, almost all managers, even the best of them, are likely to underperform for many consecutive years over a horizon of 10 years. As investors, we are too impatient. We believe a good manager is one that should outperform every year because we have been raised in an environment where we think in yearly intervals. We have a birthday each year, one national holiday and usually one yearly income tax return to file.

However, markets do not function that way. Bonds may outperform equities for several years, and then, suddenly, this positive momentum will reverse. Small-capitalization stocks may underperform large-capitalization stocks for several years, and this momentum will also reverse. The same goes for value and growth stocks, for Canadian versus US equities, for emerging (growth) markets versus developed markets and for resources versus equities. All market segments are prone to performance cycles. They vary in length and in amplitude of movements, but these cycles, although usually unpredictable, are rarely short. To outperform year after year and to have the confidence that someone can repeat this consistently requires tremendous faith. Some people may be that smart, but very few are.

There are certainly characteristics that make a good manager, but that does not mean that he or she can be successful every year. Furthermore, it also does not mean that an investor cannot replicate some of these characteristics at a lower cost, even if he or she does not have all of the knowledge of more experienced managers.

Implications of Long Performance Cycles and Management Styles

The likelihood that an average manager will outperform the market before fees is probably 50% a year. Because of this, investors often believe a manager has a one in four chance to outperform the market two years straight (50% × 50%). Thus, if a specific manager outperforms three years in a row, they assume the probability of achieving this result is one in eight (50% × 50% × 50%). Investors could conclude that such a manager is a very good one. Even if we were to accept this logic, these investors ignore that in a universe of, for example, 8,000 funds, approximately 1,000 of them would be likely to outperform their benchmark for three successive years, and 250 for five successive years, even if none of these managers had expertise. This is not different from asking 10,000 individuals to make a forecast about next year's economic growth. Even if they have no expertise, many of them are likely to have the correct answer. However, there is also the possibility that we are simply thinking about these probabilities in the wrong way. What if the right answer is that out of 100 managers operating in the same market segment, one-third are likely to outperform for at least three years straight, a second third of managers are likely to underperform for at least three years straight and the remaining third will have inconsistent yearly performance against the benchmark. This should certainly influence how we analyze historical yearly excess returns for the purpose of selecting managers. I will now develop the logic behind this argument, starting with a statement from Rice and Strotman (2007):

> Approximately 90 percent of ten-year top quartile mutual funds across 17 categories spent at least one three-year stretch in the bottom half of their peer group [1].

Three years is a very long time, and the authors are not saying the first-quartile managers underperformed for only three years during a 10-year period, but for at least three consecutive years. They also added that 51% of managers spent at least a five-year stretch in the bottom half, and these results are based on an extensive study of 1,596 funds over 10 years (December 1996 to December 2006). A 2010 update of this study covering a slightly different period changed the percentages for the three- and five-year consecutive performances to 85% (slightly better) and 62% (slightly worse). These observations were supported by similar research by Brockhouse Cooper, according to which 79% to 94% of first-quartile managers in five subgroups over the period 1999 to 2009 spent at least three consecutive years in the bottom half of their peer group. Close to 63% and 32% of them were bottom-quartile and bottom-decile managers during this three-year period [2]. Furthermore, the first study went on to specify that more than 97% of funds that finished with a 10-year first-quartile ranking within the large-capitalization blend peer group had a bottom-half performance in the three years prior to December 1999. This seems to indicate that unless investors allocated their portfolio to managers who underweighted the technology sector prior to the burst of the technology bubble, and maintained this position until after the bubble burst (probably very disciplined value managers), they had a very slim chance of ever investing with a first-quartile manager over this entire period. Therefore, what if a significant part of the reasons for managers underperforming or outperforming for several consecutive years is related to their investment philosophy, style of management and allocation principles (all of which impact the portfolio structure), and not necessarily to their ability to pick single stocks? What would be the implication?

Let's assume, for now, that managers who outperform or underperform their benchmark over successive years follow dedicated allocation processes. There is one major aspect that will differentiate a manager with a dedicated process from the market. On one hand, a process requires, by definition, discipline. On the other hand, markets are not disciplined. Shiller (1981) [3] argued that stock prices were far more volatile than warranted by expectations from the underlying dividend stream. Although greater price volatility can be explained by many rational factors, it can also indicate the creation and destruction of periodic bubbles. John Maynard Keynes is credited with saying, "The market can remain irrational [or undisciplined] longer than you can remain solvent [or disciplined]." Furthermore, I will briefly illustrate in Chapter 5 that although dividends and profit growth are major determinants of equity returns in the very long term, fluctuations in P/E (price-to-earnings) multiples, which are driven in part by changes in market sentiment and risk tolerance (i.e., time-varying risk premiums), are the major determinants of equity returns over shorter periods (although a shorter period in this case can sometimes extend to several years). Therefore, if market valuations are far more volatile than the fundamental valuations resulting from a disciplined process, and if this "excess" market volatility can extend for many years in different segments of the market, a manager with an efficient management process may underperform the market for many consecutive years, even if he or she is eventually proven right. Unfortunately, this also means that a manager with an inefficient process and no particular expertise could actually outperform the market for several years, even if he or she is eventually proven wrong. In such an environment, undisciplined and uninformed investors may constantly draw the wrong conclusions from analyzing the historical performance of managers, even over periods as long as five years.

For example, in late 1999, a colleague and I traveled to several cities across Canada to discuss the valuation of the stock market in general, and that of the technology sector in particular. At the time, the NASDAQ was trading slightly below 4,000, and our message was the following: if we assume a normalization of P/E ratios on indices and companies related to the technology sector within 10 years, the profit growth that is required to achieve this goal, and the resulting corporate profits to GDP ratio, are simply unimaginable unless the GDP grows at a pace well beyond what we have ever seen. When we were asked what we believed the NASDAQ was worth, we were

FIGURE 2.1 Valuation of Disciplined Manager Against Undisciplined Market.

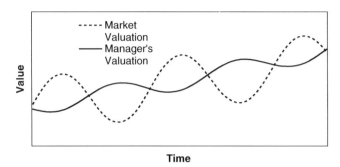

uncomfortable answering 1,200 to 1,500, considering that, at the time, it was trading at approximately three times this range.

There are two aspects I remember from this period. First, very few individuals in all of our meetings wanted to accept the idea of an overvalued market. It went against their hopes and dreams of getting rich quickly—a behavioral bias. Secondly, after we made these statements, the NASDAQ climbed to over 5,000, and reached 5,132.52 at its intraday peak several months later. Thus, even when you may be proven right in the longer term, the undisciplined market may still humble you, and may even force you to change your portfolio allocation before you are ever proven right. Betting significantly against the market and your peers requires strong convictions and courage.

Figure 2.1 illustrates this concept using a theoretical example. It compares the manager's valuation of a specific investment position over time to the actual price observed in the market over the same period. Let's assume the figure covers a 20-year horizon or more. At the beginning and end of this horizon, we assumed the manager and market had similar opinions about valuations. However, the process used by the manager leads to far more stable valuations. Sometimes these valuations are in sync with market valuations (in terms of momentum), sometimes not. If the manager believes the position is worth more or less than market price, he or she may overweight or underweight this position. Thus, sometimes the market will prove the manager right (and he or she will appear to perform well for several years), but at other times the market will prove the manager wrong (and some of his or her investors will move on to new managers).

How do we know if a manager's outperformance has been achieved by chance or by design? How can we be confident that a manager or his or her process could in fact produce an excess performance in the long term? In Figure 2.1, it seems that fluctuations in market prices were just noise around the valuations of the manager (or vice versa), and, in the end, it does not seem like the process contributed to the wealth of the average investor. Considering two different management processes—top-down and bottom-up—may help to answer these questions. A top-down process starts with a macro view of the economy, sectors and industries (it is sometimes called a factor-based approach), while a bottom-up process starts at the single security level. Top-down managers are more concerned with systematic risk, while bottom-up managers

FIGURE 2.2 Excess Performance of Energy Sector Over Financial Sector.

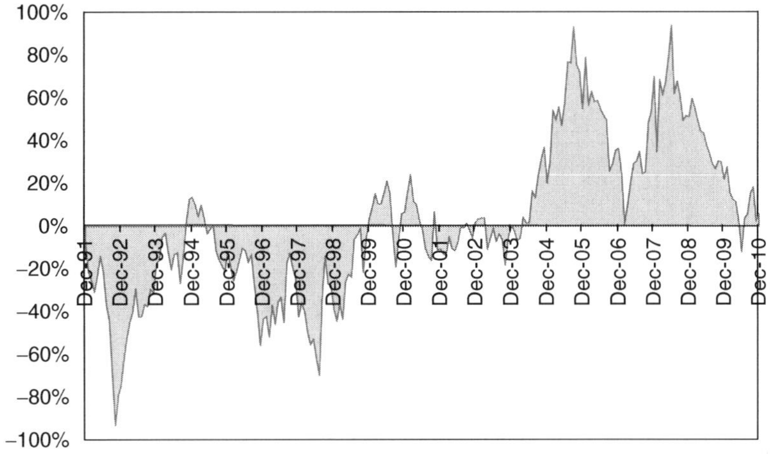

Source: Data from Bloomberg.

are more concerned with idiosyncratic risks. Note that many managers will integrate both approaches. Let's start with the top-down approach.

If there are long cycles in different segments of the financial markets, and if markets are undisciplined, some managers applying a top-down investment methodology could outperform the market on average over a period of 10 years because of a single or few strategic and significant decisions, and not because they were right on a majority of several hundred single stock-picking decisions. It would also mean that selecting a manager on the basis of his or her past returns is not a reliable approach, since we would never want to extrapolate the abilities of a manager on the basis of few material decisions. Therefore, even if the excess performance of this manager may be attributed to very insightful and successful reasoning (and not to chance, such as being right for the wrong reason), it is difficult to assume he or she will necessarily repeat this success once the economic and financial landscape has changed.

Figure 2.2 illustrates how performance could be driven by one successful macro decision. It shows the relative performance of the energy and financial sectors within the S&P 500 index from the end of 1989 to the end of 2010 using two-year cumulative rolling excess returns. A negative value indicates that the financial sector outperformed the energy sector over the previous two years.

This figure shows that the financial sector outperformed the energy sector for almost all rolling two-year periods ending from December 1991 to July 1999. It also shows that the energy sector outperformed the financial sector for almost all two-year periods ending from April 2004 to December 2010. Thus, if the manager of a large-capitalization US equity mandate had taken the macro view that the financial sector would outperform the energy sector in the 1990s, he could have been right for a very long time. Similarly, in the last decade, a manager that had taken the opposite view could also have been right for a very long time. Furthermore, once managers are proven right, it reinforces their beliefs in their own skills, which may incite them to increase or maintain their positions. The performance spread between sectors is often extremely significant, and so even a very small under and over allocation to sectors can produce a significant outperformance against the index. Must we assume a manager has persistent expertise because he or she was proven right on a single but material industry view?

Bottom-up managers also use an investment process, but at the security level. Their performance relative to an index will not be attributed to a single or a few market views, but to their ability to have selected the best single stocks on average. However, managers that use a bottom-up process could still underperform or outperform for several straight years. A bottom-up process may emphasize specific style biases or strategies. It could be an approach that favors value stocks, smaller stocks or less liquid stocks, or stocks that display positive momentum, lower volatility or more favorable balance sheets, or that benefit from better analysts revisions, etc. Therefore, although the outperformance of the manager may be attributed to many single decisions, it will reflect a specific bias, whether good or bad, at each level of this decision process. We are then left with an issue that is similar to that of the top-down manager: How do we know if a manager who emphasizes a specific bias/strategy has expertise even if he or she has outperformed for a few years?

For example, Figure 2.3 illustrates the performance of the Russell 1000 Value Index against that of the Russell 1000 Index using two-year cumulative rolling excess returns. Value stocks have outperformed Growth stocks since 1978 by about 1.5% yearly. According to Russell Investments, "The Russell 1000 Value Index measures the performance of the large-cap value segment of the U.S. equity universe. It includes those Russell 1000 Index companies with lower price-to-book ratios and lower expected growth values [4]."

Therefore, if a manager of US large-capitalization stocks is benchmarked inappropriately against the Russell 1000, and if this manager uses a process that tends to

FIGURE 2.3 Excess Performance of a Value Index against the General Index.

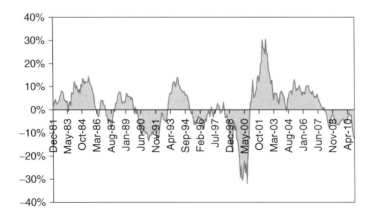

Source: Data from Datastream.

favor stocks with lower price-to-book ratios, this manager could have outperformed or underperformed for many consecutive years, and we would still not know if this manager is a good stock picker.

Thus, we have to be careful when analyzing the performance of managers. Although, in the long run, a manager may be smarter or more disciplined than the market, in the short run, it is often the less disciplined market that will determine if a manager outperforms or underperforms. If cycles in asset classes and styles last several years, even the worst managers may outperform for many consecutive years.

Our purpose thus far has not been to demonstrate that we can forecast the length of different market cycles, or even to explain what causes them. They may be related to macro factors such as business cycles and structural economic change, but they may also be related to changes in time-varying risk premiums (such as a change in investors' tolerance for risk caused by a change in economic conditions), to market inefficiencies, irrational behavior by market participants, etc. At this point, I only want to emphasize that these cycles do exist, can be significant, are rarely short, are usually unpredictable and will reward or humble many managers for several consecutive years. With so many asset managers, there will always be many among them who will have taken the right view, if even by chance, and yet we still do not know if a manager will add value after fees over 10 years. Unfortunately, the historical performance is known to significantly influence the investors' process of selecting managers.

For example, let's assume that most managers who end up with a first-quartile ranking over 10 years do, in fact, underperform for three consecutive years during this time. How likely is it that an investor will be advised to invest in a fund that underperformed for the last three years, or be advised to sell this fund if he or she already owns it? If a fund underperformed for at least three consecutive years, it could be that a fund managed according to this style may outperform in the near future. It could also be that the style of a manager that has outperformed in recent years will underperform in the near future. This is a situation where marketing objectives and our own biases may not be in line with our best interest.

There is much evidence to support this assumption. First, a study by Goyal and Wahal (2007) looked at the performance of fund managers before and after plan sponsors fired them [5]. The results are reported in Table 2.1 Most managers performed poorly prior to being fired, and performed well after being fired.

TABLE 2.1 Cumulative Performance of Managers Before and After Being Fired (1994–2003) (%)

Before Being Fired		After Being Fired	
Timing	Performance	Timing	Performance
Years –3 to 0	+2.3	Years 0 to 1	+1.0
Years –2 to 0	–2.1	Years 0 to 2	+1.5
Years –1 to 0	–0.7	Years 0 to 3	+3.3

Source: Goyal and Wahal (2007).

Second, in 2007 our asset management group looked at 146 funds that used the Russell 1000 Index as a benchmark and had reported their performances for at least 10 years [6]. The objective was to evaluate the consistency of outperformance by these managers. Results showed that 54% of the funds outperformed during the first five years, and 58% outperformed during the second five-year period. But, only 34% outperformed during the two subperiods. Fink (2012) [7] did a similar comparison, but using a more restrictive test that concluded that only 12.2%, 3.0% and 20.2% respectively of managers in the large-cap, mid-cap and small-cap equity segments were first-quartile performers in both the 2002 to 2006 and 2007 to 2011 periods—slightly more, on average, than could be accounted for by chance. Nevertheless, outperforming the benchmark, even for a period as long as five years, and being a first-quartile manager over the same period does not ensure that this performance will be repeated.

Ability to Identify Performing Managers

If we follow the teachings of Burton Malkiel, author of *A Random Walk Down Wall Street* and professor of economics at Princeton, attempting to identify the best managers is a waste of time. An article published in the *Guardian* summarizes his words:

> Markets are, broadly speaking, efficient. You can't beat them, so fire your financial adviser and put your money into index funds. These are unburdened by investment management costs, so they will always outperform the average active fund . . . There is no evidence that good performers stay at the top. Yes, there will be Warren Buffets [*sic*] in the future. But I don't know who they are, and you don't, either. You can't predict that from the past. Indexing will beat two-thirds of the market [8].

However, Warren Buffett would disagree. He is not a believer in the efficient-market hypothesis, according to which stock prices reflect all available information about companies, and investors can't beat the market indices by stock picking. In his 1984 speech at Columbia Business School, while he conceded that investment outperformance is not by itself proof of performance, Buffett nevertheless argued that we can distinguish the lucky coin flippers from the talented by analyzing their investment philosophy. In his own words:

> I'm convinced that there is much inefficiency in the market . . . When the price of a stock can be influenced by a "herd" on Wall Street with prices set at the margin by the most emotional person, or the greediest person, or the most depressed person, it is hard to argue that market always prices rationally [9].

He also added that if we were to identify those managers who outperform the market, a vastly disproportionate number would share a value-investing philosophy.

To support this statement, he presented the favorable track records of nine managers that he had identified years before.

Even if we agreed with Warren Buffett, we would still have to identify the qualities within an investment process that can lead to successful outperformance in the long run, determine if these qualities extend beyond the simple value philosophy and explain why it seems so difficult to identify managers that can deliver them. Answering these questions is possibly the main objective of this book. However, I will start with a short review of the research on manager skills and performance persistence.

A study by Barras, Scaillet and Wermers (2009) [10] discriminates among three groups of managers: those who destroy value, those who create value and those who add no value. They used a methodology designed to identify managers that may just have been lucky. The study covered 2,076 funds over a 32-year period (1975 to 2006) and accounted for fees and expenses. They concluded that 24% of managers were unskilled, 75.4% added no value and only 0.6% were skilled!

There are other studies that did find some evidence of persistence. A fairly thorough review of research completed prior to 2002 can be found in Kazemi, Schneeweis and Pancholi (2003) [11]. For example, Goetzmann and Ibbotson (1994) [12] examined if winner and loser funds over periods of two years were more likely to maintain their status over subsequent periods of two years. They found that, on average and for all years and all types of funds, 62% of winners remained winners, while 63% of losers remained losers. Further analysis shows that persistence is also greater among the best and worst funds. For example, the top quartile and the bottom quartile of funds tend to have a stronger likelihood of repeat performance than the second and third quartile of funds. Furthermore, Brown and Goetzmann (1995) [13] tested the strategy of ranking all mutual funds into eight groups (according to their annual performance) and of investing consistently within a particular group. Their study, conducted over the period of 1976 to 1988, showed much greater performance for the top two groups. They also reported that 60% of winners in one year remained winners the following year.

However, Carhart (1997) [14] studied mutual funds over the 1962 to 1993 period, and although he found evidence of some persistence, he attributed this persistence to momentum in stocks. Phelps and Detzel (1997) [15], who studied the period of 1975 to 1995, could not detect any persistence once returns were adjusted for size and style. Contradictorily, Ibbotson and Patel (2002) [16] did find that winners are more likely to remain winners, even when performances are adjusted for style (such as value versus growth), but they also found that higher persistence is generated by funds whose adjusted excess performance is greater, such as 5% or even 10%. We will come back to this observation later on.

Is persistence in returns over a period of a few years indicative of expertise? If there were market cycles that benefited the approach of specific managers for several years, we would expect that, on average, recent performers would more likely than not remain above market performers. For example, let's assume that the average cycle lasts three years (purely as an example), and that cycles are not all synchronized with one another. Under these assumptions, if we identify managers that performed well last year, we would still expect that, on average over time, about two-thirds would perform well the following year. It seems to indicate, as we will see in Chapter 5, that chasing funds, or even asset classes, with positive return momentum can be a profitable strategy. The longer the performance cycle, the more likely it is that there may be illusions of performance persistence related to expertise. Not all cycles are related to style effects that can be accounted for in tests.

However, more recent work by Cremers and Petajisto (2009) [17] seems also to support the view that it is indeed possible to identify a group of managers who are more likely to outperform. They proposed a new measure of active management called "Active Share," and it is defined as:

$$\frac{1}{2} \Sigma \mid (w_{\text{fund},i} - w_{\text{index},i}) \mid$$

Active Share measures how the portfolio holdings differ from the index holdings in terms of portfolio allocation. On one hand, a perfectly indexed portfolio would have an Active Share of zero, since the weights of each security in the portfolio and in the index would be identical. On the other hand, a portfolio made of components, which are not included in the index, would have the highest possible measure of Active Share (which is one assuming no short positions and no leverage). Cremers and Petajisto believe that Active Share not only provides a clearer picture of active management, but that it is also a useful predictor of a fund's performance against its benchmark.

According to Cremers and Petajisto, active management is done on two levels: stock selection and factor timing (such as choices of sectors and industries). Furthermore, they classify the different types of active management along five categories: pure indexing, closet indexing, factor bets (i.e., bets on sectors and industry), diversified stock picks and concentrated stock picks.

Until now, tracking error (i.e., the volatility of portfolio returns against that of the index) has been the preferred methodology for evaluating the level of a manager's activism. However, tracking error puts significantly more weight on correlated active bets. For example, shifting a 1% allocation between two sectors (such as from finance to energy) is likely to have much more impact in terms of tracking error against the benchmark than shifting a 1% allocation between two securities within the same sector. In contrast, the measure of Active Share is not impacted by such consideration. It is independent of the covariance of returns. Therefore, an investor who uses both measures would have a better understanding of the type of active management used by his or her manager. For example, according to Cremers and Petajisto, a diversified stock picker and a concentrated stock picker could both have Active Shares of 80% to 90%, but the tracking error of the concentrated stock picker would be significantly higher, such as 8% or more. A manager betting on sectors would have a high tracking error but his active share could be either low or high depending on the diversity of his holdings within sectors. Finally, closet indexers would have low tracking errors and low Active Shares (less than 60%).

Our main interest is in the conclusion reached by Cremers and Petajisto that active management, as estimated by Active Share, is a significant predictor of fund performance relative to the benchmark. Tracking error proved to be a poor indicator. Their results are based on the analysis of 2,647 funds during the period of 1980 to 2003. More specifically, they found that:

- funds in the highest Active Share quintile outperformed their benchmark, even after expenses, while funds in the lowest quintiles underperformed;
- the relationship between Active Share and relative performance is stronger for funds within the bottom three quintiles; and
- the best performing funds are the smaller funds with the highest Active Share and the highest historical 12-month returns.

The work of Cremers and Petajisto also received indirect support from Amihud and Goyenko (2009) [18]. They found that the R-square of the regression of funds performance on the Carhart four-factor model (to be discussed in Chapter 5) has significant negative predictive power. More specifically, the lower our ability to explain returns through standard risk factors, the greater the performance. Similarly, why would funds with greater excess historical returns be more likely to remain winners? Could all these observations be related?

When I first read these articles, I was puzzled with the results. More specifically, I wondered why a measure such as Active Share should predict performance, why funds whose performance is poorly explained are more likely to generate higher returns and why funds that generated the greatest excess return historically were more likely to remain winners. Of course, to outperform an index, we must hold a portfolio that is different from the index. However, in the case of Active Share, for example, why would being extremely different from the index be more likely to predict excess positive performance? Do managers with a higher level of Active Share have greater stock-picking expertise? A more rational expectation would have been that managers with high Active Share would simply have a wider range of excess returns, both positive and negative.

To solve this puzzle, I started with the recognition that Active Share is simply a measure of differentiation against the index. For example, another classification often used to reflect style of active management is the following: pure indexing, closet indexing, benchmark aware and benchmark agnostic. This categorization reflects the concern of each manager about having a portfolio that deviates from the index. A benchmark-agnostic manager has little concern for his or her security weights against those of the index, and such manager would likely have a very high measure of Active Share.

My second thought was the following: Active Share being a measure of differentiation against the index, it is possible that the excess performance of a manager may not be attributed to his or her abilities to pick stocks, but to some other statistical diversification property that is captured by Active Share. For example, as we have seen, most studies seem to indicate that persistence in mutual fund performance is more likely to occur among funds whose security positions are very different from the index. Consequently, this propensity to outperform would be more present in benchmark-agnostic managers than in other types of management approaches.

Langlois and I [19] launched a study of the measure of Active Share with an objective of supporting an alternative interpretation—an interpretation that is not necessarily linked to a manager's expertise. Since there is information relevant to this discussion that we have not yet covered, the findings of this study will not be discussed until Chapter 6. I will say here that the findings challenge the view that excess performance by funds with high Active Share is necessarily explained by a manager's expertise, and supports the idea that similar results could be achieved within a structured and systematic process. Therefore, although we may come to the conclusion that we are in fact able to predict the types of funds that are more likely to outperform their benchmark, we may also come to the conclusion that we do not necessarily need the managers of these funds to achieve those performances. Furthermore, this raises the possibility that some successful managers do not understand the reason for their success. They improperly attribute their excess performance to their specific expertise, when it is actually explained by an easily replicable process inherent to their investment approach.

Replicating the Performance of Mutual Fund Managers

Replication is a concept that basically says we can explain and reproduce much of the performance of a portfolio by trading only a few indexed products or portfolio subcomponents. For example, let's assume a balanced fund manager generates most of his or her excess returns by trading between indexed fixed-income and equity products. Even if this manager does not provide his or her daily fixed-income and equity allocations, the manager will disclose his or her daily performance. Since we have the manager's daily performance, and since we also know the performance of the two indices traded by this manager, there are econometric techniques that can be used to determine his or her most likely allocation, assuming the manager does not change position significantly every day or every week. Therefore, we can use this information to reproduce the most likely structure of risk factors present in the portfolio of this manager, and thus the manager's performance.

To illustrate this approach conceptually with a simple example, let's assume our balanced fund manager reported a performance of 0.4% yesterday. If the bond market was down 0.2% and the stock market was up 0.8% (this information is publicly available to all), we could assume that this manager currently has a two-thirds allocation to fixed income and one-third allocation to equity, because this is the only allocation that will lead to a 0.4% daily return.

$$2/3 \times 0.2\% + 1/3 \times 0.8\% = 0.4\%$$

If the next day we recalculated the most likely allocation of this manager with the performance data of this particular day and obtained a similar allocation, we could assume with relative certainty that the most likely allocation of this manager is indeed two-thirds fixed income and one-third equity. Some portfolios will have more complex structures, but, assuming we have correctly identified the most relevant explanatory factors that drive their performance, it is possible to determine the most likely allocation structure of almost any portfolio.

The principle behind the use of replication as a portfolio-management or portfolio-valuation approach is based on the idea that if a few factors are responsible for most of the performance of a manager, we may be able to "replicate" this performance by trading fewer assets. Thus, it would be interesting to find out if replication would be successful if applied to mutual fund portfolios, and to discover what conclusion could be reached from the analysis of the results.

Using a database of US large-capitalization equity managers, Langlois and I selected the managers who over the 2001 to 2010 period had a performance that would have ranked them among the top 60% to 70%, because we wanted the replication exercise to be more challenging, and to determine if few factors could explain their excess performance. This means that 60% of managers in the US large-capitalization universe had worse performances, and 30% had better performances. There were 74 managers in that group. The replication test was done over the period of 2002 to 2010 because of data availability. The excess performance of the average manager against the S&P 500 over this period was a significant 1.64%. Note that we have no idea whether the excess performance of each manager was achieved by chance or by design, only that they all outperformed the index.

Our test was simple. We attempted to replicate the performance of a portfolio of these managers month by month using only information that was available each time the replication would have been implemented. It is important to note that the test relied on monthly and not daily data. Only three products were used initially for the replication: the S&P 500, a value index (S&P 600 Value) and a small-capitalization index (S&P 600 Small-Cap). The first set of results is presented in Table 2.2. Although the replication process was applied to the performance of the portfolio of managers, we also present the relevant statistics for the average manager.

TABLE 2.2 Performance of a Mutual Fund Portfolio Replication (2001–2010) (%)

	Replication	Portfolio Managers	Average Manager	S&P 500
Return	4.01	4.96	4.85	3.21
Volatility	15.87	15.51	16.16	16.05
Tracking Error	1.48	1.62	4.75	0.00

Source: Langlois and Lussier (2011).

FIGURE 2.4   Replication Allocation Weights.

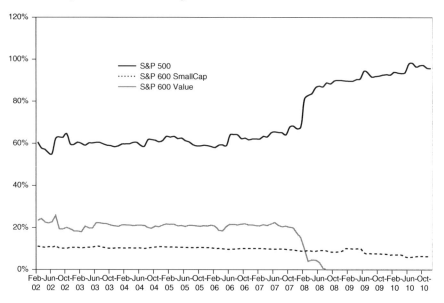

Source: Langlois and Lussier (2011).

The replication was very efficient. It captured nearly 50% of the excess return of these managers by using only three assets, one of which is the benchmark of these managers. On an after-fee basis the difference would not be as significant. The volatility of the tracking portfolio was slightly less than the index. The tracking error was also low at 1.48%. It is interesting to note that the tracking error of the portfolio of managers is far less than that of the average manager. Thus, the diversification of managers was far more efficient at reducing the tracking error than it was at reducing the volatility, which is not surprising since market risk is hardly diversifiable. This example illustrates that significant performance can be achieved without significant tracking error. It also supports the argument that managers do indeed introduce style biases in their portfolios, whether consciously or unconsciously. Finally, the correlation of excess returns of the replication versus that of the portfolio of managers (not shown in the table) is fairly high, at 61%.

What is most interesting is how this performance was achieved. Figure 2.4 shows the weights attributed to each investment product by the replication process over time.

Basically, two factors can explain much of the excess performances of these managers from 2002 to 2010. For almost seven years, the allocation to the S&P 500 index stayed at about 60%, while the allocation to the value index stayed approximately at 20%. The allocation to the small-cap index remained close to 10%. This may indicate that the performance of these managers has been achieved, on average over this period, by simply maintaining value and small-capitalization biases. However, in early 2008, when investor concerns moved from securitized products to institutions holding these products, these managers appear to have made a conscious decision to remove their value bias.

I was curious about what changes may have occurred in early 2008, and if these changes had actually been beneficial in terms of performance. The excess performance of the managers over the 2008 to 2010 period was reduced to about 1.1%, and replication explained nearly 100% of this performance. Thus, we completed a second replication and used 10 sector indices instead three market indices as factors in the replication. The replication was just as effective as the previous one, and the correlation of excess return of both replications was fairly high at 60%. However, could we explain the disappearance of a value factor in the first replication by sector shifts that may have occurred in 2008? The most significant shift was a large reduction in the combined exposure to the consumer discretionary and consumer staple sectors, two sectors that are usually almost twice as large in growth indices than in value indices. Furthermore, the allocation shift by our 74 managers added only 0.09% to their 2002 to 2010 performance.

This example illustrates that we can replicate the performance of active managers by trading a few indexed assets instead of hundreds of stocks, even without using daily data. It supports the idea that long-term performances, even by managers who have outperformed their indices, are not necessarily attributed to their stock-selection skills but could be attributed to a few decisions or to long-term persistent biases in their portfolios. For example, if the investor had simply maintained a 70% allocation to the S&P 500, a 20% allocation to the value index and a 10% allocation to the small-capitalization index over this entire period, he or she would have achieved 62% of the excess performance of these managers (before fees). In later chapters we will uncover other arguments that could explain the other 38%.

Replication is not about forecasting which manager will perform better. Replicating a bad fund should lead to a bad performance, and replicating a good fund should lead to a good performance. Unfortunately, we do not know ahead of time if the fund we are attempting to replicate will become a first- or last-quartile fund. Furthermore, replication works better on portfolios of funds than for single funds, because there are fewer idiosyncratic risks in portfolios of funds. Also, the allocation of a portfolio of funds is likely to change more gradually than the allocation of a single fund, allowing the replication to capture structural changes more efficiently, even with only monthly data.

Closing Remarks

A horizon of a few years is insufficient to conclude whether or not a manager has expertise. Furthermore, even if a manager has outperformed the market for more than a decade, his or her success could be attributed to consistent and significant structural biases that contribute to excess returns in the long term. This will be discussed further in Chapter 5. Nevertheless, even if we could agree that some style or process of management is structurally superior over long investment horizons, no management style or process consistently outperforms. Thus, good managers will be made by the market to look bad every so often, and bad managers will be made to look good.

I recently had a discussion with an active manager who raised a very significant amount of assets in less than 10 years. He indicated how his business might have turned out differently if the firm had been launched a few years later. The environment of the first two years proved very favorable to his style of management. Removing those years from his track record would have made him much less appealing to investors. In asset management, as in almost any other business, timing is everything.

The most significant issue with active management is the following. First, some managers perform by chance and others by design, but of those who perform by design, it is still possible that some of them do not fully understand why they have outperformed. It may be that they are not truly better than others at picking the right stocks, but that they have an investment process that can lead them, structurally, to outperform the market, whether they are aware of it or not. For example, if there is a behavioral pattern among market participants that leads to an overvaluation of growth stocks on average, a deep value manager could outperform the market in the long run, even if he or she is not an exceptional manager. It also means that you may not need this manager to outperform.

The replication exercise was useful if only to understand the potential dynamic of managers who have performed well. It did not explain all of the excess return of our pool of managers (before fees). However, other causes of excess performance will be discussed in Chapter 6, and, again, they have little to do with the ability of these managers to pick good stocks.

Unfortunately, although many investors are disillusioned with active management, they often draw the wrong conclusions. Bloomberg reported in late 2011 that stock pickers (presumably in the United States) suffered half a trillion dollars of losses to index trackers in five years [20]. Bloomberg reported that not only did 72% of stock-fund managers underperform the US market, but that 80% of bond managers also did. Many see this as the greatest opportunity for low-cost index trackers. Unfortunately, we should not only question the value of active management in general, but also the efficiency of standard indices. Are we making yet another mistake?

Notes

1. Rice, Matthew, and Geoff Strotman (2007), "The next chapter in the active vs. passive management debate," DiMeo Schneider & Associates, L.L.C. (An update was published in 2010.).
2. Brockhouse Cooper (2009), "Manager selection after the financial crisis—Lessons from the crash and how to apply them."
3. Shiller, R. (1981), "Do stock prices move too much to be justified by subsequent changes in dividends?" *American Economic Review* 71(3), 421–436.
4. Russell Investments, "Russell 1000® Value Index," Russell Investments official corporate website, accessed August 13, 2012, www.russell.com/indexes/data/fact_sheets/us/Russell_1000_value_index.asp.

5. Goyal, Amit, and Sunil Wahal (2008), "The selection and termination of investment management firms by sponsor plans," Goizueta Business School—Emory University, and WP Carey School of Business—Arizona State University.

6. Lussier, Jacques, and Sébastien Monciaud (2007), "Developing and investment culture," Desjardins Global Asset Management.

7. Fink, Jim (2012), "Burton Malkiel: Value investor?" *Investing Daily*, March 23.

8. Collinson, Patrick, "The index funds gospel according to Dr Burton Malkiel," *Guardian*, April 16, 2010, http://www.guardian.co.uk/money/2010/apr/17/index-funds-dr-burton-malkiel.

9. Connors, Richard J. (2010), *Warren Buffett on Business*, John Wiley & Sons, p. 233.

10. Barras, Laurent, O. Scaillet, and Russell Wermers (2010), "False discoveries in mutual fund performance: Measuring luck in estimated alphas," *Journal of Finance* 65(1), 179–216.

11. Hossein, Kazemi, Thomas Schneeweis, and Dulari Pancholi (2003), "Performance persistence for mutual funds: academic evidence," Center for International Securities and Derivatives Markets.

12. Goetzmann, W.N., and Roger Ibbotson (1994), "Do winners repeat?," *Journal of Portfolio Management 20*(2), 9–18.

13. Brown, S.J., and W.N. Goetzmann (1995), "Performance persistence," *Journal of Finance* 50(2), 679–698.

14. Carhart, Mark M. (1997), "On persistence in mutual fund performance," *Journal of Finance* 52(1), 57–82.

15. Phelps S., and L. Detzel (1997), "The non-persistence of mutual fund performance," *Quarterly Journal of Business and Economics* 36, 55–69.

16. Ibbotson, Roger G. and Amita K. Patel (2002), "Do winners repeat with style?," Yale IFC Working Paper No. 00-70.

17. Cremers, Martijn K. J., and Antti Petajisto (2009), "How active is your fund manager? A new measure that predicts performance," Yale School of Management.

18. Amihud, Yakov, and Ruslan Goyenko (2009), "Mutual fund's R^2 as predictor of performance," Stern School of Business, McGill University.

19. Langlois, Hugues and Jacques Lussier (2009), "Fundamental indexing—It's not about the fundamentals," Desjardins Global Asset Management.

20. Bhhaktavatsalam, Sree Vidya (2011), "Gross dominance in jeopardy as indexing revolution engulfs bonds," Bloomberg.

CHAPTER 3

Outperforming Which Index?

Investors make significant efforts to select the right "manager" for their equity or fixed-income portfolio. However, they often do not invest the same effort in selecting the market index they would like to match (if it is a passive portfolio) or outperform (if it is an active portfolio). Selecting the right benchmark for each mandate should be one of the most important aspects of an investment process.

We have this notion that the most well-known market indices (S&P 500, MSCI World, etc.) are based on an assembly process that is objective and efficient, and that an index should be based on a capitalization-weighted principle (cap-weighted for short) where the allocation to each security is based on its capitalization value relative to the sum of the capitalization value of all securities in the index. We have this belief, in part, because a security-pricing model developed in the early 1960s said that cap-weight portfolios are the most efficient. As we will see in this book, there is more and more evidence that this is not the case. We have mentioned previously that excessive attempts by a new breed of managers and researchers to outperform the market may no longer contribute to greater capital-allocation efficiency and investor wealth in the long term. In fact, these attempts may eventually reduce the efficiency of the allocation process at the margin by increasing its cost. We could also say that all indices are not as efficient at creating wealth for investors, but not for the same reasons.

Even if you settle for a passive approach to investment, it does not mean that you have no decisions to make. We often assume, as I just implied, that being passive means investing in a portfolio indexed to some benchmark. However, a passive approach can only exist in relation to a decision you have already made: Which benchmark will I use? Choosing a benchmark, even among cap-weight benchmarks, is an active decision. Once this decision has been made, and if you index your portfolio on this benchmark, then you have become a passive investor. However, the fact that you have chosen index X instead of index Y as a benchmark is an active decision. Since no two benchmarks are exactly the same, and since we can always decide to change a benchmark, are we ever truly passive? Furthermore, to use a metaphor, if you want to get into a race, you do not want a dressage horse; you want a racehorse. The same is true of choosing an index. Unfortunately, many benchmarks are not built for the long-term race.

In this chapter and in later chapters, the word "protocol" will often be used. A protocol simply expresses the set of systematic rules used to assemble a portfolio. For example, a cap-weight protocol means that the securities within a portfolio are allocated according to size, as measured by capitalization. Similarly, an equal-weight protocol means that securities are periodicially re-weighted toward $1/N$.

Purpose and Diversity of Financial Indices

The purpose of an index is to provide investors with a good representation of the performance and volatility of specific markets. For example, the purpose of the S&P 500 is to measure the performance of the large-capitalization segment of the US stock market. The purpose of the DEX Universe in Canada is to measure the performance of the Canadian fixed-income market.

There are hundreds of these indices, and the most popular family of indices (such as the one created by Standard & Poor's, Russell and MSCI) will be used as benchmarks for a plethora of products (ETFs, mutual funds and other active mandates). Indexed mutual funds will attempt to match the performance of the most popular indices by replicating their components. For example, a manager given the mandate to match the performance of the S&P 500 may simply buy all 500 securities and use the same weight as tht of the index for each security. Others may buy a subset of the 500 securities if they believe it will still reproduce the performance of the entire index fairly accurately.

Active managers are usually given the mandate to outperform one or a combination of those same indices. Once an index has been specified as a benchmark to an active manager, the structure of this index will become the structure of reference for the portfolio of this manager. Although some managers may adopt an agnostic approach by trying not to be significantly influenced by the structure of the chosen index as a benchmark, many other managers will continually analyze their active positions in relation to the index, and several will even attempt to manage their tracking error against the index. Thus, the same manager may deliver different performances depending on which specific index he or she is measured against. The choice of an index as a benchmark may, in many cases, have much more impact on realized performance than the choice of an active manager.

There are many different categories of indices. There are indices for equities, bonds, commodities, etc. Within the equity segment there are global indices such as the MSCI World (an index of 1600 securities and 24 countries), and there are country-specific indices for large-capitalization stocks (such as the S&P 500 (United States), the S&P/TSX (Canada) or the FTSE 100 (United Kingdom)) or small-capitalization stocks (such as the Russell 2000 (United States)). There are capped indices (such as the S&P/TSX 60 Capped) to prevent any component of the index from having too much weight. There are sector-specific indices (such as S&P Consumer

Finance Index), there are style indices (such as Russell 1000 Growth and Russell 1000 Value), there are indices built around social concerns, ethical conduct and environmental issues (such as the FTSE4 Good Index series) and there are even indices built around portfolio-assembly methodologies (such as FTSE TOBAM MaxDiv). There are probably more indices than are truly needed. The greater the diversity of products the industry wants to create, the more indices will be designed. However, to reinforce what we said in the introduction of this book, with so many indices to choose from, how can we ever be truly passive investors, especially when even capitalization-weight indices do not even represent the entire market?

Building an Index

Two main steps are required to build an index. The first is identifying the eligibility criteria that will determine which securities are eligible to be potentially included in the index (criteria such as minimal capitalization and liquidity). The second is choosing the weight mechanism. Several weighting schemes can be used to build an index, but the most popular process is to weight securities according to their market capitalization. Such indices are referred to as "cap-weight indices." Other examples of weighting principles are $1/N$ (where all the components of the index are given equal weight and rebalanced periodically to bring the components back to an equal weight) and dividend payout (where the weight of each security is determined according to the relative dividend payout). For example, there are two versions of the S&P 500 index, the S&P 500 Cap Weight (the most well-known) and the S&P 500 Equal Weight. There are many more weighting principles that are being used in the industry, but using market weights is the dominant approach.

The literature says that an index should meet some minimum requirements. It should be measurable (obviously), replicable (not very logical for an investor to use an index that cannot be acquired) and representative of the investment universe. According to Arnott, Hsu and West (2008) [1], an index process should also be transparent and rule based (anyone who would attempt to later recreate the index should have identical results) and should produce a low turnover (we do not want to reduce our long-term performance by incurring excessive transaction costs).

The concept of cap-weight indices was first introduced in 1926. There are two main reasons why it has remained so prevalent until now. First, in 1964, William F. Sharpe introduced the capital asset pricing model (CAPM), a security-pricing model. The model was developed fairly independently by Jack L. Treynor (1961, 1962), Bill Sharpe (1964), John Lintner (1965) and Jan Mossin (1966), building on the earlier work of Harry Markowitz on diversification and modern portfolio theory. Sharpe, Markowitz and Merton Miller jointly received the Nobel Memorial Prize in Economics for their contribution to the field of financial economics.

According to this model, the pricing of securities could be summarized by a single risk factor, the market, represented by a cap-weight portfolio of all risky securities available. Thus, investors would hold all of their assets in a portfolio allocated between a risk-free asset and the market portfolio. The model assumes that the required excess return on any risky security is solely determined by its sensitivity to the market factor measured by β (Beta), which is itself a function of the covariance of returns between the security and the market. In his 1964 paper, Sharpe demonstrated the superiority of the cap-weight approach, subject, however, to many assumptions. Decades of research have illustrated several inconsistencies with the CAPM. For example, Fama and French (1992) [2] concluded that the market factor could not explain the cross-sectional variation in returns, and that a model incorporating other factors, such as size of firms and market-to book-values, was more appropriate. Thus, we may have been motivated to support the dominance of cap-weight indices because of a model developed in the 1960s that does not really hold, although the CAPM was certainly an important trigger for substantial research over the last 40 years.

Another reason for the usage of cap-weight indices is simplicity. Cap-weight indices do not require any rebalancing, assuming the components of the index do not change. Within a cap-weight index, the allocation of each security evolves according to its relative price change against the rest of the index, and since all price changes are fully reflected in the market capitalization of each stock, no rebalancing is required. Rebalancing only becomes necessary if securities are being removed and added to the index. Thus, in theory, a cap-weight index meets one important requirement of an index: a low turnover. Finally, we do live in a financial universe where a company' size is determined by capitalization.

Some investors may not realize that many well-known indices do not meet some of the basic requirements that were specified above. Let's consider the S&P 500. The S&P 500 is not an index of the 500 largest companies. It is an index of large companies that must generally meet specific criteria. An index committee decides additions to and deletions from the index. Standard & Poor's keeps all index committee discussions confidential because it considers information about changes to its US indices and related matters to be potentially market moving and material. In other words, this is not a fully transparent, rule-based system. This can be better illustrated by the decisions of the index committee in the midst of the technology bubble.

In 2000, at the top of the technology bubble, 24 of 58 companies added were in the technology sector. One company, AOL, was added to the index even though it did not meet all the requirements set forth by S&P and at a time when the technology sector accounted for a growing proportion of cap-weight indices (because of the strong performance of the sector over the previous five years). Thus, the index committee contributed to increase the weight of technology within the index by adding even more companies to this sector. Committees may be subject to the same biases as many financial advisors. A financial advisor may recommend investing in funds that recently outperformed and exiting funds that recently underperformed. The decisions of an index committee to change the components of the index may also be biased by the recent popularity of securities and sectors.

This issue is not limited to equity indices. Ilmanen (2011) [3] discussed why index investors in investment-grade corporate credit in the United States over the last few decades have earned only one quarter of the spread delivered by the market.

The main culprit is the tendency of index investors to sell the assets that leave the index and subsequently perform well. It may also mean the construction rules of these indices force investors to sell too quickly, and at a loss.

Furthermore, several indices cannot be fully replicated by buying their components. This is especially true of emerging-market indices and fixed-income indices such as the DEX Universe in Canada. Many investors in Canada will not fully use the DEX Universe (the most well-known fixed-income index) as a benchmark. Rather, they will use a combination of DEX sub-indices, partly because of the large percentage of Canada bonds within the index, and because of the instability of its issuer components. For example, in the 1990s, after years of huge government deficits, the index (called Scotia Universe in those days) had a very large allocation to Canada bonds. The allocation to Canada bonds declined in the last decade (and until the recent credit crisis) because of years of fiscal surpluses. This goes to show that bond indices become less or more risky and provide smaller or greater credit premiums depending on government policy and economic regime. It does not make sense to have the structure of an index dictated by the fiscal policies of our governments.

Are Cap-Weight Indices Desirable?

My main objective thus far has not been to criticize cap-weight indices per se. I simply wish to convey that financial indices, even well-known indices, are not grounded in some universal and indisputable set of construction rules. Therefore, if, as in the case of the S&P 500, an investment committee with its own biases determines which securities are admissible or not, and if market-cap-weight indices have no foundation in theory, there is a strong possibility that better concepts for indices can be designed.

Some investors have been questioning the pertinence and value of cap-weight indices. The EDHEC conducted a survey [4] that was completed by 85 institutional respondents with average assets of $142 billion each. The survey indicated that 70% of the respondents were using customized benchmarks to compensate for the flaws of cap-weight indices. Two-thirds of respondents also agreed with two of the EDEHC's criticisms concerning market-weight benchmarks, their lack of stability and their lack of efficiency.

Let's discuss these issues. When investors use an index as a reference portfolio, there is an implicit assumption that this index represents a neutral position of sorts. However, we also know that markets may favor specific companies, sectors or styles from time to time. Therefore, because the relative price change of securities within a cap-weight index dictates the changes in weights for all securities within the index, market events will change the exposure to specific companies, sectors and styles within the index. Since we all witnessed the burst of the technology bubble in the early 2000s, we should understand how significant an issue this can be. The instability of sector exposure within an index such as the S&P 500 is illustrated in Table 3.1.

The weight of technology and telecom within the S&P 500 increased from 15.0% in 1990 to 37.1% in 1999. By 2000, their combined weights were 26.7%. It was

TABLE 3.1   Evolution of Sector Weights Within the S&P 500 (%)

Sectors	1990	1995	1999	2000	2005	2010
Financials	7.5	13.1	13.0	17.3	21.3	16.1
Technology	6.3	9.4	29.2	21.2	15.1	18.7
Health Care	10.4	10.8	9.3	14.4	13.3	10.9
Industrials	13.6	12.6	9.9	10.6	11.3	11.0
Consumer Discretionary	12.8	13.0	12.7	10.3	10.8	10.6
Energy	13.4	9.1	5.6	6.6	9.3	12.0
Consumer Staples	14.0	12.8	7.2	8.1	9.5	10.6
Utilities	6.2	4.5	2.2	3.8	3.4	3.3
Telecom	8.7	8.5	7.9	5.5	3.0	3.1
Materials	7.2	6.1	3.0	2.3	3.0	3.7

Source: Standard & Poor's.

21.8% in 2010. The financial sector was only 7.5% in 1990. The weight tripled to 21.3% in 2005. It was 16.1% in 2010. It is interesting how investors set precise percentage targets for their allocation to asset classes and yet they are willing to let the market dictate the structure of their exposure within an asset class. Canadians should know. Because of Nortel, the technology sector accounted for more than 35% of the index in the early 2000s. By 2003, with the collapse of Nortel, the sector accounted for less than 5% of the main index—and yet we attribute so much credibility to these indices. Thus, cap-weight indices have a growth bias.

Alternatives to Cap-Weight Indices and Implications

Cap-weight indices do not create a company or sector bubble, investors do. But cap-weight indices will not protect the investor against such an event, either. In fact, cap-weight indices will fully participate in the creation and destruction of such bubbles. In a cap-weight index, relatively overvalued stocks will be overweighted, and relatively undervalued stocks will be underweighted whether or not we know which stocks are relatively undervalued, overvalued or fairly priced. As an investor, you have a choice. You can benchmark and manage your portfolio according to an index methodology that will expose you to every security, style or sector bubble, or you may choose another methodology that is less likely to expose you to these bubbles—a methodology that simply does not use capitalization as a weighting mechanism. We will use the terms "nonmarket-cap protocols" or "market-indifferent protocols" to designate any of these methodologies.

TABLE 3.2 Annualized Returns of S&P 500 and S&P 500 Equal Weight (%)

Weight Structure	1991–2010	1991–2000	1998–1999	2000–2002	2001–2010	2001–2005	2006–2010
Cap Weight	9.1	17.5	24.7	−14.5	1.4	5.4	2.3
Equal Weight	11.8	17.7	12.1	−3.7	6.3	7.7	4.8

Source: Data from Bloomberg.

Let's consider a simple nonmarket-cap allocation process, $1/N$ or equal weight. An equal-weight allocation process may not be the best protocol (although it is surprisingly efficient), but it is very unlikely to overexpose you to security and sector bubbles. An equal-weight protocol will force a calendar rebalancing (for example, once a year) of all securities, whether the price of a security has risen or declined. Thus, equal weight is a mean-reverting allocation process. Table 3.2 shows comparison of the performance of the S&P 500 market Cap Weight and the S&P 500 Equal Weight.

Equal-weight indices often perform very well. An investor in the S&P 500 cap-weight index multiplied his assets by 5.8 times from 1991 to 2010. An equal-weight investor would have multiplied his assets by 9.4 times. However, the 1998 to 1999 period was not conducive to a strong performance by equal-weight protocols because the period was characterized by strong momentum in one sector: technology. Since an equal-weight protocol will revert to equal weights at rebalancing, it will not benefit as much from the creation of a sector bubble. However, it will also not be penalized as much by its destruction. Equal-weight indices have, among other characteristics, far more stable sector exposure than cap-weight indices, although some investors may be uncomfortable with the structure of the sector exposure that results from applying such a protocol (especially in countries where some industries are highly concentrated). This could potentially lead to an index structure with an unacceptable representation of the economic structure.

When we look at Figure 3.1 and notice the much greater allocation instability of cap-weight protocols, we should also be thinking about the relevance of the concept of tracking error. For example, many investors will use tracking error (i.e., the volatility of the excess performance of one portfolio against another, such as an index) as a measure of risk. However, if we were to look at the tracking error of the equal-weight S&P against the cap-weight S&P, it seems the tracking error is caused by the greater instability of the reference portfolio: the cap-weight index. We must stop thinking of cap-weight indices as superior reference portfolios. They are not.

To some investors, this may seem like a zero-sum game. Investors will not do as well in markets with positive momentum, and will do better when this momentum reverses. Furthermore, they may attribute the outperformance to a smaller capitalization bias resulting from applying an equal-weight investment protocol (within the large-cap corporate universe). However, there are many other reasons why an equal-weight protocol can or should outperform cap-weight protocols in the long run, and

FIGURE 3.1   S&P 500—Evolution of Cap (Left) and Equal (Right) Sector Weights.

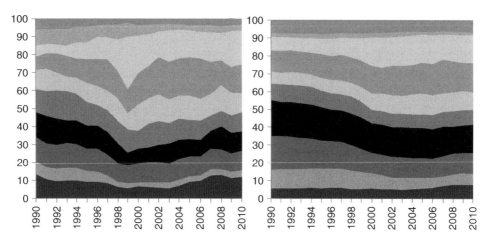

Source: Data from Standard & Poor's.

one of the arguments is related to the smoothing of price noise (also called pricing error). Furthermore, some nonmarket-cap protocols are better suited than market-cap indices to a liability-driven investor (we will come back to this issue in Chapter 10). For now, let's concentrate solely on the issue of price noise. The price of any security can be considered as the sum of two components: a fair price and a pricing error. Thus,

$$\text{Observed Price} = \text{Fair Price} + \text{Price Noise}$$

The "Fair Price" is the true theoretical price that no one really knows, but that perfectly reflects the fundamentals of the firm. For example, even if the current price of a Ford stock is $10, is it really worth $10? Maybe its true fundamental value is $8 or $12, hence the price noise. You may ask, how good is it to know that there is price noise if no one can tell you what the true fair value of any security is?

To understand why this is so important, let's assume there are only two firms (A and B), and that the shares of each firm trade at $8 each. Although we do not really know the true fair value of these securities, it will help to assume that we do know for the sake of this example. Let's also consider several scenarios as in Table 3.3a.

In this example, we have six possible scenarios of relative valuation: the shares of both companies can be equally fundamentally undervalued or overvalued (which is fairly unlikely), both can be overvalued but the shares of one firm are likely to be overvalued more and finally both can be undervalued but the shares of one firm are likely to be undervalued more.

Let's assume each firm has a million shares in circulation (to simplify). The market capitalization of each firm at fair value would be $8 million. Thus, the weight of each firm within the index should be 50%. However, since fair values are unknown, the relative weights of our two securities will be determined by market prices. Table 3.3b presents all possible relative weights according to each scenario.

The example shows that if a security is relatively overvalued, it will be overweight within a cap-weight index. If a security is relatively undervalued, it will be underweight within a cap-weight index. With only two firms it may not seem so interesting, but what is true of two securities is also true of 100 or 500 securities. If about half the securities are relatively overvalued (undervalued) with respect to the median of

TABLE 3.3a Pricing Scenarios and Over/Under Valuation ($)

Scenarios of Observed Prices	Fair Values	Price Noise*	Conclusion
A = 9 B = 10	A = 8 B = 8	A = 1 B = 2	Both overvalued but B more than A
A = 10 B = 9	A = 8 B = 8	A = 2 B = 1	Both overvalued but B less than A
A = 7 B = 6	A = 8 B = 8	A = −1 B = −2	Both undervalued but B more than A
A = 6 B = 7	A = 8 B = 8	A = −2 B = −1	Both undervalued but B less than A
A = 9 B = 9	A = 8 B = 8	A = 1 B = 1	Both equally overvalued
A = 7 B = 7	A = 8 B = 8	A = −1 B = −1	Both equally undervalued

* + = Overvaluation.
– = Undervaluation.

TABLE 3.3b Price Scenarios and Over/Under Valuation

Scenarios of Observed Prices ($)	Weights Within the Index (%)	Fair Value Weights (%)	Conclusion
A = 9 B = 10	A = 47.4 B = 52.6	A = 50 B = 50	A is underweighted B is overweighted
A = 10 B = 9	A = 52.6 B = 47.4	A = 50 B = 50	A is overweighted B is underweighted
A = 7 B = 6	A = 53.8 B = 46.2	A = 50 B = 50	A is overweighted B is underweighted
A = 6 B = 7	A = 46.2 B = 53.8	A = 50 B = 50	A is underweighted B is overweighted
A = 9 B = 9	A = 50 B = 50	A = 50 B = 50	Actual weight = fair value weights
A = 7 B = 7	A = 50 B = 50	A = 50 B = 50	Actual weight = fair value weights

mispricing, about half are relatively overweight (underweight). So, in a cap-weight index, approximately 100% of the firms that are relatively overvalued are overweight and approximately 100% of the firms that are relatively undervalued are underweight. There is nearly a 100% correlation between the relative mispricing of securities and the underweighting/overweighting within a cap-weight index. There is no diversification of price noise in a cap-weight index.

Again, we do not know which securities are undervalued or overvalued, but we do not have to know to diversify price noise. Let's assume we are using $1/N$ (equal weight) as an allocation protocol. In such a protocol, the market price of each security, its fair value and its price noise have no impact on its allocation within the index. If 0.2% is allocated to each of the 500 securities within the index, the correlation between the weight of a security and its price noise will be zero over time. Of the 50% of firms that are relatively overvalued, about half have probably been underallocated and half overallocated. Of the other 50% of the firms that are relatively undervalued, about half have also probably been underallocated and the other half overallocated. Being wrong 50% of the time is still better than being wrong 100% of the time.

Therefore, an index or portfolio based on an allocation process that is not correlated with market prices should be far more efficient in the long term. From this point of view, a cap-weight portfolio is relatively inefficient. An equal-weight portfolio rebalanced periodically is one way of achieving a low correlation between price noise and allocation weights, but it is not necessarily the most appropriate approach. There are many methodologies that can prove more efficient than cap-weights that will meet all the requirements of the investors, whether it is concentration, economic representations, cash flows, etc.

However, as we have seen with Table 3.2, it is important to understand that avoiding cap-weight does not guarantee superior performance over any horizon, but it does increase the probabilities in your favor. This statement is not based on some forecasts but on exploiting the weakness that is present in all cap-weight indices. In later chapters, we will see that smoothing price noise is not the only source of performance when designing or choosing a more efficient index or investment protocol.

Closing Remarks

We live in a cap-weight world. We cannot avoid the fact that the size of a company in the equity market (and also in the fixed-income market) is defined by its capitalization (the market values of all its equity or bonds). Therefore, a larger company accounts for a bigger proportion of all equity capitalization than a smaller company. That may explain why it seems so natural to use cap-weight indices as benchmarks. Fortunately, this is not your concern. We may, all of us, live in a cap-weight world, but you, as a single investor among millions, do not have to invest according to this principle—even if you are a very large investor.

The structure of cap-weight indices is often unstable. Market sentiment can drive the weight of a company or a sector or a style to new levels (higher or lower). This may not be in your best interest if you seek to manage concentration, diversification, representativeness and volatility. Furthermore, well-known indices are not a true representation of a market. They are an approximation of the public markets. Thus, choosing an index and an index-construction methodology is an active decision, because not all indices are created equal.

There is much evidence that indices not based on cap-weight protocols outperform. One explanation is their ability to smooth price noise, and, thus, to avoid the almost 100% correlation between price noise and the changes in allocation weights that occur within cap-weight indices. There are other reasons as well, which will be discussed in Part III of this book. There is nothing passive about investing in a cap-weight index, but it does comfort some investors to know that they are probably applying the same investment process as many others. As investors, we are concerned about absolute risk (how much we can lose) and relative risk (how much less we can make than others), and although it is always important to be concerned about absolute risk, the obsession of many with relative risk (and how they will be perceived against others in the short run) is making it extremely difficult to implement efficient structural changes to investment portfolios that are necessary to outperform. This is why there will always be opportunities for those more concerned with absolute risk and with the quality of their investment process.

A consultant once asked me what would happen if a significant proportion of investors were to use nonmarket-cap equity protocols. Would the advantage that results from the smoothing of price noise disappear? Conceptually, it should not disappear, but it could be significantly reduced. First, if investors were using methodologies that were not based on market capitalization to build and rebalance their portfolio, market momentum would be lower and market volatility would decline. There would be fewer equity booms and busts. This would be to the benefit of all investors. This is why nonmarket-cap methodologies were generally found to perform better over time in more volatile markets.

Second, there are infinite ways to build nonmarket-cap protocols. This means that it is more difficult to create a situation where specific types of securities become severely overpriced because of significant one-way trading by a group of investors. Furthermore, a process that can be implemented in many different ways is more difficult to arbitrage. However, I am far from convinced that a large segment of investors will abandon market-cap indices as a guideline for the structure of their portfolios. The obsession with short-term performance tracking against market-cap indices will not allow this to occur on a huge scale. Similarly, it is doubtful that investors in general will restrain themselves from overreacting or underreacting to momentum in securities or sectors and suddenly become more disciplined.

Notes

1. Arnott, Robert D., Jason C. Hsu, and, John West (2008), *The Fundamental Index: A Better Way to Invest*, John Wiley & Sons, Inc, p. 64.
2. Fama, Eugene F. and Kenneth R. French (1992), "The cross section of expected stock returns," *Journal of Finance* 47 (2), 427–465.
3. Ilmanen, Antti (2011), *Expected Returns: An Investor's Guide to Harvesting Market Rewards*, Wiley Finance, p. 46.
4. Goltz, Felix and Guang Feng (2007), "Reactions to the EDHEC study—Assessing the quality of stock market indices," An EDHEC Risk and Asset Management Research Centre Publication.

PART II

Understanding the Dynamics of Portfolio Allocation and Asset Pricing

CHAPTER 4

The Four Basic Dimensions of An Efficient Allocation Process

We can use two approaches to outperform the market with statistical probabilities greater than 50%. One approach requires that we become great students of the investment process, and, as Antti Ilmanen (2011) [1] said, that we develop multi-dimensional thinking on all pertinent inputs: historical average returns, financial and behavioral theories, forward-looking market indicators (such as earning yields) and discretionary views. According to Ilmanen, "the challenge is to refine the art of investment decision making in a way that exploits all of our knowledge about historical experience, theories, and current market conditions, without being overly dependent on any of these . . . Stated differently, investing involves both art and science; a solid background in the science can improve the artist."

Many managers will argue that their investment process already incorporates all of these aspects, but although almost everyone can paint by numbers, few can create a masterpiece. Few investors have the balanced discipline, depth of understanding and experience that are required to become a true artist. If you read Ilmanen's book, *Expected Returns*, you will fully appreciate the subtlety and complexity of the investment world.

A less demanding, less intimidating yet comprehensive approach (which may, in fact, be a subset of the first approach) is to exploit specific structural inefficiencies and statistical properties inherent in portfolios of assets. This will not necessarily require the ability to explicitly forecast returns, but it will nevertheless increase expected performance in the long term. In essence, instead of attempting to outperform the market, we will allow the market to underperform. This nuance will become clearer as we proceed. My main objective is not to claim that the global investment process proposed in this book is the most efficient (it can be improved), but simply that it is much less inefficient than what the market and most service providers offer. It is also more statistically reliable. A reduction in inefficiency increases expected returns.

The proposed investment process is segmented according to four main dimensions. Chapter 4 will introduce these dimensions and lay a foundation for all other chapters. However, the emphasis of this chapter is on developing a better understanding of the first dimension: volatility.

53

First Dimension: Understanding Volatility

In finance, volatility is a measure of the price variation of a financial instrument. For most individuals, volatility is undesirable because it is synonymous with risk. It is also undesirable because, as will be explained, it is synonymous with lower compounded returns. However, an understanding of volatility can be used to illustrate the benefits of diversification and rebalancing, and the benefits or danger of using leverage. It can also be used to understand the source of some of the excess performance that lower-variance equity protocols may generate, to propose investment processes that can improve the compounded return of a portfolio and to provide alternative explanations for some of the realized performances of strategies and managers (which may increase our skepticism about management expertise even further). A great many idiosyncrasies of the financial world can be explained with an understanding of volatility. Furthermore, although volatility reduces compounded returns, we unfortunately need volatility to produce excess returns. We may not like volatility, but we have to appreciate what it can do for us. Since this aspect is not necessarily well understood, we need to build a foundation in Chapter 4 that will be developed much further in the rest of this book. Let's start with the traditional comparison between two scenarios of periodic returns over two periods.

In Scenario 1, the performance is 10% both years. In Scenario 2, the performances are 20% and 0% respectively. The arithmetic mean (ARI mean) is simply the average of the yearly performance, and it can be thought of as a representation of the most likely performance in any single year. However, investors are much more concerned with the geometric return (GEO mean) on their investment, which is the average yearly return that takes into account the reinvestment rates. This is the return that will define your final wealth. Maximizing the GEO mean is equivalent to maximizing final wealth. For example, if you had invested $100 under each scenario, the value of your investment would have evolved as indicated in Table 4.1b.

TABLE 4.1a A Simple Illustration of Arithmetic and Geometric Means (%)

	Scenario 1	Scenario 2
Period 1	10	20
Period 2	10	0
Arithmetic Mean	10	10
Geometric Mean	10	9.54

TABLE 4.1b A Simple Illustration of Arithmetic and Geometric Mean ($)

	Scenario 1	Scenario 2
Initial Investment	100	100
Period 1	110	120
Period 2	121	120

The end value under Scenario 1 is greater, despite the fact that both investments have the same average arithmetic return, because the investor benefited in Period 2 from the reinvestment of the gains realized in Period 1. To be more specific, the investor in Scenario 1 has a higher terminal wealth because the ability to benefit from the reinvestment of cash flows is inversely linked to the volatility of returns. A greater volatility penalizes geometric returns. In Scenario 1, there is no volatility of returns and therefore the GEO mean is equal to the ARI mean. It can never be greater. In Scenario 2, the GEO mean is less than the ARI mean. Volatility will contribute to the decrease of your geometric returns and therefore your accumulated wealth.

The relation between the GEO mean (μ_g) and ARI mean (μ_a) is well documented [2]. Equations 4.1a to 4.1d present the basic formulas for the arithmetic mean, the geometric mean and for the relation between both performance measures. Note that Equation 4.1c is well-known but remains an approximation. The relation is more accurate in the context of assets having a normal (Gaussian) distribution (a distribution with no asymmetry and no excess fat tails). However, it remains fairly accurate in most circumstances, even when the distribution of returns is not symmetric and there is reasonable momentum or autocorrelation in the data. Equation 4.1d is a further simplification of Equation 4.1c, which is especially appropriate when dealing with low-return, low-volatility assets and high-frequency data. Fully understanding the implication of this relationship between ARI mean and GEO mean is extremely important to many aspects of the allocation process.

$$\mu_a = \Sigma(R_i) \,/\, N \tag{4.1a}$$

$$\mu_g = (\Pi(1 + R_i))^{\,1/N} - 1 \tag{4.1b}$$

$$\mu_g = \mu_a - [\sigma^2/(2(1 + \mu_a)^2)] \tag{4.1c}$$

$$\mu_g = \mu_a - [\sigma^2/2] \tag{4.1d}$$

The terms within brackets in Equations 4.1c and 4.1d represent the performance drain (i.e., the difference between the ARI mean and the GEO mean) attributed to volatility. For example, in the Langlois and Lussier case study about replication of mutual funds discussed in Chapter 2, the GEO mean of the S&P 500 for the period 2002 to 2010 was 3.21% (or 0.264% monthly). Although we did not mention the ARI mean over this period, it was 4.47% (or 0.372% monthly). Thus, the performance drain attributed to volatility was 1.26%. However, according to Equation 4.1c, if the ARI mean is 4.47% and the volatility is 16.05% (4.63% monthly), the GEO mean should be as follows:

$$0.372\% - [4.63\%^2 /\, (2 \times (1 + 0.372\%))] = 0.265\% \text{ (or 3.23\% annualized)}$$

The difference between the actual GEO mean and the GEO mean derived from Equation 4.1c is not significant (3.21% versus 3.23% annualized) considering that the S&P 500 had a skew of −0.75, a kurtosis of 4.26 (1.26 above the kurtosis of a normal distribution) and the period was characterized by strong upward and downward momentum. Nevertheless, the (negative) sign of the difference between the two values is consistent with the fact that negative asymmetry should normally lead us to underestimate the size of the performance drain attributed to volatility and overestimate (slightly) the GEO mean.

Estrada (2010) [3] has calculated the difference between the observed GEO mean and the GEO mean derived from Equation 4.1c for the equity markets of 22 developed countries, 26 emerging countries and 5 asset classes. Periods of analysis ranged from 20 years to nearly 40 years for each data set. For developed countries the average and maximum absolute deviations were only −0.1 and 1.3 bps respectively. For asset classes, they were −0.2 and 0.8 bps, while for emerging markets the values were 1.3 and 13.6 bps. The relationship is more accurate when the volatility is lower and the asymmetry is as small as possible. However, it remains highly accurate in almost all cases, especially in the context of diversified portfolios.

Someone may ask: So what? Even if this relationship is true, the pattern of market-price volatility between two periods does not necessarily influence the true long-term fundamental value of an asset at the end of the investment horizon. Let's consider two scenarios. Under both scenarios, the market volatility at the end of the investment horizon is identical. However, the pattern of market volatility under the first scenario is far more volatile because of exogenous factors (i.e., market volatility was more volatile during the investment period, but is identical at horizon end). Does it mean an asset should have a lower value at horizon end if the first scenario occurs? Not if the excess market volatility did not impact the fundamental valuation parameters. For example, on one hand a transient event may have impacted market volatility for a time, but may have had no impact on economic growth, inflation or corporate profits. On the other hand, it is likely that excessive volatility and fear between 2008 and 2009 significantly impacted confidence, thus aggravating the liquidity crisis and changing the economic scenario that would have prevailed otherwise. In this case, the pattern of volatility may have significantly and permanently impacted fundamental valuations. We will ignore this possibility in Chapter 4, but it will be considered later on. Thus, we will assume, for now, that if a stock traded for $70 five years ago, and if it were trading at its true fundamental value of $100 now, the GEO mean remains at 7.3%, whatever the pattern of volatility during the horizon of the investment. Therefore, if the course of volatility did not impact fundamental valuations at horizon end, the GEO mean will be the same, but the ARI mean will be different.

For example, assuming volatilities of 10% and 15% respectively, but identical GEO means, the ARI mean would have to be approximately:

$$7.8\% = 7.3\% + 10\%^2/2 \qquad \text{if volatility} = 10\%$$

$$8.425 = 7.3\% + 15\%^2/2 \qquad \text{if volatility} = 15\%$$

The ARI mean is greater in the second scenario, but the investor is not any wealthier in the end. He or she would probably just have been more stressed if the second scenario occurred. Accepting, for now, the argument that the pattern of volatility did

TABLE 4.2 The Effect of Diversification on GEO Mean (%)

	Equity	Fixed Income	Diversified Portfolio	Portfolio without Diversification Benefits
ARI mean	8.50	4.82	6.66	6.66
Volatility	20.00	8.00	11.82	14.00
GEO Mean	6.50	4.50	5.96	5.68
Performance Drain	2.00	0.32	0.70	0.98
Correlation	30			

not impact fundamental values at the end of the investment horizon, and that our investor was able to tolerate the higher level of volatility during the investment period, we could say, "So what?" However, what is true in the context of a single asset does not apply in the context of a portfolio of assets that are rebalanced. Let's now use another simple example in Table 4.2 with two single assets and a 50/50 allocation. Note that we will keep coming back to this example in this section.

Equity has an ARI mean of 8.5% and a GEO mean of 6.5%. The performance drain attributed to volatility is 2%. Fixed income has an ARI mean of 4.82% and a GEO mean of 4.5%. The performance drain is 0.32%. The ARI mean of a portfolio is always the sum of the weighted average of the ARI mean of its components, in this case it is 6.66%. However, the volatility of a rebalanced portfolio (11.82%) is always less than the weighted average of the volatility of its components (14%) unless the correlation is one. This is a simple result of Markowitz's diversification formula. Thus, if the volatility of the portfolio is 11.82%, its GEO mean and performance drain have to be, respectively, 5.96% and 0.7%. If we were to assume there were no diversification benefits (correlation = one), the GEO mean and performance drain would have to be 5.68% and 0.98%. The 0.28% spread is what we call the "diversification bonus" or the increase in the GEO mean that can be attributed to diversification. This is why we diversify. Diversification improves portfolio efficiency, and a more efficient portfolio generates a greater compounded return and Sharpe ratio. However, diversification in the Markowitz sense cannot exist without a rebalancing process. For a portfolio to benefit from a reduction in performance drain that can be attributed to diversification, the portfolio must be rebalanced.

The justification for this diversification bonus can be found in Equation 4.1d, which stipulates that volatility reduces the GEO mean by half the variance. For example, if the volatility of the portfolio is 11.82%, but its volatility, assuming a correlation of one, is 14%, then the increase in GEO mean attributed to lower volatility can be estimated by half the variance spread, or:

$$[14.00\%^2 - 11.82\%^2] / 2 = 0.28\%$$

FIGURE 4.1   Volatility and Performance Drain.

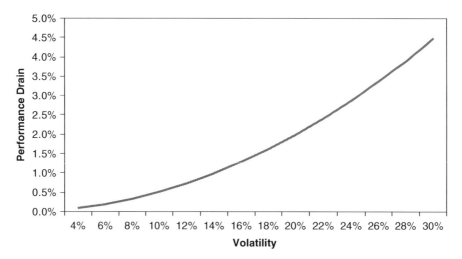

Thus, the diversification bonus is a linear function of the variance. However, if one considers standard deviation instead of variance, the diversification bonus would be a non-linear function. This relationship is illustrated in Figure 4.1, which shows the size of the performance drain according to volatilities (standard deviations) ranging from 4% to 30%. At 4% volatility, this drain is only 0.08%, but at 30% volatility it is a significant 4.5%.

The relationship between volatility and the performance drain is concave. Therefore, if we combine assets of different volatilities, and if the resulting portfolio volatility is less than the weighted average of the volatilities of its components, the performance drain will necessarily be less than the weighted average of the performance drain of its components. Reducing volatility through efficient portfolio-management processes and methodologies is extremely important.

Now that we understand the relationship between volatility, GEO mean, performance drain and the diversification bonus, I will explain how a portfolio can be structured to maximize the benefits of diversification. The answer to this question can be found in Equation 4.2a, which specifies the variance spread between a two-asset portfolio, assuming these two assets have either a correlation of one (no diversification benefits) or a correlation equal to ρ_{ab}. The equation is simply derived from the difference of two basic Markowitz equations. However, three sets of components are isolated in brackets to facilitate the interpretation. And because the diversification bonus is equal to half the variance spread, Equation 4.2b is the expression that estimates the diversification bonus for a two-asset portfolio.

$$2 \times [X_a X_b] \times [\sigma_a \sigma_b] \times [1 - \rho_{ab}] \qquad (4.2a)$$

$$[X_a X_b] \times [\sigma_a \sigma_b] \times [1 - \rho_{ab}] \qquad (4.2b)$$

where X_a and X_b are the portfolio weights, which must sum to one.

If we replace the variables in Equation 4.2b by the values specified in Table 4.2 we obtain exactly 0.28%. Equation 4.2b also reveals interesting details. The impact of diversification on the GEO mean (i.e., the diversification bonus) will be maximized if, for a given level of weighted average volatility among assets:

- portfolio weights are equally balanced because the product of $X_a X_b$ is highest when both values are 0.5;
- all assets have equal volatility (or at least similar volatilities) because the product of the volatility of two assets that have identical volatilities will always be greater than the product of the volatility of two assets that have different volatility but the same average volatility (for example, in a 50/50 portfolio, the impact would be greater if two assets of 15% volatility were combined instead of one asset with 10% volatility and another with 20% volatility); and, of course.
- if the correlation is as far below one as possible.

There is also one other important aspect. For a given correlation, the diversification bonus is greater if both assets have more volatility. We need volatility to create diversification benefits. Figure 4.2a and b illustrates how the portfolio allocation

FIGURE 4.2a Correlation, Equity Weight and the Diversification Bonus.

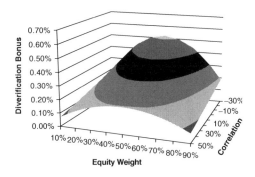

FIGURE 4.2b Correlation, Equity Weight and the Diversification Bonus.

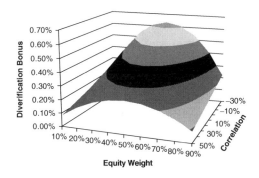

among two assets (from 10/90 to 90/10) and their correlation (from +50% to −30%) impact the GEO mean. Figure 4.2a assumes the same volatilities as in Table 4.2 (20% and 8% for each asset, respectively) while Figure 4.2b assumes both assets have equal volatilities (14%). As expected, the diversification bonus is at its maximum when assets have equal weight. It is also greater if assets have identical volatilities and correlation declines. This may explain the interest on strategies designed around equal-weight portfolios of standardized (volatility-adjusted) risk factors, a topic to be discussed in Chapter 7.

However, in both figures, much of the benefit of diversification is achieved when the allocation remains between 30/70 and 70/30—fortunately a fairly wide range. The reason is simple. According to Equation 4.2b, the product of the weights of our two assets will impact the diversification bonus. Although the value of this product is at its maximum when the weights are equal, a 40/60 allocation or a 60/40 allocation would retain 96% of this efficiency, since: (60% × 40%) / (50% × 50%) = 96%. Similarly, a 70/30 or 30/70 portfolio would retain 84% of the efficiency. However, a 20/80 or a 10/90 portfolio would only retain 64% and 36% of the efficiency of an equal-weight portfolio.

We should not confuse maximum diversification bonus and minimum performance drain with maximum Sharpe ratio and information ratio. We will see in Chapter 6 that if two assets have a different volatility, the most statistically efficient portfolio is achieved when both assets contribute an equal amount of risk. In our current example of two assets, equal risk is achieved when the allocation to equity and fixed income is respectively 28.57% and 71.43%. In other words, owning 28.57% of an asset with 20% volatility will contribute the same amount of risk to the portfolio as owning 71.43% of an asset with 8% volatility. Thus, the allocation that maximizes the diversification bonus does not necessarily lead to the most efficient portfolio allocation, except under specific circumstances.

For reasons that will be explained later, our only objective for now is to evaluate the impact of lower volatility on the GEO mean and to evaluate which portfolio allocation maximizes the diversification bonus. If the answer is 50/50 in a two-asset case (when assets have similar volatility), what is the answer if there are more than two assets in the portfolio? Since the number of pairwise correlations increases with the number of assets, the effect of diversification on the GEO mean would be determined by the sum of several equations such as Equation 4.2b, one for each pairwise correlation. In a three-asset case, there are three pairwise correlations, and in a four-asset case, there are six. Assuming, for now, that all assets have similar pairwise correlations, the portfolio structure that would maximize the diversification bonus is still the one where assets have equal weight and volatilities are similar. Furthermore, if these conditions were met, the diversification benefits would increase strongly compared to the two-asset case.

For example, assuming again that all assets have identical volatilities and pairwise correlations, an equal-weight portfolio of two assets has exactly 50% of the efficiency that could be achieved with a portfolio containing an infinite number of equally weighted assets. Fortunately, four assets would already deliver 75% of this efficiency,

FIGURE 4.3 Diversification and Portfolio Efficiency.

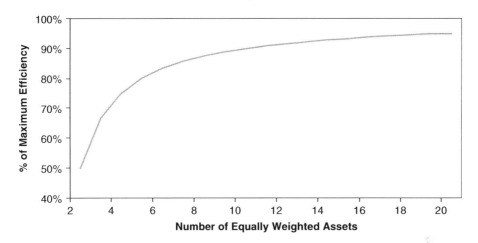

and seven assets would deliver more than 85%. The relation between the number of equally weighted assets and the efficiency of diversification, as defined by the size of the diversification bonus, is illustrated in Figure 4.3. These observations do explain, in part only, why equal-weight portfolios are often found in the literature to be return/risk efficient, but this is an aspect to be analyzed further in Chapter 6.

To illustrate the importance of portfolio structure to the diversification bonus, let's consider two portfolios as described in Table 4.3. Portfolio 1 is more concentrated, with 70% invested in one asset and the remainder equally weighted between two other assets. Portfolio 2 is equally weighted between all three assets. The volatility of assets in Portfolio 1 varies from 8.6% to 18%, while all assets in Portfolio 2 have the same volatility (16%). Both portfolios have the same weighted average volatility (16%). Finally, all pairwise correlations are identical at 0.3. We could illustrate that under those circumstances, the structure of Portfolio 2 will contribute an extra 28 basis points (bps) a year to the GEO mean, not insignificant in the current environment.

TABLE 4.3 Analysis of the Impact of Three Portfolio Structures on the GEO Mean (%)

	Portfolio 1		Portfolio 2		Portfolio 3	
	Weight	Volatility	Weight	Volatility	Weight	Volatility
Asset A	70	18	33.33	16	50	16
Asset B	15	14	33.33	16	25	16
Asset C	15	8.6	33.33	16	25	12
Weighted Average Volatility	16		16		15	
Performance Drain	96 bps		68 bps		65 bps	

It may sound unrealistic to assume that a portfolio of components of similar volatilities and weights could be created. However, many of the benefits of diversification on the GEO mean can be achieved even if the weights and volatilities of assets are not equal. Several chapters in this book also discuss methodologies that can be used to adjust the volatility of portfolio components. Portfolio 3 in Table 4.3 has achieved an even greater efficiency than Portfolio 2, while having a more balanced allocation than Portfolio 1 and a lower weighted average volatility than both portfolios 1 and 2 (15%), although the assets are not weighted equally and do not have the same volatility. The lower volatility of Portfolio 3 would reduce the performance drag that is attributed to volatility by 31 bps. We can structure asset components (i.e., equity, fixed income, commodities and others) to produce better diversification benefits. We can draw several conclusions from this discussion:

- Maximizing the diversification bonus does not necessarily imply maximum Sharpe ratio or Information ratio. Our objective at this stage is only to illustrate the portfolio structure that maximizes the diversification bonus since methodologies that attempt to create portfolios that maximize the Sharpe ratio often lead to unstable structures (high turnover, greater concentration and less-than-balanced economic structure). It can be acceptable for portions of a portfolio, but less palatable to an investment committee if applied on a large scale. We want to improve portfolio efficiency, but the global solution must appear very balanced to the investor.
- Much more can be done to improve the diversification bonus. Investors should not only seek to diversify their portfolios more efficiently, but also to structure their portfolio components to deliver a range of volatilities that will help maximize the diversification benefits. We should not accept that the volatility of an asset class within our portfolio is the volatility that the market provides for this specific asset class or index. The structure of an index should be adjusted to provide more beneficial volatility and diversification characteristics within the portfolio.
- Efficient portfolios can be built with few asset components if these components have been structured to offer the required characteristics.
- Although we would prefer to incorporate asset components that offer large expected risk premiums in our portfolios, a well-built index (or investment protocol) that offers better diversification properties than readily available indices may compensate, under specific circumstances, for a less-than-ideal risk premium. This will be illustrated in Chapters 7 and 8. This is especially true for commodities.
- None of this is possible without a systematic rebalancing process. To efficiently capture the benefits of diversification (the diversification bonus), your portfolio must be rebalanced. However, not all rebalancing processes are created equal. The efficiency of the rebalancing process is also a very significant issue, which will be covered in Chapters 7 and 10.
- Finally, and very importantly, just because a portfolio with a 50/50 allocation benefits from a greater diversification bonus than an 80/20 portfolio, it does not mean that a 50/50 portfolio will necessarily outperform. However, for the 80/20 portfolio to outperform, the ARI mean of equity should exceed that of fixed income enough

to compensate for the lower diversification bonus. A less efficiently diversified and riskier portfolio must generate a higher ARI mean to compensate for this lower efficiency before it can expect to outperform.

Benefits and Dangers of Leverage

A transformation of Equation 4.1d [4] can be used to illustrate the potential pitfalls and benefits of using leverage. Equation 4.3 stipulates the relation between GEO mean and ARI mean in the context of leverage (L) and cost of funding (r).

$$\mu_g = [(L \times \mu_a) + r(1 - L)] - [0.5 \times (L \times \mu)^2] \tag{4.3}$$

To illustrate first the danger of leverage, let's assume we are leveraging an equity investment in a 20% plus volatility environment. Let's also assume equity has an expected ARI mean of 8.5%, which dictates that in a 20% volatility environment, the GEO mean has to be 6.5%. What is the expected return if the investment is leveraged by a factor of two, and if the cost of leverage is 4%?

If we double the amount of invested capital, the ARI mean adjusted for the cost of leverage will be 13%, or $2 \times 8.5\% + 4\% \times (1 - 2)$. However, the volatility of return adjusted for leverage is now 40%. The volatility drain on the ARI mean will not double; it will quadruple from 2% to 8%. Leverage has reduced the expected GEO mean to 5%, less than that of an unleveraged investment. If the portfolio were leveraged by a factor of three, the GEO mean would be negative (−0.5%). Leverage can significantly reduce the GEO mean of a portfolio. In the context of volatile assets, leverage can only be a short-term tactical play, not a strategic long-term position.

It is important to understand that this is not a forecast. This is an unavoidable long-term mathematical relationship. If leverage is applied on an asset that has volatile returns, and if this investment structure is maintained, the long-term return will drift much lower than the investor may expect. Table 4.4 illustrates the impact of leverage and volatility on the GEO mean.

TABLE 4.4 Leverage, Volatility and Long-Term Performance Drag on Performance (%)

Volatility	Performance Drag		
	Leverage = 1	Leverage = 2	Leverage = 3
5	0.13	0.50	1.13
10	0.50	2.00	4.50
15	1.13	4.50	10.13
20	2.00	8.00	18.00
25	3.13	12.5	28.13
30	4.50	18.0	40.50

Two units of leverage applied to an asset with a 10% volatility of return will create a drain on performance of 2%. However, the same leverage applied to an asset with 25% volatility will create a performance drain of 12.5%. Leverage can be dangerous (this is why many leveraged ETFs are not advisable for investors), but there are circumstances where some type of leverage can be of use. For example, if leverage is applied to assets with volatility, such as 5% or less, the performance drag is not as significant. The most important aspect of using leverage is not being wrong about the expected volatility of the underlying asset.

Diversification, Leverage and Portfolio Efficiency

It may be useful at this point to illustrate the impact of volatility on portfolio efficiency using real data. We will keep the example simple because this aspect will be addressed in more detail and with more sophisticated methodologies in Chapters 7, 8 and 10. We will consider eight portfolios whose allocations range from 20/80 to 90/10 with 10% increments. The fixed-income component is the 10-year US Treasury, while the equity component is the S&P 500. Over the period we'll be looking at, the S&P 500 outperformed the 10-year Treasury by 2.89% (annualized). The analysis is done using weekly data from 1980 to 2010, which has not been annualized. Information on returns and volatilities is provided in Table 4.5a.

TABLE 4.5a Impact of the Diversification Bonus on Portfolio Structures (1980–2010) (Weekly Data in %)

Equity Weight (%)	20	30	40	50	60	70	80	90
ARI Mean (Weekly)	0.177	0.184	0.191	0.198	0.205	0.212	0.219	0.227
Volatility (Weekly)	1.05	1.09	1.19	1.32	1.49	1.68	1.88	2.10
GEO Mean (Weekly)	0.171	0.178	0.184	0.189	0.194	0.198	0.202	0.204
GEO Mean (Annualized)	9.30	9.68	10.03	10.34	10.61	10.85	11.05	11.21
Diversification Bonus	0.21	0.27	0.31	0.32	0.31	0.27	0.21	0.12
Correlation to Equity	53	71	84	92	96	98	99	99
Volatility Accounted by Equity	20	43	65	81	90	96	99	99

Source: Data from Datastream.

The spread between the weekly ARI and GEO means is almost exactly equal to one-half the observed variance. Unsurprisingly, the diversification bonus is at its maximum level for the 50/50 portfolio. It is also interesting to note that the diversification bonus for a 40/60 or a 60/40 allocation has 96% of the efficiency of a 50/50 allocation, as we would have expected. As well, the efficiency for a 30/70 or a 70/30 allocation is 84%. Since equity outperformed fixed income by a wide margin over this period, and since these portfolio components have not been "optimized," the diversification bonus was not sufficient to prevent a riskier portfolio to outperform a less risky portfolio. In this particular case, the 90/10 portfolio still outperformed the 50/50 portfolio by 0.015 percentage points weekly or 0.87 percentage points annually (although it is also more than 50% riskier) despite the fact that the diversification bonus is 0.20 percentage points greater for the 50/50 portfolio (0.32% versus 0.12%). However, the investor should also consider the impact of management fees, which are likely to be greater on a 90/10 portfolio than on a 50/50 portfolio. There are no fees in this example.

We can see that equity dominates the total risk of most portfolios. For example, in a 50/50 allocation, equity contributes 81% of the volatility of the entire portfolio, and its correlation to equity is, unsurprisingly, 92%. Thus, although the diversification bonus is maximized when allocation weights are equal, the portfolio itself remains poorly diversified in the Markowitz sense. There are at least five ways to deal with this issue.

The first approach may not please many investors, since it has to do with leverage. However, it will improve our understanding of the dynamics of volatility, as well as its potential role in the hedge fund industry, even if we do not use this approach. In theory, portfolios that have more balanced risk weights between equity and fixed income, such as a 30/70 or even a 40/60, are more efficient. They usually have a better Sharpe ratio. Therefore, leveraging a more efficient portfolio could be more return/risk efficient than allocating more to equity without leverage.

Let's assume an investor is comfortable with the average volatility level of a 60/40 portfolio. However, instead of buying the 60/40 portfolio, our investor considers leveraging another portfolio to achieve the same level of volatility as a 60/40. Table 4.5b presents those results.

TABLE 4.5b Diversification Bonus and Leverage (1980–2010) (%)

Equity Weight	20	30	40	50	60	70	80	90
GEO Mean not Leveraged	9.30	9.68	10.03	10.34	10.61	10.85	11.05	11.21
GEO Mean Leveraged	10.42	10.80	10.88	10.76	10.61	10.43	10.26	10.09
Level of Leverage	47	41	28	13	0	−12	−21	−29
Equity Allocation	29	42	51	56	60	62	63	64
Fixed-Income Allocation	118	99	77	56	40	26	16	7

Source: Data from Datastream.

The most efficient leverage is achieved with 30/70 and 40/60 portfolios. They outperform the 60/40 by 19 bps and 28 bps respectively over 30 years. They have identical volatilities, but their portfolio structures are entirely different. For example, the contribution of equity to the overall risk of these two leveraged portfolios is far less significant. In this case, the investor would have to decide if leveraging the 40/60 portfolio and having an allocation of 51% to equity and 77% to fixed income is preferable to a 60% allocation to equity and 40% allocation to fixed income. The second portfolio is, in theory, more appropriate to an investor with fixed cash flow liabilities, but many investors would balk at leveraging their portfolio by 28%.

Leveraging will be even more efficient if the reference portfolio is not well diversified. If the objective of the investor had been to leverage a more efficient 40/60 allocation to the same level of volatility as US equity, the excess GEO mean would have been 1.56% annually. However, the leverage would also have been 100% (i.e., the amount invested would equal two times the capital allocation). This raises the possibility that some of the excess performance of many hedge funds (but not all) can be attributed to the leverage of lower-volatility assets or strategies, and to a more balanced allocation of risk premiums than in a traditional portfolio. Investors would basically be paying higher fees to these hedge funds because the hedge fund managers deliver return characteristics that the investors find attractive. But, these characteristics are achieved using strategies that investors could implement themselves (if they wanted to), and require no particular expertise. I will come back to this issue in Chapter 7.

Fortunately, leveraging is not the only approach available to managing the issue of risk concentration within a portfolio. A second approach consists of modifying the risk structure of the portfolio components. For example, although most equity mandates have volatilities ranging from 16% to above 20%, it is possible to design mandates that have two-thirds to three-quarters of this volatility. Furthermore, this could be done in conjunction with an increase in the duration and/or the credit risk of the fixed income mandate, thus creating a more balanced set of risk premiums and a more return/risk-efficient portfolio.

Let's consider again the 40/60 allocation, which has been leveraged to the same level of risk as a 60/40 allocation. In this scenario the equity allocation would have to increase to 51%, while the fixed-income allocation would have to increase to 77%. A similar effect could be achieved without leverage. The investor could allocate 51% to equity and 49% to fixed income, but increase the duration of the fixed-income portfolio by about 50%. The investor would have to decide if he or she prefers a 60% allocation to equity and a 40% allocation to 10-year bonds, or a 51% allocation to equity and a 49% allocation to longer-duration bonds. Thus, interest rate sensitivity can be increased through traditional leverage, but also by using swaps or, in this case, by increasing bond duration. Not all these options would have the same sensitivity to a change in the slope of the yield curve, and scenario analyses would be required to determine which option is preferred. However, the purpose of this example is not to promote leverage, but simply to illustrate the significant role that (adjusted) volatility plays in designing an allocation strategy.

A third approach involves integrating more distinct and lowly correlated risk premiums than what is usually available through standard market indices (such as small-cap versus large-cap or value versus growth, etc.). Therefore, the objective of the third approach is to dilute the dominance of systemic equity market risk within the portfolios, allowing for a higher Sharpe ratio.

We already know that although global geographic exposure to equity markets does provide long-term diversification of economic risk and returns, it does not provide short-term diversification from major financial crises. Christoffersen, Errunza, Jacobs and Jin (2010) [5] showed that correlations among developed countries' equity markets have been on the rise and are quite high, and although emerging markets are showing lower correlations with developed countries, these correlations were also on the rise. Furthermore, their results illustrate that there is substantial tail risk dependence between equity markets, especially between developed markets, resulting from substantially higher correlations in down markets. This indicates that, in the case of equities, the likelihood of unfavorable events is still significant. Diversification among developed equity markets is unreliable when most needed. Risk concentration and dependence of traditional equity risk must be reduced.

A fourth strategy for managing risk concentration within a portfolio consists of modifying the return distribution of specific assets or portfolios and, implicitly, their sensitivity to specific events or regimes. This can be achieved by appropriately combining allocation to standard risk premiums with an overlay of instruments such as options and variance swaps. The objective is usually to buy appropriate protection against the financial impact of unfavorable events and pay for it by accepting lower returns during favorable events. Although I will describe in Chapter 7 a product designed to fully exploit this approach, we will not study it in as much detail as other methodologies because the product requires a higher level of complexity to be properly executed.

The final approach involves dynamically managing the portfolio volatility using a more efficient rebalancing process. This approach does not seek to reduce the average contribution of equity risk to the overall risk of the portfolio, but rather to manage and control its risk contribution over time. For example, equity exposure is often the most volatile component of a portfolio, and it dominates even more the overall risk in difficult markets. Because volatility is not stable (it is always changing), managing volatility can improve the GEO mean of a portfolio.

A more comprehensive portfolio solution would allow for all five approaches to be used in a framework that is acceptable to investors. For example, not everyone can use or wants to use leverage (or at least very much of it), not everyone wants to modify the structure of asset classes on a large scale, not everyone is comfortable with incorporating new risk premiums or has access to them and not everyone is willing to have his or her portfolio allocation dictated significantly by volatility movements. Finally, investors do not understand the implications of adjusting the traditional structures of asset classes or managing volatility in order to build investment products that are more coherent with an LDI (liability-driven investment) concern. An appropriate balance must be found and investors must be able to choose among several portfolio-management solutions. Although volatility and its impact on performance will be discussed specifically in Chapter 7, it will be a topic of discussion in almost all remaining chapters of this book. Therefore, I will not continue this discussion any further because the goal of this section was to demonstrate, at least partially, that there is more to volatility than risk alone.

Second Dimension: Increasing the ARI Mean

The GEO mean of a portfolio is a function of the ARI mean and volatility. The first dimension of our portfolio-management process was a concern for the impact of volatility on performance. The second dimension is to increase the ARI mean of the entire portfolio. In essence, we seek to increase performance for the same level of volatility. This would require a more efficient portfolio structure than what is delivered, for example, by cap-weight portfolios. This issue is covered in the following two segments:

1. Selecting investment protocols that improve the ARI mean of each asset class (Chapters 6 and 8)
2. Implementing processes that improve the ARI mean of the entire portfolio through efficient asset-allocation processes (Chapters 7 and 10)

Each of these two objectives are achieved through the following types of approaches:

1. Exploiting structural inefficiencies (such as avoiding cap-weight benchmarks)
2. Using reliable forward-looking indicators of the relative performance of components within asset classes and among asset classes

Both approaches can and should be designed with a focus on the behavioral patterns of investors and management. If a factor is related to persistent excess performance, our confidence in this factor will increase if it can be linked to human behavior. There are few things in life that are reliably persistent. Each of us may show inconsistent behavior over time, but groups of individuals usually do not. Optimism and pessimism are easily spread to a group of investors. As I will illustrate, the degree of long-term success in asset management is a function of how far investors are willing to move away from conventional wisdom. This does not require that we increase absolute risk (on the contrary, it can be reduced), but it may require that we accept a different kind of relative risk.

Investors who allocate to active equity managers are already accepting tracking-error risk, and, as we discussed in Chapter 2, tracking error is a poor predictor of excess performance. However, in Chapter 6, we will see that there are structural qualities that a systematic nonmarket-cap investment protocol should have that will statistically lead to expected excess performance (against a traditional cap-weight benchmark) in the long run. Such protocols will not behave as traditional cap-weight indices, which will create a tracking error of sorts, although the term "tracking error" is probably not appropriate to express the volatility of the relative performance between a traditional cap-weight index and a systematic nonmarket-cap investment protocol. Tracking error is a term reserved for expressing how much risk a manager is taking against his or her benchmark. There is an implicit understanding that this tracking error could be reduced to zero if an active manager decided to eliminate his or her bets against the index. That said, in the case of an alternative benchmark (i.e., an alternative systematic investment protocol), there is no such implicit assumption, since respecting the protocol after it has been adopted is the neutral position. Thus, if an investor is willing to tolerate the tracking error that results from investing with an active manager (especially a benchmark-agnostic manager), he or she should also be willing to accept a different benchmark (such as an equal-weight protocol), especially if the justification for expected excess performance is much more powerful. However, many investors have ideological issues with this transition.

Third Dimension: Efficiently Maximizing GEO Mean Tax

Taxation is not an issue for pension funds and foundations, but it is an issue for individual investors. Taxation impacts the objective of maximizing the GEO mean in two ways:

1. It has a downward impact on the ARI mean. Furthermore, this impact is asymmetric, because not all sources of income and investment vehicles are taxed according to the same rates, or even the same principles of taxation.
2. Taxation does not only impact return, it impacts risk.

It is important to understand the impact of taxation on the after-tax GEO mean. To develop this understanding we will compare the basic principles of the US and Canadian tax system. Although Canadians certainly pay, on average, higher taxes than Americans, the Canadian tax principles have been far more stable and coherent, and are less likely to distort the investment process. I will also quantify the benefits of efficient after-tax planning.

One aspect that I will cover with special attention is the tendency to postpone portfolio rebalancing in order to avoid capital gains. We already know that portfolio rebalancing creates a diversification bonus. We will see in later chapters that some forms of rebalancing can improve the performance of the portfolio well beyond the effects of the diversification bonus. Furthermore, because taxation can impact volatility, it will also impact the size of the diversification bonus. Therefore, avoiding taxation in the short-term can, sometimes, have long-term unfavorable consequences.

TABLE 4.6   Impact of Taxation on GEO Mean (%)

	Before Tax	After Tax
ARI Mean	8.5	6.8
Volatility	20	16
GEO Mean	6.5	5.52

To illustrate, let's assume a simple and rational tax system (we can always hope) where all gains and losses (whatever their source) are taxable or tax deductible on a yearly basis. In such a world:

$$\text{ARI mean (after tax)} = \text{ARI mean (before tax)} \times (1 - \text{tax rate})$$

$$\text{Volatility (after tax)} = \text{Volatility (before tax)} \times (1 - \text{tax rate})$$

For example, if an investor received a return of 10% in Year 1 and −10% in Year 2 before tax, his or her yearly after-tax returns (using a 20% tax rate) would be respectively +8% and −8%, assuming, for now, that investment losses are tax deductible in the same period that they are realized. The volatility would be reduced by 20%. Therefore, if we assume an ARI mean of 8.5%, a volatility of 20% and a tax rate of 20%, how does the GEO mean before and after tax compare? This is illustrated in Table 4.6.

The after-tax GEO mean is nearly 85% of the before-tax GEO mean, despite a tax rate of 20%. This is obviously an ideal situation, but it does illustrate that the obsession of many investors with postponing taxes for as long as possible may not always be the optimal choice. As we all know, taxation rules are far more complicated than assumed here, but in Chapter 9 we will concentrate on the basic principles of the US and Canadian tax systems, not only to introduce these principles to our portfolio-management process, but also to learn from the differences between the two systems.

Fourth Dimension: Accounting for Objectives and Constraints

All investors are not alike. Although all investors share in the common objectives of minimizing volatility, maximizing the ARI mean and maximizing the GEO mean tax efficiently, not all investors can follow the same recipe. First, even ignoring the difference in tax treatment of different investors, not all investors share the same investment goals or have the same attributes. These differences are not limited to risk, as defined by the distribution of losses, but also to requirements such as cash-flow matching, minimum periodic income, inflation protection, etc.

Such constraints should, preferably, not be treated as an overlay on the previous three dimensions of investing, but as something that is part of the process. For example, if an investor requires regular periodic cash flows, the investment processes used for this investor should incorporate both the objective of maximizing the GEO mean after tax and generating periodic and reliable cash flows. Thus, it should be coherent with an LDI concern. One of the main conclusions we will reach in this book is that there are qualities that a basic portfolio requires, but that these qualities are not exclusive to a single investment approach. For example, we can identify many investment protocols that are likely to outperform a standard benchmark (if they all offer those basic qualities that we should be looking for) and although we could never say which protocol is the best among them, we can say with relative confidence that all of them have more than a 50% chance of outperforming a standard protocol if the horizon is reasonably long.

Closing Remarks

Diversification can be characterized in different ways. Diversification can be about not having all our eggs in one basket. Diversification can also be about increasing the GEO mean and our end wealth. Markowitz [6] said that diversification] is the only free lunch in financial markets. However, how do we go about delivering our objective of a greater after-tax GEO mean in a portfolio that meets all constraints in a statistically reliable way?

In late 2010, I told a colleague working at a state pension fund that I was in the process of writing a book about what we know with relative certainty and what we do not know about the field of portfolio management. I indicated to him that my motivation for writing this book was based on the observation that, despite 60 years of modern portfolio management, the industry did not seem to be learning from its own mistakes, and was not learning from the tremendous amount of financial literature available. The spouse of this colleague is a physician, and, because of his general familiarity with this field of research, he advised me to look at the literature on evidence-based medicine and evidenced-based management.

Evidence-based medicine is an approach that advises clinicians to make decisions based on the best available evidence that is gathered, ideally, from rigorous methods using large patient samples. It is a dynamic process, because the knowledge acquired during the initial training is augmented by the clinicians' subsequent experience as practitioners through knowledge efforts that constantly and reliably convey the latest research evidence [7].

In the field of management (not specifically portfolio management), evidence-based management is defined by Bryner, Denyer and Rousseau (2009) as "making decisions through the conscientious, explicit and judicious use of four sources of information: practitioner expertise and judgment, evidence from the local context, a critical evaluation of the best available research evidence, and the perspectives of the people who might be affected by the decision [8]."Thus, evidence-based management is implemented by practitioners and not by academicians.

Bryner, Denyer and Rousseau made the argument that evidence-based management is underdeveloped, misunderstood, misapplied and implemented inconsistently. In the field of management, Pfeffer and Sutton (2006) [9] mentioned how firms often implement reengineering/restructuring processes at the cost of millions of dollars from their favorite consulting firms, while most of these consultants have very little evidence that their advice and techniques actually work. Most clients will apparently not even think to ask if such evidence exists. The authors also noted how a senior consultant admitted that the restructuring and reengineering processes implemented by his firm generated millions in revenues, and how the firm made millions again from the same clients trying to fix the organizational issues that the reengineering process had created.

Although this literature is not specific to portfolio management, we can easily relate to it. We have met with many consultants throughout our careers, and there is an aura of confidence that comes with using consultants that is sometimes not deserved. Looking at the four sources of information required to implement a good decision-making process (mentioned above), we can attempt to evaluate whether or not the financial industry is at all concerned about this process. Let's go back to the issue of active management and product development. What is the evidence?

Researchers in medicine say that the gold standard of research methodology is the double-blind, placebo-controlled study, in which patients in one group are randomly assigned to get a treatment, while patients in the other are randomly assigned to get a placebo, and neither patients nor doctors know which patient is in which group. We have had such an experiment in the portfolio-management industry for many decades. Most research on the issue of active management concludes that active managers do not create value in aggregate, that it is extremely difficult to identify managers who will outperform, that the most likely scenario is that expected performance will be equal to index performance minus fees and, thus, that investors should buy the least expensive products. These conclusions have been reached by looking at practitioners' experiences over several decades, by considering almost every local context and by relying on the best research available. Furthermore, the research was done from the point of view of the affected party: the investors. Finally, we have the benefit of knowing for a fact that investing is a zero-sum game for all investors before fees. In a normal experimentation process, decades of such evidence would have led the industry to emphasize well-diversified products with low management expense ratios. Instead, the industry has developed a wide range of ever more specialized and expensive products.

The industry is not the only party to blame. Most investors do not want to hear that they have to be patient and disciplined to get richer, and that simplicity may trump complexity over time. Although there have been research papers challenging the benefits of active management since the early 1920s, our generation of investors is now questioning the value of active management like never before.

The industry has created far more specialized and unproven products than those that are needed by investors. Just as I was writing those lines, a hedge fund based in London announced that they were launching an equity product where the securities would be selected according to investors' sentiment as measured by the use of key words on Twitter! Yet, as we will try to demonstrate in several chapters of this book, even after decades of research, it is often difficult to agree on stylized facts about portfolio-management concepts. We still cannot determine with certainty if a risk premium exists in commodities, and there is hardly a consensus about the issue of hedging currency risk. The financial industry does not follow the basic principles of evidence-based research because it is not in its own best interest, and also because investors do not want to hear that patience is essential to a good investment process.

Therefore, in response to the original question, "How do we go about delivering our objective of a greater after-tax GEO mean in a portfolio that meets all requirements in a statistically reliable way?", the answer is simple: we will follow the evidence.

Notes

1. Ilmanen, Antti (2011), *Expected Returns: An Investor's Guide to Harvesting Market Rewards*, Wiley Finance, p. 5.
2. Bernstein, William J. and David Wilkinson (1997), "Diversification, rebalancing, and the geometric mean frontier," Working Paper.
3. Estrada, Javier (2010), "Geometric mean maximization: An overlooked portfolio approach?" IESE Business School.
4. Carver, Andrew B. (2009), "Do leveraged and inverse ETFs converge to zero?" *Institutional Investors Journal* 2009(1), 144–149.
5. Christoffersen, Peter, Vihang Errunza, Kris Jacobs, and Xisong Jin (2010), "Is the potential for international diversification disappearing?" Working Paper, The Rotman School, McGill University, University of Houston.
6. Markowitz, H. (1952), "Portfolio Selection" *Journal of Finance* 7 (1), 77-91.
7. Reay, Trish, Whitney Berta, and Melanie Kazman Kohn (2009), "What's the evidence on evidence-based management?" *Academy of Management Perspectives* 23(4), 5–18.
8. Briner, Rob, David Denyer, and Denise M. Rousseau (2009), "Evidence-based management: Concept cleanup time?" *Academy of Management Perspectives* 23(4), 19–32.
9. Pfeffer, Jeffrey and Robert I. Sutton (2006), "Management half-truths and nonsense: How to practice evidence-based management," adapted from *Hard Facts, Dangerous Half-Truths, and Total Nonsense: Profiting from Evidence-Based Management*, Harvard Business School Press.

CHAPTER 5

A Basic Understanding of Asset Valuation and Pricing Dynamics

Few managers outperform consistently. Ninety percent of first-quartile managers over a horizon of 10 years underperform for at least three years straight. Thus, it appears that if there is a recipe for long-term success, it involves accepting the possibility of several years of underperformance (against traditional benchmarks). This may indicate that predictor variables (whatever they may be) are more likely to be strongly correlated with multi-year returns than with quarterly returns. Recent studies indicate that managers who have specific characteristics (such as a high measure of Active Share) are more likely to outperform their benchmark, but these studies rely on mutual fund data that covers several decades. Thus, even if some variables have predictive value, such predictors may provide a high probability (much more than 50%) of outperforming in the long term, but, over short-term horizons, the probability may not be much higher than 50%.

This is not what most investors want to hear. What we may be facing is a mismatch between the objective of most investors (systematic outperformance) and what intelligent portfolio management can potentially deliver (long-term outperformance but not systematic). Furthermore, if we add to this equation the fact that we live in a world of time-varying risk aversion and biased beliefs, it seems that the only investors who can be expected to outperform by design and not by chance are those who understand the basics of asset valuation and pricing dynamics (including behavioral patterns) combined with the necessity of investment discipline.

The purpose of this chapter is to explain why it is so difficult to forecast market returns and to discuss what level of predictability of returns, volatility and dependence can be expected from using historical returns only. We will then discuss the value of other predictor variables. The main argument of this chapter is that an investment process and horizon should be commensurate with our ability to use predictors that are statistically reliable and coherent with that horizon.

Determinants of Interest Rates

A 2010 Bloomberg article discusses [1] the different rate calls made by financial institutions in late 2009 and early 2010 for year-end 2010. For example, Morgan Stanley, the most bearish among the 18 primary dealers forecasted then that a strengthening U.S. economy would lead to private credit demand, higher stock prices and diminish the refuge appeal of Treasuries, pushing yields higher. Their chief fixed-income economist said in December 2009 that yields on benchmark 10-year notes would climb about 40 percent to 5.5 percent. The firm then reduced its forecast to 4.5 percent in May 2010 and to 3.5 percent in August. Other primary dealers were not much better at predicting yields. According to a March 2010 survey by Bloomberg News, Jefferies Group Inc. said the 10-year would yield 4.75 percent by year-end. Deutsche Bank AG, JPMorgan Chase & Co., and Royal Bank of Canada estimated a rise to 4.5 percent. The most accurate dealers were Goldman Sachs Group Inc., with an estimate of 3.25 percent, and HSBC Holdings Plc with 3.3 percent.

By August 20, 2010, Morgan Stanley was calling for a range-bound market with rates remaining between 2.40% and 2.85%. This compares with a prediction of 5.5% that was made eight months prior! We also know what has happened to interest rates since then. Why is forecasting interest rates accurately so difficult?

Let's understand their determinants. The expected nominal short-term interest rate on Treasury securities (such as one year, to simplify) is a function of expected inflation and expected real rate of return:

Expected One-Year Yield $[E(Y_1)]$ = Expected One-Year Inflation $[E(\text{Inf}_1)]$
$$+ \text{Expected One-Year Real Rate } [E(\text{RR}_1)] \quad (5.1)$$

According to the pure expectation hypothesis, forward rates are the most likely estimates of future spot rates. If this is true, the yield on a 10-year Treasury bond would be determined by an average (although normally geometrically compounded) of future short-term expectations:

$$Y_{10} = \text{Average } [E(\text{Inf})] + \text{Average } [E(\text{RR})] \quad (5.2)$$

Under such a model, an upward-sloping yield curve would be indicative of expectations of rising rates, while a downward-sloping curve would indicate the reverse. However, much evidence has shown that forward rates are not necessarily representative of market expectations of future rates. At the very least, forward rates have not been a very good predictor in recent decades. Figure 5.1 compares the 12-month forward yield (derived from one- and two-year Treasury bonds) with the 12-month yield actually observed a year later. It appears that the forward rate was almost systematically below the actual rate prior to mid-1982 (when inflation was at unprecedented levels), and almost systematically above the actual level ever since. Therefore, during the inflation era of the late 1970s and early 1980s, the forward

FIGURE 5.1 Forward One-Year Yield (1,1) versus Actual One-Year Yield.

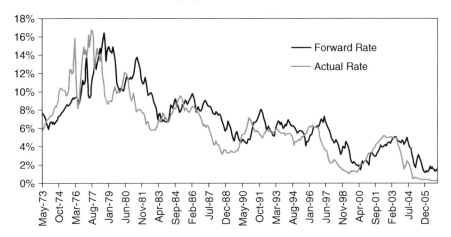

Source: Data from Federal Reserve Bank of St. Louis.

rate was, on average, 1.88% too low, and in the low-inflation era that followed it was almost 1.29% too high. We would not normally expect an unbiased predictor to systematically overestimate or underestimate the actual value being predicted over such long periods.

In fact, according to Ilmanen (2011) [2], yield curve steepness (the spread between longer-term and shorter-term yields) has been much more strongly correlated with excess bond returns than changes in the longer-terms yields. For example, Ilmanen reports the correlation of curve steepness with either excess bond returns or change in 10-year yields were respectively +0.34 and −0.25 respectively for horizons of one year since 1962. The correlation to yield is negative and contrary to expectations.

One explanation for this apparent contradiction (ignoring, for now, the possibility that expectations of future interest rates were consistently wrong for a very long time) may be that yields incorporate a time-varying bond risk premium (BRP).

$$Y_{10} = \text{Average } [E\,(\text{Inf})] + \text{Average } [E\,(\text{RR})] + \text{BRP} \qquad (5.3)$$

The BRP is a protection for duration risk. For example, the holder of a 10-year Treasury bond is exposed to a price risk approximately equal to the potential variation in the yield multiplied by the duration of the 10-year bond. Therefore, if current yields are a function of inflation, real return expectations and a risk premium, fluctuations in yields are a function of changes in all three variables. It also means that forecasting each determinant is a significant challenge.

Ilmanen used survey data about future short-term interest rates to isolate the BRP and understand its dynamics. He concluded that the risk premium has, over time, been as high as 3% to 4%, and as low as zero or even negative. More specifically, the risk premium increases when inflation concerns are greater (such as during the 1960s and 1970s) and declines to extremely low levels when Treasury securities act as a safe haven in uncertain times, such as during the late 1990s and in recent years.

In the presence of a time-varying BRP, the yield curve may be an unreliable predictor of future yields. A steep curve may indicate expectations of rising yields, or simply a compensation for bearing duration risk, and it may provide little information about market expectations of future yields. It may also combine the two effects. For example, Ilmanen explains that the inverted yield curve in the early 1980s was the result of lower rate expectations, despite the fact that the risk premium was quite high. Thus, as the risk premium declined in the following decades, yields declined by much more than would have been expected from forward rates. The consequence was that realized returns on bonds were also much higher than expected. On the other hand, Ilmanen argues that the steep yield curve between 2009 and 2010 was explained more by expectations of rising yield than by the presence of a risk premium. Therefore, in order to forecast a particular yield we must forecast the risk premium, inflation and real return. Let's first consider inflation.

There are two main sources of inflation that are not mutually exclusive: "cost push" and "demand pull." Cost push occurs when businesses respond to rising costs and must increase their prices in order to protect their profit margins. The severe increase in the price of oil in the 1970s is the best example of cost-push inflation in the last 40 years. The emergence of China as a major global low-cost producer has illustrated the impact of cost-push inflation in reverse. This illustrates that cost-push inflation can originate from an increase in commodity prices, wage increases when unemployment is low, higher taxes and significant international competitive shifts driven by currency movements or simply the emergence of new low-cost producing countries.

Demand-pull inflation occurs when excess demand in the economy, combined with scarcity of resources, allows producers to increase their prices. The basic conditions for demand-pull inflation can occur when a government launches a stimulus program of tax reductions or new expenditures, when a central bank stimulates demand through a low-interest-rate policy, when extreme confidence in the economy leads consumers to reduce their savings rate and borrow significantly, etc. Obviously all of these effects can be observed in reverse. For example, a lack of confidence may depress domestic— or even global—demand and put downward pressure on prices.

Now that we can differentiate between cost-push and demand-pull inflation, are we any closer to a decent long-term forecast on inflation? Will China remain a deflationary source, or will the country become an inflationary source if or once its export-oriented economy is converted gradually into a consumer powerhouse? Will other countries such as Vietnam become the next source of cheap manufacturing on a large scale? Will the currencies of high-growth countries appreciate significantly against those of low-growth countries? Will the current debt-management challenge in the United States and Europe and high unemployment remain a deflationary force for many years, despite monetary stimulus (especially in the United States)? Will public pension fund deficits become a fiscal nightmare that will restrict growth in one way or another? Will the duration deficit of pension funds restrict increases in long-term rates for many years? What will be the impact of new regulations (such as those concerning carbon emissions) on growth and operating costs? Can we integrate all of this information and more (such as demographic evolution) and achieve an inflation scenario that we can be confident in?

There is also one other factor to consider. The main role of central banks is to stabilize prices, although recent crises have certainly widened the scope of central bank intervention and motivation. Nevertheless, central banks in some countries such as Canada have instituted inflation targets (such as a 2% target within a 1% to 3% range), while central banks in others (such as the United States) state a desired target range without committing to this target. Central banks have significant power, but their ability to intervene to maintain inflation within the upper limit is probably greater than their ability to prevent it going below the lower limit, since this event would probably be triggered by a significant demand-related shock. It is easier to constrain economic activity with a restrictive monetary policy than it is to boost it with an expansionary monetary policy when there are significant deflationary forces at play.

Inflation forecasting is complex, and we have to consider the fact that market participants can be significantly wrong about expectations of inflation and real returns for many consecutive years. Figure 5.2 shows the 10-year inflation forecast made by professional forecasters for the United States since 1991, along with the rolling 12-month observed inflation. The graph illustrates that the 10-year forecast is fairly tainted by the most recent inflation. Also, inflation forecasters have, on average, overestimated inflation for 20 consecutive years, as if forecasters kept expecting some mean reversion that never occurred. This does not bode well for our confidence in inflation forecasts because we would normally expect rational unbiased forecasts to be

FIGURE 5.2   Twelve-Month Rolling Inflation and Ten-Year Inflation Forecast.

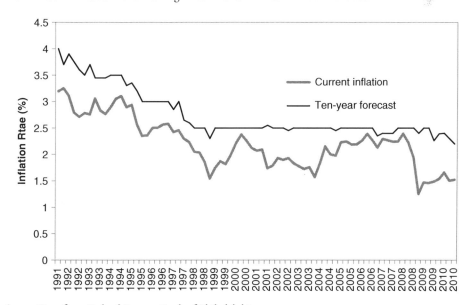

Source: Data from Federal Reserve Bank of Philadelphia.

periodically higher and lower than the true value, but not consistently higher or lower. Since the late 1990s, the 10-year forecasts have been almost a constant, at 2.5% until the end of 2009. Nevertheless, central banks have certainly been efficient at managing inflation and inflation expectations in recent years (which should help with inflation forecasting), although we have yet to digest the potential long-term impact of the recent growth of their balance sheets.

The issue of real interest rates is just as complex as the issue of inflation. Some economists link real interest rates to per capita consumption growth rate. Therefore, real rates would be expected to be higher on average in countries where consumption per capita is growing at a fast pace. Conceptually, it makes sense that we impose higher return requirements on our savings when global demand is strong.

Much research has been devoted to this issue. Lopez and Reyes (2007) [3] established that both rates (real rates and per capita consumption growth rates) appear to exhibit similar stationary behavior in the seven most industrialized countries. However, they also established that for several countries, the two rates appear to be regime-wise stationary. This means that the distributions may be stationary, but around a regime-dependent mean. Essentially, Lopez and Reyes's analysis shows more compelling results if they assume that two different economic regimes occurred over this period, one prior to the mid to late 1970s and one after. The real rate during the first subperiod appears to be significantly lower than that of the second subperiod. This implies that some significant structural change may have occurred in conjunction with the rise in the price of oil and its consequences on monetary policy.

Based on this research, we may wonder if the credit and financial crisis that was triggered in 2007 may have impacted the structure of equilibrium real rate, since it may bring consumption growth per capita in industrialized countries to a lower level than what we experienced in the 1980s, 1990s and part of the 2000s. In August 2010, Carmen and Vincent Reinhart [4] presented at the Federal Reserve's annual symposium a study of previous global and regional financial crises. Their conclusion was that even after 10 years, unemployment remained high and inflation-adjusted real estate prices remained 15% below their pre-crisis levels. Inflation and real rates of return also generally remained low, the exception being the 1970s and early 1980. Unlike other crises, the crisis in the 1970s was triggered by cost-push inflation. This study would support a low-interest-rate scenario in the current economic regime, and evidence thus far seems to support the Reinharts' view. More recently, Carmen Reinhart (2012) [5] reiterated that financial repression (negative real rates) would remain for many more years. At the very least, we should humbly admit that it is very unlikely that a forecaster can achieve accurate absolute forecasts consistently. In a later section of this chapter, we will present some evidence of interest rate predictability.

Determinants of Equity Prices

It is often said that the price volatility of equity markets is far greater than should normally be observed based on fundamental economic factors. Therefore, it may be useful to understand the source of this volatility.

In its simplest form, the performance that an investor will achieve on any investment is based on three factors: the initial price paid for the asset, the price it was sold for and the cash received from the investment during the period of ownership (such as dividends). Assuming an initial price of $100 for a stock, a single dividend of $3 (to make things simple) and an end price of $105, the investor has achieved a cumulative return of 8% before taxes and fees, or:

$$[(\$105 - \$100) + \$3] / \$100 = 8\%$$

A measure often used to determine how expensive an equity market is the price-to-earnings ratio (P/E ratio or P/E multiple)—or, the number of times investors are willing to pay current earnings to buy a stock. Thus, the price we pay for the shares of a company can be expressed in terms of earnings per share and P/E multiples. In our example, the initial price of $100 may have been the result of a company that has a current $10 earnings per share and a market that is willing to pay 10 times these earnings (P/E multiple = 10) to buy the stock ($10 x 10 = $100). When the stock was sold a year later at a price of $105, it could have been because earnings remained at $10 a share and the P/E multiple somehow increased to 10.5, or earnings increased to $10.50 and the P/E multiple remained at 10 or because of any other appropriate combination of earnings and P/E multiple (linked to future dividend growth rates, changes in discount rates, risk aversion, etc.).

Therefore, both the beginning and end price are a function of profits and P/E multiple at the time the investment is made and sold. Table 5.1 segregates the different sources of total return on the S&P 500 in terms of three components: dividends, profit growth and change in P/E multiple. The dividend growth rate is also indicated.

From 1979 to 1999, the total annual return on the S&P 500 was 17.88%, but dividends and growth in earnings only accounted for 9.65% of this return, a still-impressive result, but significantly shy of 17.88%. Thus, almost half the performance

TABLE 5.1 Average Yearly Sources of Performance (S&P 500) (%)

	1979–1999	1999–2006	2006–2009	1999–2010
Dividends	3.94	1.63	2.08	1.81
Earnings Growth	5.71	8.50	−45.42	4.52
P/E Multiple Change	8.23	−9.00	37.71	−5.92
Total	17.88	1.13	−18.47	0.41
P/E Beginning and End	7.4–33.3	33.3–18.2	18.2–19.6	19.6–17.5
10-Year Treasury Yield	10.8–6.7	6.7–4.8	4.8–2.5	2.5–3.4
Dividend Growth Rate	5.78	5.53	0.04	2.96

Source: Data from Federal Reserve Bank of St. Louis, Standard & Poor's, Datastream.

of the S&P 500 can be explained by the fact that investors were only willing to pay 7.4 times earnings to purchase stocks in 1979, but were willing to pay more than four times as much in 1999. Was investor optimism simply based on an extrapolation of historical returns, even though much of these returns were not necessarily attributed to improved expectation of profit growth, but to P/E expansion caused by irrational exuberance? Did investors understand that in order to maintain similar returns in the future, P/E would have to expand even more? Why did P/E multiples expand so much? Were they too low in 1979 and too high in 1999? These are questions we will attempt to answer in this chapter.

From 1999 to 2006, the performance of equity was dismal, but, strangely enough, the growth in earnings was stronger than during the 1979 to 1999 period, despite the burst of the technology bubble between 2000 and 2002. Dividends did not contribute as much to returns because, although the P/E multiple contracted significantly from 1999 to 2006, it was still much higher in 2006 than in 1979. Furthermore, dividends did not grow as fast as profits during this period, and many firms relied more substantially on share buybacks instead of dividend adjustments.

In the following period (2006 to 2009), the ongoing credit crisis decimated corporate earnings (especially in certain industries) and impacted dividends, something that rarely happens because most firms have a policy to keep their dividends as stable as possible. Finally, from 1999 to 2010, the S&P 500 delivered almost no return. A small dividend return and 4.5% annual growth in profits was canceled out by the decline in P/E multiple. It should be obvious by now that changes in P/E multiple play a significant role in equity returns.

P/E multiples are a representation of how much we value future earnings, their potential growth and risk. It is a real value concept since both the numerator and the denominator incorporate nominal variables, price and earnings. It is also a present value concept of sorts. For example, how much should we be willing to pay to receive $100 a year for 10 years? Assuming that the discount rate used to present value this stream of cash flows is 6%, the value of this investment would be $736. We could express this price as a 7.36 multiple on the $100 yearly cash flow. Furthermore, if we assumed the cash flows were less uncertain because of a better economic environment, investors may be willing to accept an even lower discount rate. The P/E multiple would expand in this case. Theoretically, if interest rates decline (or increase), and if the risk premium declines (or increases), we should be willing to pay a higher (or lower) P/E multiple for this stream of cash flows. However, in the case of equities, it is actually somewhat more complicated than this.

To understand the dynamics of equity prices, we need a simple equity valuation model such as the Gordon growth model. The Gordon model is a cash flow discounting model that assumes perpetual constant dividend growth. The equation is as follow:

$$P_0 = d_1 / [k - g] \tag{5.4}$$

Equation 5.4 implies that the present value (P_0) of a continuous stream of future dividends is a function of the dividend in one period (d_1), of the discount rate (k) (which incorporates a risk premium) and of the constant dividend growth rate (g). Equation 5.5 shows that the discount rate is a function of long-term inflation (I), of the long-term real rate of return (RR) and of an equity risk premium (ERP):

$$P_0 = d_1 / (I + RR + ERP - g) \tag{5.5}$$

However, we also know that the long-term dividend growth (g) is a function of growth in earning (per share), and that nominal earning growth is related to nominal GDP growth. In the long run, earnings cannot continuously grow faster than GDP. Table 5.2 illustrates the growth in all three variables since 1979.

Dividend growth has almost matched earning growth, but not nominal GDP. This is further confirmed by Arnott and Bernstein (2002) [6] who showed that not only did growth in real earnings per share not match real GDP growth since the 1950s or the 1900s, it did not even match real GDP per capita, although dividend growth stayed pretty much in line with earnings. Therefore, the tendency of many investors to estimate earnings growth and equity appreciation based on expected nominal GDP growth could be mistaken. However, we should not confuse the observation that growth in earnings per share did not match GDP or GDP per capita with the idea that nominal profits as a share of GDP decline over time. Figure 5.3 illustrates that it is not the case.

The ratio of financial corporations' corporate profits to GDP and the ratio of total profits to GDP have both increased in the 2000s. It also appears that the financial sector accounts for a growing proportion of all profits. In the early 1950s, financial corporations accounted for no more than 15% of all corporate profits. This ratio increased to about 30% in the early 1970s, 40% in the late 1980s and nearly 50% in the 2000s. This is consistent with John C. Bogle's statements discussed in Chapter 1 that the financial industry now extracts significant financial resources from the overall economy. It may have become a drag on the global economy [7].

Total nominal profits as a share of GDP have gone beyond the level observed in prior decades, and yet earnings per share has not tracked nominal GDP growth. One possible explanation is that new and younger firms, whose stocks are not yet listed, capture a significant share of profits at the expense of listed established firms.

TABLE 5.2 Dividend, Earnings and GDP Growth (%)

	1979–1999	1979–2010
Dividends	5.78	4.77
Earnings	5.71	4.52
Nominal GDP	6.69	5.76

Source: Data from Datastream, U.S. Department of Commerce: Bureau of Economic Analysis.

FIGURE 5.3   Corporate Profits as a Share of GDP 1947–2010.

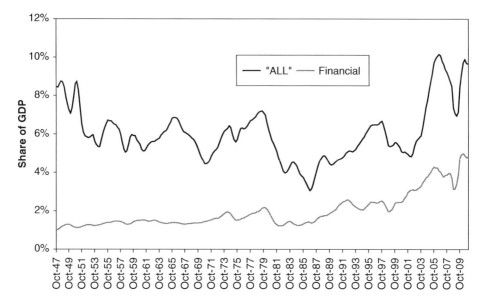

Source: Data from NIPA.

Furthermore, new share issuances may contribute to a dilution of earnings per share, although share buybacks have also been significant in recent decades. Finally, most equity indices are becoming less and less representative of the domestic corporate economy, because many large corporations are generating more of their profit growth from overseas markets, specifically from emerging markets. This could lead, in some cases, to profits that grow faster than the domestic economy—a reversal of the situation observed in Table 5.2. Therefore, global growth may become more relevant than domestic growth when determining the long-term evolution of the nominal profits of securities within some domestic benchmarks.

Nominal profits are related to nominal GDP in the long term and are influenced by inflation and real GDP growth. Consequently, if we write the growth rate (g) in Equation 5.6 as a function of earning inflation (I_g) and earning real growth (RG_g), the Gordon model takes the form shown in Equation 5.7:

$$g = I + RG_g \tag{5.6}$$

$$P_0 = d_1 / (I - I_g + RR - RG_g + ERP) \tag{5.7}$$

We can conclude from Equation 5.7 that three factors significantly determine equity valuation:

1. Whether or not markets conclude (rightly or wrongly) that earning inflation (the ability of corporations to pass cost increases to their clients) would not equal the general level of inflation. It could be higher or lower.

2. Whether or not expectations of real growth in earnings exceed or fall short of the expected real return.
3. The size of the ERP.

Significant shifts in market prices can be explained by the time-varying nature of these variables. Therefore, the P/E multiple would be expected to decline (or rise) if the ERP were to rise (or decline), if the spread between general inflation and earning inflation were to rise (or decline) and if the spread between real rates of return and real earning growth were to increase (or decrease). We can use this equation to understand what happened to stock market prices and P/E multiples over the last 30 years. For example, in the late 1970s:

- investors may have been suffering from irrational money illusions (the idea that the stream of discounted expected dividends would not nominally increase with the level of inflation);
- inflation uncertainty and economic uncertainty at the time may have contributed to raising the ERP; and
- there may have been an interaction between high levels of inflation and real economic growth that contributed to lower levels of expected real earnings growth.

None of these concerns were present in the late 1990s. Inflation was low and stable; any risk premium related to inflation uncertainty would have been considerably lower, and any concern about the impact of high inflation on real growth would have been almost nonexistent. Furthermore, investors had just been through two decades of rising asset values in a full-employment economy, which may have led to overconfidence, over-optimism and irrational expectations based on extrapolations of historical returns. This is also the era when the United States was projected to generate fiscal surpluses for many years, and pay off its entire national debt within 15 years!

The fact that, from time to time, hoards of investors are behaving irrationally is often considered a justification for active management. More rationally, this should be a justification for implementing consistent and systematic portfolio-management processes. Market dynamics in the 1980s, 1990s and 2000s illustrate that market prices are not only a function of long-term changes in fundamentals, but also of time-varying risk premiums and, sometimes, irrational fears and expectations. The latter may explain why, according to Shiller (1981) [8], Cutler, Poterba and Summers (1989) [9] and many others, only a small fraction (less than a third) of price volatility could be accounted for by fundamental information. Investors' psychology is difficult to model. This is partly why we need a confident investment philosophy to protect us from ourselves and from others. Nevertheless, we have to ask the question: What and how much information can we reliably predict, and what predictors should we use?

Historical Returns as a Predictor

Correlation is a measure of the strength of the linear relation between two sets of observations. It can be between two securities within the same asset class (Audi versus BMW) or between two asset classes (equity versus fixed income). Autocorrelation will also measure the strength of a linear relation, but for the same variable across time. For example, instead of measuring the strength of the relation between the returns on Canadian and US stocks or bonds and equities, we measure the strength of the relation between today's performance on the S&P 500 and yesterday's performance on the S&P 500, or between today's performance and the performance of two days ago. The first case would be a measure of autocorrelation of the first order, and the second case a measure of the second order. We could also go back a hundred days (100th order) or more. When we use the terms "market momentum," "trends" or "persistence," we are implicitly discussing autocorrelation. The presence of autocorrelation helps to make statistically reliable forecasts, although this is certainly not the only form of serial dependence that can support forecasting. It is, however, the simplest one.

Autocorrelation is not only relevant to the measurement of persistence in returns. It can also be used as a measure of the persistence in volatilities or correlations. For example, we could ask what the strength of the relation is between today's volatility of return and yesterday's volatility of return, or between today's correlation of returns and yesterday's. Since the objective of any investment process is to improve the return-to-risk trade-off, the process would be much improved by an ability to forecast other moments beyond returns. In this chapter we only seek to demonstrate the ability to predict. Chapters 7, 10 and 11 will address specific predicting methodologies. Therefore, in this section, we evaluate the degree of autocorrelations in returns, volatilities and covariance for equity and fixed income.

Figure 5.4a illustrates the time-varying nature of annualized volatilities of equity and 10-year Treasuries using a 250-day horizon, while Figure 5.4b illustrates the relative volatility. Finally, Figure 5.4c illustrates the autocorrelation (of the 1st to 100th order) of returns (r) and volatilities (r^2) of both series.

Although the volatility of equity was 2.5 times the volatility of Treasury bonds on average, both measures of volatility have fluctuated significantly in the long run, but have shown persistence in the short run. Any portfolio allocation process would be strengthened by an ability to forecast volatility (and correlation). Figure 5.4c indicates, as we would expect, an absence of autocorrelation between returns. As we've discussed previously, this does not mean that historical returns cannot be used to detect useful information about price momentum, but simply that serial dependence is more easily detected in volatility and correlation than in returns.

Volatility displays strong autocorrelation, especially in the case of equity. The autocorrelation for equity remains significant and persistent even after 20 or 30 days. This indicates that a more sophisticated approach, such as GARCH models, could potentially be used successfully to forecast volatility. Although the autocorrelation in fixed income is substantially lower, it does not mean this information is not statistically significant in the context of a long-term allocation process.

Forecasting volatility is important for two reasons. First, we have discussed at length the impact of volatility on the GEO mean, and the fact that the impact is not linear. Keeping the volatility of a portfolio relatively constant through a dynamic allocation process (between bonds and equity, for example) is more efficient than allowing volatility to fluctuate over time even if the average volatility is similar. However, in order to manage this volatility, we must be able to forecast it.

FIGURE 5.4a   Rolling Volatility Using 250-Day Moving Average (1988–2010).

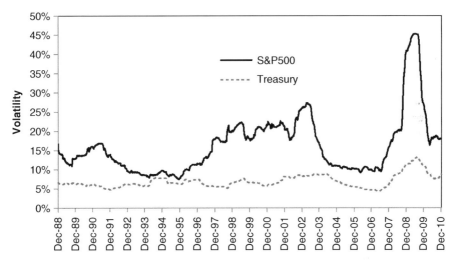

Source: Data from Datastream.

FIGURE 5.4b   Relative Volatility Using 250-Day Moving Average (1988–2010).

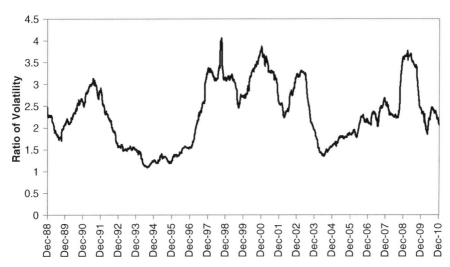

Source: Data from Datastream.

FIGURE 5.4c   Autocorrelations of Returns and Volatilities (1988–2010).

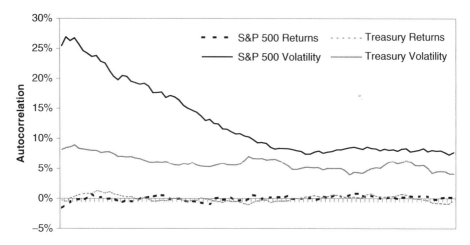

Source: Data from Datastream.

It is also important to forecast volatility because of the potential link between volatility and adverse returns. More specifically, if extremely negative performances usually occur when volatility is abnormally high and risk aversion is increasing, forecasting and managing volatility would be even more important. Therefore, the impact of managing volatility on the GEO mean would go beyond the statistical benefits discussed in Chapter 4.

Despite the intuitive appeal of this relation, there is no absolute consensus on this aspect. First, many pricing models (such as CAPM) imply a positive relationship between return and risk, though the reported findings from studies that attempted to document this relation are conflicting. Brandt and Kang (2002) [10] found strong and robust negative contemporaneous correlations between conditional mean and volatility. However, the unconditional return-to-risk relation remains large and positive because of strong lag volatility in mean effect. More specifically, they argue that the contemporaneous correlation $[\rho(\mu_t, \sigma_t)]$ could be negative (indicating a tendency to observe lower returns when volatility is high) even though the long-run correlation $[\rho(\mu, \sigma)]$ could be positive (indicating a tendency of riskier assets to deliver large returns in the long term). This would occur if current returns were correlated with lagged volatility, and lagged returns were correlated with current volatility. For example, a series of successive negative returns could lead to greater volatility $[\rho(\mu_{t-1}, \sigma_t)]$. Similarly, a period of low volatility could lead to increasing returns $[\rho(\mu_t, \sigma_{t-1})]$. This would be entirely consistent with the existence of a time-varying risk premium.

To illustrate the negative contemporaneous correlation between returns and volatility, Figure 5.5a shows a scatter plot of the trailing 250-day volatility on the vertical axis and the trailing 250-day return on the horizontal axis. The graph shows that negative returns are rarely observed at low levels of trailing volatility, while the distribution of observations appears positively skewed at average levels of volatility. However, the most negative performances (our Black Swans) are observed at high levels of volatility.

To better visualize the relationship between trailing volatility and return, Figure 5.5b illustrates the same data but after it has been ranked in increasing order of return, and after using a moving average of 20 days to smooth the data. Although the period incorporates a wide range of performances (from less than –40% to more than +50%), the volatility was, on average, much higher for extremely low returns than for normal to extremely high returns. This observation would be consistent with a time-varying risk premium that increases substantially in weak equity markets, causing greater fluctuations in asset prices. If in fact such a relationship exists, incorporating volatility forecast into an allocation model could significantly enhance performance. Furthermore, even if this apparent relationship were spurious, we would still want to manage the volatility of the portfolio anyway.

FIGURE 5.5a Scatter Plot Trailing Volatility versus Trailing Return (1998–2010).

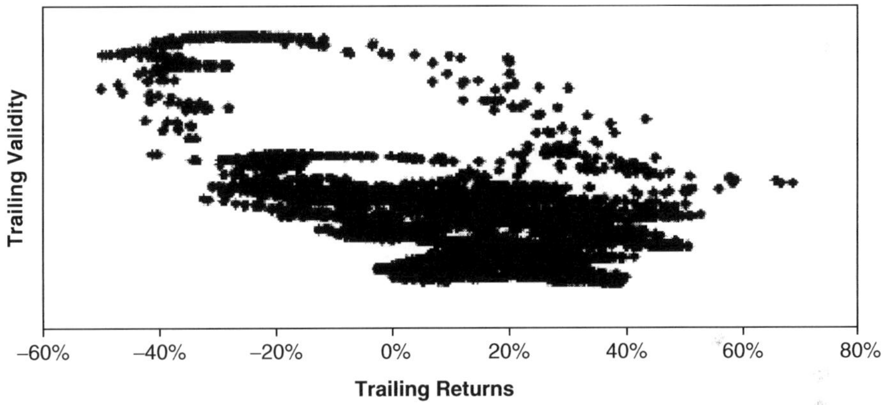

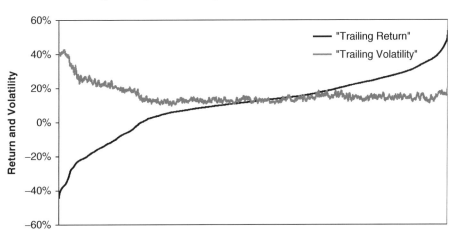

Source: Data from Datastream.

FIGURE 5.5b Trailing Volatility versus Trailing Return (1988–2010).

Source: Data from Datastream.

FIGURE 5.6a   Rolling Correlations (Equity and Fixed Income) (1988–2010).

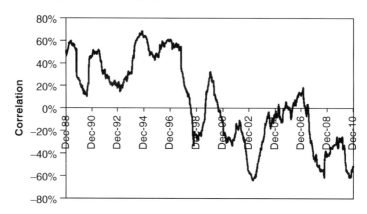

Source: Data from Datastream.

Lastly, Figure 5.6a illustrates the time-varying nature of correlations. Unlike volatility, which can only be positive, correlations are not only time varying, but they can also switch signs. In the 1990s, correlations were time varying but positive, while in the 2000s they were time varying but mostly negative. Although we do not illustrate correlations in prior years, they were also strongly positive in the 1960s and 1970s.

We can refer to the discussion in the first section of this chapter to understand the changes in economic regime that can occur between equity and fixed income. Fixed income is positively affected by declining inflation, and negatively affected by rising inflation. The case for equity is more complex. Equity may react negatively to rising inflation if investors do not believe corporations will be able to pass all of their cost increases to their clients, or if, for some reason, investors suffer from money illusions and do not properly account for increasing nominal cash flows caused by inflation. There is also the possibility that low and stable inflation may have a positive impact on expected growth and lead to a lower risk premium. Obviously, both asset classes over the 1980s and 1990s have benefited from the secular decline in inflation in a positive economic environment. However, in the 2000s, the correlation dynamic changed. That decade was characterized by two major events (the tech bubble implosion and the credit crisis) that led to a policy of low interest rates. This was also the period when Treasuries became a safe haven for investors.

Thus, it should be obvious by now that the "optimal" allocation from a return-to-risk point of view should be significantly impacted by the time-varying nature of volatility and correlations. In essence, diversification in the 2000s between equity and fixed income became more efficient (although an investor facing rising liabilities because of declining interest rates would not agree). This is unlike what is usually observed among equity markets where correlations between different markets rise significantly in difficult times.

FIGURE 5.6b Autocorrelations of Covariance (1988–2010).

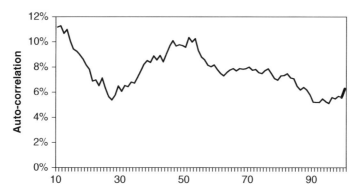

Source: Data from Datastream.

However, we cannot always expect that correlations between equity and fixed income will remain low when the environment is challenging. For example, in an inflationary environment, correlations would likely rise. Furthermore, if government bonds were to lose their safe haven characteristic for some reason, correlations could also rise. Again, the issue is whether or not we can forecast correlations. Figure 5.6b helps answer this question. Although the autocorrelation is weaker than for equity, it can still lead to statistically significant forecasts.

This section illustrates that while it may be difficult to rely on past returns to forecast future returns, there is still significant information in historical returns. Historical returns can be used to forecast volatility and dependence—an aspect that is extremely important to the allocation process. Even if we were totally unable to forecast returns using daily data, the ability to forecast other distribution moments would still improve the Sharpe ratio of any portfolio. Furthermore, I have used the simplest and least sophisticated illustrations of the ability to forecast. Much better methodologies are available.

Other Predictors

Financial advisors and economists are often asked to forecast the absolute yearly performance of fixed income, equity, currency, gold, oil and other commodities. However, the belief that anyone could precisely forecast absolute returns for specific horizons (especially shorter horizons such as a few years) reliably and systematically is unrealistic. There are too many changes in public policy, as well as too many unforeseen structural, social and political changes. There are economic and financial shocks, technological changes and mostly undisciplined changes to investors' risk tolerance.

That said, even if precise absolute forecasts are unrealistic, we could still be satisfied if we had a process that explained even a small fraction (much less than 5%) of future returns. For example, Campbell and Thomson (2007) [11] indicated that even if a predictor explains a very small proportion of future returns, this information would still greatly improve the Sharpe ratio of a portfolio. In this section, we discuss some of the most important predictors related to equity pricing, and conclude with a summary of several equity and interest-rate predictors covered by Ilmanen (2011).

Dividends

In 2008, J.P. Morgan paid a dividend of $1.52 per share. This dividend was slashed to only 20 cents per share (annualized level) in early 2009 in order to help rebuild the capital base of the firm. With about 3.5 billion shares in circulation, the dividend payment made in 2008 was slightly more than $5 billion. The dividend payment of 2009 was slightly more than $2 billion. In 2010, it was about $800 million—a decline of more than $4 billion from 2008. Coincidently, the company paid $4.2 billion more total compensation in 2009 than in 2007, despite revenues from continuing operations that were 25% lower than in 2007. Even in 2008, the bonus pool was still $8.7 billion, and total compensation was similar to the level of 2007, while revenues from continuing operations were down by 75% from the previous year. This sequence of events is troubling, even though the firm eventually raised its annualized dividend to $1.00 and $1.20 in early 2011 and 2012 and has announced a share buyback program.

There is definitely something wrong with the business model of many corporations, and even of some industries. How can investors agree to a long-term commitment in corporate entities that believe that only shareholders should bear the brunt of the long-term adjustments required to increase the capital base during a crisis? How can investors properly value their investment if they have no understanding of the guidelines that dictate the compensation practice during good and bad years? The management of these firms will argue that they need to pay such compensation to maintain their expertise, but, although it is obvious that management benefits from this situation, it is far from obvious that investors benefit in the long term from such a high cost structure.

One of the reasons we are interested in dividends and share buyback or debt repayments is that investors should positively value firms that demonstrate a strong alignment of interest between management and investors. To better understand this argument, it may be useful to know more about the history of dividend policy in the United States and elsewhere.

Corporate behavior that is related to dividend policy (and vice versa) has been a significant factor in the evolution of the tax codes in the United States and in other countries. Steven A. Bank (2004) [12] of the UCLA School of Law wrote an interesting paper discussing the historical reasons behind the different evolutions of corporate taxation principles of UK and US firms. Bank states:

> During the nineteenth century, when corporations in both countries distributed virtually all of their profits each year, it was reasonable to view a tax on corporations as a mere proxy for taxing shareholders individually on their allocable share of corporate profits. This proxy, which allowed for the collection of the tax at the source, was considered a significant innovation for tax

systems suffering under the burden of tax evasion. Not surprisingly, therefore, the United States and the United Kingdom were aligned in their use of a pass-through or integrated approach to corporate income taxation. During this period The United Kingdom, under the Income Tax Act of 1803, and the subsequent Income Tax Act of 1842, integrated the company and individual income taxes through an imputation system. Companies were subject to an income tax. Shareholders then received a credit for taxes paid on the income at the company, level and companies were entitled to deduct from the dividends paid an amount sufficient to cover the company-level tax. In this sense, the company tax operated as a withholding tax for the individual income tax.

Although the United Kingdom has remained true to this tax principle for most of the past century, tax principles in the United States have been less stable. For example, in the United States, corporate and individual income taxes were also integrated during the nineteenth century, but the system was based on a different approach. During the Civil War and Reconstruction, shareholders were taxed on the undivided profits of the corporation. However, in the Tariff Act of 1894, a corporate income tax was imposed and dividends were exempt from the individual income tax. Then, in 1913, Congress introduced a corporate income tax in conjunction with an individual income tax in the form of a normal tax rate and a surtax based on the level of income. Under this scheme, the corporate income tax rate was equal to the normal individual tax rate, and dividends were exempt from the normal tax rate but not from the surtax. Although this ensured that corporate and noncorporate income would be taxed similarly at the individual level (as far as the normal tax rate was concerned), if corporations retained more and more profits and distributed less and less dividends, rich individuals could use corporations to avoid the surtax. In fact, US corporations were retaining their profits internally to a much higher degree than UK corporations.

When President Franklin D. Roosevelt proposed replacing the corporate income tax with an undistributed profits tax and a shareholder-level tax on dividends in 1936, it was under the assumption that corporate hoarding was at least partially to blame for the crash and the ensuing depression. Rexford Tugwell, a member of Roosevelt's "Brain Trust" (the name used to refer to his advisory group) and a Columbia economics professor, argued that because of managerial control over retained earnings, corporations "grow overconfident of the future and expand their own activities beyond all reason [13]." Another member of Roosevelt's brain trust, Adolf Berle, argued that the growing separation between ownership and control meant that managers increasingly became interested in using retained earnings to fund expansion plans or further their own job security, rather than to support dividends to stockholders. Thus, in his July 1932 acceptance speech at the Democratic National Convention, Roosevelt attributed the Depression to heavy "corporate surpluses" used to finance "unnecessary plants" and rampant pre-crash stock market speculation. There may be some parallels with the circumstances of the technology bubble in the late 1990s and early 2000s, as well as with the more recent credit bubble.

The increase in retained earnings did not occur in the United Kingdom to the same degree because separation of ownership and control generally came much later than in the United States. Moreover, even where separation of ownership and control did occur, shareholders in the United Kingdom have maintained a degree of influence over dividends in British corporations that did not exist in the United States. From early on in the history of British companies, shareholders of most companies were accorded the right to vote on the board's recommendation to declare a dividend.

As we read about the debates on tax frameworks in the United Kingdom and the United States over the past century, it is clear that legislators were trying to find the tax approach that would lead to a proper balance between earnings retention (required for reinvestments) and dividend payout (required when investment opportunities are insufficient). The United States was worried about excessive earnings retention, whereas the United Kingdom was worried, at some point, about excessive dividend distribution. Although the United States has maintained its classical corporate income tax since 1936, concern about excessive retained earnings has helped prompt legislators to revisit this issue. In January 2003, President George W. Bush announced a proposal to eliminate the double taxation of corporate income. His proposal would have been subject to the corporate income tax as under the current economic regime, but dividends on that income would have been exempt from the shareholder income tax. According to Bush, the goal was to eliminate the double taxation of corporate income.

Bank (2004) explains that a significant factor that prompted the Bush proposal was the perception that corporations were unnecessarily retaining earnings due to the tax disincentive for dividends, and that this was harming the economy. The Treasury's *Blue Book on Integration*, which was released in connection with the Bush announcement, made the argument that "double taxation of corporate profits encourages a corporation to retain its earnings rather than distribute them in the form of dividends [14]." This would lessen "the pressure on corporate managers to undertake only the most productive investments because corporate investments funded by retained earnings may receive less scrutiny than investments funded by outside equity or debt financing." The Council of Economic Advisers concluded that the president's proposal might resolve this issue by increasing the percentage of corporate profits paid out as dividends. As we know, the president's proposal was rejected in favor of a more modest, but still significant, tax relief. Nevertheless, as this historical series of events shows, we should not assume that the interests of corporations and investors are aligned. Investors may be better served by investing in corporations whose interests are better aligned with their own. Since conflicts of interest of this nature originate from behavioral issues, we can be confident that they will be persistent. Corporate behavior usually does not change unless it is properly regulated. According to Brock (2012) [15]:

> The moral is that, if society does not like the behavior that results from an existing set of incentives, then legislators and regulators must change and improve the incentive structure. Instructing people to act "better" given unchanged incentives is hypocritical and will not succeed. This is as true at the level of the family as it is of entire societies.

We have talked previously about how corporate earnings remain in line with GDP growth in the long term. However, as equity investors, we should be more interested in the growth in earnings per share. William J. Bernstein [16] published an essay which shows that, contrary to reasonable expectations, if we look at 70 years of history, it appears that growth in profits per share lagged behind total profit growth. On average, investors lost 1.5% yearly at the hands of management, possibly through earning dilution. The last decade of the last millennium had reversed this trend, but this reverse was achieved through share buyback programs at a time when P/E multiples were abnormally high. Bernstein makes the argument that if P/E multiples were 30, in order to increase profitability for investors by a bit more than 1%, it required 30% of the annual profits of these corporations! If you add the annual dividend payout, it does not leave much capital for reinvestment. This was unsustainable, and we paid the price in the following decade in more than one way. Therefore, an investor could be disappointed if he or she expects equity performance (before fees) in the long run to be equal to dividend yield plus inflation plus real growth.

Since the credit crisis occurred, I have become fairly convinced that the source of our performance does matter. I intuitively prefer dividends to capital gain. As they say, "A bird in the hand is worth two in the bush." Or, even more to the point, "How little you know about the age you live in if you think that honey is sweeter than cash in hand." Our long-term expectations may not be consistent with the motivations of management. That is one reason why we have to diversify, and why dividends (and share buybacks) are attractive. A strong dividend policy may impose a level of discipline on the officers of a corporation and a more responsible culture throughout the organization. There may be less value destruction on average at the hands of the managers of dividend-paying firms than at the hands of the managers of non-dividend-paying firms.

Arnott and Asness (2003) [17] investigated whether low payout ratios (i.e., the share of profits paid as dividends) by firms was a good indication of future profit growth over the 1946 to 2001 period. They had two main objectives in mind:

1. To discover if periods of low dividend payouts are indicative of stronger profit growth in future years. For example, do aggregate profits grow faster over 10 years if the payout ratio was lower at the beginning of the period?
2. To discover if firms with lower payout ratios produce greater profit growth over the following 10 years, whatever the period under study.

Figure 5.7 deals with the first objective. It is a schematic representation of the results obtained by Arnott and Asness (2003) that shows the dividend payout at the beginning of a period on the x-axis, and the 10-year growth rate in profits on the y-axis. The results contradict expectations. Periods of low payout rates are followed by lower growth, not stronger growth. This supports the assumption that some managers are more concerned with empire building than efficient use of capital, and suggests that investors should be concerned when payout ratios fall.

FIGURE 5.7   Dividend Payout Ratios and Subsequent Corporate Earnings.

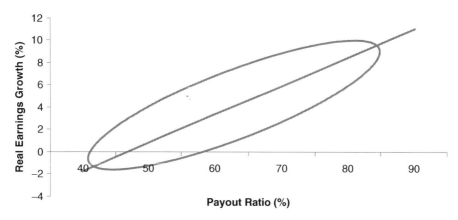

Source: Inspired From Arnott and Asness (2003).

On the other hand, we have to realize that, despite the existence of a dividend policy, the payout ratio will not remain stable in the short term because dividends are usually a lot more stable than net income. For example, we know from experience that managers will resist reducing the dividend when profits decline, or resist increasing the dividend too quickly when profits rise. They want to be convinced that recent profit trends are not an aberration. Furthermore, during an economic slowdown, when profits decline, the payout ratio will automatically increase. In this case, a higher payout rate may coincide with declining short-term profits, paving the way for a profit recovery later on. The reverse argument could also be made. If profits are extremely high, the payout ratio may decline, paving the way for lower profit growth in future years. However, overall, Arnott and Asness do conclude that high payout ratios lead to stronger profits notwithstanding any change in the profit cycle.

The study also looked at the effect of dividend payout among different types of firms. Arnott and Asness's sample of firms was divided into four quartiles in order of increasing dividend payout. Results are presented in Table 5.3, and clearly indicate that profit growth among firms that have higher payout ratios was significantly stronger.

TABLE 5.3   Dividend Payout Ratios According to Payout Quartile and Subsequent Corporate Earnings (1946–2001)(%)

Starting Payout Quartile	Average	Worst	Best
1 (Low)	−0.4	−3.4	+3.2
2	+1.3	−2.4	+5.7
3	+2.7	−1.1	+6.6
4 (High)	+4.2	+0.6	+11.0

Source: Arnott and Asness (2003).

We may speculate as to why we have these results. It could be that higher and lower dividend payout ratios are an indication of managers' confidence. Less confident managers may be afraid of paying dividends. It could also be arrogance and an overconfidence in their own ability. Or, perhaps managers' needs enforced discipline. Some managers may value their ambitions of building a corporate empire more than they value higher return on capital. Another possibility is that our window of analysis is too short, and these results are not truly representative. However, the recent credit crisis, why and how it occurred and how it was dealt with, illustrates that the interests of managers and investors are not necessarily aligned.

It is important to understand that a higher dividend payout ratio should not normally be an indication of better corporate earnings. The fact that we do observe this contradiction may be indicative of behavioral and policy differences between managers of organizations that pay large dividends and managers of organizations that pay little or no dividends. It may even be related to exaggerated compensation for management based on option programs that eventually dilute earnings. Whatever the reasons, persistence in management behavior and self-interest are probably characteristics we can count on.

The relationship between payout ratios and future earnings should raise two more questions.

1. Do investors recognize that periods of low payout ratios lead to lesser growth in long-term (10-year) earnings? In other words, is equity valuation lower when payout rates are low?
2. Do investors recognize that firms that have lower payout ratios (whatever the market context) usually deliver lower profit growth in long-term (10-year) earnings?

We probably already know intuitively that the answer to these questions is no. The excessive volatility of equity prices shows that most investors are not capable of such long-term rationality, even though low interest rates have triggered in recent years an interest in dividend-paying firms. We also know from Sorensen and Ghosh (2010) [18] and several other authors that the securities of corporations whose year-over-year earnings increases are higher than year-earlier expectations tend to significantly outperform. Thus, if higher payout rates lead to higher realized profits, and if unexpected increases in profits lead to relatively stronger stock performance, higher payout stocks would be a good long-term investment.

The literature on payout rates did not specifically address the direct relationship between payout rates and stock price performance, but there is a significant body of literature that addresses the issue of dividend yields, payout yields (dividend yield plus yields attributed to repurchases and new issues of stocks) and equity performance. We will start with Fama and French (1988)[19].

Fama and French used the dividend-to-price ratio (dividend yield) to forecast returns on NYSE stocks for horizons ranging from one month to four years over the period 1926 to 1985. Although they found that dividend yields (DY) explain less than

5% of the variance of quarterly or monthly stock returns, they did find that it explains as much as 25% of the two to four year variance. This is entirely consistent with the view that price volatility is far greater than what fundamental factors would justify, thus weakening the short-term efficiency of predictor variables.

Campbell and Ammer (1992) [20] looked at the importance of dividends with a different approach. They started with the assumption that the variance of excess stock returns can be attributed to three factors: news about cash flows (dividends), real interest rates and future excess returns. This view is entirely consistent with our prior decomposition of the Gordon growth model, where price is a function of the growth rate of earnings and dividend policy (news about dividends), real returns (news about real returns) and risk premium (a proxy for news about future excess returns). The authors concluded that changes in the risk premium could explain much of the volatility of asset prices in the short term (i.e., the volatility of the P/E multiple), although profits and dividend policies should be the main determinant of prices in the long term.

Using monthly interval data, Campbell and Ammer found that the real interest rate component does not explain much of the variance in excess stock returns. Rather, news about future excess returns explains three to four times more of the volatility of excess returns (about 70%) than does news about dividends (less than 20%). Although this appears to contradict the conclusion of other studies concerning the role of dividends, when Campbell and Ammer did the same analysis using quarterly data (instead of monthly), they found that almost 40% of the variance in excess returns could be accounted for by dividends.

The dividend approach was criticized in the 1990s when its value as a predictor seemed to weaken. Based on this observation, some even argued that prior conclusions about the value of dividends as an investment variable were the result of spurious circumstances. I find it rather peculiar that we would not have attributed much of this decline in predictive power to the creation of the largest equity bubble in history—a period when investors considered the four characters ".com" more relevant to value than the absence of any positive cash flows. Therefore, if markets behave irrationally, it is likely that rational models will lose some of their efficiency during that period.

However, there are some aspects that weaken the power of dividends as a predictor. Companies with excess cash flows can pay dividends, but they can also buy their own securities, thus increasing the earnings per share and the values of remaining securities. Share repurchase can also be indicative of a stronger commitment to shareholders and of alignment of interests. Thus, selecting stocks on the basis of a measure that calculates net payout yields instead of dividend yield only could provide a better measure of corporate responsibility and alignment with shareholders. For example, Boudoukh, Michaely, Richardson and Roberts (2007) [21] found that stock return predictability is much stronger using gross (dividend plus share repurchase) and net (dividend plus share repurchase minus new issuance) yields than simply using dividend yields.

We will complete this segment with Table 5.4, which compares the performance between the S&P 500 and the S&P High-Yield Dividend Aristocrats Index, an index of companies that have shown a history of increasing their dividends.

TABLE 5.4 Annualized Performance S&P 500 versus S&P High-Yield Dividend Aristocrats Index (1994–2010) (%)

	Aristocrats	S&P 500
Return	10.33	8.04
Volatility (5 years)	16.82	17.82
Dividend Yield	2.82	1.81

Source: Standard & Poor's.

The Aristocrats Index had a stellar performance over the 17-year period. Investors in this index accumulated 42% more capital than investors in the S&P 500. This is not active management; these are simply two indices with two different allocation protocols. Nevertheless, there can be substantial performance deviations in the short run. For example, the Aristocrats Index underperformed the S&P 500 in the two years prior to the credit crisis (June 2005 to June 2007) by about 8.25% (not shown here).

It is important to realize that the Aristocrats Index is not an index of firms that pay the highest dividends. It is an index of firms that have a history of increasing their dividends. The construction process of the index is biased toward firms that have a very specific corporate culture, and there is nothing wrong with building an index around criteria that incites or demonstrates a better alignment of interests between managers and shareholders. There may be investment protocols that are conceptually even better. For example, we will see in Chapter 6 that the dividend culture is not necessarily sector specific, but can also be country specific. Thus, although critics of the dividend/payout approach will argue that it leads to structurally biased, sector-specific portfolios, this argument holds much less in the context of global portfolios.

Size, Book Value, Momentum and Liquidity

Much of the literature on equity forecasting originated from literature on equity risk premiums—basically, the development of models designed to explain the returns that investors require on risky assets. The most well-known pricing model for equities is the capital asset pricing model (CAPM), a model that assumes, under many restrictive assumptions, that equity prices should be related to a single factor, the market. Beta represents the linear sensitivity of a security's return to the market excess return (ERM) in a world assumed to be mean-variance efficient.

$$\text{Excess return on single stocks} = \text{fct (Beta, ERM)} \tag{5.8}$$

Since the early 1970s, financial literature has raised some contradictions to the model. However, I will concentrate initially on the breakthrough article of Fama and French (1992) [22]. The authors found that equity risk is multidimensional. Two variables, "firm size" and "book value to market value" explain a significant portion of returns. Results strongly show a negative relation between return and size (there is a greater risk premium on small firms) and a positive relation between return and book to market. The pattern may illustrate a persistent psychological bias by investors to overestimate the potential of what they consider growth firms or growth industries.

$$\text{Excess return on stocks} = \text{fct (Market, Size, Book/Market)} \qquad (5.9)$$

Fama and French (2007a) [23] attempted to explain the size and value premiums by studying the yearly migration dynamics among six groups of US stocks formed on the basis of size (small and large) and book value to market value (low, average and high as a proxy for growth, neutral and value stocks) from 1926 to 2005. They split each portfolio using four migration groups:

1. Same: stocks that remain in the same portfolio at rebalancing
2. Size: small-cap stocks that become big-cap stocks and vice versa
3. Plus: stocks that move toward growth or are acquired
4. Minus: stocks that move toward value or are delisted

They found that the small-cap premium is almost entirely attributed to small-cap stocks that become big-cap stocks (not to the reverse). They also found that three of four types of migration contribute to the value effect. First, value stocks that remain in the "Same" portfolio have greater returns than the matching growth stocks. Second, value stocks are more likely to benefit from the "Plus" transition. Third, growth stocks are more likely to be penalized by the "Minus" transition. These positive effects are somewhat offset by the "Size" effect of small stocks that become big, since small-cap growth stocks are more likely to become large-cap than small-cap value stocks are.

Fama and French (2007b) [24] furthered their understanding of the value premium by breaking down the returns of value and growth stocks into three components: dividend yield, change in the growth rate of book equity (primarily from earning retention) and change in book to market. With this analysis, they hoped to get a better understanding of the root cause of the migration across styles described in the previous article. They found that although growth stocks have had a significantly greater increase in book equity than value stocks, they suffered from a rising ratio of book to market (market value is rising less than book value), while value stocks benefited from a declining ratio.

The authors explain this observation by describing the dynamic of growth and value companies. Growth companies are highly profitable and fast growing, but they eventually face competition that erodes their performance, which leads to a higher ratio of book to market. Value companies are less profitable and do not grow as fast, but they eventually restructure and improve their profitability.

Fama and French believe the value effect is simply the result of value stocks being more risky. They do not necessarily accept the argument that the excess return in value stocks is the result of mispricing caused by persistent behavioral biases. However, there is the possibility, as I explained earlier, that growth companies eventually become complacent and invest in less desirable projects instead of simply increasing dividends. This may partially explain the increasing ratio of book to market.

Recent studies conclude that the dynamics of size and book-to-market effects have evolved. The book-to-market effect has been found to be even more significant recently, while the size effect has been mitigated. However, Zhang (2008) [25] found that the size effect retains its importance after 1992, and even increases its explanatory power prior to 1992 if two size factors are used, one for growth firms and one for value firms. Again, this illustrates how central the issue of growth firms and value firms is to portfolio management.

In the late 1990s, the three-factor model (Market, Size and Book/ Market) became a four-factor model [26], with the inclusion of momentum as an explanatory variable. Momentum is usually defined in most studies as the cumulative performance over the last two to twelve months. Thus, although we could not detect autocorrelation of returns in daily data, it appears to be more present in lower frequency data. Therefore, under the four-factor model:

$$\text{Excess return on stocks} = \text{fct (Market, Size, Book/ Market, Momentum)} \qquad (5.10)$$

The impetus to incorporate momentum as a risk premium originated from the work of Jegadeesh and Titman (1993) [27] and others who found that selling recent losers and buying recent winners had been a fairly consistent winning strategy. The best performance had been achieved by going long on the top 10% of the best-performing stocks and short on the bottom 10% over the last 12 months, and holding this position for three months. It yielded an excess annual return of 1.31%. Many other horizons for selecting and holding stocks also yielded good results. For example, Jegadeesh and Titman (2001) [28] reported that the same strategy, using a standard six-month historical period for selecting the long and short positions and holding this position for six months, had remained profitable for every five-year period since 1940. Their research also showed that the profits of a momentum strategy tend to increase monotonically for the first 12 months and then to decline afterward, an aspect we will use indirectly in our portfolio-rebalancing strategy later on. Since several studies of momentum showed that the Fama and French three-factor model could not explain the excess returns generated by this factor, the four-factor risk model was proposed. Furthermore, recent studies show that the momentum factor is still alive and well.

I have a special interest in momentum because momentum may be attributed, in part, to behavior (i.e., psychological biases), and anything related to behavior may show persistence. Many authors have attempted to determine whether specific types of stocks exhibit greater or lower momentum. A few studies are particularly interesting.

• Daniel and Titman (1999) [29] found that momentum is stronger on low book-to-market stock (stocks that may be more difficult to value), which may lead us to conclude that investors find it easier to be optimistic about what is less tangible.

- Chan, Jegadeesh and Lakonishok (1996) [30] reported that price momentum and earnings momentum are positively correlated, but that the effect of earnings momentum is more short-lived than that of recent price performance. The horizon is six months for earnings momentum and 12 months for price momentum. The authors argued that portfolios built on the basis of prior return trends may reflect much greater revisions of expectations for the future outlook of companies than simply a recent change in profit trends.

Why is momentum a profitable strategy? One interpretation is that stocks underreact to information. If a firm releases favorable news and stock prices react partially to this information, buying this stock after the information has been released will generate profits. However, the explanation does not fit with the observation that price volatility in the stock market is far greater than is justified by the fundamentals. There are, however, some behavioral theories that can better explain both the existence of momentum profits and the excess market volatility.

Daniel, Hirshleifer and Subrahmanyam (2000) [31] argued that informed investors have a cognitive bias. Investors attribute investments in winning bets as a demonstration of their skills, but attribute losing bets to bad luck. As a result, these investors are overconfident about their ability to pick stocks, and they will push the price of ex-post-winning bets above their fundamental value. Their trading activity is creating the momentum that we observe. Hong and Stein (1999) [32] considered that the market is composed of two groups of investors: informed traders (who rely on fundamental information) and followers or technical traders (who look at price trends). The impact of the informed traders on the market will gradually be incorporated and push security prices toward their fundamental value, while the technical traders will push the security prices above their fundamental value. Avramov, Chordia and Goyal (2006) [33] showed that informed (contrarian) trades lead to a reduction in volatility, while uninformed (herding/momentum) trades lead to an increase in volatility.

What if all these theories are valid? For example, informed investors push the price of securities toward their fundamental values and initiate positive or negative momentum. Followers push prices beyond or below their fundamental values, and even reinforce the confidence of informed traders in their own abilities. We could even make the argument that, when momentum is positive, followers are slower to follow than when momentum is negative, contributing to higher volatility on the downside.

Much of the literature we have covered so far deals mostly with equities and the US market. However, Asness, Moskowitz and Pedersen (2009) [34] have demonstrated that the importance of value and momentum (they did not study size) is not limited to equities, and is not limited to the US market. Their study covered five asset groups: bonds (10 countries), stocks (United States, United Kingdom, Japan and continental Europe), equity indices (18 countries), commodities (27 commodities) and currencies (10 exchange rates). They tested for high and low value portfolios (a value proxy was defined for each asset group), high and low momentum (based on 12-month prior returns) and a combination of both effects on each asset group, as well as on a combination of all asset groups. The data covered the period of January 1975 to October 2008. Here are their findings:

- Value-based strategies (such as buying high book-to-market stocks and selling low book-to-market stocks) are positively correlated across all asset classes.
- Momentum-based strategies (such as buying securities with more positive momentum and selling securities with less positive or more negative momentum) are positively correlated across all asset classes.
- Value-based strategies are negatively correlated with momentum-based strategies. Therefore, a combination of value and momentum strategies (50%/50%) offers a better Sharpe ratio than either value or momentum alone. The volatility of a combo strategy is about half that of either value or momentum strategies.
- A combination of value and momentum strategies across all asset classes is statistically and economically superior than any portfolio subset.
- The negative correlation between value and momentum appears to be related to market liquidity. Value strategies appear positively correlated with liquidity risk (they do worse when market liquidity declines) and momentum strategies appear to be negatively correlated (they do better when market liquidity declines).

The analyses of value-based strategies show statistically significant results and also significant excess returns. For example, a 50/50 combination of equally weighted portfolios of all asset groups shows that the top third of value and momentum assets outperformed the bottom third of value and momentum assets by as much as 3.1% yearly, on average, over nearly 33 years. The excess performance was evenly divided between long and short positions, indicating that a long-only portfolio benefits substantially from assets with attractive valuation and momentum. We can conclude that value and momentum approaches are extremely important to the allocation process. Chapter 6 will illustrate that relative momentum can also be detected in portfolios that use different structuring processes. If anything, the content of this book probably does not exploit enough the benefits that can be obtained from exploiting momentum.

One of the objectives of any new research on risk premiums and return forecast is to determine whether or not a new explanatory factor or a process remains significant when considered in conjunction with the three- or four-factor model. For example, as we will examine more closely in Chapter 6, portfolios weighted by fundamental measures such as dividend and payout often outperform that market capitalization counterpart. Does this outperformance remain when Market, Size, Book to Market and Momentum are also taken into account? Francis, Hessel, Wang and Zhang (2009) [35] applied a four-factor model to the excess returns of portfolios whose security weights are based on several investment protocols, such as dividends or total payout, and determined if the portion of return unexplained by the four factors (the Alpha) is statistically significant. Such a result would support the pertinence of other "factors" in the allocation process. Furthermore, I have already indicated in Chapter 3 that using cap-weights to allocate a portfolio may not be efficient, and that there is no reason why alternative allocation protocols could not be used as long as they satisfy the basic requirements that most investors would want, such as low concentration, sector representation and stability (although not all investors may require it). Table 5.5 illustrates a range of weighting protocols from the Francis et al. study and their factor-adjusted performance.

The cap-weight portfolio is our reference portfolio for this comparison. Its mean return was 11.75%. The strongest Alphas are related to repurchase and total payout, indicating that this aspect is not captured within the four-factor model. Although most Alphas were not significant, every single investment protocol achieved a better performance than the cap-weight portfolio. This supports the argument made in Chapter 3 that cap-weight protocols are not efficient. This study also shows that Size, Book to Market and Momentum remain significant explanatory variables. We will explain in Chapter 6 why market-cap protocols are outperformed by so many weighting schemes.

However, investors and academicians may have to incorporate another factor into their analysis. More recently, Ibbotson, Chen and Hu (2011) [36] made the argument that the liquidity investment style—the process of investing in relatively less liquid stocks (as measured by turnover) within the liquid universe of publicly traded stocks—produced risk-adjusted returns that rival or exceed those of the three previous anomalies/factors. Ibbotson, Chen and Hu attributed the potential gain from liquidity-based portfolios not only to a normal compensation premium paid to liquidity providers, but also to the potential dynamic between a stock's popularity, its

TABLE 5.5 Allocation Protocols and Statistical Significance (1973–2007)

Weighting Variable	Mean Return (%)	Sharpe Ratio	Alpha (%)	Factors		
				Size	Book	Momentum
Equal	13.60	0.450	0.23	**	**	
Assets	13.61	0.465	−0.54	**	**	**
Book	12.60	0.447	0.45	**	**	**
Earnings	13.13	0.499	0.80**	**	**	**
Employees	13.63	0.471	0.33	**	**	**
Cash Flows	13.94	0.513	0.78	**	**	**
Sales	13.90	0.516	0.47	**	**	**
Dividend	13.00	0.529	0.45	**	**	**
Repurchase	16.36	0.642	2.77**	**	**	
Total Payout	13.51	0.554	1.08**	**	**	**

** Indicates the variable is significant at the 95% level.
Source: Francis, Hessel, Wang and Zhang (2009).

trading volume and its return. For example, when a stock falls into disfavor, sellers dominate buyers, leading to low volume and low price. The reverse is observed when a stock becomes popular.

Ibbotson, Chen and Hu found that the liquidity premium remains regardless of size, but that it is more important among smaller-cap stocks. The same conclusion applies to value versus growth, and combining high value/low liquidity stocks far outperformed high growth/high liquidity stocks. Finally, high momentum/low liquidity stocks far outperformed low momentum/high liquidity stocks. Liquidity is an independent factor and Ibbotson, Chen and Hu call it a missing style.

The authors also studied the effect of migration from low to high turnover and the reverse on portfolio performance. They found that much of the positive performance of stocks in the lowest liquidity quartile is attributed to the yearly migration of about 25% of these securities to higher turnover quartiles. Similarly, much of the negative performance of stocks in the highest liquidity quartile is attributed to the yearly migration of about 30% of these stocks to lower turnover quartiles. Finally, Idzorek, Xiong and Ibbotson (2011) [37] found that the liquidity premium is also present in mutual funds. Funds that hold less liquid stocks outperform, even though the managers of these funds may not specifically focus on this factor.

Nominal Rate Versus Nominal GDP Growth

Equation 5.7 identified several variables that influence equity pricing: dividend, risk premium, inflation and the differential between real rates and real earnings growth. This relationship could also have been expressed as the difference between nominal interest rates and nominal GDP growth. Thus, when nominal rates are higher than nominal GDP growth, this could be seen as a buy signal for equity versus fixed income.

Morgan Stanley (2010) [38] indicated that such a signal is not only intuitively appealing and economically grounded, but has also historically been a strong buy-and-sell signal. According to Morgan Stanley, an investor using this signal would have sold equity in Q2 of 1998, bought them back in Q3 of the same year and sold them again in Q4 of 2000 to buy them back in the Q3 of 2003. A weak sell signal would have been received in Q1 of 2007, but a really strong sell signal would have been received in Q2 of 2008. At the time of their writing (at end of 2010), the indicator would still have been in equity holding mode in the United States, but not in all of the European countries, including the United Kingdom and Germany.

As I indicated, such a signal is consistent with the valuation principles described in the early section of this chapter. I have replicated that signal in Figure 5.8a and 5.8b. Figure 5.8a indicates if we have a signal for being long equity (positive) or fixed income (negative). Figure 5.8b illustrates what the cumulative performance would have been if we had applied a full allocation to either fixed income or equity using this signal.

If an investor had used this signal, he or she would have held fixed income assets for most of the 1980s and 1990s. The investor would have sold off in the early 2000s, and would have gone long until the recent crisis. He or she would have missed the 2009

FIGURE 5.8a   Signal for Going Long Equity (Positive) or Fixed Income (Negative) (1979–2010).

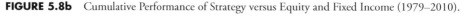

Source: Data from NIPA and Datastream.

FIGURE 5.8b   Cumulative Performance of Strategy versus Equity and Fixed Income (1979–2010).

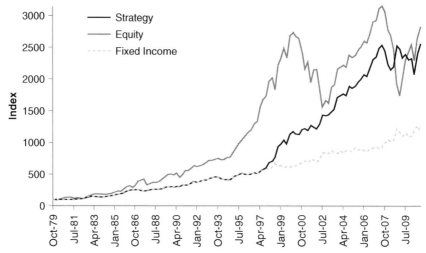

Source: Data from NIPA and Datastream.

rally, however. Both the strategy and equity had about the same cumulative returns, although the strategy was far less risky most of the time, being out of the equity market. Its performance was also extremely stable, with only 70% of the volatility of the S&P 500.

However, the investor would have lagged the equity market until the tech bubble occurred. This indicator may actually have been a sign that something was wrong with the relative value of fixed income and equity assets. On the other hand, the fixed-income asset in this simulation is the 10-year Treasury, and a more appropriate comparison should have been made with a longer-duration portfolio incorporating a high-quality corporate credit component. Furthermore, the allocation between fixed income and equity was based on a simple rule of thumb, and the process itself can be refined.

Review of Predictors

Using data from 1962 to 2009, Ilmanen (2011) [39] evaluated the correlation between specific predictors and future excess returns for equity and Treasuries over the next quarter, the next year or the next five years. Table 5.6 summarizes some of his results.

These results confirm several aspects that we have discussed so far. First, most correlations are much stronger as the horizon is increased, with one exception: the

TABLE 5.6 Correlations of Predictors with S&P 500 and Treasuries

	Correlation to S&P 500		
	Next Quarter	Next Year	Next 5 Years
Dividend Yield	0.11	0.23	0.35
Real Smoothed Earnings	0.10	0.19	0.34
Yield Curve	0.12	0.20	0.37
Long-Rate Momentum	−0.15	−0.15	−0.11
Unemployment Rate	0.15	0.21	0.53
Real GDP Growth Rate	−0.15	−0.23	−0.51
Consumption/Wealth Ratio	0.21	0.40	0.69
Stock Market Volatility	0.05	0.07	0.03
	Correlation to Treasuries		
Yield Curve	0.21	0.34	0.06
Survey-Based BRP	0.19	0.38	0.67
Ex Ante Real Yield	0.28	0.48	0.69
Expected 10-Year Inflation	−0.02	0.01	0.31
Bond Volatility	0.11	0.22	0.64
Equity Market Volatility	0.11	0.08	0.27
Corporate Profits/GDP Ratio	−0.13	−0.25	−0.52
Unemployment Rate	0.11	0.18	0.24

Source: Ilmanen (2011).

yield curve as a predictor of Treasury returns over five years. However, this is not surprising because strong upward or downward sloping curves will usually not last for more than a few years. Eventually, the curve will flatten, whether the adjustment comes from the long end or the short end of the curve.

For equity, the strong correlation with dividend yield and real smoothed earnings is a value trade since such ratios will usually be higher when markets have been weak. Similarly, the positive correlation with unemployment and negative correlation with GDP growth rate is also indicative of the effect of time-varying risk premiums. For example, it is likely that investors underestimate growth when unemployment is high (and require a higher risk premium) and overestimate the ability to maintain strong growth (thus requiring a lower risk premium) when the cycle has recently been favorable. Although stock market volatility appears to have low correlation, Chapter 7 will illustrate that we can still benefit from a control of volatility because of the impact on the GEO mean. Furthermore, it is possible that the correlation is weak because the relation between performance and volatility is far from linear.

Many other predictors are also strongly correlated with fixed income. The signs of the correlation coefficients are also intuitive. For example, we would expect a negative correlation with the ratio of corporate profits to GDP, since an increase in this ratio would normally indicate a stronger economy (although it is not obvious that this relation would remain as strong in an economy where the corporate sector is healthy but the public sector is dealing with huge fiscal imbalances). Nevertheless, all of this evidence points toward the idea that investors could benefit from this information if it is used within a medium- to long-term process.

Closing Remarks

The evidence shows that correlation and volatility can be forecasted even from daily historical returns. It is also likely that this evidence is not spurious but a reflection of behavior by investors and markets. Thus, we have the capacity to integrate this information into an investment and allocation process. Forecasting returns is more complex. Short-term returns cannot be easily forecasted from high-frequency data, and the predictors that appear to have potential work best over a medium-term to long-term horizon. This is also coherent with the observation that price volatility is much higher than justified by fundamentals. Therefore, an allocation model that uses predictors of returns should be based on a forward-looking horizon that is consistent with the efficiency of the predictors over this particular horizon. One of the reasons for the failure of so many allocation models is the attempt to build short-term models with data that is only statistically relevant in the medium- to long-term—another behavioral bias.

As I indicated in the Preface, this book is all about process. The next six chapters are devoted to describing and implementing investment processes that have persistent characteristics and offer a high likelihood of superior risk-adjusted performance over medium-term to long-term horizons. The overall approach may also help investors deal with the daily stress related to their investment portfolio.

Notes

1. Walker, Susanne (2010), "Morgan Stanley issues a mea culpa on Treasuries forecast that was 'wrong'," Bloomberg, August 20, http://www.bloomberg.com/news/2010-08-20/morgan-stanley-issues-a-mea-culpa-on-treasuries-forecast-that-was-wrong-.html.
2. Ilmanen, Antti (2011), *Expected Returns: An Investor's Guide to Harvesting Market Rewards,* Wiley Finance, p. 161.
3. Lopez, Claude and Javier Reyes (2007), "Real interest rates stationarity and per capita consumption growth rate," University of Cincinnati.
4. Reinhart, Carmen M. and Vincent R. Reinhart (2010), "After the fall," Federal Reserve Bank of Kansas City, Jackson Hole Symposium.
5. Kirkegaard, Jacob F. and Carmen M Reinhart (2012) "The return of financial repression in the aftermath of the great contraction," Peterson Institute Working Paper.
6. Arnott, Robert D., and Peter L. Bernstein (2002), "What risk premium is normal?," Financial Analyst Journal 58(2), 64–85.
7. Bogle, John C. (2005), "The relentless rules of humble arithmetic" in "Bold thinking on investment management," *The Financial Analysts Journal 60th Anniversary Anthology*, CFA Institute, 127–144.
8. Shiller R. (1981), "Do stock prices move too much to be justified by subsequent changes in dividends?" *American Economic Review* 71(3), 421–436.
9. Cutler, D.M., J.M. Poterba, and L. H. Summers (1989),"What moves stock prices?" *Journal of Portfolio Management* 15(3), 4–12.
10. Brandt, Michael W., and Qiang Kang (2002), "On the relationship between the conditional mean and volatility of stock returns: A latent VAR approach," *Journal of Financial Economics* 72(2), 217–257.
11. Campbell, J. Y., and B. Thompson (2008), "Predicting Excess stock returns out of sample: can anything beat the historical average?", *Review of Financial Studies* 29(4), 1509–1531.
12. Bank, Steven A. (2004), "The dividend divide in Anglo-American corporate taxation," University of California Los Angeles—Law & Economics Research Paper Series, Research Paper No. 04–3.
13. Tugwell, Rexford G. (1933), "The Industrial discipline and the governmental arts".
14. The United States Department of Treasury (2003), "General explanation of the administration fiscal year 2004 revenue proposals, 50.
15. Brock, Woody (2012), *American Gridlock: Why the Right and Left are Both Wrong—Commonsense 101 Solutions to the Economic Crisis*, John Wiley & Sons, Inc., p. 141.
16. Bernstein, William J. (2002), "How much pie can you buy?," Efficient Frontier.
17. Arnott, Robert D. and Clifford S. Asness (2003), "Surprise! Higher dividends = Higher earnings growth," *Financial Analysts Journal* 55(1), 70–87.

18. Sorensen, Eric H. and Sanjoy Ghosh (2010), "Rewarding fundamentals," *Journal of Portfolio Management* 36(4), 71–76.
19. Fama, Eugene F. and Kenneth R. French (1988), "Dividend yields and expected stock returns," *Journal of Financial Economics* 22(1), 3–25.
20. Campbell, John Y., and John Ammer, "What moves the stock and bond market? A variance decomposition for long-term asset returns," *The Journal of Finance* 48(1), 3–37.
21. Boudoukh, Jacoband, Michaely Roni, Matthew Richardson, and Michael R. Roberts (2007), "On the importance of measuring payout yield: Implications for empirical asset pricing," *Journal of Finance* 62(2), 877–915.
22. Fama, Eugene F. and Kenneth R. French (1992), "The cross section of expected stock returns," *Journal of Finance* 47(2), 427–465.
23. Fama, Eugene F. and Kenneth R. French (2007a), "Migration," *Financial Analysts Journal* 63(3), 48–58.
24. Fama, Eugene F. and Kenneth R. French (2007b), "The Anatomy of Value and Growth Stock Returns," *Financial Analysts Journal* 63(6), 44–54.
25. Zhang, Chu (2008), "Decomposed Fama-French factors for the size and book-to-market effects," Department of Finance—Hong Kong University of Science and Technology.
26. Carhart, M. M. (1997), "On persistence in mutual fund performance," *Journal of Finance* 52(1), 57–82.
27. Jegadeesh, Narasimhan and Sheridan Titman (1993), "Returns to buying winners and selling losers: Implications for stock market efficiency," *Journal of Finance* 48(1), 65–91.
28. Jegadeesh, Narasimhan and Sheridan Titman (2001), "Momentum," University of Illinois; University of Texas and NBER.
29. Daniel, Kent., and Sheridan Titman, 1999, "Market efficiency in an irrational world," *Financial Analyst Journal,* 55, 28–40.
30. Chan, Louis K. C., Narasimhan Jegadeesh, and Josef Lakonishok (1996), "Momentum strategies," *Journal of Finance* 51,1681–1713.
31. Daniel, Kent D., David Hirshleifer, and Avanidhar Subrahmanyam (2000), "Covariance risk, mispricing and the cross section of security returns," NBER, Working Paper 7615.
32. Hong, Harrison and Jeremy C. Stein (1999), "A unified theory of underreaction, momentum trading and overreaction in asset markets," *Journal of Finance* 54(6), 2143–2184.
33. Avramov, Doron, Tarun Chordia, and Amit Goyal (2006), "The impact of trades on daily volatility," *Review of Financial Studies* 19(4), 1241–1277.
34. Asness, Clifford S., Tobias J. Moskowitz, and Lasse H. Pedersen (2009), "Value and momentum everywhere," AQR Capital Management, Graduate School of Business—University of Chicago and NBER, Stern School of Business—New York University, CEPR, and NBER.

35. Francis, John Clark, Christopher Hessel, Jun Wang and Ge Zhang (2009), "Portfolios weighted by repurchase and total payout," Zicklin School of Business, Long Island University.

36. Ibbotson, Roger G., Chen Zhiwu, and Wendy Y. Hu (2011), "Liquidity as an investment style," Yale School of Management and Zebra Capital Management LLC.

37. Idzorek, Thomas M., James X. Xiong, and Roger G. Ibbotson (2011), "The Liquidity Style of Mutual Funds," Morningstar Investment Management and Zebra Capital Management.

38. Leibowitz, Martin, and Anthony Bova (2010), "Portfolio strategy – Policy portfolios and rebalancing behavior," Morgan Stanley Research North America.

39. Ilmanen, Antti (2011), Expected Returns: An Investor's Guide to Harvesting Market Rewards, Wiley Finance, pp. 146 and 175.

PART III

The Components of An Efficient Portfolio-Assembly Process

CHAPTER 6

Understanding Nonmarket-Cap Investment Protocols

It seems that a new equity-investment protocol is created every few weeks. Although there are unlimited ways to build more efficient protocols than those based on cap weights, several products are conceptually similar. The diversity comes from the fact that many service providers would like investors to believe that their protocol is the best, when in fact the philosophical differences are sometimes minimal. It does not mean that all protocols will generate the same excess performance, but it does mean that many can be similarly ex ante efficient.

This chapter seeks to clarify what are the general characteristics of efficient nonmarket-cap protocols (also called market-indifferent protocols in the industry) and to explain what aspects differentiate one protocol from another. In theory, in a Gaussian world, investors would seek to invest in the portfolio that offers the highest Sharpe ratio. In practice, identifying the optimal portfolio requires that we forecast returns, volatilities and correlations among securities, which can lead to unstable portfolio structures. There may be too much noise in the market to derive stable and reliable parameters, especially for expected returns. If we do not have confidence in our ability to forecast expected returns, we should avoid any process that requires modeling expected returns. Chapter 6 explores the different types of investment protocols that are available. A classification based on the following three categories is used: risk based, fundamental and factor based. These categories are not necessarily mutually exclusive. Several approaches can be used within a single investment protocol. This chapter also attempts to bridge the literature on mutual fund performance with that of nonmarket-cap protocols and discuss the possibility that the pattern of excess performance of some protocols may be conditioned by specific factors. Therefore, by the end of this chapter, investors should be in a better position to make a more informed decision about the types of protocols to use and why.

Risk-Based Protocols

Some investment protocols are solely based on assemblage processes that do not require information about expected returns and do not impose any requirement on the economic structure of the portfolio, such as maintaining a representative sector exposure. At most, they will use information that is related to the covariance matrix. The following are the protocols being studied in this chapter:

- equal weight
- equal risk
- minimum variance
- maximum diversification

However, for the purpose of understating these protocols, I will use a traditional mean variance optimization protocol (maximizing the Sharpe ratio) as a reference. Unlike the four other protocols, the maximization of the Sharpe ratio requires information about expected returns. We will discuss optimization protocols in more details in a later section, but for now I will do a quick introduction.

Maximizing the Sharpe Ratio

The Sharpe ratio is the ratio of excess return to volatility.

$$[(R_p - R_f) / \sigma_m]$$ (6.1)

In order to maximize the Sharpe ratio, we need to forecast returns, volatilities and all pairwise correlations. However, the solution to any optimization process can be very sensitive to its underlying assumptions. Let's assume the following expectations about two assets. Assets A and B have respective volatilities of 16% and 8%. Asset B has a 4.5% expected return and the risk-free rate is 2%. The following table shows the optimal allocation to both assets depending on their correlation (either 0.3 or 0.5) and the expected return on Asset A (either 5%, 7.5% or 10%).

The optimal weights are extremely sensitive to estimated returns, and even more so if the correlation of returns is high. Therefore, if we were to use this process to allocate within an equity portfolio where the components are volatile and highly correlated

TABLE 6.1 Optimal Weights Under Returns and Correlations Assumptions (%)

Correlation	Return on Asset A	Weight Asset A	Weight Asset B
0.3	5	15	85
	7.5	37	63
	10	56	44
0.5	5	7	93
	7.5	40	60
	10	73	27

with one another, the optimal weights could be extreme and unstable, and trading requirements could be significant. Such an approach, although conceptually superior (since it takes into account return as well as risk), could lead to disastrous performance if not properly implemented. For example, DeMiguel, Garlappi and Uppal (2007) [1] showed that although mean variance optimization produces high Sharpe ratios "in sample," these Sharpe ratios decline in most cases by 65% to 100% (a nil Sharpe ratio) "out of sample" because of errors concerning estimates of future expected returns, volatilities and correlations. However, the failure of the optimization approach could also be attributed to an improper implementation, such as using a forward-looking horizon to forecast returns, which is inappropriate with the ability of a predictor to forecast returns over such a horizon.

Introduction to Risk-Based Protocols

A minimum variance protocol seeks to use the information on volatilities and correlations (i.e., the entire covariance matrix) to determine the weights that would create a minimum risk portfolio (min σ_p). An equal risk protocol seeks to determine the weights that would create a portfolio in which each component would contribute the same amount of risk. For example, in the context of a portfolio of two assets, we would seek the weights in which each asset contributes 50% of the total risk. A maximum diversification protocol seeks to find the weights that maximize the ratio of the weighted average volatility of all securities to the volatility of the portfolio itself [2]. Assuming P_i represents the weight of each security in the portfolio, σ_i its volatility and σ_p the volatility of the entire portfolio, we must determine the appropriate security weights such that:

$$[\Sigma P_i \, \sigma_i] \, / \, \sigma_p \tag{6.2}$$

is maximized. Unlike a minimum variance portfolio, a maximum diversification portfolio is more likely to incorporate volatile securities as long as they have low pairwise correlations.

Choueifaty (2006) introduced the concept of maximum diversification, in the context of portfolio construction. The intuition behind Equation 6.2 can also be found in the work of Christoffersen, Errunza, Jacobs and Langlois (2011) [3]. As we did in Chapter 4, they started with the general Markowitz diversification formula presented in Equation 6.3a. They then considered two extreme scenarios. The first case is that of a portfolio with no diversification benefits, where all cross-correlations are one (as we did in Chapter 4). In this case, the portfolio volatility is simply a weighted average of the volatility of all components. However, they also considered the opposite extreme, that of a correlation matrix where all cross-correlations are minus one. In this case, it is possible to create a portfolio whose volatility would be nil. They found that by combining both extremes, the diversification benefit (DB) is determined by Equation 6.3b. This equation normalizes the diversification benefit between zero (when all correlations are one) and one (when all correlations are minus one). We can easily see that minimizing Equation 6.3b is identical to maximizing Equation 6.2.

$$\sigma_p = [P_t^T \, \Sigma_t \, P_t]^{1/2} \qquad\qquad (6.3a)$$

$$\text{DB} = 1 - \sigma_p \, / \, [P_t^T \, \sigma_t] \qquad\qquad (6.3b)$$

Investors using any of these protocols make implicit assumptions about the structure of the variance–covariance matrix. Therefore, to have a better understanding of these protocols, it is necessary to understand how these assumptions can influence the output of a portfolio optimization process. More specifically, I am trying to determine the structural conditions that would lead to an equal weight, a minimum variance, an equal risk or a maximum diversification portfolio allocation. The analysis is done for both portfolios of two assets (such as two asset classes or two securities) and portfolios of two or more assets.

Table 6.2 presents the results of the analysis. It indicates which investment protocols would yield the same allocation if all portfolio components are assumed to have the same characteristics specified in the first line. An "N" indicates that the findings apply to portfolios of two or more components. A "2" indicates that the findings apply only to a two-component portfolio. The two-components case is obviously not as interesting within an asset-class context (our current interest in this chapter) since we will always have much more than just two securities.

If securities have identical volatilities and pairwise correlations (a totally hypothetical scenario), all risk-based protocols would lead to the same allocation: an equal-weight portfolio. Thus, an equal-weight approach may be advisable if we believe that there is too much noise in the market to obtain appropriate estimates of expected returns, volatilities and correlations. If returns and volatilities were identical, all protocols would lead to the same allocation, but only in the two assets case. Equal risk and equal weight would not lead to the same allocation in a portfolio that has more than two components. This makes sense because, if we have only two assets, we obviously

TABLE 6.2 Implicit Assumptions of Risk-Based Protocols

	Rd. Vol. Corr.	Rd. Vol.	Vol. Corr.	Rd. Corr.	Rd.	Vol.	Correlation
Maximum Sharpe Ratio	N	N		N	N		
1/n	N	2	N			2	
Equal Risk	N	2	N	N	2	2	N
Minimum Variance	N	N	N			N	
Maximum Diversification	N	N	N	N	N	N	N

have a single correlation. Finally, if we made the assumption that the returns expected on all securities are identical, maximum diversification would yield the same results as optimizing the Sharpe ratio.

We can easily see from Equation 6.2 that this is an unnecessarily restrictive condition. If the volatility of each security within a portfolio (σ_i) were proportional to its risk premium, maximum diversification would also maximize the Sharpe ratio. Demey, Maillard and Roncalli (2010) [4] summarized the specific statistical characteristics of all four protocols:

- Equal weight: all securities have the same weight.
- Minimum variance: all securities have the same marginal risk.
- Equal risk: all securities have the same marginal risk weighted by their respective weight.
- Maximum diversification: all securities have the same marginal risk scaled by their respective volatility.

We also know for a fact that equal-weight protocols will have greater volatilities than equal risk. Minimum variance will have the lowest volatility. Maximum diversification will have a greater volatility than minimum variance. Since we know that volatility and correlation show some persistence, and that returns are more difficult to forecast, maximum diversification could be an interesting allocation process, since it exploits more fully all the information in the variance–covariance matrix. However, can we really say that any of these protocols is truly superior to the others, and superior to an ordinary cap-weight approach once other considerations are taken into account? Let's now look successively at these options, starting with the equal-weight and equal-risk protocols.

Equal-Weight and Equal-Risk Protocols

An equal-weight protocol would obviously have a bias toward smaller-cap stocks. Therefore, some of the excess return of an equal-weight protocol could be attributed to a small-cap risk premium. However, it could also be attributed to smoothing of price noise (see Chapter 3). In fact, an equal-weight protocol would be particularly efficient at smoothing price noise because it benefits from the law of large numbers and the absence of any active bets. In essence, there is probably no price noise smoothing process that could be more statistically neutral. Although the S&P 500 is one of the least concentrated indices, Exxon Mobile and Apple each account for more than 3% of the index, and the top-10 companies for nearly 20%. In an equal-weight protocol, each security would have a 0.2% weight. By comparison, in Canada, the top-10 securities account for approximately one-third of the S&P/TSX Composite.

Figure 6.1 illustrates what the volatility of an equal-weight index would be if the number of securities ranged from 10 to 10,000, if the volatility of each security was 30% and if all pairwise correlations were 20% or 40%. We can see from Figure 6.1 that almost all the statistical benefits of diversification of the S&P 500 have been achieved with 100 equally weighted securities.

FIGURE 6.1   Volatility of Equal-Weight Protocols According to Correlation and Number of Securities.

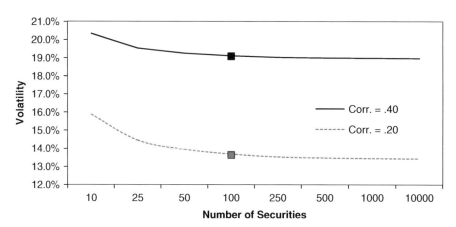

Pollett and Wilson (2006) [5] have shown that the average market volatility on an index such as the S&P 500 can be almost entirely explained by the average volatility and average correlation of its constituents (97% between 1963 Q1 and 2004 Q2). This supports the inferences that were made from Figure 6.1 by using average volatilities and correlations, and illustrates that we can build efficiently diversified portfolios using only subsets of all the securities available. Therefore, equal-weight protocols may be performing in the long term for three reasons: first, because they benefit from a smaller-cap bias (although the benefit of a small-cap bias has been found not to be consistent in the literature), second, because they are statistically very efficient at diversifying idiosyncratic risk and third, because they are very efficient at smoothing price noise. The main criticisms that could be made of a pure equal-weight protocol (although it applies to all risk-based protocols) is the lack of concern for economic (sector) representation and liquidity. If applied to the population of securities of some market indices, this approach could lead to sector allocations that are not representative of the economic reality. For example, although the sector allocation of the S&P 500 equal weight remains fairly balanced, this would not necessarily be the case for the index of a less diversified market like Finland or even Canada. Therefore, despite its greater efficiency, an equal-weight protocol could theoretically underperform a cap-weight protocol for many years.

All of the previous comments could apply to an equal-risk protocol. Although an equal-risk protocol would not lead to an equal-weight allocation, in an index of many securities, such as the S&P 500, the allocations resulting from an equal-risk protocol would be far closer to equal weight than cap weight.

Maillard, Roncalli and Teiletche (2009) [6] have compared equal risk and equal-weight protocols. There is something comforting about the idea that all components within a portfolio contribute equally to the total risk. But, as I implied, does it really make a significant difference against an equal-weight protocol in the context of a diversified equity portfolio? We already know that if all securities had similar volatilities and pairwise correlations, both protocols would lead to the same alloca-tion—an equal-weight allocation. We also know that the volatility of an index such as the S&P 500 can largely be explained by average volatilities and correlations. Maillard, Roncalli and Teiletche studied the performance and characteristics of both protocols in the US market over the period 1973 to 2008. The analysis was completed on US sector indices (instead of single stocks), because building large-scale equal-risk proto-cols can be computationally problematic. Some of their results are presented in Table 6.3. The results for the minimum variance protocol are also presented for comparison purposes. Although equal risk and equal weight do not lead to the same specific allo-cations, their risk/return characteristics are incredibly similar. An equal-risk protocol is hardly worth the greater complexity in the context of a diversified equity portfolio.

The intrinsic appeal of an equal-weight protocol is also supported by the work of DeMiguel, Garlappi and Uppal (2007). Their research compared the performance of an equal-weight strategy against 14 other strategies, including minimum variance, but not equal risk or maximum diversification. Their analysis was applied to eight differ-ent data sets. They concluded the following:

- No strategy (among those tested) surpassed a simple equal weight.
- An equal-weight strategy is most efficient when the number of assets (n) is large. When n is large, the diversification potential of an equal-weight strategy increases, while the number of parameters that must be estimated by other protocols grows significantly. Thus, the estimated errors of these parameters (returns and/or vola-tilities and correlations) are so important that they overwhelm the diversification benefits. The authors concluded that more effort must be invested to improve the estimates of moments, especially expected returns.
- A minimum variance approach does not consistently outperform an equal-weight pro-tocol, but its relative performance improves significantly and can be an efficient alter-native to equal weight if weight constraints, such as no short sales, are imposed on the components of the portfolio. The issue of using constraints will be covered later on.

This is not to say that an equal-weight protocol does not have its detractors. Kritzman, Page and Turkington (2010) [7] have come to the defense of optimization

TABLE 6.3 Equal Risk versus Equal Weight—Equity US Sectors Portfolios (1973–2008) (%)

	$1/n$	Equal Risk	Minimum Variance
Average Return	10.03	10.01	9.54
Volatility	16.20	15.35	12.41
Sharpe Ratio	0.62	0.65	0.77
One Month Value-at-Risk	−12.67	−12.17	−10.22
One Month Worst Drawdown	−30.28	−28.79	−23.31

Source: Maillard, Roncalli and Teiletche (2009).

protocols (such as maximizing the Sharpe ratio). They argued that criticisms of optimization protocols are misplaced, and the conclusion that equal-risk protocols can outperform a reasonably designed optimization process is erroneous. I will come back to this article and others later on, but, although I agree with their observations, our current argument is not that equal weight is necessarily the best protocol, but that it is a better protocol than market capitalization if applied to a diversified and balanced universe of securities.

Minimum Variance and Maximum Diversification Protocols

Equal-risk and equal-weight protocols will lead to low portfolio concentration. However, a minimum variance (MinVar) or maximum diversification (MaxDiv) protocol will be based on an optimization process that will determine how many securities will actually be included in the portfolio. Such protocols can lead to portfolios of less than 30 to 100 securities, even for a global mandate. They may also lead to portfolios that are not representative of the economic structure (although this interpretation could be conditioned by the fact that investors have traditionally been educated to analyze the economic structure of portfolios through sector weights, a topic to be discussed later on). Some investors may have issues with these two aspects, but, in most cases, it should not lead to a rejection of these protocols (on the contrary, there is strong value in these approaches). Rather, it should lead to a proper dosage within the overall allocation that takes into account the circumstances of the investors.

Some investment protocols may incorporate constraints to manage these issues. For example, Rajamony and Puchtler of Numeric Investors (2011) [8] have shown that it is possible to design protocols that impose constraints on sector exposure (against cap weights) and still achieve a low level of portfolio volatility. This indicates that, although there may be a single allocation structure that leads to a minimum variance portfolio (for a given set of data and methodology), there are many more portfolio structures that can deliver both a low volatility (although slightly higher than minimum variance) and a more balanced sector and concentration exposure. When all factors and concerns are considered, a minimum variance objective may not be optimal for all investors.

MinVar and MaxDiv lead to structurally different portfolios. The example in Table 6.4 is meant to explain the nuance between the two concepts. Three securities, A, B and C have respective volatilities of 20%, 20% and 30%. The pairwise correlation between A and B is 0.5, while both A and B have a 0.3 correlation with C. Table 6.4 indicates which weights would either minimize the volatility or maximize the diversification.

Although the MinVar protocol is allocated to the riskier security, the approach implicitly favors securities with lower volatilities and Beta coefficients. The MaxDiv protocol is more concerned with the combination of volatilities and correlations that will maximize the distance between average volatility and portfolio volatility. In essence, it does not lead to a MinVar portfolio unless all securities have the same variance, but it is more efficient at reducing the difference between average security

TABLE 6.4 Weight Minimum Variance versus Maximum Diversification (%)

	Minimum Variance	Maximum Diversification
Security A	43	35
Security B	43	35
Security C	14	30

volatility and portfolio volatility. Also, it will not necessarily bias the portfolio allocation toward the least volatile sectors, as would an MinVar protocol. Both types of protocols should lead to a less volatile portfolio than a market-cap protocol, and, thus, both approaches would benefit from the effect of lower volatility on the GEO mean.

Rajamony and Puchtler attribute the performance of MinVar protocols to the fact that the relationship between return and risk (as measured by Beta) is not as predicted by the CAPM. The empirical relationship between Beta and return is much flatter than expected. Higher Beta securities do not necessarily deliver higher returns. They explain this apparent anomaly by outlining several causes, but, again, most of them are related to human behavior and preferences (such as overconfidence in high-growth securities and sectors, which leads to mispricing). Thus, if behavior explains part of the excess performance of MinVar protocols, we may assume that this benefit will be persistent. This argumentation may also apply to MaxDiv protocols with the added argument that investors may also not properly price correlations.

Choueifaty and Coignard [9] tested their MaxDiv protocol against an equal-weight protocol in the United States and in the Eurozone from 1992 to 2008. They obviously needed information on volatility and correlation of single stocks to apply their concept, but, interestingly enough, they discovered that their results were not very sensitive to the methodology used to obtain measures of volatility and correlation (250 days of historical returns were used to derive volatilities and correlations). They believed that their results were driven much more by relative volatilities and correlations. Therefore, although volatilities and correlations are unstable, the authors make the argument that the correlation between BMW and Audi will almost always be greater than the correlation between BMW and J.P. Morgan, and that the volatility of securities in the resource sectors will almost always be greater than that of securities in the utility sector. Consequently, they implicitly make the assumption that there is persistence in relative volatility and relative correlation and that fact is enough for the protocol to be successful even if simple methodologies are used to derive volatilities and correlations.

Table 6.5 presents the results of this analysis. The performance of a MaxDiv protocol is impressive even though the portfolios usually contain no more than 30 to 60 stocks. Its volatility is much lower than either an equal-weight or market capitalization protocol and its Sharpe ratio is also much higher, although the equal-weight protocol still outperforms significantly a capitalization weight protocol. Why is a MaxDiv protocol outperforming?

TABLE 6.5 Performance of Maximum Diversification Against Two Other Protocols (1992–2008) (%)

	Annualized Data	Maximum Diversification	Equal Weight	Capitalization Weight
United States	Return	12.7	12.0	9.6
	Volatility	12.7	14.3	13.4
	Sharpe Ratio	0.66	0.54	0.39
Eurozone	Return	17.9	14.0	11.3
	Volatility	13.9	18.1	17.9
	Sharpe Ratio	0.96	0.52	0.37

Source: Choueifaty and Coignard (2008).

From the material we have covered so far, there are four factors that could explain the excess performance of a MaxDiv protocol against a cap-weight protocol. The volatility of a MaxDiv portfolio is less than that of a cap-weight portfolio, which improves the GEO mean. However, this factor could hardly account for more than 20 bps to 70 bps of excess return per year on average, far less than the generally reported excess return. It may also implicitly smooth price noise (although the high turnover of MinVar and MaxDiv protocols makes this assertion less certain). Furthermore, in the previous example, MaxDiv outperformed equal weight, even though the latter is very efficient at smoothing price noise. The third and fourth arguments are related to volatility. A MaxDiv protocol may lead to a more efficiently diversified portfolio than a cap-weight approach (because investors misprice volatility and correlations). It may also be more efficient at controlling tail risk.

Choueifaty and Coignard make the argument that MaxDiv protocol is the most efficient unbiased risk-based protocol that can be built. Conceptually, they may be right, but market noise, estimation errors and simple bad luck would probably stop most investors from concentrating all their allocation in a single protocol. However, there is also one aspect that may help understand the structure and fundamental source of performance of MaxDiv portfolios, what Choueifaty, Froidure and Reynier [10] call the core properties of MaxDiv (or MDPs):

Any stock not held by the MDP is more correlated to the MDP than any of the stocks that belong to it. Furthermore, all stocks belonging to the MDP have the same correlation to it.

This statement has strong implications. For example, I have indicated previously that the optimization process applied to a MaxDiv protocol could lead to a concentrated portfolio (for example, 50 securities), which may not be representative of the economic structure. However, let's assume a MaxDiv portfolio of 50 securities is built from an index of 500 securities. In this case, the core properties would indicate that the 450 securities that are not included in the portfolio have, in fact, greater correlation to the portfolio than the 50 securities that are in the portfolio. This is an important aspect because it means that MaxDiv portfolio may be statistically less concentrated and more representative of the economic structure than traditional measures related to security concentration and sector representation would indicate. Furthermore, as indicated, these are not assumptions, but properties that result from the maximization of the MaxDiv ratio, which can easily be supported empirically. Thus, MaxDiv portfolios are statistically very diversified, and no other portfolio could offer a higher MaxDiv ratio.

In their 2008 article, Choueifaty and Coignard specified what the MaxDiv ratio would have been over time for both a MaxDiv protocol and for a cap-weight protocol. Although the ratio is volatile in both cases, the relative ratio of both remains around 1.5. This means that if, for example, the ratio of the average stock volatility to the volatility of the portfolio is 1.5 for a cap-weight portfolio, this ratio would be approximately 2.25 for the MaxDiv portfolio, even though this portfolio contains far fewer securities. Consequently, MaxDiv portfolios can have volatilities that are 25% less than a cap-weight portfolio. Finally, the authors determined that an unexplained excess return still existed once we took into account the market, size factor and the book-to-market factors. Thus, there are definitive factors other than traditional risk factors that explain the performance of a MaxDiv protocol.

We have mentioned before that volatility and correlation show persistence. It appears that investors do not properly integrate this information in the pricing of securities. More specifically, according to Choueifaty and Coignard, forecasts of volatility by market participants could be fairly accurate, and investors may be rational at the single-security level, meaning that all else being equal, investors require higher returns for higher risk (although we could easily challenge the idea that volatility is well priced). However, investors would not incorporate or would only partially incorporate the information about cross-correlations among securities. Securities offering low average pairwise correlation would be undervalued, while those offering high average pairwise correlation would be overvalued. This implies that investors do not properly price diversification.

This aspect should not surprise us. Whenever security analysts provide a target pricing range for specific securities, their valuations almost never incorporate the diversification benefit they provide. Nevertheless, Choueifaty and Coignard implicitly recognize the uncertainty of the parameters that are required for the optimization by imposing constraints. Single-security weight is limited to 10%, cumulative weight is limited to 40% for the sum of weights above 5%, the contribution of each security to total risk is also limited at 4% and no short sales are allowed.

Thus, the MaxDiv protocol exploits all of the information in the covariance matrix in a most efficient way. Choueifaty, Froidure and Reynier (2011) illustrated how the maximum diversification ratio (DR) can be expressed using two important factors: $\rho(W)$, which represents the volatility weighted average correlation of the assets in the portfolio, and CR(*W*), which represents the volatility weighted average concentration ratio of the portfolio. More specifically:

$$DR(W) = [\rho(W) (1 - CR(W)) + CR(W)]^{-1/2} \qquad (6.4)$$

Thus, DR will increase as the volatility weighted average correlation and the volatility weighted average concentration ratio declines. Conceptually, the fact that the MaxDiv ratio is dependent on $\rho(W)$ leads to a more efficient solution than equal risk. However, as indicated, using this conceptually very efficient approach may lead to the most diversified portfolio, but this portfolio may have fewer than 50 or 75 securities, will most likely have a very different sector allocation than traditional benchmarks and will have a fairly high turnover. If the investor has no issue with any of these aspects, MaxDiv is an efficient concept for a long-term investment.

It may be important at this point to explain the parallel between the MaxDiv concept and the diversification bonus that was discussed in Chapter 4. If all volatilities and pairwise correlations were equal, the MaxDiv protocol would recommend an equal-weight allocation, and this allocation would also lead to the maximum diversification bonus that can be achieved. However, the argument made in Chapter 4 was simply that we should seek, if we can, to structure asset classes in order to minimize the differentiation in volatilities between them. Furthermore, if we can go one step further and control volatility within some asset classes (a topic for a later chapter), this would lead to more stable allocation solutions and less turnover between asset classes. Finally, we also wanted to illustrate that diversification can be improved with more balanced risk allocations, even if these solutions were not the most efficient. The concept of maximum diversification bonus is used more as a portfolio-construction guideline in our allocation process.

Closing Remarks on Risk-Based Protocols

Equal-weight and equal-risk protocols are probably similarly ex ante efficient when applied to diversified markets. Both would lead to portfolios that have low single-security concentration and that are very efficient at smoothing price noise. However, both protocols can also lead to portfolios that are not representative of the economic structure of the market. Some investors could be uncomfortable with this aspect. Minimum variance and maximum diversification protocols are even less concerned with the issue of economic representation, as defined by sector weights (unless constraints are imposed), and the portfolio turnover can be significant and detrimental to tax efficiency. However, they will lead to lower-volatility portfolios that could be efficient at increasing the GEO mean, and MaxDiv is particularly efficient at exploiting the covariance matrix. Although these protocols may offer the benefit of lowering volatility, if an investor is concerned with maintaining a proper economic/sector representation, he or she should scale the allocation within his or her comfort zone.

MinVar and MaxDiv also differ in concept in one important way. MinVar is only concerned with total risk reduction. Since volatility usually plays a greater role in risk reduction than does correlation (something we will demonstrate in Chapter 10), MinVar is biased toward lower-volatility sectors and stocks. Therefore, the potential benefit of MinVar would largely be explained by the fact that investors do not, in fact, properly price riskier (more volatile) assets, and, thus, that the relation between Beta and excess return is much flatter than expected. This is what allows the GEO mean of low-volatility protocols to outperform the market. By comparison, MaxDiv may benefit from the same issue, but it is much more concerned with maximizing the benefits of diversification by fully exploiting the variance–covariance matrix. One methodology (MinVar) concentrates on volatility mispricing at the single-security level, while the other (MaxDiv) concentrates on both volatility and correlation mispricing. As we will illustrate at the end of this chapter, both approaches are interesting.

Even if minimum variance and maximum diversification protocols are simple concepts, not everyone can be a manager of such products. First, there are technical challenges. We may get inappropriate readings on volatilities and correlations because some securities are illiquid, may be targeted for acquisition, may have paid significant special dividends, may be traded on different time zones, etc. As a result, many factors can affect volatilities and correlations in a permanent or in a transient fashion, and can make the estimates noisy. However, it is common practice, when structuring a portfolio to use a number of filter rules (such as minimum liquidity requirements, exclusion of securities subject to a merger or acquisition proposals, etc.) which may help improve the quality of the data.

Second, if the number of securities within the portfolio is large in relation to the number of observations, the empirical covariance matrix may be unstable. Therefore, different techniques (such as factor models or shrinkage) may be required to improve the estimates of the matrix. Furthermore, constraints or cost functions may also be required to reduce turnover to a reasonable level.

Third, with an equal-weight protocol and most fundamental protocols (to be discussed later), we are usually not concerned with idiosyncratic risks because the portfolios tend to contain a large number of securities. However, with minimum volatility or maximum diversification, idiosyncratic risks are an issue because the recommended portfolios contain fewer securities. Sector concentration may also be a greater issue with MinVar protocols. This aspect can also be managed with constraints on security and sector concentration, and a proper allocation within the overall portfolio of the investor.

Fourth, since MinVar and MaxDiv are among the purest forms of risk-based protocols, the optimizer could, from time to time, select what may appear to be a less balanced set of securities. However, the dynamic optimization process ensures that the desired statistical and/or core properties are realized over time. Furthermore, the investor must understand that this is what he or she is paying for. Such protocols will have significant tracking error against traditional market-cap indices, and investors must understand that significant underperformance can occur over specific periods. This is why MinVar and MaxDiv protocols must be one of several strategic approaches within a portfolio. Furthermore, we should expect MaxDiv to provide a more heterogeneous assemblage of securities than MinVar, and avoid concentration in low-volatility securities as MinVar normally would.

Fifth, the main objective of the managers of such protocols is to exploit the statistical properties of assets, not to express a view on the appreciation potential of specific securities. Let's not forget that the justification for the design of so many nonmarket-cap protocols is because of our lack of confidence in traditional active management. We should not recreate the flaws of active management within these protocols. Thus, the role of a manager in this case is to intervene as little as possible with the process. Because of these implementation issues, it may be preferable to design investment protocols that have a stricter initial security screening and lead to more diversified portfolios, even if this is achieved at the expense of slightly higher volatility.

Although the reduction in volatility may be less, we may also be more confident in allocating relatively more to this protocol. Again, it is my experience that investors analyze these protocols in silos without consideration for their overall integration within the portfolio, and that several firms that design such protocols also ignore the greater allocation agenda of the investor. That is because no single firm offers a comprehensive range of such products. As we combine two or three different protocols based on different underlying concepts with other asset components, and overlay a rebalancing methodology, the concern with idiosyncratic risks declines.

Finally, if we believe that diversification opportunities are greater internationally than domestically (a logical assumption), the benefits of using risk-based protocols, especially those that exploit the covariance matrix more fully (such as MaxDiv), should be even greater on international portfolios. However, the implementation in a global context is certainly more complex.

Fundamental Protocols

As I indicated previously, I use the term "fundamental protocols" to designate protocols that seek to smooth pricing error while targeting a specific allocation structure. Therefore, the objective of these protocols is not necessarily limited to the smoothing of price noise at the expense of any other concern. The pioneer work on fundamental protocols comes from Arnott, Hsu and West, who have devoted an entire book to their investment management approach. All investors should read it, since it provides not only a better understanding of their approach, but also a deeper understanding of the flaws of cap-weight indices [11]. Many products that use Arnott, Hsu, and West's specific approach are offered as ETFs under the acronym RAFI (Research Affiliates Fundamental Index). They use the term "Fundamental Indexing" to refer to their approach, and, therefore, we will also use this terminology to refer specifically to the RAFI approach.

The issue with fundamental protocols is not the basic principle underlying the approach: the smoothing of price noise. That principle has a solid conceptual foundation [12]. The issue is determining how we allocate in a way that reduces the correlation between price noise and changes in allocation weights (something that is easy to do with a simple equal-weight methodology) while retaining a balanced portfolio of securities and sectors (or any other relevant investment requirement). Arnott, Hsu and

West opted for an approach that seeks to create a portfolio that has a representative footprint of the overall economy.

To build their RAFI indices, Arnott, Hsu and West used a five-year moving average of four equally weighted metrics. They are sales, cash flows, book value and dividends. It is important to understand that the authors did not use these metrics because they believed they offered some intrinsic information about the value of the companies. In fact, these particular metrics usually offer no real valuation information, per se. For example, what do the amounts of Ford and Walmart sales tell us about the relative or absolute value of each company? Really, they tell us nothing. Book value (the authors did not use book-to-market, but simply book value) also contains no specific valuation information. The authors used four metrics because the average of all four indicators provides, in their opinion, an acceptable representation of the economic footprint of a company in the overall economy.

They also used four metrics because they were afraid that any single one may bias the portfolio and unfairly favor a specific industry or company. For example, using only cash flows may overexpose or underexpose the portfolio to cyclical firms. Sales may favor the retail industry, dividends may favor the financial industry and book value may favor older established firms. Thus, the four metrics may allow a smoothing of price noise while limiting the portfolio tracking against a cap-weight index. It also implicitly means that the process, much like equal weight, ignores any information regarding expected returns, volatilities or correlations. Therefore, the true objective of the RAFI methodology is to create a family of market-value-indifferent products whose main purpose is to smooth price noise (like equal weight) while maintaining a representative economic footprint (unlike equal weight). But what could be the argument to maintain a representative footprint?

In Chapter 3 we explained that the price of a security is the sum of its true fundamental value and of price noise. We do not know the true fundamental value of any security, and the noise is responsible for the over and under weight of securities within a market-cap index. Thus, the objective of the RAFI protocols is not to take an active view on the weighting of securities, or to introduce a specific bias on purpose (such as a value or small-cap bias), but simply to maintain security weightings, which are consistent with the true long-term fundamental value of securities (without the noise).

Arnott, Hsu and West believed that the average of their four metrics is an appropriate proxy for an approximate economic weight in the long run. It certainly does not mean that this weighting mechanism is the only one that could be used, but, as I just mentioned, simply that it is appropriate. Some may also argue that such protocols may introduce a value bias, but it is actually more likely that it is market-cap protocols that reflect a growth bias because of the behavior of investors, as discussed in Chapter 5. For example, fundamental protocols will usually avoid most of the pitfalls resulting from P/E expansion and P/E contraction that are caused by investors' overreaction and underreaction to events. The RAFI approach is more neutral to behavioral biases than a market-cap index is. Finally, since a large firm will still receive a relatively larger allocation within the RAFI framework, we may assume that most liquid securities are likely to receive a larger allocation.

TABLE 6.6 Performance of Fundamental Protocols According to the Metrics (1962–2007)

	End Value $1 ($)	GEO Mean (%)	Volatility (%)	Sharpe Ratio	Excess Return (%)	Tracking Error (%)
S&P 500	90	10.3	14.6	0.37	0.1	1.7
Cap 1000	88	10.2	14.8	0.36		
Book	176	11.9	14.6	0.47	1.7	3.5
Cash Flow	214	12.4	14.6	0.50	2.2	3.8
Sales	248	12.7	15.4	0.50	2.5	4.8
Dividend	174	11.9	13.3	0.50	1.7	5.1
Average	207	12.3	14.4	0.50	2.1	4.0

Source: Arnott (2008) [13].

Table 6.6 illustrates the simulated performance of protocols using the four RAFI metrics individually (as well as that of the average of all four) from 1962 to 2007 on a population of 1,000 US stocks. The use of any of these metrics would have resulted in a profitable strategy against a market-cap-weight index. How reliable is this approach? The fundamental indexing methodology (the RAFI methodology) has been tested extensively within academic and professional circles, not only in the United States and not only on equities. In fact, fundamental protocols in general can be valuable to any asset class that has volatility. The reason is simple: if an asset class has very little volatility, it is likely that the range of the price noise of its components is small, and although a theoretical gain may be achieved, it would be negligible. Fortunately, there is no lack of volatility in equities and in high-yield bonds.

The firm Nomura Securities [14] tested fundamental indexing on the equity markets of 23 countries from January 1988 to August 2005. The analysis was completed for all single countries and for global portfolios of 23 countries and 22 countries (i.e., ex-Japan). Furthermore, they tested the performance against several cap-weight indices. All portfolios outperformed their respective market-cap-weight benchmarks. Table 6.7 presents some initial results for the global portfolios.

The Cap Global and Cap ex-Japan portfolios are simply cap-weight portfolios that were built using the same securities as those of fundamental indexing portfolios. The performance of the RAFI methodology with or without Japan is excellent, since it delivered excess spreads of 2.0% to 2.75% annually on average. Also, the tracking error, at 2% to 3%, is reasonable, assuming that the investor is even concerned with this aspect. Nomura Securities also tested the RAFI methodology on all single countries. Excess performance varied from very little (0.13% annually in New Zealand) to a lot (4.32% annually in Canada), but the important point is that it worked everywhere. In their book, Arnott, Hsu and West also reported favorable results for a similar analysis over the period 1984 to 2007. Their fundamental protocols outperformed cap-weighted indices by 2.6% annually on average. They underperformed in one country,

TABLE 6.7 Fundamental Indexing—Performance of Global Portfolios (1988–2005)

	Index	GEO Mean (%)	End Value $100	Volatility (%)	Sharpe Ratio	Tracking Error (%)
Global Index	MSCI World	6.08	293	14.26	0.12	2.70
	FTSE Developed	6.06	292	14.40	0.11	2.72
	Cap Global	5.55	267	14.19	0.08	3.23
	RAFI Approach	8.78	472	13.14	0.33	—
Global ex-Japan	MSCI Kokusai	8.30	433	13.67	0.28	1.96
	FTSE World ex-Japan	8.29	433	13.68	0.28	1.97
	Cap ex-Japan	8.42	443	13.60	0.29	1.84
	RAFI Approach	10.26	612	13.44	0.43	—

Source: Nomura (2005).

Switzerland, by 0.2% annually. In Scandinavian countries such as Finland and in the Netherlands it outperformed, but by less than in other countries. Walkshausl and Lobe (2009) [15] did an even broader study but arrived at similar conclusions.

Understanding why the strategy did not work as well in Switzerland, or why it was less effective in Finland and the Netherlands, helps to understand what is required for this approach to work. Fundamental indexing is a concept that benefits from the law of large numbers. It will be more efficient if a market has lower single-security concentration. Therefore, in countries such as the Netherlands and Finland, one company in each of these countries (Nokia in Finland and Royal Dutch Shell in the Netherlands) accounts for a very large percentage of the total market capitalization (much like Nortel did in Canada in the early 2000s). If a very large company becomes more successful than the entire market, not having invested enough in that very dominant company can cancel out all the benefits of smoothing price noise. Thus, fundamental protocols may not work as well in very concentrated equity markets. Fortunately, global market indices have very low concentration. For example, the most important security within an index such as the MSCI World usually has an allocation smaller than 2%. An investor with a global portfolio would not face this issue.

Furthermore, fundamental indexing may not work as well if there is a significant and resilient shift in investor sentiment. For example, according to Arnott, Hsu and West, there was such a shift toward value and growth stocks in Switzerland. Basically, they argued that Swiss investors, known for being very conservative, became much less conservative over this period and favored growth stocks consistently. A neutral statistical process cannot necessarily win against a global shift in investor sentiment, whether it is growth stocks in Switzerland or technology stocks around the world in the late 1990s. Thus, consistent and concentrated momentum in returns, which can be beneficial to many allocation processes, is not a favorable factor for a smoothing process.

How systematic is the outperformance of the RAFI protocols? Figures 6.2a and 6.2b have been provided by Research and Affiliates. Each data point in Figure 6.2a compares the five-year annualized performance of RAFI protocols against traditional indices. The period analyzed is 1984 to 2011. If the fundamental indexing approach were no more profitable than a cap-weight index, the data points would have remained on or below the diagonal line. However, a much greater percentage of dots are actually above the diagonal line. We also notice that the methodology did well in poor markets, and did very well in rising markets. However, its worst performances were recorded in extremely strong markets (where annualized returns were

FIGURE 6.2a   Rolling Five Year Excess Returns (RAFI versus the World) (1984–2011).

Source: Research Affiliates.

FIGURE 6.2b   Evolution of Sector Weights—Cap Weights versus RAFI Weights.

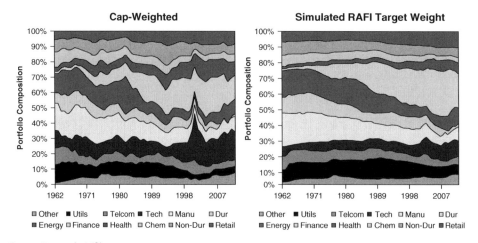

Source: Research Affiliates.

above 30% yearly). We can probably conclude that these observations are due mostly to the technology bubble era, since this would be the only period that produced such strong performances worldwide after 1984. As we already indicated, an allocation protocol that does not rely on market capitalization is much less likely to participate in the creation of an equity bubble, and it will suffer during the creation of this bubble. Therefore, the sector allocation of a RAFI protocol should be more stable. This is also confirmed in Figure 6.2b.

Looking at figure 6.2b, our intuition would lead us to the possibility that simply smoothing the volatility of market weights (such as using a moving average) could improve returns. This idea was actually evaluated by Chen, Chen and Bassett (2007) [16], who found that using the median of cap weights over a 120-month look-back window did increase returns by 1% a year. Again, this illustrates the importance of smoothing market noise, even if the methodology is quite simple. However, smoothing historical cap weights is not as efficient as the RAFI approach.

All of the analyses on fundamental indexing presented thus far dealt with the equity markets. However, price noise is not limited to equities. It applies to any asset class that has significant volatility, since the volatility of mispricings around true fundamental asset values is likely to be higher in assets that have greater volatility. Arnott, Hsu, Li and Shepherd (2010) [17] applied the fundamental indexing approach to three types of bond investments: investment grade US corporate, high-yield US corporate and emerging-market sovereign bonds. The authors used four metrics to allocate among US bonds: total cash flows, total dividends (including preferred), book value of assets and sales. Thus, the metrics were slightly adjusted (compared to those of equities) in order to use more global accounting measures. However, these metrics are not appropriate in the case of emerging market bonds. Therefore, the authors used other measures related to the current and potential importance to the world economy, such as total population, land area, GDP and energy consumption.

Table 6.8 presents the annual geometric performance for the period of January 1997 to December 2009 for all three portfolios against published indices: the Merrill Lynch Corporate Master Index, the Merrill Lynch High Yield Master II Index (without the C- and D-rated securities) and the Merrill Lynch (USD) Emerging Market Sovereign Plus Index. Since the authors could not perfectly match the universe of bonds from their study to the composition of the Merrill Indices, they also built their own cap-weight indices from the same universe of securities.

TABLE 6.8 Performance of Valuation-Indifferent Fixed Income Portfolios (1997–2009) (%)

	Investment Grade	High Yield	Emerging
Fundamental Index	6.76	8.79	12.07
Benchmark	6.52	7.06	11.06
Published Index	6.33	6.25	10.80

Source: Arnott, Hsu, Li and Shepherd (2010).

As expected, the excess return appears less important for an investment-grade portfolio where, presumably, the price noise would be less. They also tested for the presence of significant Alpha (excess returns) using the three-factor model of Fama and French augmented by two more factors: a measure of yield slope and yield spread. They found a positive Alpha in all cases. This analysis supports the conclusion that price noise is not limited to equities, but can be present in any volatile asset class.

Closing Remarks on Fundamental Protocols

The concept of price noise is appealing. Some critics argue that fundamental indexing is simply a strategy that loads on other risk premiums that have yet to be identified. Considering the argument that market prices are far more volatile than warranted by fundamentals, that investors as a group are emotional and undisciplined, an approach that would smooth these excesses seems appropriate.

Arnott, Hsu, Liu and Markowitz (2010) [18] went even further in arguing that risk premiums such as size and book value to market are in fact inefficiencies created by market noise. In other words, market-cap protocols would accentuate growth and large-cap biases, allowing reasonable investors to outperform with a more balanced portfolio. The authors explained this intuitively, saying the following:

> A stock with a positive noise should have a lower expected return. Although noise is unobservable, it can be inferred from prices: noise for a stock is more likely positive if its price is high. The same intuition applies for price to book as well as a variety of other fundamental ratios.

Although the work of Arnott and Hsu has dominated the fundamental protocol literature, the four metrics of RAFI are not the only ones that can be used to smooth price noise. One could use moving averages of historical weights. For some institutional investors we successfully used a very simple approach of averaging sector weights over five years, and using equal security weights within the sectors. This allows for an effective smoothing of price noise while maintaining economic representation. Investors who are interested in developing a greater understanding of the dynamics of excess returns (against cap weight) related to a smoothing process should read Langlois and Lussier (2010) [19].

As indicated, the criteria used for smoothing price noise may be fairly irrelevant to the success of the strategy as long as we avoid a significant and undesired bias. A European manager mentioned to me that allocating according to the number of letters in the name of the company (allocating more to companies with longer names), its reverse (allocating more to companies with shorter names) and many other irrelevant factors still lead to a smoothing process and better performance than a cap-weight index.

Researchers have mostly tested fundamental protocols on portfolios of securities. Estrada (2006) [20] tested fundamental indexing with country indices and used the measure of dividend per share to allocate among countries. The period he covered was December 1973 to December 2005, and he rebalanced once a year in December. Since Estrada applied the strategy to country indices, transaction costs were much less of an issue in this case.

The author compared the strategy to two indices: a cap-weight average of the Datastream indices of 16 countries that were also used for the fundamental protocol, and the Datastream World Index. The fundamental approach outperformed the first cap-weight index by 1.9% yearly and the second by more than 2.0%. However, the outperformance was not systematic. When the period was split into 7 subperiods of 5 years each, the fundamental approach underperformed the two cap-weight indices from 1979 to 1983 and one of them from 1994 to 1998. However, this is still fairly impressive considering that we do not have the law of large numbers on our side with simply 16 countries and not hundreds or dozens of securities. Jim O'Neill of Goldman Sachs (2012)[21] has also been selling the idea of a GDP weighted global fixed-income index, arguing that it moderates exposure to highly indebted countries while increasing exposure to growing economies. This illustrates that market noise can be exploited (smoothed) at the macro level and not only at the single-security level. This may be useful when we discuss allocation among countries, commodities or even asset classes.

However, just as interesting is the fact that Estrada tested two other allocation metrics against the traditional fundamental index approach: a simple equal-weight protocol (the simplest form of valuation-indifferent protocol) and a dividend yield weighted protocol (not a valuation-indifferent protocol). Both protocols outperformed the more traditional fundamental approach, by 0.5% in the first case and 1.5% in the second case. Thus, although smoothing price noise is an essential objective because it basically delivers superior portfolio efficiency, we may also want to design protocols that do more than just smooth price noise. However, doing so will introduce a stronger allocation bias than the RAFI approach, which attempts to maintain a representative economic footprint. Furthermore, the manager and the investor would have to be convinced that this bias has persistent qualities. The work of Arnott and Hsu has been extremely valuable in understanding the sources of inefficiencies in traditional benchmarks.

(Risk) Factor Protocols

We already covered some material related to risk premiums in Chapter 5. In the case of equity, Fama and French and subsequently Carhart assumed that investors receive compensation for exposing themselves to securities with low book to price, smaller capitalization and momentum. However, Arnott and Hsu made the argument that many risk premiums are a manifestation of price noise. In the end, there are two possibilities. Either these factors are representative of specific risks for which compensation is to be received, or exposure to these factors generates excess gains because of mispricing that is caused by persistent behavioral or structural biases. We will not try to resolve this issue, but rather we will try to determine whether or not the risk premiums of the four-factor model (except for Beta), size, book value to market and momentum are in fact useful to an allocation process. Already, in Chapter 2, we used a portfolio replication approach to show that a group of managers benchmarked against the S&P 500 had potentially outperformed in large part because of fairly persistent biases in value and small-cap securities. We could also consider other biases such as dividend yield or payout yield.

The statistical significance of the four-factor model has been well covered by the financial literature. However, an article by Brandt, Santa-Clara and Valkanov (2009)[22] explores the relevance of these factors using an innovative methodology. The authors agreed that traditional mean variance optimization may lead to extremely unstable allocations due to the instability of the parameters. However, what if, instead of using information on volatilities and correlations to design a portfolio using a traditional Markowitz approach, we attempted to model the security weights directly using the characteristics of these securities? For example, let's assume we are attempting to create a better protocol using the 500 securities in the S&P 500. Each security in the S&P 500 has a cap weight at any specific time (cw_{it}) and characteristics (x_{it}) such as size (S), book value to market (BVM) and momentum (M). In this case, we could build a protocol where the weight we would attribute to a security (fw_i) would be a function of its current cap weight and its specific characteristics (x_{it}). Therefore:

$$fw_{it} = cw_{it} + 1/N_t \, \theta \, x_{it} \qquad (6.5)$$

The characteristics are standardized to have, cross-sectionally, a mean of zero. This is essential because we want the weight adjustments to sum to zero. θ is a vector of coefficients derived in the optimization process that maximized the expected utility of the portfolio return. The coefficients θ are fixed across assets.

Brandt, Santa-Clara and Valkanov applied the strategy successfully, out of sample, to the US market for the period January 1974 to December 2002. The results of the study illustrate the relevance of Carhart's four factors, whether or not they are, in fact, a representation of some specific risk. First, the authors found that the coefficient for size is negative and that coefficients for book value to market and momentum are positive, much like Carhart (1997) did. This means that the weights attributed to securities relative to a cap-weight approach are:

- smaller for large-cap securities and larger for small-cap securities;
- larger for high book value to market and smaller for low book value to market; and
- larger for high momentum securities and smaller for low momentum securities.

On average, the protocol is invested in 54% of all stocks and the concentration is low. No security ever accounted for more than 2% of the entire portfolio. The outperformance is close to 4% annually, even though the portfolio has a lower Beta than a cap-weight index. It seems that there is relevant information that can be exploited in these risk premiums.

This approach has a significant advantage since it does not require deriving an entire covariance matrix, although it is fairly computationally demanding. The resulting allocation recommendations are relatively stable. Furthermore, it offers great flexibility. For example, if we wanted to create a high-payout, low-volatility portfolio, we could incorporate these characteristics into the protocol (instead of book value to market, for example). If we wanted to restrict any single security or sector from exceeding a certain percentage of the entire portfolio, it could easily be accommodated. Although the authors kept the coefficients constant in the initial simulations, a more elaborate optimization can also accommodate time-varying coefficients. For example, in one of their analyses, Brandt, Santa-Clara and Valkanov obtained even better results when they allowed the coefficients to change according to whether or not the yield curve was positively sloped or negatively sloped. Furthermore, although their protocol is based on adjusting cap weights, there is no reason why it should be so. For example, we already know that an equal-weight protocol is more efficient than a cap-weight protocol, especially if the underlying securities belong to a diverse universe. Therefore, if an equal-weight protocol is already efficient as a way to diversify price noise, it may even be more profitable to apply the weight adjustments to an equal-weight index instead of a cap-weight index. We will come back to this aspect later on.

Although the Brandt, Santa-Clara and Valkanov article is in fact an optimization approach, I only wanted to use this article at this point to illustrate the relevance of specific (risk) factors to the allocation process. However, I will come back to this methodology in the section on optimization protocols later in this chapter, and oppose it to the more traditional mean/variance optimization.

High Payout and High Dividend Yield Protocols

In Chapter 5 I discussed the justification for a dividend- or payout-based protocol. Some may argue that a high-payout or high-dividend yield protocol would restrict the diversification that could be achieved and limit the potential appreciation of the portfolio. We have already covered evidence showing that firms who reinvest most of their available cash flow (instead of paying some of their cash flow in dividends or to repurchase their shares) do not provide better growth prospects.

It is also possible to challenge the view that diversification among high-payout firms would be limited, especially in a global context. Over the last few years, I have been involved in the design of high-dividend/high-payout-based products and I was surprised to discover how many firms actually pay high dividends in the developed world. I also found that firms belonging to the same industry in different countries could have a very different dividend policy. For example, in Canada, firms in the oil and gas sector often pay high dividends, while firms in the materials sector do not. However, in Australia, many firms in the materials sector pay much higher dividends than in Canada. It is globally feasible to build balanced portfolios of securities that pay high dividend yields globally (or have a high-payout yield). Furthermore, the global economy has become more integrated and the benefits of geographic diversification in the context of global firms may no longer be as important as the benefits of sector diversification.

Christoffersen, Errunza, Jacobs and Jin (2010) [23] showed that correlations among developed countries' equity markets have been on the rise and are quite high, and although emerging markets are showing lower correlations with developed countries, these markets were also on the rise. Furthermore, the authors' results illustrate that there is substantial tail risk dependence between equity markets that results from substantially higher correlations in down markets, especially among developed markets. In such a context, it becomes possible to create portfolios of securities that are well diversified on a sector basis and still offer dividend yields as high as 4.0% to 5.5%.

Finally, there is no reason why we could not combine a high-payout protocol with a price noise smoothing process. Already, several existing products that offer high dividend yields do not use market weights to determine security allocations. For example, the S&P 500 Dividend Aristocrats Index uses an equal-weight allocation with quarterly rebalancing. The following product, designed by a Canadian firm and launched in 2011, is an example of a process that combines the smoothing of price noise with the alignment of interest that a high payout ratio provides.

The product is inspired by the work of Chen, Chen and Bassett (2007), according to which, smoothing market weights using a historical moving average is a simple but efficient way to smooth price noise. We also know that equal weight is a very efficient process but it does not lead to a representative economic footprint, assuming this objective is important to the investor. Therefore, the investment protocol is based on three concepts:

- a five-year sector moving average to provide a representative economic footprint but also an efficient smoothing process
- an equal-weight allocation within each sector to reinforce the efficiency of the smoothing process
- a stock selection process using total payout to establish the ranking within each sector in order to improve the alignment on interest

Rebalancing occurs yearly, and a credit check process is used at rebalancing to eliminate firms that have a high dividend yield but where the dividend may be in jeopardy. Since the portfolio has about 150 stocks, if a sector has a 20% allocation, this sector will have 30 securities with respective weights of 0.66% at rebalancing. Tables 6.9a and 6.9b present the simulated performance and some characteristics of this protocol against the S&P 1200 between December 1999 and March 2011. The protocol has an active risk of 6.8%, which is consistent with the level of a benchmark-agnostic active manager. The concentration is appropriate and the sector exposure will be representative of the investment universe since it is based on a moving average of five years. Although the volatility of the product is greater than that of the index, this volatility is caused by greater upside performance, as illustrated in Table 6.9b. For such a simple process, the performance would have been spectacular.

TABLE 6.9a Characteristics of a Protocol: Smoothing of Price Noise and Payout Yield (December 1999–March 2011)

	Global Large Cap	S&P 1200
Number of Securities	150	1,200
Weighted Average Market Cap ($M)	37,946	77,775
Top 10 Holdings	6.9%	8.5%
Dividend Yield*	4.2%	2.5%
Active Risk	6.8%	—
Volatility	17.9%	13.6%
Return	11.8%	2.2%

* Payout yield is approximately 6.0%
Source: Desjardins Global Asset Management (2011).

TABLE 6.9b Annual Performance of a Protocol: Smoothing of Price Noise and Payout Yield (%)

	2010	2009	2008	2007	2006	2005
Protocol	21.4	58.4	−40.6	5.9	27.5	12.0
S&P 1200	11.9	31.7	−40.1	10.2	21.5	10.8
Value Added	9.5	26.7	−0.5	−4.34	6.1	1.81
	2004	2003	2002	2001	2000	
Protocol	25.8	49.2	−14.0	2.7	15.8	
S&P 1200	14.9	32.9	−19.6	−15.0	−10.1	
Value Added	10.9	16.3	5.6	17.6	25.9	

Source: Desjardins Global Asset Management (2011).

Optimization Protocols

Earlier in this chapter, we saw an example of how the optimal weights are sensitive to the estimation of parameters: expected returns, volatility and correlation. DeMiguel, Garlappi and Uppal (2007) tested 14 allocation models on seven different data sets, including some models that do not rely on any estimate of future returns, such as equal weight and minimum variance. All of the models except equal weight required some optimization process. The authors found that most performing models were those that did not require any return inputs, such as equal weight and minimum variance. Excluding returns from the process also reduced the risk of extreme portfolio weights. DeMiguel, Garlappi and Uppal concluded the following:

- The estimation errors on returns are so large that it is actually preferable to ignore returns from the optimization process and to concentrate on the dependence structure.
- The imposition of constraints on the covariance matrix is useful in reducing potential harmful effects from estimation error in the covariance matrix.

More recently, Tu and Zhou (2011) [24] furthered this debate. They showed that the optimal combination of an equal-weight protocol with an optimized Markowitz-type protocol can outperform the equal-weight protocol, and that the solution converges to the true optimal rule. Kritzman, Page and Turkington (2010) also came to the defense of optimization, arguing that very simple optimization processes can outperform equal weight. The authors not only found that a minimum variance portfolio outperforms an equal-weight portfolio, but also that an optimized portfolio of asset classes that uses expected returns based on long-run historical risk premiums outperforms an equal-weight portfolio. Finally, a process that uses common sense long-term excess returns against cash did even better. These excess returns were as follows: US and foreign equity (+5%), US government bonds (+2%), US corporate bonds (+3%), REITS (+5%) and commodities (+1%).

Furthermore, the DeMiguel, Garlappi and Uppal and Kritzman, Page and Turkington studies are not that far apart. They both agree that the information in the covariance matrix is important, and, although DeMiguel, Garlappi and Uppal argue that it is better to ignore returns, Kritzman, Page and Turkington are simply using very long-term returns for expectations that are a representation of an appropriate long-term risk premium. Therefore, if we assume steady expected returns, the covariance matrix is basically driving the changes to the portfolio allocation. A relevant question at this point would be to ask if it is possible to develop an optimization process that relies on forecasted returns that could outperform results obtained from a simple long-term historical average. For example, according to Goyal and Welch (2008) [25], the poor out-of-sample performance of predictive regressions versus the historical average is a systemic problem.

I have already indicated that tilting a portfolio allocation toward certain factors, such as high payout yield or a value bias, can improve long-term returns. However, we have also seen that such considerations can be integrated within very simple allocation processes that do not require explicit forecasts or optimization. But, is there any benefit to using more complicated processes?

A significant issue with the forecast of returns is the very low level of out-of-sample R-square that is usually achieved over monthly and even annual horizons. Campbell and Thompson (2008) [26] indicated that unconstrained forecasts of excess returns based on 12 well-known factors such as dividend-to-price, book-to-market, term spread, etc. have a low and meaningless R-square. However, if restrictions are placed on the process, such as imposing the theoretically expected sign, restricting the value of the coefficients and requiring a positive equity risk premium, the out-of-sample predictability is improved. Although the R-square remains very low, Campbell and Thompson argue that the forecasts are statistically meaningful and often outperform the historical average. Kong, Rapach, Strauss and Zhou (2011) [27] also illustrated the potential of predicting returns. Using combination forecasts (a simple average of individual regression forecasts using 39 predictors) they analyzed the predictability of 25 size/value-sorted portfolios. They found stronger predictability for small-cap/high-book-to-market firms and, more importantly, that return forecasts could be used to rotate efficiently across portfolios. However, as with the previous study, we do not know if using these return predictions leads to wide fluctuations in allocations. Most likely, they do.

Furthermore, we may ask what would be the purpose of using a process of prediction returns within a mean/variance type of optimization when we can directly optimize the weights using the approach of Brandt, Santa-Clara and Valkanov that I described previously. Their approach does not require forecasting the entire covariance matrix, and it does not require forecasting returns prior to the optimization. The relation between factors and expected returns is directly reflected in the weights of the securities.

I am a proponent of simple portfolio-assembly methodologies, such as the ones developed by RAFI and by Desjardins Global Asset Management (presented in Tables 6.9a and 6.9b), because they combine the efficiency of the smoothing process with economic representation and alignment of interest with shareholders. However, the parametric optimization approach of Brandt, Santa-Clara and Valkanov has the potential to be a superior methodology because it can be adapted easily to fit any requirement. It can be made to smooth price noise, to reflect a particular portfolio tilt, to exploit relevant (risk) factors, to deliver a specific volatility requirement and to create a portfolio that has a meaningful economic representation. Furthermore, the process is not sensitive to the estimation errors in the covariance matrix. It can do it all. Investors simply have to decide what characteristics they want in their portfolio.

Langlois (2011) tested the parametric approach of Brandt, Santa-Clara and Valkanov using the securities within the S&P 500 from September 1992 to November 2010. Five characteristics were used for each stock: payout ratio, book value, momentum, downside Beta and idiosyncratic volatility. As I explained earlier, the characteristics are standardized to have cross-sectionally a mean of zero. The coefficients were also conditioned by one variable, the term spread. Table 6.10 compares the parametric approach to the S&P 500 Cap-Weight and S&P 500 Equal Weight.

TABLE 6.10 Parametric Process versus S&P 500 Cap-Weight and S&P 500 Equal Weight

	S&P 500 Cap-Weight	S&P 500 Equal Weight	Parametric Portfolio
Annualized Return	8.74	11.90	15.91
Annualized Volatility	15.15	17.08	17.60
Tracking Error		6.09	10.90
Skewness	−0.735	−0.565	−0.002
Correlation to S&P 500		0.93	0.78

Source: Langlois (2011).

The parametric portfolio has much greater performance for slightly greater volatility and almost no negative skew. However, the tracking error against the S&P 500 is significant. Thus, as long as investors keep hoping for great excess performance without tracking error, and evaluate their performance potential over short horizons, rational and patient investors will still have the opportunity to outperform in the long run.

Comparing and Analyzing Protocols

Chow, Hsu, Kalesnik and Little (2011) [28] compared the performance of several protocols for US and global equity portfolios. Some of the protocols that they tested were equal weight, equal risk, fundamental weighting (RAFI), minimum variance and maximum diversification. They applied the equal-weight methodology on sectors and countries. Table 6.11a and 6.11b illustrate their results.

All of the protocols that the authors tested outperformed a standard cap-weight index. Unsurprisingly, the equal-weight protocol usually delivers among the highest

TABLE 6.11a   Comparing Investment Protocols (US) (1964–2009)(%)

	Return	Volatility	Tracking	Turnover (One-Way)
S&P 500	9.46	15.13	–	6.69
Equal Weight	11.78	17.47	6.37	22.64
Equal Risk	10.91	14.84	4.98	25.43
Fundamental	11.60	15.38	4.50	13.60
Minimum Variance	11.40	11.87	8.08	48.45
Maximum Diversification	11.99	14.11	7.06	56.02

Source: Chow, Hsu, Kalesnik and Little (2010).

TABLE 6.11b   Comparing Investment Protocols (Global) (1987–2009) (%)

	Return	Volatility	Tracking	Turnover (One-Way)
S&P 500	7.58	15.65	–	8.36
Equal Weight	8.64	15.94	3.02	21.78
Equal Risk	10.78	16.55	6.18	32.33
Fundamental	11.13	15.30	4.77	14.93
Minimum Variance	8.59	11.19	8.66	52.95
Maximum Diversification	7.77	13.16	7.41	59.72

Source: Chow, Hsu, Kalesnik and Little (2010).

volatility. This comparison also illustrates that nonmarket-cap protocols do not necessarily have high turnover. In fact, the average active manager has a higher turnover than the average nonmarket-cap protocol. For example, the protocol presented in Tables 6.9a and 6.9b has an average turnover of less than 15%.

In September 2011, Goldman Sachs introduced yet another equity protocol, called Equity 3.0 (now called S&P GIVI, for Global Intrinsic Value Index)[29]. It may be helpful to our understanding to challenge and or explain some of the justifications for this protocol. According to Goldman Sachs, S&P GIVI exploits two pervasive phenomena. The first aspect is the tendency of high-risk stocks to underperform low-risk stocks, where risk is defined by Beta. The second aspect is related to a measure of overvaluation related to some accounting data. The general process of S&P GIVI is simple. First, the riskiest 30% of stocks, as defined by market weight, are removed, and second, the remaining 70% of stocks are allocated according to a measure of valuation. First Goldman Sachs analyzed the specific performance impact of each aspect, and then it illustrated the impact of combining both. Let's start with the low/high Beta issue.

As we have already discussed, many studies, such as Baker, Bradley and Wurgler (2011) [30], have documented that low-volatility and low-Beta portfolios offer better performances and smaller drawdowns. They justify this observation through behavioral biases (preference of investors for lotteries, and overconfidence) and by arbitrage limitations (the so-called smart money is insufficient to offset the price impact of irrational participants). The same argument can be used for the tendency of the value style to outperform the growth style on average.

In their presentation of S&P GIVI, Goldman Sachs compared the historical performance of the highest 30% of Beta stocks with the lowest 70% for a global portfolio over the period of 1993 to 2011. Their results are presented in Table 6.12. The performance spread between the two portfolios is 3.7%. However, the relative performance drag attributed to a volatility of 23.6% versus a volatility of 13.0% is 1.93%, which explains more than half of the performance spread. Thus, what Goldman Sachs created is, in part, a portfolio that benefits from a smaller performance drag attributed to a lower volatility.

The second component of their process is based on a measure that is a variation of the dividend discount model. It is meant to incorporate growth opportunities and

TABLE 6.12 Comparing the Performances of Riskier and Less Risky Stocks (1993–2011) (%)

	Highest Beta	Lowest Beta
Return	3.8	7.5
Volatility	23.6	13.0
Maximum Drawdown	−72.0	−47.3
Excess Return	−2.8	0.9

Source: Goldman Sachs (2012).

used to determine security weights within the portfolio. Inputs to the model are book value to common equity, return on equity, dividend payout ratio and a discount rate. Goldman Sachs found that this approach improves performance for their global market universe by about 2% annually over the same period that was used in Table 6.12. Volatility was also slightly lower. They also mentioned that their results were not so sensitive to the methodology that they used to compute intrinsic value or the inputs. This raises an interesting question. Is it possible that the added value is simply caused by a smoothing of price noise, as with a RAFI approach, and not so much by the particular valuation indicator being used? Since the excess performance and the pattern of this excess performance over time are not so different from other similar investment protocols, this is entirely possible.

When both aspects of their protocol are combined, the excess return was 2.3% while the volatility was lower than that of a cap-weighted index by about 2%. Thus, overall, what Goldman Sachs has designed is a process with lower volatility tilts that smoothes price noise—two attractive qualities.

Bridging the Gaps and Improving on the Existing Literature

Building more efficient equity portfolios is all about process. I believe in the power of an efficient investment process because we consistently witness examples of why investors fail. In 2011, a consultant asked my opinion about a project he was working on. His objective was to offer the client an investment program that would be in line with many of the principles that we have discussed in this book: using nonmarket-cap investment portfolios and seeking securities with high payout ratios. However, the program would still be based on traditional external managers instead of investment protocols that could have been managed more cheaply (because an active manager is often easier to sell to a client than a protocol). He also told me which managers he was considering. I knew most of those managers and I commented that the style of one of them did not match the desired characteristics detailed in his proposal. He explained that he had picked that manager over others who met the requirements because that manager had recently performed better!

The objective of this section is to go beyond the existing literature and develop a greater understanding of the aspects that influence portfolio and manager performance in the long term. Much of the content is based on research by Langlois and Lussier (2009) [31], which seeks to clarify some aspects of the existing literature and reinforce our belief in the use of investment protocols. No long-term process can ever be implemented and maintained if the decision makers (investors) do not fully understand why they have made this decision in the first place. A long-term and coherent process means that we must not necessarily pick the managers or investment processes that recently outperformed the most. It also means that it may be easier to develop three or four investment protocols that are all likely to outperform cap-weight indices in the long run and are efficient at diversifying excess performance (such as combining lower-volatility and normal-volatility protocols) than it is to find three or four managers who will remain in the portfolio for 10 years. It will certainly cost less to an institutional investor.

Active Management, Active Share and Price Noise

Cremers and Petajisto (2009) [32] developed the measure of Active Share that we initially discussed in Chapter 2. They presented this measure as "a new intuitive and simple way to quantify active management." Active Share can vary from zero (for an index fund) to one and it is a measure of differentiation between the structure of a portfolio and that of its reference index.

$$\tfrac{1}{2} \, \Sigma \, \left| (w_{\mathrm{fund},i} - w_{\mathrm{index},i}) \right| \qquad\qquad (6.6)$$

According to Cremers and Petajisto, funds that have performed better have been shown to have a greater level of Active Share, often above 0.7. There are three questions that should be addressed:

- How is the level of Active Share influenced by the structure of the reference index and the structure of the portfolio of managers? For example, does an Active Share of 0.7 mean the same to a US manager benchmarked against the S&P 500 as it does to a Canadian manager benchmarked against the S&P/TSX?
- Is it possible that a high Active Share is also an indication of a greater emphasis on smoothing price noise? If yes, is it possible that some of the excess performance of managers is simply explained by the intensity of the smoothing process, which a measure of Active Share would capture?
- Do investment protocols, such as the ones discussed in the previous chapter, have a high level of Active Share? In other words, do they share some of the same characteristics as those performing active managers?

Table 6.13 illustrates the active share of equal-weight portfolios against two indices, the S&P 500 and the S&P/TSX (the Canadian index). An equal-weight portfolio does not necessarily have to incorporate all securities in the index. The table indicates the average Active Share from a simulation of portfolios with 25, 50, 100 and 250 securities. It also indicates the Active Share assuming all securities in the index were included, 500 for the S&P 500, and 260 for the S&P/TSX.

TABLE 6.13 Active Share of Equal-Weight Portfolios (%)

Number of Securities	All	250	100	50	25
S&P 500	44	64	81	88	94
S&P/TSX	52	53	72	84	92

The Active Share of a portfolio of all securities against the Canadian index is greater than that of such a portfolio against the S&P 500, illustrating the greater concentration of securities within the Canadian index. However, as we move to more concentrated portfolios, the Active Share increases and remains higher for a US portfolio. Investors with portfolios of 50 securities or less would have a very high Active Share. From this point of view, a portfolio that has a low concentration in single securities but also a much lower number of securities than the index could be assumed to both smooth price noise and have a high measure of Active Share. Therefore, could we explain some of this reported excess performance of managers who have high Active Share by a price noise smoothing process?

To test this hypothesis indirectly, we simulated 10,000 large-cap portfolios whose Active Share against the Russell 1000 varied from very low to extremely high. The portfolios were ranked by quintile and their relative performances were adjusted for the Carhart four factors. Some of the results of Langlois and Lussier (2011) against those of Cremers and Petajisto (2011) are presented in Table 6.14. Both sets of results are based on gross returns (before fees).

How can we make sense of these two sets of results? First, the level of Alpha in the Langlois and Lussier analysis increases with the level of Active Share. The portfolios within the highest Active Share quintile recorded a yearly Alpha of 1.11%, but all quintiles generated a positive Alpha. A strategy of building random portfolios of equally weighted securities appears to create value. Since we created all of these portfolios randomly and controlled for the four Carhart factors, the excess performance could be attributed to a smoothing of price noise. However, at lower levels of Active Share the simulated portfolios necessarily look more and more like the benchmark, and the opportunity to benefit from a smoothing process is reduced. The difference in return between the highest and lowest quintile is 0.98 percentage points and the difference is statistically significant ($t = 1.87$).

The results of the Cremers and Petajisto study are different from Langlois and Lussier in many ways, and similar in one aspect. First, the average manager has destroyed value before fees (–0.36% on average). The average fee in their population of 1,678 managers was 1.24% while a random process, such as the one we tested, could obviously not justify such fees. This is entirely consistent, again, with the findings in Chapter 2. The only portfolios that added value to investors were those that had a very high level of Active Share (usually 70% or higher). The performance spread between the top quintile and bottom quintile is significant because managers in lower quintiles destroyed value.

TABLE 6.14 Four Factor Alpha: Active Managers and Stimulated Portfolios (%)

	Low	2	3	4	High	All	High-Low
Cremers and Petajisto 1980–2003	−0.63	−1.17	−0.89	−0.63	1.51	−0.36	2.13 (3.29)
Langlois and Lussier 1979–2009	0.13	0.38	0.61	0.88	1.11	0.62	0.98 (1.87)

Source: Cremers and Petajisto (2009), Langlois and Lussier (2011).

The differences between the two sets of results may be related to the structure of portfolio management styles within the industry. Managers with a high Active Share have to be, by definition, benchmark agnostic. If their management style is consistent across time, it could lead to portfolios that have the required structure to smooth price noise. However, at a lower level of Active Share, it is much less likely that the manager is smoothing price noise, since his or her positions are more and more similar to the index. We may be in the presence of "bad" closet indexers. This may also explain why managers among the worst quartile of performance (as reported in Chapter 2) are likely to remain losers. "Closet indexers" would, more often than not, destroy value.

We can create portfolios that smooth price noise and have an average level of Active Share, but it is unlikely that we will find many active managers who offer a portfolio structure that would be consistent with such an objective. For example, we will see later on that minimum variance or maximum diversification protocols have a high Active Share (which is consistent with the portfolio structure of these protocols). In contrast, RAFI products perform well even though they have a much lower level of Active Share. However, the RAFI protocols contain a large number of securities. As an example, the ETF of the RAFI US has nearly 1,000 securities. How many active managers have that level of diversity in their portfolio? Very few. Thus, a high Active Share may often be consistent with a smoothing process, whether the manager is aware of this or not, but a low Active Share may often be inconsistent with a smoothing process simply because very few managers in the low-to-average level of Active Share group have a management style consistent with such a process. This may explain, in part, why the results of the simulation and of our own analysis are so different at low levels of Active Share.

Although there is no information on tracking error in Table 6.14, Cremers and Petajisto argue that the best performances were realized by concentrated stock pickers (high Active Share and high tracking error) followed by diversified stock pickers (high Active Share but low tracking error). However, in the Langlois and Lussier analysis, tracking error has almost no relevance. Similar excess performances are recorded whether the tracking error is very high or average. Again, we obtain these results because, in the Langlois and Lussier analysis, a single approach of portfolio construction is used to create all portfolios, while in the industry there are, on average, different styles of management at different levels of Active Share. What are the implications?

First, Cremers and Petajisto may be right. A high level of Active Share may be desirable. However, it may not be an indication that a manager has any particular ability to select stocks, even if that manager outperforms his or her benchmark. It may be that the manager's process leads to a smoothing of price noise, which provides the manager with an advantage, whether he or she is aware of this or not. This would be even more obvious in the context of a multi-manager portfolio. For example, a multi-manager portfolio of benchmark-agnostic managers will lead to a diversified portfolio of small positions that will be very different from the index. Unless these managers engage in unnecessary trading, this may lead to a portfolio that is efficient at smoothing price noise. This also means that the investor can easily recreate a portfolio structure that will achieve the same objective at a much lower cost. Investors do not need experienced managers to achieve the benefits that come with having a high Active Share. Furthermore, the same benefits can also be achieved through protocols that have a lower Active Share. Unfortunately, there are very few active managers who have a process that leads to low Active Share and the smoothing of price noise. This is a rare style among active managers.

A Test of Several Investment Protocols

Although many articles have compared the performance of nonmarket-cap protocols, I found it necessary to evaluate and compare different methodologies with our own data. The main reason is to control the test environment, since individuals and firms that have a personal commercial interest have done much of the research on this topic. Furthermore, we need to have access to our own data for the purpose of analyzing the performance of these protocols over time, as well as their potential sensitivity to market factors.

The test is based on a recreated index of 1,000 large-cap US stocks between July 1973 and December 2009. The data were extracted from CRSP (University of Chicago's Center for Research in Security Prices), which contains daily data on all stocks listed on NYSE, AMEX and NASDAQ. In essence, the data set is a fairly close replication of the Russell 1000 Index during that period. We tested five methodologies and eight protocols. They are equal weight, diversity weight (Diversity 25 and 50), smoothed market cap using 60 and 120 months' moving averages (Smoothed 60 and 120), RAFI and minimum variance.

The diversity weight methodology is based on Fernholz (1998) [33]. It can be viewed as a method of interpolating between cap weight and equal weight. Equation 6.7 expresses the stock market diversity (D) where $w_{market'i}$ represents the cap weight of each security within the index, p is a desired level of portfolio tracking error (between 0 and 1) and $w_{diversity'i}$ is the weight of each security in the investment protocol. When p is equal to one, the weight of each security is determined by its cap weight. When p equals zero, the investment protocol is equal weight. The approach is tested with p values of 0.25, 0.50 and 0.75.

$$w_{diversity'i} = (w_{market'i})^p / [\Sigma\ w_{market'i}{}^p]^{1/p} \tag{6.7}$$

Table 6.15 presents all relevant statistics for this test. If we ignore risk, all investment protocols outperformed the cap-weight index by an average of 1.5% annually. This spread would have been sufficient to increase final wealth after 20 years by more than 30%. The most performing protocol was minimum variance, followed by equal weight, although equal weight had the highest volatility, while minimum variance had the lowest. The smoothed cap-weight protocols outperformed the least, although a protocol based on a moving average of historical market weights is probably not as efficient as others in smoothing price noise. This is why the approach used by Desjardins Global Asset Management (presented in Tables 6.9a and 6.9b) uses smoothed cap-sector weights mixed with equal weights for securities within sectors. Finally, the RAFI approach performed fairly well while maintaining economic representation. The Beta of most protocols remains close to one except for minimum variance, which has a Beta of only 0.44.

All protocols, with the exception of minimum variance, have low levels of Active Share. This is not surprising, since minimum variance leads to portfolios of less than 100 securities, while all other protocols have the same number of securities as the index. It supports the assertion that it is not necessary to have a high level of Active Share to outperform a cap-weight index. As I explained earlier, the reason why a high level of Active Share in mutual funds has been associated with outperformance is simply that most benchmark-agnostic managers own a small fraction of the securities in their reference index. Closet indexers may also only own a small subset of the securities, but they are also likely to maintain allocations to the largest securities that are similar to those in the index to avoid generating too much tracking error. Table 6.15 also presents the level of Active Share related specifically to sectors and to security exposure within sectors. The evidence shows that much more Active Share is attributed to allocation within sectors than across. Interestingly enough, the three investment protocols with the lowest performances (Diversify 75, Smoothed 60 and Smoothed 120) are also the protocols with the lowest levels of Active Share within

TABLE 6.15 Analysis of Eight Investment Protocols Against a Cap-Weight Index (1973–2009)

	Weighting Mechanisms							
	Cap	Equal	Diversity 25	Diversity 75	Smoothed 60	Smoothed 120	RAFI	Minimum Variance
Annualized GEO Means (%)	10.4	12.7	12.3	11.1	11.0	11.2	12.2	13.3
Annualized Volatility (%)	16.0	17.5	17.1	16.3	15.8	15.6	15.4	13.9
Skewness	–0.48	–0.63	–0.61	–0.54	–0.49	–0.49	–0.53	–0.52
Excess Kurtosis	2.03	2.64	2.52	2.20	2.33	2.35	2.78	2.89
Average Active Share	0.00	0.50	0.40	0.15	0.15	0.20	0.30	0.97
Average Active Share across Sectors	0.00	0.11	0.09	0.04	0.05	0.06	0.11	0.30
Average Active Share within Sectors	0.00	0.46	0.36	0.13	0.14	0.19	0.25	0.94
Average Tracking Error	0.00	0.04	0.03	0.01	0.01	0.02	0.02	0.06
Average Beta	1.00	0.93	0.94	0.98	0.97	0.95	0.91	0.44

Source: Langlois and Lussier (2011).

sectors. It seems that an efficient smoothing process requires a sufficient level of differentiation (against the market-cap index) within sectors.

Table 6.15 compared the performance of investment protocols over a very long period. However, our interest is also in their performance and risk profile across time. Table 6.16 illustrates the relative performance of these protocols against the market-cap index over five time periods. The decade of the 1990s was not appropriate to a smoothing process. The significant momentum in the technology sector allowed a cap-weight index to outperform all nonmarket-cap investment protocols during this period. In retrospect, we understand why. Equal weight did remarkably well considering the circumstance of the 1990s, while RAFI and minimum variance did worse. However, minimum variance was an efficient defensive strategy in the 2000s, and it still performed well in a more "normal" growth environment in the 1980s.

Although we tested five methodologies and eight protocols, many of these protocols are conceptually similar. For example, as we indicated, Diversity 25 and 50 are basically a mix between equal weight and market-cap weight, and their performances are in line with a blended approach. Therefore, we will no longer consider the Diversity protocols in our analysis. To gain a better understanding of the other protocols and of their performances, we will concentrate on four methodologies: equal weight, Smoothed 60, RAFI and minimum variance.

Table 6.17 presents the correlation between the 12-month rolling excess performance and the 12-month rolling market returns over five periods. Smoothed 60, RAFI and minimum variance all had strong negative correlations of excess returns to market returns over the entire period. Equal weight had almost no correlation. Furthermore, the correlations across subperiods were not stable and sometimes switch signs. However, although RAFI and Smoothed 60 reported different performances over these periods (see Table 6.16), they have a very similar correlation of excess returns.

TABLE 6.16 Relative Performance of Eight Investment Protocols Against a Cap-Weight Index (%)

	Weighting Mechanisms						
	Equal	Diversity 25	Diversity 50	Smoothed 60	Smoothed 120	RAFI	Minimum Variance
1973–2009	2.30	1.87	1.33	0.54	0.79	1.77	2.83
1973–1979	6.58	5.30	3.72	0.26	1.09	4.07	1.53
1980–1989	0.30	0.30	0.28	0.58	1.09	1.87	3.31
1990–1999	−1.88	−1.63	−1.23	−1.18	−1.53	−3.06	−4.36
2000–2009	5.07	4.17	2.96	2.13	2.34	4.47	9.68

Source: Langlois and Lussier (2011).

TABLE 6.17 Correlation of Protocols' Excess Returns Against Market Returns (Cap Weight)

	Weighting Mechanisms			
	Equal	Smoothed 60	RAFI	Minimum Variance
1973–2009	–0.06	–0.31	–0.29	–0.34
1973–1979	0.40	0.47	0.50	–0.32
1980–1989	0.36	–0.44	–0.46	–0.02
1990–1999	–0.09	–0.42	–0.35	0.01
2000–2009	0.22	–0.25	–0.27	–0.46

Source: Langlois and Lussier (2011).

It may help you understand the excess return profile of investment protocols if we consider three subcategories:

- risk based (market structure indifferent) and covariance indifferent, such as equal weight
- risk based (market structure indifferent) but conditional on the variance–covariance matrix, such as minimum variance, equal risk or maximum diversification
- fundamental (market structure dependent), such as RAFI and Smoothed 60

Let's start with RAFI and Smoothed 60. Both approaches attempt to maintain a portfolio structure that has some economic representation (market structure dependent). In other words, a large company or sector will retain a larger weighting than a smaller company or sector, even if some smoothing process is at play. Thus, it is not surprising that the correlations of excess returns across different periods for these two approaches are similar, although it does not mean that both are as efficient since the two protocols use different methodologies to achieve their objective. Smoothed 60 relies on historical market weight information while RAFI uses accounting information that relates to the size of a company. Thus, RAFI is a more market-indifferent process and, therefore, is probably more efficient at smoothing price noise. Both strategies would suffer from strong positive (or negative) momentum in a sector or dominant security, although RAFI would likely suffer the most (or least) since Smoothed 60 would capture some of that momentum within its weighting mechanism. This probably explains why Smoothed 60 outperformed RAFI in the 1990s.

By comparison, equal weight is the purest form of market-indifferent strategy. The excess performance of equal weight over a short period is a function of the structural bias (against market cap) that equal weight would introduce. This bias would be different from market to market, and it will change according to changes in economic structure, relative performances of smaller-cap companies and rules of inclusion within a cap-weight index. Thus, we could not easily generalize how equal weight would perform across markets and time.

FIGURE 6.3   Excess Returns Against Portfolio Returns and Periods of Occurrence of Negative Excess Returns.

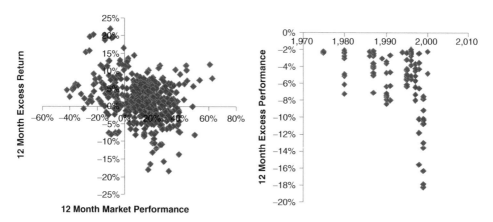

Source: Langlois and Lussier (2011).

Finally, minimum variance (as well as equal risk and maximum diversification) is also a form of market-indifferent strategy, but it does use information about the variance–covariance matrix. The process may smooth price noise (although this aspect is uncertain because of the high turnover and it is not the main objective) and it will impact the GEO mean through a lower average volatility. It will also lead to concentrated portfolios. There may also be an implicit assumption that investors will not price volatility and dependence appropriately on average. However, minimum variance is also ill equipped to capture strong momentum in companies or sectors.

Figure 6.3 illustrates a scatter plot of the rolling 12-month excess performance of an average of all three strategies (against market returns). It also illustrates when the weakest relative performances (lower than a negative 2% excess return) have occurred. The first graph clearly illustrates the negative correlation, but also the fact that most below-market performances occurred in positive markets. The second graph illustrates how concentrated (in time) the below-market performance occurred. The impact of the tech bubble is clearly apparent.

Although equal weight, RAFI and minimum variance are based on different assembly methodologies, are their excess returns related to market volatility? For example, significant changes in volatility could be linked to significant breaks in price momentum, whether related to the entire market, or to sectors, styles or dominant security positions. Figure 6.4 presents four scatter plots of 12 months' excess returns for those three protocols and for a blend of all three against the 12 months' annualized trailing market volatility (using daily data). The period under study is still 1973 to 2009.

The correlation of excess return to volatility for each protocol is, on average, very close to nil. However, some patterns are discernible at different levels of volatility. Let's consider the observations related to extremely high levels of volatilities, such as 30%

FIGURE 6.4 Excess Returns of Investment Protocols Against Volatility.

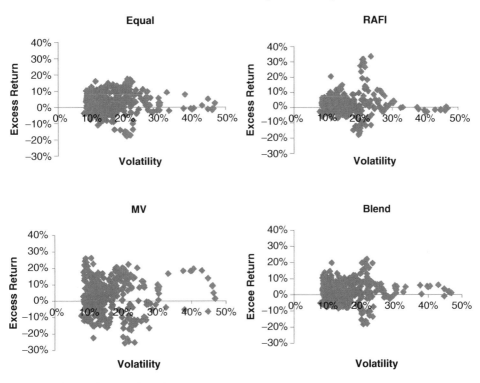

Source: Langlois and Lussier (2011).

or greater. Most of these observations are accounted for by the 12-month period ending between late 2008 and early 2009. The RAFI protocol did not benefit from this period, but equal weight and minimum variance both did. However, this analysis is based on very few observations.

In the case of RAFI, we can observe several significant high-excess returns for the range of volatility between 20% and 25%. All of these observations are related to the burst of the technology bubble. On average, the correlation of excess return to volatility is similar across all three approaches at this level of volatility. However, when volatility is low or normal, RAFI has a higher correlation of excess return to volatility. Therefore, overall, RAFI appears to perform relatively better at a low and average level of volatility, similarly at a high level of volatility and not quite as well when the volatility is extremely high.

The evidence at high levels of volatility is based on few observations. Nevertheless, since the excess performance of nonmarket-cap investment protocols can differ over time, blending several protocols, as we did above, may be a good approach. In fact, a blend of three protocols produced, as we would expect, a higher information ratio than any single protocol. The information ratio of a blend of all three protocols is about 0.36, while most protocols had an information ratio below 0.25. Can we do even better?

Do Some Equity Protocols Display Persistent Excess Performance?

Very often a research project leads to counterintuitive results. Whenever this happens, the logical analytical process is to study the structure of the data and the nature of the relationships between the variables to try to make sense of the results. This effort may lead to a moment when the researcher first says, "Well, those results actually make sense." And then, "Why didn't I think of this before?" Finally, the researcher will attempt to determine the implications of his or her finding.

I had one of these significant moments while writing this book. Chapter 6 was initially going to end with the previous section. However, as I was writing Chapter 11 and performing several portfolio simulations, I observed some unusual results. Basically, I found that the objective functions that I would use to allocate between asset components did not favor investing in equity protocols such as RAFI, MaxDiv or MinVar; they favored allocations to standard cap weight indices, even though the realized performance would almost always be less. The analysis of this issue indirectly led me to think that there could be persistence in the excess returns of investment protocols against standard cap-weight indices.

There are actually implicit precedents in literature to support the idea of persistence of excess returns. In Chapter 2, I indicated that there are long performance cycles in asset classes, sectors, styles, etc. We have also discussed that there is strong empirical evidence that multiyear performance by mutual fund managers can be attributed to long-run factors (Malkiel 2005), and that styles of mutual funds typically explain more than 90% of the variations in returns (Ibbotson). Therefore, equity managers, whether they have a bottom-up or top-down approach, create implicit structural biases in their portfolio relative to a cap weight benchmark, and these biases will cause them to outperform or underperform for several consecutive years. Finally, let's also remember the observations of Amihud and Goyenko (2009), who found that funds that recently added value and had lower sensitivity to market returns were more likely to create value in the following year. Thus, the excess performance of managers over different cycles is explained by structural portfolio differences between their own portfolio and market-cap weight indices. How does all this relate to the excess performance of equity protocols having persistence?

One of the main themes of this book is that there are general (structural) qualities that an active manager or an equity protocol must offer in order to produce excess performance in the long term. These qualities may be the smoothing of price noise, the geometric effect on returns created by lower or more stable volatility, a mispriced risk premium explained by persistent behavioral biases and the ability to forecast volatility and dependence and to integrate this information efficiently within the allocation process, etc. Although these qualities may be found in active managers, there is a fundamental difference between investing in an active manager and investing in an equity protocol.

When investing in an equity protocol, we can not only clearly isolate the qualities that this protocol offers (for example smoothing of price noise for RAFI, geometric effect on returns and tail risk management for MinVar and TOBAM, more efficient use of the information related to the covariance matrix for TOBAM, etc.), but we can also assume that this protocol would have offered the same general qualities five years ago as it offers now and will offer five years in the future. The structural qualities that a protocol offers are consistent across time. However, when investing with an active manager, we have to analyze the implicit qualities that we believe are offered by the manager's style and process, determine if the manager has been consistent over time and be reassured that he or she will remain consistent in the future. And if there is turnover among managers, we must remain convinced that the culture of the organization has not been significantly altered.

Furthermore, if excess performance is determined by structural differences between the allocation structure of the protocol and the market-cap index, and if markets are subject to long-term cycles, excess performance should have some persistence. Therefore, recent performance could be a good predictor of excess performance by a systematic protocol.

I tested this hypothesis using data on three equity protocols that I gathered for the case studies discussed in Chapter 11. The analysis covers the period of 1980 to September 2011. The three types of protocols are RAFI, MinVar and TOBAM for the large-cap US market. The test compares the performance of an equal-weight portfolio of all three protocols against a portfolio that dynamically allocates between protocols. In order to avoid extreme solutions, the allocation to any protocol had to remain between 20% and 60%, versus a 33% allocation for each of the protocols in the base case. The methodology is simple. The protocol that has the most momentum in excess performance receives the highest allocation. I could and have designed better processes, but the idea remains to determine if the simplest process works.

Figure 6.5 illustrates the dynamic allocation among all protocols. It appears at first glance that the RAFI protocol was the most prevalent over the entire period. It received the maximum allocation approximately 40% of the time against 30% each for MinVar and TOBAM. The relative dominance of RAFI is explained by the late 1990s, a period of substantial momentum and overvaluation, and also a period where even the worst performer delivered high absolute returns. If we were to eliminate the late 1990s from our analysis, the percentages become 32% respectively for RAFI and MinVar and 36% for TOBAM. Therefore, it is difficult to determine which protocols could dominate in the future. It all depends on the specific dynamics of asset returns. However, a notable benefit is the fact that turnover among equity protocols is not so significant—less than once a year on average.

The approach delivered significant performance improvements. The statistics are presented in Table 6.18. Not only did the protocols add 2.01% of annualized return against the S&P 500, the dynamic allocation also added an extra 1.53% of excess return. Furthermore, the volatility in both cases is significantly less than that of the S&P 500 and the dynamic allocation improved the kurtosis. Overall, the information ratio almost doubled! But was this excess performance achieved in a stable fashion?

Figure 6.6 answers this question. It presents the excess performance of the dynamic portfolio over the equal-weight portfolio using 250-day rolling averages. The dynamic allocation outperformed in 74% of all rolling periods using daily data. The example

FIGURE 6.5   Dynamic Allocation to Equity Protocols

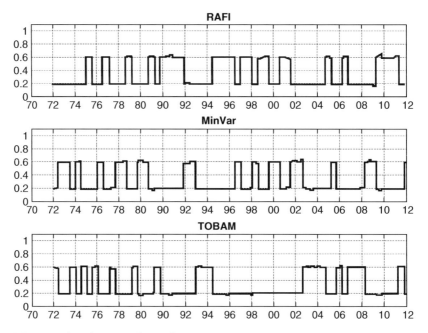

Source: TOBAM, Bloomberg, Langlois and Lussier.

FIGURE 6.6   Relative 12-Month Rolling Performance of Dynamic Versus Equal-Weight Allocation.

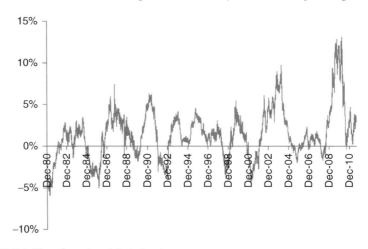

Source: TOBAM, Bloomberg, Langlois & Lussier.

illustrates the value of combining several protocols within an allocation process. It also illustrates how important it can be not to have the allocation process dictated by recent performance. For example, TOBAM did not do as well as the other two protocols in the 1990s, but it was an essential component in the 1980s and the 2000s. If some investors are true believers in the importance of building structurally sound

TABLE 6.18 Comparative Performance of S&P 500, Equal-Weight Protocols and Dynamically Managed Portfolio of Protocols (1980–September 2011)

	S&P 500	Equal-Weight Portfolio	Dynamic Portfolio
GEO Mean	11.29	13.30	14.83
Volatility	18.64	13.44	13.25
Information Ratio	0.61	0.99	1.12
Skewness	−1.21	−1.21	−0.84
Kurtosis	28.98	28.60	18.00

portfolios, and if they believe in the qualities of their approach, they must consider their investment approach as a package of components, and not the sum of single components, each of which could be fully removed when a rough period is observed. It is also potentially easier to maintain discipline when using transparent investment protocols instead of active managers whose styles may evolve over time.

Closing Remarks

By now, investors should realize that there are many ways to outperform a market-cap index. But, in all cases, investors must have a reasonable investment horizon. Some methodologies are quite simple, while others, such as the parametric approach, require a more evolved but still manageable optimization process. Most nonmarket-cap portfolio-assembly processes seek to combine one or several of the following elements: smoothing price noise, exploiting the benefits of specific factor tilting, managing volatility and optimizing diversification benefits. Furthermore, many different approaches can be used to smooth price noise. Some methodologies are market-structure indifferent; others are not. Some are conditional on volatility and dependence while many are not. Finally, although the parametric approach appears to be a superior methodology because of the flexibility it offers in exploiting all relevant basic qualities of portfolio construction, in the end, no protocol can be truly superior in all market conditions. Since different methodologies lead to different patterns of excess returns, one should consider a blend of different approaches, such as combining protocols that are efficient at diversification, smoothing price noise and exploiting risk factors. A blend of approaches is also likely to support the longevity of an investment program, although a "super" protocol that would incorporate all relevant qualities could conceptually be built.

An advisor should tell the investors to pay attention to the performance of their entire portfolio of nonmarket-cap protocols and not be obsessed with the performance of any single protocol over the short term. What has to be sold to investors is the idea of statistically efficient nonmarket-cap protocols—not any single concept. Doing so may cause investors to lose patience and eliminate a mandate at the very worst time. For example, an investor once asked me how I would present minimum variance protocols to an investment committee. This investor had never allocated to a nonmarket-cap protocol. My recommendation was that they should explain to the committee the notion of nonmarket-cap protocols and then position the minimum variance approach as one among many. My concern was that, if the investment did not do well initially (timing is everything) and if the initial investment in a single strategy was significant, the committee could be very displeased after two years, and the effort to diversify among other methodologies would become impossible.

Despite all that has been said, investors who believe in the concepts of nonmarket-cap protocols should not necessarily ignore all active managers. However, it does appear to indicate that if investors want to retain active managers, they should favor benchmark-agnostic managers who have a strong, coherent and very disciplined process offered at a competitive cost. An investor could find in some active managers that the qualities that we have identified in this chapter are relevant to long-term performance. However, based on all the evidence we have covered thus far in this book, if I were confronted with the decision to invest for the next 10 years either in three active equity managers who have performed very well over the last five years or in three distinct and well-designed nonmarket-cap investment protocols, I would choose the latter without any hesitation.

Notes

1. DeMiguel, Victor, Lorenzo Garlappi, and Raman Uppal (2007), "Optimal versus naive diversification: How inefficient is the $1/N$ portfolio strategy?" London Business School, McCombs School of Business—University of Texas at Austin.
2. Choueifaty, Yves (2006), "Methods and systems for providing an anti-benchmark portfolio," USPTO No. 60/816,276 filed June 22, 2006.
3. Christoffersen, Peter, Vihang Errunza, Kris Jacobs, and Hugues Langlois (2011), "Is the potential for international diversification disappearing?" Working Paper, The Rotman School, McGill University, University of Houston.
4. Demay, Paul, Sébastien Maillard and Thierry Roncalli (2010), "Risk-based indexation," Lyxor Asset Management.
5. Pollet, Joshua M. and Mungo Wilson (2006), "Average correlations and stock market returns," University of Illinois; Hong-Kong University.
6. Maillard, Sébastien, Thierry Roncalli and Jérôme Teiletche (209), "On the properties of equally-weighted risk contributions portfolios," SGAM Alternative Investments and Lombard Odier.
7. Kritzman, Mark, Sebastien Page, and David Turkington (2010), "In defense of optimization: the fallacy of 1/N," *Financial Analysts Journal* 66(2), 31–39.
8. Rajamony, Jayendran and Shanta Puchtler (2011), "What is minimum variance and how does it work?" Numeric Investors.
9. Choueifaty, Yves and Yves Coignard (2008), "Toward Maximum Diversification," The Journal of Portfolio Management 35(1), 40–51.

10. Choueifaty, Yves, Tristan Froidure, and Julien Reynier (2011), "Properties of the most diversified portfolio," TOBAM.

11. Arnott, Robert D., Jason C. Hsu, and John M. West (2008), *The Fundamental Index: A Better Way to Invest*, John Wiley & Sons, Inc.

12. Hsu, Jason C. (2006), "Cap-weighted portfolios are sub-optimal portfolios," *Journal of Investment Management* 4(3), 1–10.

13. Arnott, Robert (2008), "Where does finance theory lead us astray?" EDHEC Symposium, Nice.

14. Tamura, H. and Y. Shimizu (2005), "Global fundamental indices—Do they outperform market-cap weighted indices on a global basis?" Global Quantitative Research, Nomura Securities Co., Ltd., Tokyo.

15. Walkshausl, Christian and Sebastian Lobe (2009), "Fundamental indexing around the world," University of Regensburg.

16. Chen, C., R. Chen, and G. Bassett (2007), "Fundamental indexation via smoothed cap weights," *Journal of Banking and Finance* 31(12), 3486–3502.

17. Arnott, Robert D., Jason C. Hsu, Feifei Li, and Shane Shepherd (2010), "Valuation-indifferent weighting for bonds," *Journal of Portfolio Management*, 36(3), 117–130.

18. Arnott, Robert, Jason C. Hsu, Jun Liu, and Harry Markowitz (2010), "Does noise create the size and value effects?" University of California at San Diego and Research Affiliates.

19. Langlois, Hugues and Jacques Lussier (2009), "Fundamental indexing—It's not about the fundamentals," Desjardins Global Asset Management.

20. Estrada, Javier (2006), "Fundamental indexing and international diversification," IESE Business School.

21. O'Neill, Jim (2012), "Monthly Insights – April 12th", Goldman Sachs Asset Management.

22. Brandt, Michael W., Pedro Santa-Clara, and Rossen Valkanov (2009), "Parametric portfolio policies—Exploiting characteristics in the cross-section of equity returns," *Review of Financial Studies* 22(1), 3411–3447.

23. Christoffersen, Pete, Vihang Errunza, Kris Jacobs, and Xisong Jin (2010), "Is the potential for international diversification disappearing?" McGill University, Houston University.

24. Tu, Jun and Guofu Zhou (2011), "Markowitz meets Talmud—A combination of sophisticated and naïve diversification strategies," *Journal of Financial Economics* 99, 204–215.

25. Goyal, Amit and Ivo Welch (2008), "A comprehensive look at the empirical performance of equity premium prediction," *The Review of Financial Studies* 21(4), 1455–1508.

26. Campbell, John Y. and Samuel B. Thompson (2008), "Predicting excess stock returns out of sample: Can anything beat the historical average?" *Review of Financial Studies* 21(4), 1509–1531.

27. Kong, Aiguo, David E. Rapach, Kack K. Strauss, and Guofu Zhou (2011), "Predicting market components out of-sample—Asset allocation implications," *Journal of Portfolio Management* 37(4), 29–41.
28. Chow, Tzee-men, Jason Hsu, Vitali Kalesnik and Bryce Little (2011), "A survey of alternative equity index strategies," *Financial Analysts Journal* 67(5), 37–57.
29. Goldman Sachs Asset Management (2012), "GIVI—Active insight plus passive efficiency," Perspectives (April).
30. Baker, Malcolm, Brandon Bradley, and Jeffrey Wurgler (2011), "Benchmarks as limits to arbitrage—Understanding the low-volatility anomaly," *Financial Analysts Journal* 67(1), 40–54.
31. Langlois, Hugues and Jacques Lussier (2009), "Fundamental indexing—It's not about the fundamentals," Desjardins Global Asset Management.
32. Cremers, Martijn K.J. and Antti Petajisto. (2009), "How active is your fund manager? A new measure that predicts performance," Yale School of Management.
33. Fernholz, R., R. Garvy and J. Hannon (1998), "Diversity-weighted indexing," *Journal of Portfolio Management* 24, 74–82 .

CHAPTER 7

Portfolio Rebalancing and Asset Allocation

The asset allocation process is driven by liability requirements, return objectives, risk tolerance and, for some investors, taxation. In this chapter, we discuss the different methodologies by which the portfolio allocation and the rebalancing process can be managed and the GEO mean improved. At this point, we are not attempting to determine which portfolio allocation is appropriate to the liability stream and risk tolerance of investors. The objective is only to discuss different methodologies that can be used, and their relative efficiency.

Most investment policies and guidelines will usually consider the issue of asset allocation and portfolio rebalancing separately. As we will see in a later section of this chapter, it is possible and generally preferable to use an approach that fully integrates these two aspects. However, I will start with a review of the traditional literature on portfolio rebalancing, and then present my own comprehensive research on this issue. Then, I will complete this chapter with a discussion and analysis of different allocation models. We will consider two types of allocation methodologies: unconditional methodologies (such as rebalancing periodically toward a fixed allocation target structure like 60/40 or 40/60), where the rebalancing process is independent of the chosen portfolio allocation, and conditional methodologies (such as maintaining a constant 6% or 8% volatility), where the rebalancing and allocation process is fully integrated.

Introduction to Portfolio Rebalancing

The issue of portfolio rebalancing is usually covered from the point of view of an investor who is seeking to restore his or her asset allocation after market forces have caused the weight of each portfolio component to move away from the desired strategic policy benchmark. For example, if the current and targeted portfolio structure is 50% equity and 50% fixed income, the respective weights of these two assets will move away from the initial allocation over time. According to Plaxco and Arnott (2002) [1], a portfolio that began with such a mix in January 1950 would have ended with a 98/2 mix 50 years later if no rebalancing took place. Although this is an extreme example, it illustrates that some form of rebalancing is required to control the desired allocation and portfolio risk.

The practitioners' literature usually addresses this issue from a single analytical angle. More specifically, it seeks to understand how different rules of rebalancing will impact risk, return, turnover and tracking error under different market environments and target portfolio allocation structures. Although this literature is pertinent, it is almost always built around the assumption that investors specify their portfolio allocation and express their risk tolerance through fixed investment weights such as a 40/60 equity bond allocation. It also often assumes that the rebalancing methodology is static (such as rebalancing every quarter) and, thus, is not conditioned by market factors.

It is true that most portfolio allocation options that are offered to investors are usually defined in this fashion by financial service providers. Financial advisors usually offer their clients four to six portfolio structures that correspond to four to six risk-tolerance levels. However, this may not be the most optimal approach.

First, we know that volatilities and correlations are not stable. Therefore, when we choose a strategic asset allocation based on fixed investment weights, and rebalance periodically toward that allocation, we are in fact rebalancing toward a target allocation that has an evolving risk. Managing the overall portfolio risk (for example, maintaining a constant 5% or 8% portfolio volatility, or managing the entire return distribution) may be more efficient than managing fixed investment weights (such as 40/60 or 60/40 allocations). It is also more coherent with the objective of meeting the investor's tolerance for risk. The risk of a portfolio built and rebalanced around fixed weights usually increases in downward markets (as market volatility often spikes up), while the investor's risk tolerance usually declines in such circumstances.

Second, we have also mentioned that volatilities and correlations show persistence, and that significant drawdowns are usually observed in volatile markets. Thus, if a portfolio structuring and rebalancing process is not conditioned by risk factors, we are ignoring very pertinent and significant sources of market information.

In this first section of the chapter, we will review the literature that is concerned with the more basic rules of unconditional portfolio rebalancing. However, we will also attempt to improve on it. First, this literature is fragmented. Different methodologies have been tested on different portfolio structures over different periods, making it difficult to draw robust conclusions. Second, a proper justification for the results of these studies is lacking. Finally, although we will present simple allocation rules that are more efficient than a traditional periodic rebalancing (and that most investors could apply), we mostly want to use this literature to steer the discussion toward more robust and coherent rebalancing and allocation methodologies that will be covered later on in this chapter.

Why Rebalance?

There are two major reasons why rebalancing is essential. First, a failure to rebalance will surely modify the return and risk structure of a portfolio, gradually bias its allocation toward riskier assets and increase its sensitivity to significant market corrections. In other words, the value at risk of a drifting portfolio will usually increase over time.

FIGURE 7.1 Equity Weight and Volatility (1973–2010).

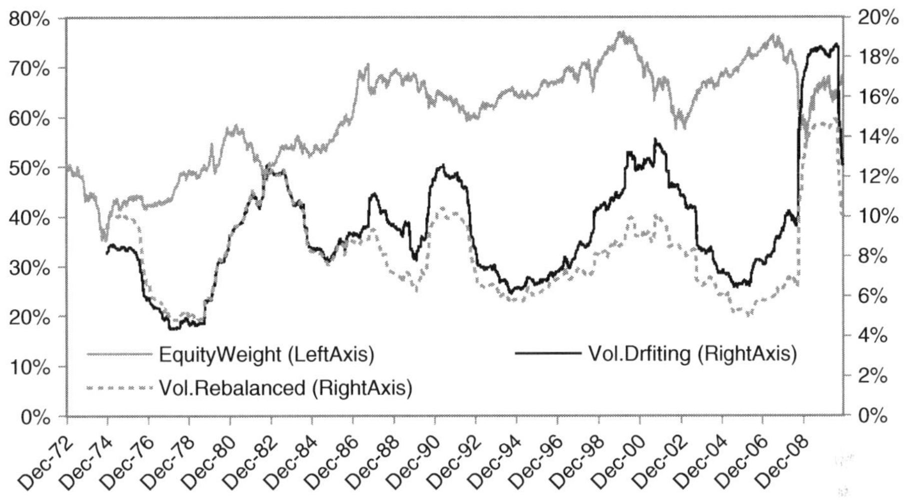

Source: Data from Datastream.

The Consulting Group of Smith Barney (2005) [2] discussed the issue of "drifting into danger." To follow up on their argument, Figure 7.1 illustrates how the asset allocation of a 50% global equity and 50% fixed-income portfolio (at inception) would have evolved from 1973 to 2010 if left unbalanced. It also illustrates how the volatility of this portfolio, as measured with a simple two-year rolling annualized volatility of weekly returns, has evolved over time, and how it would have evolved if, instead, the portfolio had been rebalanced on a monthly basis.

As we can see, the allocation to equity drifted from 50% toward 70%, and would have been much higher if not for the two significant periods of equity decline, 2001 to 2002 and 2008. However, although the volatility of the drifting portfolio was significantly greater than that of the rebalanced portfolio in recent years, we can also see that the volatility of both portfolios was not stable. The volatility of the rebalanced portfolio ranged from 4.76% to 14.78%, while that of the drifting portfolio ranged from 4.35% to 18.62%. Therefore, as we expected, rebalancing toward fixed weights does not imply that portfolio risk remains constant, but it is still an improvement over a drifting portfolio.

Another reason for rebalancing is its impact on risk-adjusted performance. The choice of a rebalancing methodology may actually be a source of added value. We already know that rebalancing allows a portfolio to benefit from imperfect correlations among asset classes, and, therefore, it contributes to lower portfolio volatility and higher GEO mean. I already mentioned in Chapter 4 that the impact on the GEO mean of a more efficient diversification can only occur if a portfolio is rebalanced. But although most rebalancing processes improve portfolio efficiency, the argument of many authors on this issue is that rebalancing can also allow a portfolio to benefit from momentum/mean reversion effects and/or from asynchronous cycles in asset classes, thereby enhancing the financial benefits of rebalancing. Furthermore, although the existence of momentum/mean reversion and asynchronous cycles may be a sufficient condition to improve portfolio efficiency through a particular rebalancing methodology, it is not a necessary condition. For example, if a traditional rebalancing process helps manage the volatility in the long term (although imperfectly), we have already shown that it will improve the GEO mean.

Excess Return Required to Balance the Diversification Bonus

When I give a seminar to investors or their advisors, I often confront them with the following question. From 1973 to 2010, the GEO mean of fixed income and equity portfolios were 7.7% and 9.8% respectively. We know for a fact that equity outperformed fixed income by 2.1 percentage points annually. If an investor had started with a 50/50 portfolio and never rebalanced, equity would have accounted for 68% of the allocation in 2010, and the annualized performance (GEO mean) of the portfolio would have been 8.9%. If we assume now that the portfolio would have been rebalanced periodically, and thus that equity would not have been allowed to drift to a higher allocation, would the performance have been higher or lower?

Almost all participants believe that the performance would have been lower, since equity outperformed significantly. In fact, the performance of the rebalanced portfolio would have been higher at 9.5%. Furthermore, volatility would have been lower on average. So although we understand the benefits of a simple Markowitz diversification, this example puts it in perspective. A 2.1% excess return of equity over fixed income is not sufficient to avoid rebalancing. With a more efficient rebalancing methodology (than a simple calendar methodology), it is even possible that a 50/50 portfolio could outperform a full allocation to equity, even though equity outperformed fixed income by 2.1%.

The example illustrates that a drifting portfolio can underperform a rebalanced portfolio, even if we allow the risk of the portfolio to increase. We will now determine how significant the performance spread must be between two asset classes in order to justify rebalancing or not rebalancing purely from a GEO mean point of view (i.e., ignoring the rising risk of the drifting portfolio). The analysis is based on the assumption of a GEO mean and volatility of 4.5% and 8.0% respectively for fixed income. Correlation with equity is assumed to be 0.30.

Tables 7.1a and 7.1b illustrate the excess return that rebalancing produces (against a drifting portfolio) according to the excess return and volatility of equity for two horizons, 15 and 30 years. Three scenarios of GEO excess return of equity against fixed income are used: 2%, 3% and 5%. Volatility of equity varies from 14% to 30%. As indicated, return and volatility of fixed income remain constant under all scenarios.

Table 7.1a, shows that, notwithstanding the potential impact that a drifting portfolio has on risk, an investor with a 30-year investment horizon must expect equity to outperform fixed income by at least 3.0% yearly in order to expect the performance of a drifting portfolio to exceed that of a rebalanced portfolio. This is consistent with the example that I provided earlier. Furthermore, the excess performance required is positively correlated with equity volatility. Although I do not illustrate this aspect, the excess performance is negatively correlated with correlation itself. Therefore, the greater the volatility of equity—and the lower the correlation of equity to fixed income—the greater the required excess performance of equity to compensate for the loss of the diversification bonus. Finally, the gains will be greater for portfolios that have an initial equity allocation in the 40% to 60% range.

Over a shorter horizon, such as 15 years (see Table 7.1b), a larger expected equity return is required to justify not rebalancing the portfolio. We get this result simply because a drifting portfolio of shorter maturity has a lower GEO mean, since the drift in equity weight will not be as significant. These results are consistent with Pliska and Suzuki (2004) [3], who commented on the underlying market conditions that would make a rebalancing process more relevant. According to them, it is all a function of the returns of the portfolio components (asset classes), their volatilities and correlations and the time horizon.

- **Volatility:** Although different portfolio components will perform differently over time, unless the volatility of returns of the portfolio components is significant, the need to rebalance may not be as relevant. Furthermore, as discussed in Chapter 4, the size of the rebalancing bonus is a linear function of the variance of asset classes. Thus, all other things being equal, an asset class with half or a third of the volatility (measured by standard deviation) of another asset class contributes only a quarter or one-ninth as much to the diversification bonus.
- **Return and Time Horizon:** If an asset component outperforms others, the allocation of the portfolio to this asset will gradually increase. Furthermore, the greater the time horizon, the greater the potential allocation drift. Although the effect of a portfolio drift on return may eventually be more important than the diversification bonus, the drifting portfolio will become significantly riskier. Thus, the investor must remain confident that equity will significantly outperform fixed income.
- **Correlation:** If asset components are highly correlated, there will be less need to rebalance. For example, a perfect correlation would obviously completely eliminate the benefits of rebalancing.

To the previous explanatory factors, another should be added: asset weights. I explained in Chapter 4 that an equal-weight portfolio is more likely to generate a greater diversification bonus. Again, all else being equal, as Equation 4.2a shows, a portfolio with a 10/90 asset mix would only provide 36% of the diversification bonus of an equal-weight portfolio. However, a 60/40 or a 40/60 portfolio would provide nearly as much benefit (96%) as a 50/50 portfolio.

As indicated previously, most reasonable rebalancing rules will allow a portfolio to benefit from the diversification bonus. It may be unrealistic to assume that an investor will not rebalance his or her portfolio for 15 or 30 years, but it does illustrate the importance of the rebalancing process. A better understanding of the power of rebalancing may lead to performance benefits that are significantly greater than the basic diversification bonus.

TABLE 7.1a Relative Performance of Rebalanced and Drifting Portfolios (30-Year Horizon (in bps))

Volatility / Equity Weight	Excess Spread: 2%								
	10%	20%	30%	40%	50%	60%	70%	80%	90%
14%	3	6	8	10	11	11	10	8	4
16%	5	10	13	16	17	17	15	12	7
18%	8	14	19	23	24	24	21	16	9
20%	11	20	26	31	32	32	28	22	12
22%	14	26	34	40	42	41	36	28	16
24%	18	32	43	49	52	50	44	34	19
26%	22	39	52	60	63	61	54	41	23
28%	26	47	63	72	76	73	64	49	28
30%	31	56	74	85	89	86	75	58	33

Volatility / Equity Weight	Excess Spread: 3%								
	10%	20%	30%	40%	50%	60%	70%	80%	90%
14%	(5)	(7)	(8)	(7)	(6)	(4)	(2)	(1)	(0)
16%	(3)	(3)	(3)	(1)	0	2	3	3	2
18%	(0)	1	3	6	8	9	9	8	5
20%	3	7	10	14	16	17	16	13	8
22%	6	12	18	23	25	26	24	19	11
24%	10	19	27	33	36	36	32	25	15
26%	14	26	36	43	47	47	42	33	19
28%	18	34	47	55	59	58	52	41	23
30%	23	43	58	68	73	71	63	49	28

Volatility / Equity Weight	Excess Spread: 5%								
	10%	20%	30%	40%	50%	60%	70%	80%	90%
14%	(35)	(52)	(59)	(59)	(55)	(47)	(37)	(25)	(13)
16%	(33)	(48)	(54)	(53)	(48)	(41)	(31)	(21)	(10)
18%	(30)	(44)	(48)	(46)	(41)	(34)	(25)	(16)	(8)
20%	(27)	(38)	(41)	(38)	(33)	(26)	(18)	(11)	(5)
22%	(24)	(32)	(33)	(29)	(23)	(17)	(10)	(5)	(2)
24%	(20)	(26)	(24)	(19)	(13)	(7)	(2)	1	2
26%	(16)	(19)	(15)	(9)	(2)	4	8	9	6
28%	(11)	(11)	(5)	3	11	16	18	17	11
30%	(7)	(2)	7	16	24	29	29	25	15

TABLE 7.1b   Relative Performance of Rebalanced and Drifting Portfolios (15-year Horizon (in bps))

Volatility / Equity Weight	Excess Spread: 2%								
	10%	20%	30%	40%	50%	60%	70%	80%	90%
14%	6	11	14	17	17	17	15	11	6
16%	8	15	20	23	24	23	20	15	9
18%	11	20	26	30	31	30	26	20	11
20%	14	25	33	38	39	38	33	25	14
22%	17	31	41	47	49	47	41	31	18
24%	21	38	49	57	59	57	50	38	21
26%	25	45	59	67	70	68	59	45	25
28%	30	53	69	79	83	79	70	53	30
30%	34	61	80	92	96	92	81	62	35

Volatility / Equity Weight	Excess Spread: 3%								
	10%	20%	30%	40%	50%	60%	70%	80%	90%
14%	3	5	7	9	9	9	8	7	4
16%	5	9	12	15	16	15	14	11	6
18%	8	14	19	22	23	22	20	15	9
20%	11	19	26	30	31	30	27	21	12
22%	14	25	33	39	41	39	35	27	15
24%	18	32	42	48	51	49	43	33	19
26%	22	39	51	59	62	60	53	40	23
28%	26	47	62	71	74	72	63	48	27
30%	31	55	73	84	88	85	74	57	32

Volatility / Equity Weight	Excess Spread: 5%								
	10%	20%	30%	40%	50%	60%	70%	80%	90%
14%	(9)	(14)	(17)	(17)	(16)	(14)	(11)	(7)	(4)
16%	(7)	(10)	(11)	(11)	(10)	(8)	(5)	(3)	(1)
18%	(4)	(6)	(5)	(4)	(2)	(1)	1	1	1
20%	(1)	(0)	2	4	6	7	8	7	4
22%	2	6	9	13	15	16	15	13	8
24%	6	12	18	23	25	26	24	19	11
26%	10	20	28	34	37	37	34	26	15
28%	14	27	38	45	49	49	44	34	20
30%	19	36	49	58	62	62	55	43	25

Now we turn ourselves to the next issue. Are there rebalancing rules that are more likely to outperform? We will initially limit ourselves to unconditional rebalancing methodologies built around fixed allocation weight targets.

Momentum/Mean Reversion and Asynchronous Asset Class Cycles

In principle, a rebalancing process, while still allowing the portfolio to benefit from the relative momentum in asset classes, remains implicitly contrarian. Let's illustrate with a simple example. An investor with $1 million maintains a 50/50 target allocation. The performance of equity is 5% in the first month and 5% in the second month. The performance of fixed income is 0% in both periods. Table 7.2a illustrates the performance that results from a calendar rebalancing approach. The portfolio is rebalanced either every month or every two months.

When the investor opts to rebalance after two months, the performance is increased by 0.0625 percentage points because, by rebalancing less often, the investor allows his or her portfolio to capture more of the positive performance of equity. The same would be true if equity had underperformed fixed income during these two periods.

When there is positive or negative relative momentum in the market, rebalancing less frequently could become very profitable, especially if the relative momentum between two assets persisted for long periods on average, such as for several months or even years. Consequently, a less frequent rebalancing would only be penalized if a positive relative momentum between two assets was suddenly reversed, and if this reversal was very significant. An example could be a sudden relative rise of 10% in equities followed by an even more sudden relative decline of 25%. In such circumstances, if

TABLE 7.2a   Impact of Rebalancing Frequency on Performance: Positive Momentum

Case 1: Rebalancing Every Month

	T = 0	T = Month 1 (Before Rebalancing)	T = Month 1 (After Rebalancing)	T = Month 2
Equity	500,000	525,000	512,500	538,125
Fixed Income	500,000	500,000	512,500	512,500
Total	1,000,000	1,025,000	1,025,000	1,050,625
Performance				5.0625%

Case 2: Rebalancing Every Two Months

	T = 0	T = Month 1 (Before Rebalancing)		T = Month 2
Equity	500,000	525,000		551,250
Fixed Income	500,000	500,000		500,000
Total	1,000,000	1,025,000		1,051,250
Performance				5.125%

the portfolio had been rebalanced more quickly, its exposure to equities would have been lower when equities underperformed. This example is illustrated in Table 7.2b. Shifting momentum can produce greater losses at lower rebalancing frequency, although such circumstances are fortunately much less frequent than the norm.

Although there is little evidence that we can accurately forecast the length of asset class cycles, we can observe that asset classes are prone to long periods of substantial relative outperformance or underperformance. Furthermore, it may be possible to detect persistence in relative returns. Table 7.3 illustrates the performance ranking of six asset classes over seven successive periods of five years, as well as the annualized performance for the entire period. Over the 35-year period, equities dominated fixed income, and small-cap equity had the best overall performance. Thus, most historical performances were in line with relative expectations over the long horizon. The S&P GSCI had the poorest performance of all assets, an aspect I will discuss in the next chapter. However, relative performances over shorter periods were very unstable. For example, small-cap equity produced the best performance in only three of the seven five-year periods, and had the worst performance between 1986 and 1990. Similarly, although the commodity index had the worst long-term performance, it performed best during the period 1986 to 1990. Why?

The long-term performances of financial assets are affected by structural changes (such as the growing dominance of emerging markets, the rise of sovereign risks in developed markets and the concerted effort to develop energy alternatives) and by fundamental factors (such as new expectations for economic growth and inflation). However, performances are also influenced in the short and medium term by investors' mood swings (time-varying risk premiums) and noisy events. Although riskier assets should have more significant embedded risk premiums that should allow them

TABLE 7.2b Impact of Rebalancing Frequency on Performance: Shifting Momentum

Case 1: Rebalancing Every Month

	T = 0	T = Month 1 (Before Rebalancing)	T = Month 1 (After Rebalancing)	T = Month 2
Equity	500,000	555,000	525,000	393,750
Fixed Income	500,000	500,000	525,000	525,000
Total	1,000,000	1,050,000	1,050,000	918,750
Performance				−4.1538%

Case 2: Rebalancing Every Two Months

	T = 0	T = Month 1 (Before Rebalancing)		T = Month 2
Equity	500,000	550,000	—	412,500
Fixed Income	500,000	500,000	—	500,000
Total	1,000,000	1,050,000	—	912,500
Performance				−4.4751%

TABLE 7.3   Relative Performance of Major Asset Markets (1976–2010)

	Return (%)	Ranking						
	1976–2010	1976–1980	1981–1985	1986–1990	1991–1995	1996–2000	2001–2005	2006–2010
10-Year Treasury	8.0	5	2	4	4	5	5	2
30-Year Treasury	7.9	6	1	5	3	6	4	3
Commodities	7.4	4	6	1	6	3	2	6
Global ex-US	12.1	2	3	2	5	4	3	1
Large-Cap US	11.2	3	5	3	2	1	6	5
Small-Cap US	13.6	1	4	6	1	2	1	4

Source: Data from Datastream.

to outperform over long periods, those performances will not be achieved consistently. Thus, when tracking the relative performance of two assets over time, there will always be periods when one asset will have a greater positive or negative performance until market preferences and circumstances reverse this pattern.

Although it may be difficult to forecast how long favorable or unfavorable asset cycles will last, and when they will revert, we know these patterns keep repeating, we know they are rarely short and we know the performance spreads between asset classes can be significant. For example, the annualized spread between the best and worst assets was 6.2% during the entire period (1976 to 2010), while it varied between 12.3% (2006 to 2010) and 30.8% (1976 to 1980) over shorter periods of five years. It seems intuitive that less frequent or smarter rebalancing methodologies, which allow one to capture the favorable relative momentum among asset classes, may be more efficient on average than more frequent and stringent rebalancing methodologies, especially when adjusted for transaction costs.

The Empirical Literature on Rebalancing

There are generally two categories of standard rebalancing triggers:

1. Calendar Based: The triggers force a rebalancing to take place at specific time intervals, such as monthly, quarterly, annually and even biennially.
2. Threshold Based: There are two types of threshold-based rebalancing. The first type is initiated whenever an asset weight exceeds a predetermined threshold. The trigger may be different for each asset class. It may be a fixed value such as ±3% or ±5%, or it may be determined by its volatility (such as a half standard

deviation, etc.). A second type of rebalancing may be based on an objective criterion that applies to the entire portfolio, such as exceeding a specific level of tracking error.

The two approaches (calendar and threshold) can also be combined. For example, the portfolio could be reviewed at different time intervals, but rebalancing would only occur when the allocation deviates from the target by a stated threshold level. When an event does trigger a rebalancing, the methodology may not require that the entire portfolio be rebalanced to the allocation target.

According to Riepe (2007) [4], there are three possible configurations that can be used as targets when rebalancing a portfolio: back to the strategic target, to the threshold, or to a tolerance band (such as half the distance between the strategic target and the threshold). For example, assume that the strategic target for an asset class is 40% and its threshold is 44%. If market forces raise the allocation to 45%, the rebalancing process could be used to bring the allocation back to 40% (the strategic target), 44% (the threshold), or to some level in between (the tolerance level).

However, this discussion would be merely academic if there was no evidence of sufficient momentum that could be captured through a rebalancing process. Clark (1999) [5] of Dimensional Fund Advisors conducted a study that addresses this issue. Clark compared several rebalancing triggers, including monthly, quarterly, semiannually, annually and biennially, as well as a form of rebalancing triggered by tracking error. He looked at several dimensions such as tracking error, turnover, return and risk for portfolios with different risk levels (60%, 70% or 80% equities) over a period of 25 years (1971 to 1996). The equity allocation had domestic and international as well as large-cap and small-cap components. Our interest in this study is that Clark also tested the impact of rebalancing using a bootstrap approach—a form of data shuffling. This means that simulations were conducted by randomly drawing sequential returns from the actual monthly data sets. Bootstrapping preserves the risk and return properties of each asset class portfolio as well as their correlations, but it also eliminates any autocorrelation/momentum effects if such effects do indeed exist. Thus, if we compare the performance of different rebalancing methodologies applied to the real data set with those obtained from a bootstrapping approach, we should expect the returns realized from the bootstrapping approach to be less than those observed with the market data set if, for example, there were momentum patterns. Table 7.4 presents the results for the 70/30 portfolio.

Returns under the bootstrap methodology are lower. The level of risk is also lower. Because of this, we cannot reject the possible presence of momentum in the market. However, the difference in return among different intervals of rebalancing is not that significant, except under biennial rebalancing. The data indicate that frequent rebalancing (monthly) is not required when a calendar rebalancing approach is used. An investor could rebalance every one or two years and expect to do just as well as if his or her investment horizon was fairly long. Long-interval rebalancing processes are also useful because they do not create a high asset turnover, which may help to manage taxes on capital gains.

TABLE 7.4 The Impact of Momentum on Performance (%)

Interval	1971–1996			Average of 100 Bootstraps		
	Return	Risk	Turnover	Return	Risk	Turnover
Monthly	12.59	12.93	11.80	12.58	11.65	11.81
Quarterly	12.71	12.93	7.19	12.63	11.69	7.17
Semiannually	12.77	13.00	5.48	12.66	11.73	5.19
Annually	12.76	12.97	4.08	12.68	11.83	3.72
Biennially	13.13	12.98	3.66	12.71	11.89	2.68

Source: Clark (1999).

There have been many studies on rebalancing, but they each cover different periods, different rebalancing methodologies, and different portfolio structure and components. They often consider the cost of rebalancing, but some of the older studies use assumptions about trading costs that are no longer realistic today, especially when even individual investors can trade ETFs at less than $10 a trade, whatever their size. Many ETFs are now large and highly liquid, which even allows many institutional investors (those with several billion dollars in assets) to adjust their portfolio if EFTs are used in combination with other mandates. Nevertheless, these studies generally come to similar conclusions.

For example, calendar-based rebalancing is usually found to be less efficient than threshold-based rebalancing. Furthermore, studies find that once a trigger has been reached, it is not necessary to rebalance back to the strategic benchmark. Rebalancing to a tolerance band located between the strategic target and the range limit is sufficient, and the rebalancing process may perform almost as well. Finally, McCalla (1997) [6] found that the threshold approach performs better if the trigger point for each asset class is based on its respective volatility, although this conclusion is contradicted by Cao (2008) [7] and by my own research, which will be presented later.

This approach is often referred to as using equal-risk thresholds. It means that thresholds for different asset classes are set so that the probability of hitting any trigger is approximately equal. There is also one consistent observation: all methodologies are more risk/return efficient than a drifting portfolio. We will only discuss a few of these studies for two reasons. First, this is an area of literature where it may be preferable to look at the most recent studies because of differences in fees, data coverage or methodologies. Second, the current research on rebalancing is moving beyond the traditional approach of rebalancing around a fixed dollar allocation target and, thus, this is not an area of research where much innovation can be expected. Therefore, I will only present the results of Cao (2008), Daryanani (2008) [8] and Lee (2008) [9].

The study by Cao is not as complete as those by Daryanani and Lee, but it does cover a much longer history, 1952 to 2007. Cao studied three portfolio structures: 30%, 60% and 80% equity. The balance is invested in fixed income with some cash. Because of the greater length of the data set, the diversity of asset classes and risk factors is limited. The study tested fixed and equal risk thresholds using checking frequencies of one month and one to eight quarters (nine frequencies). Cao found that the rebalancing process that seems to offer the best performance over different subperiods for the portfolios with 30% and 60% equity allocations is usually the three-month checking frequency with a 5% nominal band, such as 55% minimum and 65% maximum for a 60% equity allocation target. This approach has a very low turnover, less than four rebalancings on average per decade. For the 80% allocation, the conclusion is not as clear cut. An equal-risk approach using a six-month checking interval with a threshold equal to 0.20 standard deviation was more efficient from a risk-adjusted perspective. It may be that equal probability rebalancing methodologies are more suitable to portfolios where one component dominates the total risk.

The studies by Daryanani and Lee come to different conclusions but they incorporate more asset classes (large-cap equity (25%), small-cap equity (20%), REITS (10%), commodities (5%) and bonds (40%)). They were also completed over a much shorter test period (1992 to 2004). Both Daryanani and Lee used a 60/40 portfolio and tested rebalancing bands of 0% (continuous rebalancing), 5%, 10%, 15%, 20%, 25% and 100% (drifting portfolio) with look intervals of 1, 5, 10, 20, 60, 125 and 250 days. Daryanani also imposed a 5% maximum deviation against the 60% strategic target for equity (as Cao did), although this constraint was not binding for the 0% to 20% band.

If a rebalancing process is required for one or more asset classes, weights would not be adjusted to the strategic target, but to half the distance between the band and the target. For example, if a 20% band is used and the target allocation is 10%, the minimum and maximum band are set at 8% and 12%. If the allocation goes outside this corridor, the weight would be adjusted to either 9% or 11%. Performance measures were also adjusted for trading costs, although, as we will discuss later on, this is no longer an issue for many investors, unless they use an extremely tight rebalancing process. Table 7.5 presents the basic results from the Daryanani study.

TABLE 7.5 Excess Performance Against a Drifting Portfolio (%)

Bands (%)	Look Intervals (Days)						
	250	125	60	20	10	5	1
0	0.26	0.19	0.18	0.07	−0.05	−0.29	−2.32
5	0.27	0.22	0.19	0.20	0.21	0.20	0.19
10	0.30	0.25	0.27	0.24	0.27	0.27	0.24
15	0.29	0.33	0.33	0.35	0.35	0.32	0.31
20	0.31	0.36	0.38	0.40	0.45	0.43	0.50
25	0.17	0.30	0.27	0.32	0.37	0.44	0.43
100	0.00	0.00	0.00	0.00	0.00	0.00	0.00

Source: Daryanani (2008).

These results indicate that a 20% band with a one- to ten-day look interval is optimal. A wider band may not allow the rebalancing process to capture some of the momentum/mean reversion occurrences. Daryanani also looked at nine subperiods of five years and four subperiods of ten years, but the 20% band with one- to ten-day look intervals was almost always preferable. Like Clark (1999), Daryanani used a boot-strapping approach to isolate the source of this excess performance. Unsurprisingly, the reshuffling of the data set removed the pertinence of using a specific look interval. Overall, this supports the view that there are transient momentum/mean reversion occurrences in the market that a rebalancing process can capture. Finally, Daryanani found that the rebalancing benefits appear to reach a maximum for portfolios with 60% to 70% equity allocation.

Lee basically completed the same study but extended the range of tests. The results confirmed those of Daryanani. A 20% band with a short look interval (one to ten days) performed best. However, Lee also compared the performance of rebalanc-ing processes under two different scenarios for the US equity component: in one, it was fully invested in the Russell 3000 (45%), and in the other, it was split between the Russell 1000 (25%) and the Russell 2000 (20%). She observed that under those conditions, rebalancing processes that used a 25% threshold sometimes outperformed those based on a 20% threshold. However, this is one area where the literature fails. The issue with unconditional rebalancing methodologies should not be whether there exists a rebalancing rule that is superior to all the others all the time and in all circum-stances. This would be unrealistic. Rather, we want to determine what factors drive the performance of these different rebalancing methodologies and why some approaches may be more successful on average so that we can improve on them.

Thus far, we have avoided much of the literature on trading cost and its impact on rebalancing. This literature discusses the impact of fixed and variable cost on the appropriateness of rebalancing. In essence, it indicates that rebalancing should be con-sidered only if the gain that is expected from rebalancing covers its cost. Therefore, because of trading cost, there is a no-trading zone that should exist around the strate-gic benchmark. We are not going to spend much time on this aspect because, although it should be considered, it is now often irrelevant to many investors. Within an asset class, we advocate either the use of low-cost indexed investments or low-cost index protocols. Many of these investments do not require expensive rebalancing, even in a taxable account. Furthermore, it is expected that nonmarket-cap investment protocols will outperform traditional indexed investments by a margin that is much greater than the impact of facing earlier taxable capital gains. The transition of a portfolio from a specific asset structure to a very different one may require more attention, but this would have to be treated on a case-by-case basis anyway.

Among asset classes, there are also many ways to rebalance without facing signifi-cant costs. First, during an accumulation phase, new contributions can significantly reduce the cost of adjusting a portfolio. Second, even if the assets are invested in specific investment protocols, dividends and coupon revenues can often be invested temporarily in liquid and appropriate ETFs until the rebalancing within and among asset classes is synchronized. Third, for many investors (except maybe for very large institutional investors), ETFs have contributed to the reduction of the fixed/variable cost issue because ETF trading involves mostly fixed costs. Most of the time, underlying securities are not purchased or sold when an ETF is traded. The ETF unit and its contents are simply transferred from the seller to the buyer at a very low fixed cost. Fourth, even an investor that uses indexed protocols for most of his or her portfolio should retain some low-cost liquid investments, such as ETFs and low-cost indexed funds, for liquidity purposes and for rebalancing. Fifth, the use of a rebalancing process that incorporates tolerance bands around the strategic allocation target also reduces the cost of rebalancing. And sixth, although most investors wish to postpone taxation of capital gains for as long as they can, Daryanani found that the time value of money that is saved by postponing taxation is less than 10% the size of the benefits from rebalancing. I have come to similar conclusions in Chapter 9.

A Comprehensive Survey of Standard Rebalancing Methodologies

To complete the prior discussion and open the door to other more effective rebalancing alternatives, I completed a comprehensive study of unconditional rebalancing methodologies. Past research looked at either a few asset classes over long periods or at many asset classes over short periods. Different studies also tested different methodologies, which makes comparison and interpretation of results difficult. My study was completed using four time periods over more than 30 years, six portfolio structures, seven look intervals (from weekly to biannually), two trading concepts (calendar and threshold), two types of thresholds (constant and conditioned by asset price volatility) and two rebalancing targets (to the benchmark and to a tolerance band). The impact of global equity exposure limits was also evaluated. Each test profile was completed 12 times, since I used 12 different starting months to make sure that my results were not driven by the beginning and end months in the data samples. Table 7.6 summarizes most of those tests.

TABLE 7.6 Range of Tests on Rebalancing

Periods + 1- to 12-Month Lag	Portfolios	Look Interval (Weeks)	Type of Thresholds		Global Equity Limit
			Constant (%)	Volatility (Units of Standard Deviation)	
1981–2010	40/60 Components	1	0.0	0.25	No limit
1981–1990	60/40 Components	2	5.0	0.50	−10%/+5%
1991–2000	80/20 Components	4	10.0	0.75	for 40/60
2001–2010	60/40 Core	12	15.0	1.00	and 60/40
	60/40 Core	26	20.0	1.25	and
	80/20 Core	52	25.0	1.50	−10%/+10%
		104	None	2.00	for 80/20

For example, the first test period is the average of 12 30-year periods starting with January 1980 to January 2009 and ending with December 1980 to December 2010. This ensures that our results are not explained by the choice of specific start and end dates. Three equity/fixed-income asset allocations were used, but the core portfolios are solely based on the S&P 500 for equity and the 10-year Treasury for fixed income. The component portfolios are much more diversified. The equity portion of each portfolio is allocated between US equities, international equities, US small-cap and commodities. The fixed-income portion is allocated between the 10- and 30-year bonds. The first trading methodology is based on constant thresholds. For example, if a target allocation is 20% and the constant threshold is 5%, a rebalancing is triggered if the allocation of that component is outside a 19% to 21% range. The rebalancing can be triggered by any of the portfolio components. Notice that using a 0% threshold is equivalent to applying a calendar rebalancing methodology. Not applying a threshold is equivalent to allowing the allocation to drift continuously.

Finally, global equity limit (minimum and maximum) is considered on each portfolio. This constraint, if applied, supersedes any other constraint. For example, if the global equity allocation of a portfolio with a 40/60 target allocation goes outside the range of 30% (−10%) to 45% (+5%) at any look interval, a rebalancing is automatically triggered.

Seven variables are reported for each test: the geometric mean against a simple one-month calendar rebalancing (our base case), the volatility, the tracking error against a one-month rebalancing, the number of rebalancings per year and the average, lowest and highest equity allocation observed during the test period. I did not consider transaction costs initially. I first wanted to determine which methodology is preferable in the absence of transaction cost. Then I set out to determine how relevant transaction costs are to the recommended set of solutions.

Because of the large amount of data (thousands of simulations), I will concentrate on the most important observations. The periodic monthly rebalancing is used as a reference scenario. Therefore, the objective is not to determine the size of the diversification bonus, since it would already be embedded in the base case of monthly rebalancing, but to determine how much further the performance can be improved using other methodologies. Table 7.7a considers the calendar rebalancing first. The best performance was realized by semiannual rebalancing, although quarterly or annually also improved the performance against a monthly rebalancing. Rebalancing every two years is not recommended. Therefore, to profit from the momentum/mean reversion effects in the market, a range of three months to one year is advisable. The component portfolios benefited more from rebalancing than the core portfolio. It could be specific to the US market (core portfolio), or, more logically, it could be attributed to the expectation that rebalancing will work even better if there is a multitude of asset classes. Overall, the six-month calendar rebalancing added 11 to 15 bps per year to the component portfolios, but the impact on the core portfolios was negligible. I have not presented risk-adjusted performances because the relative impact of different rebalancing methodologies on volatility was insignificant. Volatility was even lower

TABLE 7.7a   Excess Performance: Six-Month Pure Calendar Rebalancing (bps)

Periods	Component Portfolios			Core Portfolios		
	40/60	60/40	80/20	40/60	60/40	80/20
30 Years	11	14	15	2	2	2
1980s	15	18	19	−2	−3	−2
1990s	−1	0	1	3	2	1
2000s	21	26	24	10	11	9

when the rebalancing frequency was less, since more infrequent rebalancing protected the portfolio even more in a downward equity environment.

The best performance under a constant threshold rebalancing usually occurs when a 20% to 25% threshold is used. As expected, the look interval becomes less significant. Anything below 12 months is appropriate. Furthermore, the performance is almost always superior to a pure calendar based rebalancing. Table 7.7b presents the results for the three-month look interval and 25% threshold. Again, performances are better for the component portfolio and for portfolios that have higher equity allocations, but the approach was not profitable for the core portfolio in the 1980s. Risk, again, was not a factor.

The volatility threshold also outperformed a monthly calendar threshold, but its performance was not any better than the constant threshold, possibly because the assets with the most volatility drive the relative change in allocation. Thus, so far, the results of this test are consistent with those of Daryanani and Lee. Constant thresholds are better than calendar thresholds. But although the two authors recommended short look intervals, I do not find the look interval to be a significant decisive factor as long as it is not greater than six to twelve months. Tables 7.7c and 7.7d present the average level and minimum and maximum level of equity observed for all horizons and portfolios.

TABLE 7.7b   Excess Performance: Three-Month Look Interval and 25% Threshold (bps)

Periods	Component Portfolios			Core Portfolios		
	40/60	60/40	80/20	40/60	60/40	80/20
30 Years	23	31	34	15	8	10
1980s	20	19	32	−17	−17	−3
1990s	22	36	36	31	35	16
2000s	31	38	36	27	18	28

TABLE 7.7c Average Total Equity Weight: Three-Month Look Interval and 25% Threshold (%)

Periods	Component Portfolios			Core Portfolios		
	40/60	60/40	80/20	40/60	60/40	80/20
30 Years	40.7	60.8	80.6	42.2	61.2	81.4
1980s	40.8	60.4	79.9	41.7	61.5	81.1
1990s	41.3	61.4	80.8	43.6	63.8	82.0
2000s	40.3	60.8	80.6	40.5	60.2	80.8

TABLE 7.7d Minimum and Maximum Total Equity Weight: Three-Month Look Interval and 25% Threshold (%)

Periods	Component Portfolios			Core Portfolios		
	40/60	60/40	80/20	40/60	60/40	80/20
30 Years	27.9/48.0	44.9/67.9	69.2/85.2	26.6/51.7	45.7/71.1	70.9/85.9
1980s	33.1/46.7	52.8/66.4	75.0/84.9	34.5/49,5	53.9/69.0	75.3/85.5
1990s	35.4/46.8	55.2/68.3	76.7/85.2	37.9/50.9	57.7/71.0	77.7/85.7
2000s	28.1/47.5	47.1/67.9	70.6/85.5	27.3/49.5	46.2/68.3	71.0/85.1

The impact of the 2008 credit crisis is apparent in Table 7.7d because this is the period where the minimum level of equity prior to rebalancing was at its lowest. For example, the 60/40 portfolio reached a minimum equity allocation of 47.1% during the 2000s, almost 13% below the target. Surprisingly, the volatility for each of these portfolios (not presented) was not substantially different from that of a portfolio with a monthly calendar rebalancing. This may occur for two reasons. First, a process that allows a deleveraging of the portfolio in bad markets is actually protecting the portfolio from the rising market volatility that often occurs in such an environment. The same process will allow equity weights to increase in good markets, but this is likely to occur in an environment where equity volatility usually remains at more normal levels. The tracking error against a calendar monthly rebalancing is also fairly small, usually at less than 0.75%. Finally, trading frequency is also minimal, at less than once a year on average, and a full rebalancing is slightly more profitable than a partial rebalancing.

As indicated in Table 7.6, I also tested the impact on performance of imposing total equity minimum and maximum limits. However, it did not change the overall conclusion. Constant thresholds of 20% to 25% remain preferable. Such results are possible because of the presence of momentum in asset classes. However, momentum alone is insufficient. In order to benefit from a performance effect related to momentum, we also need volatility. For example, I adjusted the data series of each asset in order to maintain the same GEO mean while reducing the volatility of each asset by half. This adjustment would not change the correlation between asset classes. Results indicate that if the volatility of the riskier asset is cut by half, the benefit of a constant threshold approach is reduced by a factor of three to six times. Thus, the benefits of constant threshold rebalancing increase with the volatility of the portfolio components. Although this may not be the best rebalancing approach, it is simple to implement and intuitively appealing.

Asset Allocation and Risk Premium Diversification

The objective of asset allocation is to appropriately diversify risk premiums in order to create a portfolio that is return/risk efficient and that meets the liability stream of the investor and his or her constraints. Most traditional portfolio allocations, such as the 60/40, are built around few asset classes and thus around few risk premiums, which limits the efficiency of the diversification process. This issue is even more problematic because risk premiums that are embedded in equity are significantly more volatile than those embedded in fixed income. To illustrate this aspect, Figure 7.2a illustrates the percentage of the total risk in a portfolio of equity and fixed income that is accounted for by equity if the allocation to equity ranges from 0% to 100%. The example assumes 16% volatility for equity and 6% for fixed income, and a correlation of either 30% or 0%.

At less than 20% allocation, equity already accounts for a majority of the total portfolio risk, and at 40% or 50%, it dominates total portfolio risk. This is why portfolios with 30/70 allocations often have higher Sharpe ratios than portfolios with 60/40 allocations. Furthermore, lower correlations actually increase the dominance of equity risk at high levels of equity allocation. Diversifying the equity risk geographically may not significantly reduce this issue because equity markets are highly correlated, especially during difficult environments. Thus, the investor in a traditional

FIGURE 7.2a Equity Weight and Equity Risk.

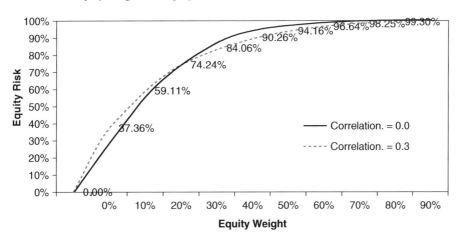

FIGURE 7.2b   Equity Weight, Equity Risk and Range of Volatility.

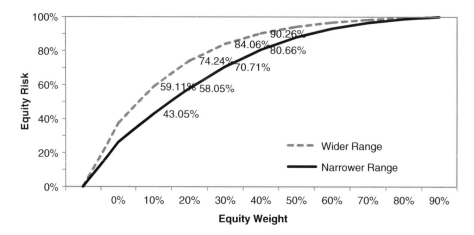

portfolio who wants more returns and is willing to endure more risk has often no other choice but to tolerate a higher concentration of equity risk.

Unless the investor is a great tactician and can anticipate bear markets in any asset class, the options available to reduce risk concentration (other than the leveraging and deleveraging of specific assets) have already been mentioned in Chapter 4. First, we can use asset components that have more similar risk, such as lower-volatility equity portfolios (which may have two-thirds to three-quarters of the volatility of normal equity) and fixed-income portfolios that have a longer duration and a more significant credit component than traditional indices (which may have one-quarter to one-third more volatility than a standard fixed-income portfolio). For example, Figure 7.2b compares the contribution of equity risk to total portfolio risk if the volatility of equity is 12% and that of fixed income is 8%, instead of, respectively, 16% and 6%. The correlation is assumed to be 30% in both cases.

This approach reduces the contribution of equity to total risk fairly significantly, and contributes to creating more efficient portfolios. For example, at 30% allocation to equity, the contribution of equity to total risk is reduced from 75.24% to 58.05%. Therefore, we have just illustrated that lower-volatility equity protocols bring another benefit to the process of portfolio construction: the potential for a more efficient global allocation. It may not resolve the entire issue of equity risk concentration, since among other aspects, investors would hesitate to implement fully such an approach, but it is another step in the right direction.

Second, we can attempt to build portfolios around a larger number of risk premiums and use a methodology that allows for a more balanced set of risk premiums. We will address this aspect from the point of view of BARRA, Bridgewater and hedge funds.

A third solution is to manage the contribution of specific asset classes to total portfolio risk through management of its volatility or of its tail risk. We will also find support for this approach. Finally, we can attempt to tailor the distribution of an asset classes through the use of options and other financial tools. However, as I indicated in Chapter 4, this approach will not be explored in details in this book.

Obviously, we can attempt to integrate all of these solutions into a single process. We can integrate more risk premiums, manage their contribution to total portfolio risk and integrate portfolio components that have volatility characteristics that will ease the process of building a more efficient portfolio.

The MSCI Barra Approach

Briand, Nielsen and Stefek of MSCI Barra Research Insights (2009) [10] made the argument that portfolios built on the basis of a diversification of risk premiums may be more efficient than the traditional 60/40 allocation. Most of the risk premiums used by Briand, Nielsen and Stefek in their analysis are similar to those found in the traditional equity and fixed-income literature on asset pricing (see Chapter 5). The authors divided risk premiums among three groups: asset class, style and strategy. Table 7.8 presents the list of risk premiums defined by Briand, Nielsen and Stefek. The style risk premiums are created by going long one risk premium and short another one. For example, the "value" risk premium is created by going long and short on value and growth equity components respectively.

Briand, Nielsen and Stefek only specified two categories of asset class risk premiums: interest rate and equity. Among style risk premiums, we recognize three premiums from the Carhart model: value, size and momentum. Three other premiums related to credit and yield curve are added. The strategy risk premiums, such as the currency carry trade, are also well-known among traders and hedge fund managers.

The authors compared the performance of a 60/40 portfolio of asset class risk premiums to an equally weighted portfolio of only style and strategy risk premiums over the period of 1995 to 2008. Table 7.9 illustrates that the diversified portfolio of style risk premiums generated greater excess returns with one-third the volatility of the traditional 60/40 portfolio, and had much smaller drawdowns. The effect of lower volatility on GEO mean can explain nearly 70% of the excess return of the strategy.

TABLE 7.8 List of MSCI Barra Risk Premiums

Asset Class	Style	Strategy
Equity US	Value = Value − Growth	Convertible Arbitrage
Equity EAFE	Size = Small-Cap − Large-Cap	Merger Arbitrage
Equity Japan	Momentum = World Momentum − MSCI World	Currency Carry Trade
Equity Emerging	Credit = Corporate AAA − Treasury	Currency Value
Fixed-Income US	High Yield = High Yield Corporates − Quality Corporates	Currency Momentum
	Term Spread = $(10^+$ Year Treasury$)$ − $(1$ to 3 Year Treasury$)$	

Source: Briand, Nielsen and Stefek (2009).

TABLE 7.9   Comparison Between 60/40 Portfolio and Equally Weighted Portfolio of Risk Premiums (1995–2008)

Statistics (Annualized)	60/40 Index	Risk Premia Index
Excess Return	2.2%	2.7%
Volatility	8.4%	2.8%
Sharpe Ratio	0.26	0.94
Maximum Drawdown	−30.6%	−11.8%

Source: Briand, Nielsen and Stefek (2009).

The great majority of investors would have been extremely satisfied to generate such a performance. Does this mean we should abandon the traditional portfolio model of asset class risk premiums to invest solely in a portfolio of style and strategy risk premiums, assuming this approach could even be sold to investors and investment committees? Not necessarily, but let's first consider the justification for these results.

Briand, Nielsen and Stefek indicated that correlations among style and strategy risk premiums are generally low. In fact, most of these correlations are below 0.25, although a few are more significant, indicating that some of these risk premiums are embedded in others. For example, the credit and high-yield credit risk premiums are strongly correlated. Thus, considering that most correlations are low, even an allocation process as simple as an equal-weight process would be statistically very efficient. Furthermore, the fact that some risk premiums are redundant (i.e., highly correlated) indicates we could still achieve an efficient portfolio even if we were using a less complete set of risk premiums. Nevertheless, such an approach is successful against a traditional portfolio partly because it allows for a much more efficient diversification of risk premiums. It is likely that no risk premium in this structure dominates total portfolio risk.

However, it is not obvious that investors are ready to apply such a process on a large scale. Isolating risk premiums requires the construction of long/short portfolios. It is operationally not that complicated, but it may still be difficult to sell the concept to investors and investment committees. Nevertheless, whether we feel comfortable or not with the MSCI Barra approach, their research illustrates that much work can be done, and must be done, to improve the allocation process before we should even think about building more complex and/or specialized portfolios of asset classes. Thus, instead of adding specialized products and investing with active managers who may or may not add to the performance of the portfolio, we should exploit more intelligently the simple but sufficient set of risk premiums that we are often already invested in.

The Bridgewater Approach

An argument could be made that although the size of the risk premium varies among asset classes, most asset classes should yield similar excess returns, adjusted for risk and liquidity over long horizons. Rational investors should require similar risk premiums per unit of risk on average. The assumption that absolute returns are not easily predictable and that the most reasonable expectation is for asset classes to yield similar risk-adjusted excess returns in the long term are the basic principles behind the All Weather product designed by Bridgewater Associates.

The objective of the All Weather program is also to deal with the traditional overconcentration of portfolio risk related to equity exposure. Whether we will agree or not that the All Weather concept offers all the qualities we should seek in an efficient portfolio, the underlying principles on which the product is built addresses many of the issues that we have discussed so far, such as overconcentration of risk in equities and the need to create a statistically more efficient diversification of risk premiums.

Bridgewater started with the principle that there are three sources of portfolio returns: the risk-free rate, the risk premiums that are being offered for taking Beta (market) risks and the Alpha generated by managers. However, although Bridgewater also manages a very well designed Alpha product (one of the few products that may be built around a true Alpha platform and does not offer Beta risks dressed as Alpha), they agree that, on an aggregate basis, Alpha is a zero-sum game, and that only Beta offers a relative certainty of generating excess returns in the long run.

According to Ray Dalio, the founder of Bridgewater Associates (2005) [11], there are fundamental issues with the process of building Beta portfolios. First, although there are many sources of Beta risks (global equities, nominal bonds, inflation-linked bonds, corporate spreads, emerging market spreads, real estate, private equities, commodities, etc.) Dalio argued that the Sharpe ratio of most of these asset classes is relatively low (0.2 to 0.3), while the volatility of some of these asset classes is fairly high. Thus, an investor who seeks a riskier portfolio has no other choice, within the traditional portfolio management context, but to allocate significantly to riskier asset classes such as equities. Therefore, the investor who seeks higher returns will end up with an overconcentration of his or her total portfolio risk in equities and private equities, and his or her portfolio will be anything but diversified.

Figure 7.3a illustrates the traditional relationship between return and risk. The graph is inspired by the work of Rocaton for Bridgewater (2005) [12], and although the data is dated, it is used for the purpose of illustrating Dalio's argument. According to this graph, commodities are not considered an efficient asset class. However, as we have seen in the first section of this chapter, an asset with a lower expected return (and, thus, a lower expected risk premium) can still benefit a portfolio through the rebalancing process.

We have explained previously that in order to benefit from low correlation among assets, we need these assets to have volatility. Furthermore, the diversification process will be more efficient if these assets contribute similarly to the overall risk of the portfolio. Figure 7.3b illustrates what the expected risk of assets in Figure 7.3a would be if all assets were leveraged in order to provide an identical expected return (in this case, 10%) and, thus, an identical expected risk premium.

FIGURE 7.3a   Expected Returns and Risk for Various Asset Classes.

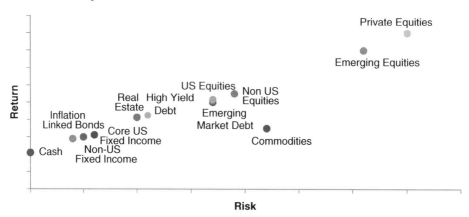

Source: Inspired by Rocaton for Bridgewater

FIGURE 7.3b   Expected Returns and Risk for Various Leveraged Asset Classes.

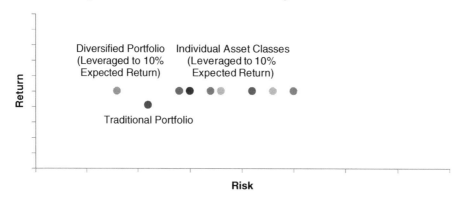

Source: Inspired by Rocaton for Bridgewater.

Since most asset classes are expected to have Sharpe ratios between 0.2 and 0.3, it is not surprising that the volatilities ranged from 15% to 25% in Figure 7.3b, instead of 5% to 35% as in Figure 7.3a. Much like the MSCI Barra approach, a combination of these assets should lead to a more return/risk-efficient portfolio than a 60/40 mix.

We also know that risk premiums are time varying. Thus, asset returns may be volatile because of changes in fundamentals, or because of a change in the price of risk, which may also be motivated by a change in fundamentals. Bridgewater assumed that there are four dominant regimes that will determine the long-term returns of asset classes: rising growth and rising inflation, rising growth and declining inflation, falling growth and rising inflation and falling growth and falling inflation. Their objective was to balance risk across all four types of environments, taking into account which asset classes performed best in each environment. The principle of this process is presented in Table 7.10.

TABLE 7.10 Balancing Risk Across Environments

	Growth	Inflation
Rising	25% of Risk	25% of Risk
	Equities	Inflation-linked bonds
	Emerging market debt spreads	Commodities
	Commodities	Emerging market debt spreads
	Corporate spreads	
Declining	25% of Risk	25% of Risk
	Nominal bonds	Equities
	Inflation-linked bonds	Nominal bonds

TABLE 7.11 Bridgewater All Weather versus Typical Allocation (1970–2005)

	Typical Portfolio	All Weather
Total Return	10.7%	10.7%
Excess Return	3.5%	3.5%
Risk	10.3%	5.4%
Sharpe Ratio	0.34	0.65
Worst Year	−30.3%	−7.5%

Source: Bridgewater.

A track record for the All Weather program since June 1996 is available. However, Table 7.11 presents a back-testing of the product calibrated to an expected return of 10% against a typical 60/40 allocation but for a much longer period of time (since 1970).

Bridgewater still expects All Weather to deliver a Sharpe ratio of 0.60. In an October 2010 presentation to the Commonwealth of Pennsylvania Public School Employees' Retirement System, they forecasted a net expected risk premium of 7.2% (after fees of 0.37%) on a targeted volatility of 12%. Over the past few years, many other firms (AQR Capital Management, Barclays, PanAgora Asset Management, Putnam Investments, First Quadrant, Invesco, BNY Mellon, SSGA) have been launching/proposing products that are expected to compete with All Weather, products that seek to allocate to asset classes on the basis of risk budgets.

Concluding Remarks on the MSCI Barra and Bridgewater Approaches

The traditional approach used in most investment products is to combine asset class risk premiums as the market (through standard indices) is offering them. The main weakness of this approach is that it does not lead to a diversified and balanced set of risk premiums. As we have seen, risk premiums can be divided into three groups: asset class, style and strategy. Style risk premiums are implicitly embedded within the risk premiums of specific asset classes. Although many risk premiums are available, the main issue is the ability to control the desired level of exposure to each one. To expand and control the allocation to specific risk premiums, we must extract them using portfolios of long/short positions combined with leveraging or deleveraging. Nevertheless, we can see that there are several options available to the investor to create more efficient static portfolios of risk premiums. Different portfolio management approaches seek to exploit the set of risk premiums in different ways.

The Bridgewater approach combines both asset class and some style risk premiums and uses, among other means, leverage to help achieve the proper balance of risk premiums. Although we explained the danger of leverage in Chapter 4, in the case of the All Weather program, it is used in a responsible manner. Highly volatile assets are deleveraged, while assets with low volatility are leveraged. Such a process will remain efficient from a GEO mean point of view.

The MSCI Barra approach puts more emphasis on style and strategy risk premiums and requires a greater use of long/short portfolios. Although Briand, Nielsen and Stefek's approach is conceptually interesting, it is likely that most investors would be uncomfortable allocating a significant portion of their portfolio to a concept that ignores the traditional asset class risk premiums, although the concept could be used to allocate an alternative segment within the global portfolio. Overall, these examples illustrate that the efficiency of a portfolio can be improved through a proper balance of risk premiums. All concepts are represented in Figure 7.4. We will see later on that portfolio efficiency can also be improved through proper management of the exposure to risk premiums over time, even if the contribution of specific risk premiums to total portfolio risk is not perfectly balanced.

FIGURE 7.4   Building Static Portfolios of Risk Premiums.

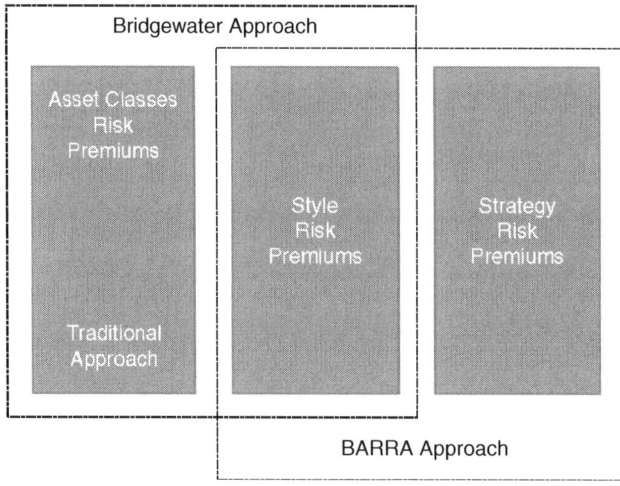

Ilmanen and Kizer (2012) [13] have further validated the vision of Briand, Nielsen and Stefek and Bridgewater. Ilmanen and Kizer demonstrated the validity of moving away from a strict asset class diversification toward a more balanced factor diversification. They argued that portfolio efficiency is determined by two characteristics: the efficiency of each asset class or style factor (for example, the Sharpe ratio) and the cross-correlations. However, not only are the Sharpe ratios of asset class risk premiums lower than those of style risk premiums, but their cross-correlations are significantly higher.

The authors compared two portfolios over the 1973 to 2010 period. The asset class portfolio has an equal-weight allocation to US stocks, non-US stocks, global government bonds and global nongovernment bonds, and to another component comprised of emerging stocks, small-cap stocks, commodity futures and global property stocks. All components are rebalanced monthly. The style-diversified portfolio has an equal allocation to four style premiums and to US large-cap equity. The average Sharpe ratio and cross-correlations within the asset class portfolio are respectively 0.40 and 0.38. Those values are 0.70 and −0.02 for the more efficient factor diversification. Overall, the Sharpe ratios of both portfolios are 0.48 and 1.44, a stunning difference. The style-diversified portfolio delivers smaller drawdowns, better recession hedging ability and better tail performance in bear markets. Finally, Ilmanen and Kizer found that an equal-risk approach, instead of equal weight, is even more profitable. We find more and more evidence of the necessity of diversifying efficiently.

Learning about Allocation from Hedge Funds

How many risk premiums do we need to achieve an efficiently diversified portfolio? To help answer this question, we will draw on the literature about hedge fund replication. Portfolio replication is a concept whose purpose is to reproduce the performance of complex portfolios by trading a smaller set of factors. Underlying the concept of portfolio replication is the idea that much of the performance of many portfolios can be explained by the most significant asset-based factors such as equity risk, interest rate risk, credit risk, etc. We saw an application of replication of mutual fund performance in Chapter 2.

Hedge funds are a particularly interesting case to study, even if an investor does not intend to invest in them. First, hedge funds are among the most complex portfolios that exist. As an industry, they incorporate just about every risk premium (asset, style and strategy). They also put more emphasis on the management of volatility. However, there is a debate about the true benefits of hedge funds—at least, of most of them. For example, many investors and specialists have made the argument that hedge fund returns incorporate two components: a Beta component related to standard market risk and an Alpha component related to the expertise of managers. However, others, such as Kat and Palaro (2006) [14], have argued that perpetual Alpha generation is impossible, since hedge funds operate in near efficient markets. According to them, what makes hedge funds of value to investors is not excess returns, but the return distribution. Therefore, the only value of hedge funds would be their ability to transform return distributions, and, thus, to offer a more efficient allocation and management of risk premiums. If Kat and Palaro were right, it would make hedge funds very expensive investment vehicles, considering their high fees, their liquidity constraints and the headline risks they pose to investors. This view would also be consistent with all that we have covered so far in this book.

If replication technologies were successful at replicating a large segment of hedge fund performance, it would mean that even complex portfolios of assets and of strategies could be replicated using few asset classes or risk factors. This would support our recommendation that investors would be better off improving their allocation process than adding complex and specialized portfolio components. Furthermore, it would also mean that Alpha is not a significant component of their performances, and that investors would be better off avoiding hedge funds as an asset class and limit their interest to the few and rare managers who can truly be expected to provide Alpha returns.

Our interest does not lie in the replication of single hedge funds. Single hedge funds, much like single mutual funds, have their own idiosyncrasies. The performance of every manager, whether good or bad, will have systematic (market) components and nonsystematic components. The nonsystematic component will be much greater in single hedge funds than in a portfolio of hedge funds. Fortunately, most investors want to hold a portfolio of funds to diversify single manager risk.

Hasanhodzic and Lo (2007) [15] used a simple linear model to replicate 1,610 single hedge funds belonging to 11 categories, including 355 funds of funds. They used only five factors: the S&P 500, the GSCI, Lehman Corporate AA Intermediate Bond Index, the spread between Lehman BAA Corporate Bond Index and the Lehman Treasury Index and a US dollar index. Regression coefficient factors were determined using 24-month rolling windows. Results clearly indicated that a significant portion of the performance of hedge funds is related to standard risk factors, but overall, results were not satisfactory since a large portion of returns remained unexplained.

However, these results are not necessarily caused by a faulty set of factors, or because hedge funds are not, in fact, replicable. It may be that the standard ordinary least square regression (OLS) approach based on rolling windows fails to capture the tactical asset allocation of hedge fund managers (Roncalli and Weisang (2008)) [16]. Furthermore, it is also possible that linear models fail to capture the non-observable dynamic trading strategies that result in nonlinear hedge fund return profiles.

Finally, there are two other issues that may impede hedge fund replication. First, hedge funds may exploit high-frequency trading strategies while replication is constrained by the monthly reporting frequency of most hedge fund returns. Second, many hedge funds invest in illiquid or less liquid markets (distressed debt, real estate, private equity, convertible securities). This means that several hedge funds may extract liquidity premiums that are not present in the liquid components usually used for replication. The presence of illiquid assets may also understate the true volatility of hedge fund portfolios when compared with their replication counterparts.

To allow for time-varying allocation to asset factors, and to better capture the asset allocation of hedge fund managers, Roncalli and Weisang used a Kalman filter. They also limited the exercise to the replication of hedge fund indices, not of single hedge funds, since replicating an index may average out much of the return noise present in single hedge funds. Although they tested several subsets of factors, I will only report the result for their basic six-factor model, which includes asset and style risk premiums: S&P 500, Russell 2000 minus S&P 500, Dow Jones Euro Stoxx 50 minus S&P 500, TOPIX minus S&P 500, 10-year Treasury and EUR/USD exchange rates. However, it is worth mentioning that incorporating an emerging-market equity component improved their results.

Roncalli and Weisang found that 75% of the performance of the HFRI Index over the period of December 1994 to September 2008 could be explained by the six-factor tracker, while another 10% could also be explained by an implementation delay that was related to the lag in reporting hedge fund performances. They also found that using nonlinear factors such as options were unnecessary in capturing the dynamic of hedge fund returns. Conceptually, this means that only 15% of the performance could potentially be attributed to Alpha, unless this so-called Alpha could be attributed to other risk factors: liquidity, strategy risk premiums, strategy related to higher-frequency trading, management of volatility, etc.

To answer this issue, Roncalli and Weisang created a portfolio of two components: a core component and a satellite component. The core component is made of the six-factor tracker. The satellite component is made of an equally weighted portfolio of the following illiquid assets and strategy risks:

- two real estate indices
- one venture capital index
- two strategy indices (a volatility index and a carry trade index)

The combination of the six-factor trackers and the above assets explained most of the performance of the HFRI index, despite the fact that the replication process did not incorporate any adjustment for a factor related to higher-frequency trading and despite the fact that the hedge fund indices that were being replicated often suffer from several biases that overstate their performances. In summary, the performance of an imperfect index of several hundred hedge funds that are active in more than 10 strategy groups and using distinctive management approaches was replicated using a core tracker of six standard components, and a satellite component of five indices related to illiquid assets and some well-known quantitative strategies.

In the end, this illustrates that a portfolio that combines exposure to large-cap equity, long/short positions between small-cap and large-cap, domestic versus foreign equity, interest rate, exchange rate, real estate, venture capital and volatility could pretty much replicate the performance of the most complex portfolios of assets, assuming that we can control the exposure to each of these risk premiums. Again, the greater Sharpe ratios of hedge funds may be explained by the flexibility given to hedge fund managers to manage their exposure to specific risk premiums through long/short positions and leverage.

This also raises one important question: What is it that investors expect from their hedge fund investments? Do they believe in their superior expertise, or are they looking for exposure to risk premiums to which they do not currently have access? Do investors realize that they are potentially paying significant fees, not to gain access to new risk premiums, but to invest in portfolios of risk premiums that offer a more efficient mix of the same risk premiums they are already exposed to? It is also possible that some of the excess performance of hedge funds is explained by their ability to increase the GEO mean through the control of volatility (i.e., by adjusting leverage). This illustrates again that investors should start paying more attention to their allocation process than to the possibility of adding more components to their portfolios. In the next section, we will explore ways in which an investor could substitute his or her hedge fund exposure and achieve the same overall portfolio efficiency at a much lower cost.

Volatility and Tail Risk Management

Over the past 10 years, numerous articles have discussed the benefits of managing portfolio volatility. There is strong evidence that volatility is, to some degree, predictable across a broad range of assets. Fleming, Kirby and Ostdiek (2001) [17] tested the portfolio benefits of targeting a fixed volatility using a simple methodology where expected returns are treated as a constant. Since return forecasts are known to be unreliable, this approach allows the variations in portfolio weights to be driven entirely by the conditional covariance matrix. Furthermore, the conditional covariance matrix was estimated using rolling data, which has some advantages because, if it is successful without using more sophisticated and complete models, it will provide a baseline for further improvements. The authors applied a test to a portfolio of stocks, bonds, gold and cash. Their benchmark was a static portfolio with the same average volatility as the volatility targeted by the conditional portfolio. They found volatility management to be economically significant and raised the possibility that part of the performance of hedge funds may be attributed to volatility timing.

Managing volatility becomes more complicated when two changes occur. First, incorporating more than two asset groups will necessarily require a more complex objective function than simply setting volatility at a specific level, such as maximizing returns (even if returns are treated as a constant) subject to some risk measures. It may also require the use of constraints to avoid solutions that may be undesirable from a policy standpoint. Second, risk models can also become more complex. For example, we may use functions such as copulas that describe dependence between random variables in a more exhaustive manner (than, for example, a simple measure of linear dependence, such as the Pearson correlation) and higher moments than simply standard deviation. The more precise our understanding of risk and dependence between sets of variables, the more efficient the risk-management process.

It may also be possible to improve on the risk-management process by using regime-switching models. Such models could still be based on simple normal (Gaussian) distributions described by two parameters (expected return and volatility), but these two parameters would change depending on the market regime we are assuming we're in.

The same goes for correlations, which could still be expressed by linear (Pearson) correlations. The number of predefined regimes is determined by what best fits the historical data. Because we do not know with certainty which regime we are in at any point in time, a transition probability matrix is required, which helps determine the likelihood of remaining in the current regime or of switching to another. Since volatility shows persistence, such models are likely to assume that the current assessment will also be persistent. Furthermore, if the model is based on three predefined regimes, it is likely that our assessments will attribute more weight to one or two of those regimes at any point in time.

I have cited two reasons for wanting to manage portfolio volatility. The first is that managing volatility improves the GEO mean, even if we could assume that distributions of asset returns are normal and dependence is linear. Second, we know that dependence breaks in crisis situations, and risky assets will become more correlated, while assets that are considered a safe haven may become less correlated. We have also observed that large drawdowns in risky assets usually occur when there is a significant spike in volatility. Thus, if volatility and dependence are predictable to some degree, volatility management will likely improve performance.

Papageorgiou, Hocquard and Ng (2010) [18] of Brockhouse Cooper presented a white paper on the issue of constant volatility management that used the approach described above. The emphasis of their approach was on the control of tail events using a constant volatility overlay strategy of long and short futures contracts. Papageorgiou, Hocquard and Ng used, as an example, a Canadian pension fund whose asset allocation to equity is 50% S&P/TSX, 25% S&P 500 and 25% MSCI EAFE. They observed over the 1990 to 2010 period three types of volatility regimes. The high volatility regime occurred 8% of the time, and equity performance was worst during those periods. The best equity performances were recorded during low volatility regimes. Those results are presented in Table 7.12a.

Papageorgiou, Hocquard and Ng tested the constant volatility approach by targeting 12% volatility and managing the entire distribution. Table 7.12b summarizes the statistics of both portfolios. The methodology was very successful at controlling tail risk. It allowed for efficient control over negative skewness and excess kurtosis. Brockhouse [19] provides regular updates of its approach and it remains effective.

Wang, Sullivan and Ge (2011) [20] also proposed a dynamic portfolio construction framework that determines asset weightings conditioned by changing market

TABLE 7.12a Volatility Regimes and Performances (1990–2010) (%)

	Low	Normal	High
Average Volatility	6	12	33
Frequency	47	45	8
Performance Annualized	19	12	−38

Source: Papageorgiou, Hocquard and Ng (2010).

TABLE 7.12b Descriptive Statistics of a Constant Volatility Strategy (1990–2010)

	Equity Portfolio	Constant Volatility
Annualized Returns (%)	7.48	8.36
Annualized Volatility (%)	14.53	11.80
Sharpe ratio	0.23	0.36
Skewness	−0.88	+0.15
Kurtosis	5.07	3.01
Drawdown Tech Bubble (%)	−43.32	−31.82
Drawdown Financial Crisis (%)	−48.10	−23.95
Worst Year (%)	−36.43	−17.53

Source: Papageorgiou, Hocquard and Ng (2010).

volatility and covariances. Their framework assumed two states of the world (normal risk and high risk), and their objective function consisted of maximizing expected return (they used a static return for each asset class) for a given target level of conditional value at risk (CVaR). Their tests showed significant outperformance and allowed the simulated portfolios to significantly reduce drawdowns. This indicates that a CVaR approach could be an acceptable alternative to a constant or range-bound managed volatility program. Opposing managed volatility and CVaR approaches is one of our objectives in Chapter 11.

Despite the intuitive appeal of regime-switching models, it remains to be proven that this approach is truly superior to others in all circumstances (Marcucci 2005) [21]. In fact, many methodologies could be used with relative success to forecast volatility and dependence. Each has its own pros and cons. For example, a RiskMetrics approach is easy to use and does not require any estimation. However, it does not allow for the mean reversion that is observed in volatility data, and may result in poor volatility forecasts for long horizons.

A GARCH model will express variance as a polynomial of past squared returns, where the conditional variances of the returns are not equal. The most widely used GARCH specification asserts that the best predictor of the variance in the next period is a weighted average of the long-run average variance, the variance predicted for this period, and the new information in this period that is captured by the most recent squared residual (Engle 2001). [22] Unlike a RiskMetrics approach, this process allows GARCH forecasts to eventually revert toward the long-run mean comparison. Mixed data sampling (MIDAS) is an economic regression that allows the predicted variable to have a lower frequency than the predicting variables, such as using daily data to make monthly forecasts. Contrary to a regime-switching approach, which requires a system of equations, MIDAS regressions involve a (reduced form) single equation. It is an easier approach to implement, and it is less prone to specification errors.

Although much of this discussion has been centered on the use of volatility, other variables could be integrated into the allocation framework. Jondeau and Rockinger (2008) [23] showed that allocating on the basis of all four moments of a distribution could potentially lead to risk-adjusted performance that is even better than volatility alone. Furthermore, I illustrated in Chapter 5 how specific factors, such as nominal interest rate versus nominal GDP growth, can be powerful indicators for asset allocation. For example, Arun Muralidhar of mCube has developed a process called SMART rebalancing that combines factor-based rules with discipline. Although many investors can probably identify the relevant investment factors by simply completing a proper review of literature, what is truly lacking among most investors is the discipline that can only come with a truly good understanding of the investment world, because discipline requires conviction. Although I do not intend to cover tools and processes such as SMART (for lack of time and space), they are essential in helping to enforce discipline because they empower the user with a greater understanding and transparency of their own process.

Combining a volatility-based approach with a process that uses factor-based rules can lead to a powerful allocation system. Tukington (2011) [24] built a regime-switching model that assumes two regimes for each of a set of four factors: equity, currency, inflation and economic growth. He then adjusted his target allocation to a set of 10 risk premia (upward or downward) based on how these risk premia have reacted historically to turbulent event regimes. Unfortunately, these approaches will not be covered in this book.

There is also one other approach that will not receive the attention it should: tailoring and "optimizing" the expected return distribution of an entire portfolio. Vinay Pande (formerly of Deutsche Bank) has done significant work on this methodology. The product is basically created as a two-step process. First, DCF models are used to evaluate the performance of several hundred financial instruments/risk premiums in all categories (equities, credit, rates, inflation-linked bonds, commodities, derivatives, etc.) under many single scenarios, which range from high-return favorable environments to geopolitical crises. Second, several of these instruments will be combined into a portfolio in order to achieve a return pattern (for all scenarios) that would be more acceptable to investors than investing, for example, in the S&P 500. Although this is a valuable approach, it is a very demanding process to put in place, and, thus, it is beyond the intended scope of this book.

Comparing Allocation and Rebalancing Methodologies

The MSCI Barra and Bridgewater strategies discussed previously are based on an assembly of risk premiums. Their objective is to improve portfolio efficiency by creating a more balanced set of risk premiums. However, this is not always possible. Therefore, even if a well-designed portfolio of asset classes may not allow us to specifically isolate (and efficiently balance) all style and strategy risk premiums (unless shorting is allowed), our previous discussion was meant to indicate that we can control the relative risk contribution of a more limited set of risk premiums by dynamically managing the total volatility of the portfolio. This approach would also answer some of Martellini and Milhau's (2010) [25] criticisms concerning the concept of most life-cycle products being offered to retail investors.

Martellini and Milhau found that the deterministic allocation process used in most of these investment programs is inefficient, and that changes in volatility should be considered. Again, such an approach could be even more efficient if shorting was authorized, but, as we will see later on, the portfolio performance characteristics can be improved even without shorting.

This section compares the performance statistics of several asset allocation methodologies. Two asset groups are used: a fixed-income asset group represented by 10-year Treasuries, and an equity group represented by a monthly rebalanced portfolio of 50% S&P 500, 40% MSCI Global and 10% MSCI Emerging. In the case of two asset groups, there can be only one allocation solution that leads to a specific volatility. If the number of asset groups increases beyond two, there is an infinite number of allocation solutions that lead to a specific volatility (unless we are looking for a minimum variance allocation) and it becomes necessary to maximize some objective function or add constraints. If we are successful with such a simple portfolio and simple approach, more complex portfolios and portfolio management processes could be considered, although simplicity has its advantages. Our reference portfolio is a 60/40 allocation. Table 7.13 compares the performance statistics of a number of allocation strategies against a rebalanced 60/40 portfolio. The allocation strategies that were evaluated are:

- a drifting portfolio;
- a control volatility portfolio whose volatility is equal to the average volatility of the 60/40 portfolio;
- a control volatility portfolio whose volatility is equal to the average volatility of the 60/40 portfolio, but whose allocation to equity is capped at 50% on the low side and 70% on the upside;
- a 30/70 portfolio leveraged to have the same volatility as the 60/40 portfolio; and
- a portfolio of five equally weighted risk premiums leveraged to have the same volatility as the 60/40 portfolio. There are two asset class risk premiums (fixed income and equity) and three style risk premiums (small-cap versus large-cap, value versus growth, and momentum).

There are many interesting observations and conclusions to be made from these results. First, as we expected, a drifting portfolio did not outperform a rebalanced portfolio. However, it is useful to specify that fixed income did outperform equity over this period by about 1.17% annually. Nevertheless, the performance spread was not significant enough to allow the drifting portfolio to outperform. Furthermore, despite the fact that portfolio weights in the drifting portfolio should have increased in favor of fixed income, the volatility of the drifting portfolio was still higher, mostly because equity significantly outperformed fixed income prior to the implosion of the technology bubble and contributed to its volatility. Again, it pays to rebalance, even if it is done using a simple calendar methodology.

TABLE 7.13 Statistics Portfolio and Portfolio Components (01/09/1990 to 09/08/2011)

	Excess Return (%)	Volatility (%)	GEO Mean to Volatility	Skewness	Kurtosis	Leverage
Basic 60/40	—	9.25	0.69	−0.34	9.58	1
Drift	−0.29	11.07	0.55	−0.36	9.21	1
Control Volatility	+0.81	9.25	0.77	−0.24	9.67	1
Control Volatility with Constraints	+0.96	7.96	0.92	−0.15	8.50	1
30/70 Leveraged	+3.01	9.25	1.03	−0.01	6.96	1.43
Risk Premiums Leveraged	+0.99	9.25	0.80	−0.34	8.83	0.90

However, all other allocation strategies outperformed the simple calendar rebalancing. The controlled volatility portfolios were created using a simple RiskMetrics methodology. Better results could be achieved using other models. Both of these portfolios (with and without constraints) generated excess returns beyond those that could be achieved with a fixed-threshold approach, despite the fact that we are only rebalancing using two asset groups (rebalancing within equity is still being accomplished with a fixed-calendar approach). It is also interesting that the constrained approach performed even better than the unconstrained. A constrained approach may actually protect us from excessively allocating to equity during low-volatility periods that may precede market meltdowns, or under-allocating to equity during high-volatility periods that may precede significant market recoveries. Furthermore, it also means that it is possible to market portfolio solutions to investors on the basis of a fixed-weight target allocation while applying a managed volatility allocation process.

Unsurprisingly, the leveraged 30/70 portfolio performed extremely well. This is expected because fixed income outperformed equity over the period, despite a much lower volatility (7.44% versus 15.72%). Furthermore, to achieve the required volatility, the portfolio had to be leveraged by approximately 43%. Thus, the actual allocation was 42.9% equity and 100.0% fixed income. The portfolio also benefited from the fact that leverage could be obtained relatively cheaply (because of the slope in the yield curve). We could also attempt to achieve similar results (in terms of risk distribution) by allocating 42.9% to equity and 57.1% to a fixed-income component whose duration would be slightly less than twice that of 10-year bonds. The decision to use leverage instead of a longer-duration component should be based on the slope of the yield curve, and it requires a scenario analysis. However, both approaches lead to a more appropriate contribution of both assets to the overall risk of the portfolio.

Finally, the equal-weight portfolio of five risk premiums also performed very well.

These examples illustrate two significant points. First, it is important to rebalance, and rebalancing by managing volatility is a far superior approach when compared to calendar or threshold rebalancing. Furthermore, it is also more consistent with the objective of delivering a more stable risk profile to the investor. Second, it is important to create a more diversified portfolio of risk premiums, and to have a more balanced risk contribution from these risk premiums. It is possible to improve the risk structure of the portfolio, even if shorting is prohibited, by properly designing the underlying portfolio components.

Risk Premiums, Volatility Management and Hedge Funds

If Kat and Palaro (2006) are correct in assuming that perpetual Alpha generation is impossible, many hedge funds (with the exception of a few true Alpha managers) would simply be providing a more balanced package of Beta risks with an overlay of volatility management at a high price. To provide support for this assumption, I have compared two portfolios. The first portfolio has a 45% allocation to both fixed income and equity, and a 10% allocation to hedge funds represented by the HFRX index (an investable index of hedge funds).

We rely on an investable index for the obvious reason but must remain aware that hedge fund indices have strong structural biases. These biases include end-of-life reporting biases (funds that stop reporting performance when returns go south) and backfill biases (funds that report performance retroactively after a strategy proves successful). Global Fund Exchange reports that the 16.45% compounded annual performance that was reported from the 3,500 funds in the Lipper TASS database between 1995 and 2006 falls to 8.98% when many of these biases are removed. Furthermore, this situation may have worsened because of the high attrition rate reported since 2008. The investable index has underperformed the non-investable index significantly every year since 2003 by an average of 560 basis points.

The second portfolio has the same allocation to fixed income and equity, but the 10% allocation to hedge funds is replaced by an equal-weight portfolio of three standard risk premiums, small-cap versus large-cap, value versus growth, and momentum. The allocation was scaled in order to produce the same volatility as fixed income. The strategy could have been scaled based on the volatility of the HFRX, but that seemed somewhat unfair since we are comparing a portfolio of only three risk premiums to an index of 250 funds. Furthermore, there is a fair amount of stale pricing in some hedge funds that helps to maintain lower apparent volatility. Interestingly, Table 7.14a shows that our very simple portfolio of risk premiums has similar correlations to fixed income and equity as do hedge funds.

Table 7.14b presents the comparison with and without the leverage adjustment. The risk-adjusted portfolio of risk premiums had to be deleveraged in order to achieve

TABLE 7.14a   Correlations to Fixed Income and Equity (04/2003 to 09/2011)

	HFRX	Risk Premiums Portfolio
Correlation to Equity	0.61	0.77
Correlation to Fixed Income	−0.16	−0.29

TABLE 7.14b   Statistics of Portfolio with HFRX and with an Assembly of Risk Premiums (01/09/1990 to 09/08/2011)

	Excess Return (%)	Volatility (%)	GEO Mean to Volatility	Skewness	Kurtosis	Leverage
HFRX	—	8.06	0.88	0.34	12.27	1
Risk Premiums	+0.27	8.91	0.83	−0.29	12.06	1
Risk Premiums Deleveraged	−0.04	8.45	0.84	−0.29	12.16	0.57

the volatility of fixed income. The gross return to volatility ratio of the portfolio remains slightly higher at 0.88, versus 0.83 and 0.84, but the difference is not so significant. Furthermore, it can be attributed to a higher portfolio volatility, which could be explained by a lesser correlation related to stale pricing, and obviously to a much more complex portfolio in the case of the HFRX. However, even if the correlation of the HFRX were less, most investors could not fully benefit from it since it would require constant rebalancing. Furthermore, a more diversified and more dynamic portfolio of risk premiums could certainly match the enhancements of the HFRX index. This raises questions about the benefits of introducing hedge funds within a portfolio. Again, the objective is not to argue that all hedge funds provide an assembly of standard risk premiums, but simply that it is unavoidable that most do, now that the industry has grown significantly in size.

Volatility Management versus Portfolio Insurance

The previous section was centered on the financial benefits of volatility and tail risk management. It showed that a more stable risk exposure might not only be beneficial to the investor from a pure risk point of view, but also from a return point of view. There is substantial literature related to portfolio insurance, more specifically concerning the use of option-based portfolio insurance (OBPI) and constant proportion portfolio insurance (CPPI). What are the nuances between volatility management (or VaR management) and portfolio insurance? There are four major differences: objective, pattern of exposure level to the risky asset, exposure triggers and cost to the investor.

The objective of portfolio insurance is usually to impose a portfolio floor value at a specific point in time. For example, if the current value of a portfolio is $100, the purpose of portfolio insurance could be to guarantee that the portfolio value five years from now does not fall below a percentage of the initial contribution amount. In the case of a principal-protected product, the floor level would be 100%. By comparison, volatility management does not impose a floor value at any point in time. It simply states that the asset allocation will be adjusted in order to maintain a predetermined level of volatility (or VaR) over a predetermined horizon. Although volatility management does not impose a portfolio floor value, the investor could infer from the level of targeted volatility the probabilities associated with specific returns over specific horizons. For example, assuming an 8% targeted annualized volatility, a 6% annualized expected return, a normal distribution and a monthly horizon, the investor could infer that there is a 2.5% probability of observing a return less than approximately −4.0% over a single month. Thus, the objective of the first approach is to manage a floor guarantee, while the objective of the second approach is to manage downside risk. We will see later on that these two very different objectives are likely to impose substantially different costs.

The pattern of exposure to the risky asset and exposure triggers are also different. With OBPI, the desired level of principal protection is achieved by either the combination of a portfolio invested in the risky asset with a put option, or the combination of a portfolio invested in a low-risk fixed-income asset with a call option on the risky asset. These two structures are essentially identical. The maturity and the strike of the option will determine the timing and level of the desired protection. The level of exposure to the underlying risky asset at maturity of the option is determined by the notional of the option and by the market price of the risky asset in relation to the strike price of the option. In the case of a call option approach, the exposure to the risky asset at maturity is as follows:

[Notional × Market Price / Strike Price] if market price > strike price

[Zero] otherwise

Prior to maturity, there are many other factors, such as time to maturity, funding cost, volatility and cash return on the risky asset that determine the level of exposure. The relation between exposure to the risky asset and market price against the strike price is nonlinear. It becomes linear (delta of one) as we approach maturity, unless the market price is very close to the strike price.

Perold (1986) [26] and Perold and Sharpe (1988) [27] introduced CPPI. The methodology first requires setting a floor for the portfolio value. This floor is basically the amount that would be required to achieve principal protection (or any level of desired protection) at a future date *if* all assets were invested in a low-risk fixed-income instrument until maturity. Thus, the level of the floor is a function of the horizon of the guarantee and level of interest rates. As maturity approaches, the level of the floor increases. It will be equal to the set amount of the guarantee at maturity. Furthermore, prior to maturity, rising (declining) interest rates will contribute to the reduction (rise) of the floor.

The difference between the portfolio value and this floor is called the "cushion"—the maximum amount by which the entire portfolio can be allowed to decline. The exposure to the risky asset is then determined by the size of the cushion multiplied by a multiple. For example, assuming assets of $100, a current floor of $80 (i.e., the current amount required to achieve principal protection "X" years from now if a low-risk asset was purchased), a $20 cushion and a multiple of five, the allowed exposure to the risky asset would be $100. Since the multiple might be constant (but not necessarily), the exposure to the risky asset over time will solely depend on the value of the cushion.

The cushion itself varies according to the value of the floor and the performance of the risky assets.

Similar to OBPI, CPPI can be implemented using two approaches. First, the portfolio can be invested more fully in the risky asset, and an implicit cushion calculation can be determined periodically. If the cushion diminishes, a portion of the risky asset would be sold to invest in the low-risk asset (and vice versa). The second approach consists of immediately buying the entire amount of the low-risk asset (required to achieve the capital protection desired at maturity), and using a funding mechanism to invest in the risky asset. This approach has the advantage of removing the uncertainty related to changes in interest rates, which may affect the floor.

However, our objective is not to debate the efficiency of CPPI versus OBPI. Both approaches target a similar objective but vary in implementation. Those interested in analyzing the nuances in expected payoffs can read Bertrand and Prigent (2002) [28]. We are more interested in the fundamental differences between CPPI/OBPI and the approaches related to volatility or tail risk management.

First, with CPPI and OBPI, market price fluctuations directly drive the exposure to the risky asset. Both approaches lead to an increase (decrease) in exposure after market prices have moved up (down). Buying after an up price movement and selling after a down price movement can become very expensive in a volatile environment. These transactions are what drive the cost of managing an option. With volatility management, the level of exposure to the risky asset is driven specifically by movement in volatility, and is only indirectly affected by movements in market prices (assuming we can infer a relation between market price and volatility). For example, although rising volatility would lead to a change in allocation, once the volatility is already high, new transactions are not necessarily triggered. Therefore, volatility management offers several advantages over principal protection in the long run:

- The cost of transacting is likely to be significantly less than with CPPI or OBPI. Volatility management does not necessarily require buying after a price rise and selling after a price decline.
- It allows for the potential of a greater GEO mean by stabilizing volatility.
- If volatility and correlations are persistent, volatility management is designed to exploit this information more efficiently.
- It allows investors to exploit the relation between volatility and returns in a stressed environment while allowing them to remain invested.

A managed volatility program will better serve a long-term investor as long as he or she can accept the absence of principal protection at specific intervals.

Closing Remarks

We have illustrated in Chapters 6 and 7 how investment processes can be used to significantly and persistently impact the long-term performance of a portfolio. In Chapter 6, we showed that asset class portfolios can be made more efficient by using assembly processes that can smooth price noise and exploit predictive variables that are related to long-term excess performance. We also showed that different processes can be used to manage the same asset class in order to combine assembly protocols that have different sensitivities to volatility regimes. In Chapter 7, we have demonstrated that the asset allocation process among asset classes can be made more efficient by using better rebalancing processes and by adding a larger number of more balanced risk premiums. Although we cannot say with certainty if a regime-switching approach is truly superior to other methodologies in all circumstances and for all horizons, the investor would still benefit from any approaches that manage risk. It seems that we are continuously reminded that exploiting the information in volatilities and dependence can impact performances at all levels of the asset allocation process. Chapters 8 to 11 will illustrate that risk management can play an even greater role than what has been discussed thus far.

Notes

1. Plaxco, Lisa M. and Robert D. Arnott (2002), "Rebalancing a global policy benchmark," First Quadrant.
2. The Consulting Group of Smith Barney (2005), "The art of rebalancing—How to tell when your portfolio needs a tune-up."
3. Pliska, Stanley and Kiyoshi Suzuki (2004), "Optimal tracking for asset allocation with fixed and proportional transaction costs," *Quantitative Finance* 4(2), 233–243.
4. Riepe, M.V. and B. Swerbenski (2007), "Rebalancing for taxable accounts," *Journal of Financial Planning* 20(4), 40–44.
5. Clark, Truman A. (1999), "Efficient portfolio rebalancing," Dimensional Fund Advisors Inc.
6. McCalla, Douglas B. (1997), "Enhancing the efficient frontier with portfolio rebalancing," *Journal of Pension Plan Investing* 1(4), 16–32.
7. Cao, Bolong (2008), "Testing methods and the rebalancing policies for retirement portfolios," Ohio University—Department of Economics.
8. Daryanani, Gobind (2008), "Opportunistic Rebalancing," Journal of Financial Planning 18(1), 44–54.
9. Lee, Marlena I. (2008), "Rebalancing and returns," Dimensional Fund Advisors.
10. Briand, Remy, Frank Nielsen, and Dan Stefek (2009), "Portfolio of risk premia: a new approach to diversification," MSCI Barra Research Insights.
11. Dalio, Ray (2005), "Engineering targeted returns and risks," Bridgewater.
12. Dalio, Ray, "Engineering targeted returns and risks," Bridgewater.
13. Ilmanen, Antti and Jared Kizer (2012), "The death of diversification has been greatly exaggerated," *Journal of Portfolio Management* (Spring), 15–27.
14. Kat, Harry M. and Helder P. Palaro (2006), "Replicating hedge fund returns using futures – A European perspective," Cass Business School.

15. Hasanhodzic, Jasmina and Andrew W. Lo (2007), "Can hedge-fund returns be replicated? The linear case," *Journal of Investment Management* 5(2), 5–45.
16. Roncalli, Thierry and Guillaume Weisang (2008), "Tracking problems, hedge fund replication and alternative Beta," SGAM Alternative Investments and University of Evry.
17. Fleming, Jeff, Chris Kirby, and Barbara Ostdiek (2001), "The economic value of volatility timing," *Journal of Finance* 56(1), 329–352.
18. Papageorgiou, Nicholas, Alexandre Hocquard, and Sunny Ng (2010), "Gestion dynamique du risque: Une approche par contrôle de la volatilité," Document technique, Brockhouse Cooper.
19. Hocquard, Aleaxandre, Nicolas Papageorgiou and Ralph Uzzan (2011–2012), "Insights corporate newsletter - Constant volatility strategy update," Brockhouse Cooper.
20. Wang, Peng, Rodney N. Sullivan, and Yizhi Ge (2011), "Risk-based dynamic asset allocation with extreme tails and correlations," Georgetown University, CFA Institute.
21. Marcucci, Juri (2005), "Forecasting stock market volatility with regime-switching GARCH models," University of California at San Diego.
22. Engle, Robert (2001), "GARCH 101: The use of ARCH/GARCH models in applied econometrics," *Journal of Economic Perspectives* 15(4), 157–168.
23. Jondeau, Eric and Michael Rockinger (2008), "The economic value of distributional timing," Swiss Finance Institute.
24. Turkington, David (2011), "Regime shifts and Markov-switching models: Implications for dynamic strategies," State Street Associates.
25. Martellini, L. and V. Milhau (2010), "From deterministic to stochastic life-cycle investing—Implications for the design of improved forms of target-date funds," Edhec-Risk Institute.
26. Perold, A. (1986), "Constant portfolio insurance." Harvard Business School, unpublished manuscript.
27. Perold, A. and W. Sharpe (1988), "Dynamic strategies for asset allocation," *Financial Analysts Journal* (January–February), 16–27.
28. Bertrand, Philippe and Jean-Luc Prigent (2002), "Portfolio insurance strategies: OBPI versus CPPI," GREQAM, Université Montpellier.

CHAPTER 8

Incorporating Diversifiers

Over the last decade, many investors have been disappointed with their equity investment, and, in the current low-rate environment, bonds are probably looking less and less attractive on a long-term basis. Thus, investors, both private and institutional, have turned to alternative investments. However, before we turn to other asset categories, it may be useful to remind ourselves of the qualities and characteristics we should be looking for in a new diversifier. Harry Kat (2006) [1] identified several questions that should be asked when considering a new diversifier. They are:

- What is the size of the risk premium? Is there one?
- How volatile are the returns?
- Are the returns skewed? Are they capped on the upside or downside?
- How certain are we of the answers to the above questions?
- What is the liquidity?
- Are the fees fair?
- What is the correlation and co-skewness to existing assets?
- What is the correlation and co-skewness to the liabilities?

In all honesty, when we consider the events of the last few years, we should also ask how certain we are of the level of liquidity, correlation and co-skewness. However, this chapter will deal with the conditions that would allow another asset class to be incorporated into a standard portfolio of equity and fixed income. We have shown that allocating to an asset class that offers a small risk premium can still be justified within a rebalanced portfolio if it acts as an efficient diversifier. We will discuss three diversifiers in Chapter 8: commodities, currencies and private market assets. We already discussed hedge funds in Chapter 7, and although there are doubts about their true value as a diversifier, my most significant objection is related to their excessive fees, especially in the current low-interest-rate environment. Some hedge funds may be appropriate on an individual basis, but the argument is more difficult to make now for diversified funds of hedge funds than five or ten years ago. Thus, before we turn to these other potential diversifiers, we will discuss first the issue of fees and second the required minimal qualifications of an asset class as a diversifier.

Finally, I do not intend to start a philosophical discussion about what is and what is not an asset class. For example, we could make the argument that hedge funds are an assembly of known risk premiums and strategies, and, therefore, do not constitute an asset class. For now we will simply accept the argument that if an asset is representative of an economically meaningful category, and if incorporating this asset can improve the risk-adjusted return of a portfolio in a meaningful way, then we will consider this asset to belong to an asset class, or, at least, an asset group to be considered on a stand-alone basis from an asset allocation and rebalancing point of view.

Fair Fees

According to Kat (2006), one of the requirements of a good diversifier is a reasonable management fee. When it comes to fees, common sense should prevail. The issue of fees is obviously relevant to retail investors. In Chapter 1 I compared the impact of fees on the relative cumulative returns of expensive and low-cost investment solutions, and found this aspect to be potentially very significant. Fees are also relevant to more wealthy investors and institutions.

Let's consider the case of hedge funds. Hedge funds usually charge fixed fees of 1% to 2%, and performance fees of 20%, often with no minimum hurdle rate. Assuming that we expect equity to deliver a return of 7%, how much gross return should a hedge fund generate to deliver the same expected return as equity if fixed fees are 1.5%? The answer is 10.25%, or 3.25% more than the expected performance of equity. An investor in a fund of hedge funds would need even more, perhaps as much as 12.0%.

Although such a performance may be possible on a case-by-case basis, it is unlikely that it could be achieved with a diversified portfolio of hedge funds, especially considering the significant changes to the structure of the industry. For example, in the 1980s and 1990s, the industry was dominated by long/short equity funds during a time when equity performed strongly, but also by global macro managers whose business model was fairly unique. As the number of hedge funds grew to 9,200 at the end of 2010, and net assets reached nearly $2 trillion, more and more new strategies developed around standard risk premiums (credit, liquidity, volatility, etc). As with the mutual fund industry, the larger a particular segment of the financial industry becomes, the more difficult it is to extract value from other investors on an aggregate basis, and the more similar to the market this industry becomes. Therefore, it is now more difficult to believe in the ideals of Alpha creation and low sustainable correlations, and easier to be convinced that most hedge funds simply offer a different packaging of Beta risks. This is why replication is possible, and why the evidence of hedge fund excess performance is so mixed, especially in light of backfill and survivorship biases in the reported performance data [2]. Normally, as the ability of the industry to deliver true Alpha and low correlations is curtailed, fees should decline.

In 2011, I had a discussion with an expert in the private equity area related to infrastructure investments. The discussion was centered on the types of investment vehicles that could be used to access the infrastructure market. For example, investment in a primary fund can be very expensive. Fixed fees of 1% to 2% are common, often excluding the cost of running the funds. Performance fees of 20% are also common, although a hurdle rate is usually applied. Therefore, in order to show investors expected net returns that are attractive, the managers of these funds must invest in riskier, more leveraged assets. High fees usually lead to higher financial risks.

More recently, Simon Lack (2012) [3] completed a devastating analysis of hedge fund gains attribution since 1998. Although the industry posted positive yearly gains on average, the greatest returns occurred when the industry was much smaller (assets were only $143 billion in 1998) while the tremendous losses recorded in 2008 occurred just after the industry had peaked in size ($2.1 trillion). Thus, according to Lack, in dollar terms, investors only captured $9 billion in gains, while managers and advisors collected $440 billion in fees. This again illustrates that the hedge fund industry of today has matured and does not have the same potential that it did, on average, when it was much smaller.

It is surprising how many investors do not challenge the idea of paying substantial fees for some investments, but they will question, for example, more forcefully the idea of not using a cap-weight benchmark or of using a dynamic volatility-based allocation process. A global equity manager once told me that he could not convince a large pension fund to invest in a nonmarket-cap equity protocol because, after the liquidity crisis, the management of that pension fund had publicly positioned itself against active management and in favor of index (market-cap) products. However, this particular organization is heavily invested in products that require substantial management fees and active management, such as hedge funds.

Investors should constantly remind themselves that fees are certain but excess return is not. They should evaluate these fees in relation to the size of the risk premiums being offered on the asset class, and simply refuse to pay excessive fees. Investors can no longer afford to pay 3.25% in fees for an assemblage of standard risk premiums in the current low-interest-rate environment, and they should not assume that superior expertise would eventually cover high fees. Reasonable fees must be paid to access true Beta risks or true Alpha expertise (assuming it even exists on a significant scale), not standard Beta risks packaged as Alpha.

Risk Premium and Diversification

The expectation of long-term excess return (above the risk-free rate) on an asset class can only be assumed in the presence of a risk premium. The risk premium is a reward and incentive for taking risk, but it is not a guarantee that an excess return will be realized. For example, let's assume that an investment promises a single cash flow a year from now, and that the value of this cash flow is $100. The cash flow is certain. Therefore, if the yield required on a riskless investment is 2%, the price an investor would pay for this cash flow is $98.04 ($100/1.02).

Let's remove the certainty assumption and assume a 50% probability of realizing either a cash flow of $110 or $90. Although the expected cash flow is still $100, the investor will require a risk premium to compensate for this uncertainty. If the risk premium was 3%, the investor would pay $95.24 ($100/[1.02 + 0.03]) for this investment. Although, the investor now has a 50% probability of realizing a gain of $14.76, he or she also has a 50% probability of realizing a loss of $5.24. Despite the existence of a risk premium, the investor can still realize a loss.

No investment can guarantee an excess return beyond the risk-free rate. First, we have to accept the presumption that a risk premium exists. In the case of fixed-income investments, the total risk premiums (credit, liquidity, etc.) are easily identifiable. Standard nominal corporate bonds with maturities similar to sovereign bonds will usually trade at higher yields to maturity, although the credit quality of many sovereign issuers is now in question. Since equities have no maturity and no fixed cash flows, it is much more difficult to evaluate the size of the risk premium that is required by investors at any point in time. But, the existence of a risk premium is also undeniable because there is no incentive other than an investment purpose to hold equity. In both cases (fixed income and equity assets), investors must be compensated for the risk of adverse performance. However, not all assets necessarily offer a risk premium.

Second, even if the investor requires a risk premium commensurate with the risk, the unfavorable scenario may still occur and the investor will realize a loss. Third, the investor could improperly estimate the required size of the risk premium. For example, he or she might have improperly estimated the probabilities of different scenarios (some relevant scenarios might have even been ignored) or he or she could have improperly evaluated the payout specific to each scenario. Fourth, there is the issue of time-varying risk premiums. Therefore, the risk premium might have been satisfactory to the investor when the investment was made, but other market circumstances might have caused the risk premium to increase, creating a capital loss.

Investing in an asset that offers a substantial risk premium is desirable but not necessarily essential in a portfolio context if it offers strong diversification potential and if the portfolio is rebalanced and managed using an efficient methodology. As we saw earlier, lower volatility portfolios benefit from a smaller drain of their GEO mean, and a rebalanced portfolio can still benefit from an asset that offers a lower risk premium if it is a good diversifier.

Let's assume that an investor owns a balanced portfolio of fixed income and equity, and ponders the possibility of incorporating a third asset class. Let's also assume that the new asset class has the characteristics described in Table 8.1a. We will assume that this new asset class is commodities. Currently, the investor has an equal allocation to fixed income and equity, but he or she considers a 10% allocation to commodities. The investor adjusts the allocation of fixed income and equity in order to maintain approximately the same current volatility. Table 8.1b shows what the expected portfolio risk premium and volatility would be under each option, assuming that commodities don't offer a risk premium.

In this example, in the absence of a risk premium, introducing commodities would not significantly modify the expected portfolio return and its volatility. However, if we

TABLE 8.1a Characteristics of Asset Classes

	Fixed Income	Equity	Commodities
Risk Premium (%)	1	4	Unknown
Volatility (%)	8	20	20

Correlations			
	Fixed Income	Equity	Commodities
Fixed Income	1	0.30	−0.20
Equity		1	0.00
Commodities			1

TABLE 8.1b How Large of a Risk Premium Is Required? (%)

	Base Case	Scenario
Allocation*	50–50–0	54–10–36
Expected Excess Return	2.50	2.52
Volatility	11.83	11.81

*Fixed Income–Equity–Commodities.

were to assume that commodities do offer a risk premium, even a small premium, in this case, one could argue in favor of adding commodities to a portfolio.

This example raises another question. To improve our GEO mean, are we indifferent to the choice between a risk premium and superior diversification benefits? The potential gains from both are uncertain. It is often very difficult to measure the size, or even, in some cases, to prove the existence of a risk premium. The existence of a risk premium on some asset classes is measurable and undeniable (corporate bonds). For other asset classes, a risk premium cannot be directly observed, but the presumption of its existence is also undeniable (equities). Finally, there are cases in which we can only attempt to prove the existence of a risk premium empirically, but we will never be able to prove its existence without a reasonable doubt (commodity futures).

We would obviously prefer to have the relative certainty that an asset class offers to both a risk premium and diversification benefits, but if we are in doubt, this understanding may influence if and how this asset class should be used. For example, we may be more comfortable introducing an asset that offers a small expected risk premium if the portfolio management process exploits efficiently the diversification benefit of this asset. Therefore, the relevance of an asset class within a portfolio should never be determined without consideration for the portfolio allocation and rebalancing process.

Commodities as a Diversifier

In 2006, a senior consultant at Watson Wyatt told the *Financial Times*:

> Commodities are a relatively easy asset class to understand and to invest in, so they provide low-hanging fruit for pension funds' diversification purposes [4].

In fact, the more we learn about commodities, the more complex the asset class appears. There is even a distinctive possibility that much of what has been published to convince investors to invest in commodities is based on flawed research, inappropriate conclusions or a no-longer-appropriate historical context. This does not mean that commodities are not an interesting asset class, but how and how much (if at all) one invests in commodities should be based on an understanding of stylized facts (what we know with great certainty), not spurious and incomplete results. It is important to understand commodities for two other reasons. First, studying commodities can serve to illustrate how easy it is to make a favorable argument for an asset class based on insufficient information. Second, an understanding of the source of returns in this market will help to understand other portfolio allocation issues and build a better global allocation process.

Do commodity futures offer a risk premium? Unfortunately, there is no single theory/model that can convincingly explain the pricing of commodity futures and prove beyond a reasonable doubt that a risk premium can exist in a market where all positions sum to zero. It is even likely that all commodity futures are not sensitive to the same pricing factors. Nevertheless, we have to start with the most well-known theories and some basic understanding of the sources of returns before we can move forward on an approach to commodities.

The difference between the initial and final futures prices determines the excess return that is generated on a long commodity futures position. Since futures contracts do not require a cash outlay (we will ignore the issue of posting margins to simplify the argument), the total return on a commodity investment is equal to the following:

$$\text{Cash Return} + (\text{Final Futures Prices} - \text{Initial Futures Price}) \qquad (8.1)$$

Since we are interested in the possible presence of a risk premium, we will ignore the cash component in order to concentrate on the excess return generated by the futures position. When the futures price is greater than the spot price, the contract is said to be in contango. However if a futures price is less than the spot price, the contract is said to be in backwardation. Why should a contract be in contango or in backwardation? Let's look at the main theories on commodities.

The Theory of Normal Backwardation

According to Keynes's (1930) [5] theory of normal backwardation, the futures market is a risk-transfer mechanism. Keynes argued that the commodity market allows operators to hedge their exposure to potential price fluctuations by selling futures contracts. Since hedging is a form of insurance, hedgers would have to pay investors a compensation for taking the price risk related to commodity futures, hence the existence of a risk premium. Therefore, the theory stipulates that the futures price of a commodity should be less than the expected spot price for that same commodity. More specifically:

$$F_{t,T} = E_t(S_T) - RP_{t,T} \tag{8.2}$$

The current price (F) of a futures contract of maturity (subscript T) is a function of the current expectation for the spot price minus a risk premium (RP_t). Since the risk premium reduces the value of the futures contract, the assumption is that long-term investors would, on average, benefit from the discount on the expected spot price and capture a risk premium. However, it is difficult to prove the existence of a risk premium without a doubt when both components of the equation, the expected spot price and the risk premium, are unobservable. Furthermore, if investing in the futures contracts of a specific commodity over a long period did provide an excess return, it could also be attributed to a market that systematically underestimated the expected spot return, not necessarily because of a risk premium.

For example, let's consider a scenario where the spot price for a single barrel of West Texas Intermediate (WTI) oil is $80, and the futures price is $81. This futures price could be the result of an expected spot price at maturity of $82 minus a required risk premium of $1. Since the futures price at maturity will be equal to the spot price, if the observed spot price at maturity is really $82, the investor will realize a $1 gain. However, even assuming this theory is appropriate, we can neither observe the risk premium of $1 nor the expected spot price of $82. As far as we know, the futures price may be $81 simply because the expected spot price is $81 and there is no risk premium. Table 8.2 summarizes these two scenarios.

Let's now consider that the market has underestimated the spot price at maturity, and that it is $83. The investor who bought the futures contract at $81 will make a $2 gain, and he or she could be duped into believing that this gain is partly attributed to a risk premium, when, in fact, the increase in spot price was caused by an unexpected change in oil supply dynamics. Furthermore, since expected changes in the price of a commodity are already priced into futures contracts, in the absence of a presumed risk premium an investor can only realize an excess return if the spot price rises by more than the current expectation. Thus, to reinforce this aspect and make sure it is well understood, an investor should not buy commodity futures

TABLE 8.2 Structure of Futures Prices ($)

	Scenario 1	Scenario 2
Expected Spot Price	82	81
Expected Risk Premium	1	0
Futures Price	81	81

because he or she expects the spot price of the commodity to increase, but because he or she expects the spot price to be greater than what is already reflected in the futures price.

Therefore, a historical excess return, even over a long period, is not necessarily indicative of a risk premium. However, according to the theory of normal backwardation, the futures price must, on average, be set at a discount against current spot price (because of the presumed existence of a risk premium). Thus, according to this theory, commodities should be in backwardation more often than not.

There is something conceptually incomplete with the theory of normal backwardation because it is based on the assumption that hedgers (such as commodity producers) usually hold a long position in the physical commodities and are net sellers of futures contracts. However, hedgers could easily be net buyers of physical commodities (such as a firm like GM that needs aluminum for its cars), and consequently be net buyers of futures contracts. This possibility led to the hedging pressure theory of Cootner (1960) [6] and Hirshleifer (1990) [7].

The Hedging Pressure Theory

According to this theory, it may be perfectly normal to observe commodities in contango (futures price greater than spot price) and in backwardation (spot price greater than futures price) and still make an argument for the existence of a risk premium. For example, the futures price could be greater than the spot price, and a risk premium would still be present. Furthermore, the same commodity could move from contango to backwardation and vice versa.

As we have already discussed, hedgers could be net short futures contracts and in need of a net long investor group. In this particular scenario, there would be downward pressure on futures prices, and commodities would be much more likely to be in backwardation. However, hedgers could also be net long futures contracts and in need of a net short investor group. In this second scenario, there would be an upward pressure on futures prices, and commodities are much more likely to be in contango.

In both cases, the investor group that fills the void could be paid a risk premium. In the first case, a positive risk premium exists because net long investors acquire long futures contracts at less than the expected spot price. In the second case, a negative risk premium would exist because net short investors sold futures contracts at more than the expected spot price. Thus, this theory is consistent with having some commodities in contango and some in backwardation, and also with having commodity futures switch from contango to backwardation and vice versa. But is the hedging pressure theory a valid one? It remains a difficult theory to test for the same reasons as I outlined before: the expected spot price and risk premiums are not observable. Furthermore, I doubt that Keynes, Cootner and Hirshleifer ever envisioned a world where investors and speculators would represent many times the trading volume of hedgers.

The Theory of Storage

Kaldor (1939) [8] and Brennan's (1958) [9] theory of storage focuses on the impact of inventories on commodity futures pricing. More specifically:

$$F_{t,T} = S_t(1 + r_t) + w_t - c_t \qquad (8.3)$$

Equation 8.3 is an arbitrage process between spot price and futures price. Basically, the futures price is equal to the spot price of the commodity, adjusted for the cost of funding the physical commodity, plus the cost of storage (w), minus a term called the convenience yield (c). Therefore, in a high-interest-rate environment, the futures price should increase in relation to the spot price. The futures price of commodities, which are more expensive to store, should also be higher. The convenience yield requires more explanation.

The convenience yield is a form of risk premium that is linked to inventory levels. If the inventory level is very high, it is unlikely that a production disruption will affect prices. However, the reverse is true if the inventory level is low. Furthermore, disruptions are more likely to occur for hard-to-store inventories than for easy-to-store inventories.

Gorton, Hayashi and Rouwenhorst (2007) [10] studied the potential link between inventory level and the term structure of futures prices using data on 31 commodities from 1969 to 2006. They used publicly available information on inventory levels to evaluate if backwardated or contango term structures of futures prices can be linked to inventory levels. One hypothesis is that low inventory levels are consistent with backwardation and higher inventory levels with contango. Another hypothesis is that commodity price volatility should be higher in a low-inventory environment, and hedgers would be willing to pay more for insurance.

Gorton, Hayashi and Rouwenhorst, and others, do find evidence of a link between inventory levels and the term structure of futures prices, but not between positions held by traders and the term structure, which they measured using the data on positions of large traders published by the US Commodity Futures Trading Commission (CFTC). These data segment the market between commercial users (assumed to be hedgers) and noncommercial users (assumed to be investors/speculators) of commodity futures. Thus, they reject the validity of the hedging pressure theory and provide stronger support for the theory of storage. The evidence also supports the heterogeneous characteristics of commodities. For example, the term structure of prices is very sensitive to inventory levels for energy-related commodities, while the sensitivity appears much more muted for easy- and cheap-to-store commodities such as industrial metals. After further tests, they also concluded that sorting commodities according to the spread between spot and futures prices primarily captures time variation in futures returns associated with time variation in inventories.

A more recent study by Basu and Miffre (2010) [11] tested the hedging pressure theory using the same data source on traders' positions as Gorton, Hayashi and

Rouwenhorst, but with a different methodology. As is often the case with studies on commodity futures, their results contradict Gorton, Hayashi and Rouwenhorst because they did find support for the hedging pressure theory and concluded in favor of a time-varying risk premium. Again, the literature is not conclusive.

The Capital Asset Pricing Model

Grauer and Litzenberger (1979) [12] developed a commodity-based version of the CAPM. However, the CAPM is a *capital asset* pricing model, and as we have already explained, a commodity future is not a capital asset—it is normally a hedging instrument in a market where all positions sum to zero. It is far from obvious that the CAPM is an appropriate pricing model.

Is There Any Empirical Evidence of a Risk Premium in Commodity Futures?

The economic function of securities is to raise financial resources for an entity, whether it is a firm, a government, a trust, etc. Investors bear the risk that expected cash flows generated by their investment might be less than expected, and the claims of investors are discounted to take into account the time value of money and a risk premium. Therefore, the existence of a risk premium is usually not in question for almost all asset classes.

As I have already indicated, attempting to prove the existence of something that cannot be observed is an empirical issue. It becomes even more complicated when it is recognized that the risk premiums of most asset classes are time varying, and, in the case of commodity futures, could be of different signs (positive and negative risk premiums). Furthermore, can there be a risk premium in a market where all positions sum to zero? For example, in the equity market, the sum of all long and short positions is still the market capitalization of that market. In the futures market, long positions are always equal to short positions.

There is much contradiction in the empirical literature on the issue of commodity risk premiums. Let's start with the CAPM. According to the CAPM, a risk premium should only exist in the presence of risks that cannot be diversified. Dusak (1973) [13] found that average returns and Beta for grain futures are both about zero. Bodie and Rosansky (1980) [14] found that all but one of 23 commodity futures from 1949 to 1976 had positive mean returns but mostly negative Betas. According to this evidence, commodity futures have either no risk premium or a time-varying risk premium, or the CAPM is simply not an appropriate model for commodities, or the market portfolio is ill defined.

There is also little evidence that supports the theory of normal backwardation. Kolb (1992) [15] studied 29 commodities and concluded that only seven appeared to offer a risk premium over the period: three of these commodities were in contango and four in backwardation. This evidence goes against the view that backwardation should be the norm. Furthermore, Deaves and Krinsky (1995) [16] speculated that some of the evidence of a risk premium may simply be due to trends in real spot prices, and therefore to persistent one-sided pricing errors. This possibility should not be overlooked when we consider how consistently inaccurate and overstated forecasts of interest rates and inflation have been over the past 20 years. It can happen.

Many studies of commodities have been conducted, but some of the most pertinent studies were those of Kat and Oomen (2006a, 2006b) [17], Gorton and Rouwenhorst (2006) [18], Gorton, Hayashi and Rouwenhorst (2007), Erb and Harvey (2006) [19] and, finally, Basu and Miffre (2009).

What is so interesting about the Gorton and Rouwenhorst and Erb and Harvey articles is that both were published side by side in the same issue of the *Financial Analysts Journal*, but their conclusions about investing in commodity futures could not be more different. Gorton and Rouwenhorst studied the long-term performance of an equal-weight index of (eventually) 36 commodity futures over the period of 1959 to 2004 and concluded that this index offered a risk premium similar to equities with less volatility and positive asymmetry. However, using the same data over the same period, Erb and Harvey concluded that commodities do not offer a risk premium. As we would expect, the Erb and Harvey study did not receive the same attention as the Gorton and Rouwenhorst study, which was used by consultants to justify investing in commodities. How do we explain how two studies by credible researchers could come to such different conclusions?

As indicated, Gorton and Rouwenhorst (2006) used an equally weighted index of commodities using monthly data over the period of 1959 to 2004. The concluded that commodity futures outperformed the physical commodities by 2.32% annually on average (9.98% versus 7.66%), and that the excess return on commodity futures at 5.23% almost matched that of equity at 5.65%, despite a lower volatility. From their analysis, the authors concluded the following:

- There is a risk premium in commodities, and this premium is statistically significant.
- Compared to equities, commodities have offered similar returns, but the volatility of equity is greater than that of their commodity index.
- The commodity index has positive skew, whereas equity displays negative skew.
- Both equity and commodities have excess kurtosis.
- Commodity futures are negatively correlated to stocks and bonds, and the negative correlation tends to increase with the length of the holding period.
- Commodity futures are positively correlated to inflation (expected and unexpected), and the positive correlation tends to increase with the length of the holding period, whereas bonds and equity display a negative correlation to inflation.

Although the negative correlation of commodities to equity and fixed income could be explained by the positive correlation of some commodities to inflation, when the portion of returns linked to inflation is isolated, the residual returns of commodities are still negatively correlated. A popular explanation is that the performance of equity, fixed income and commodity futures varies according to the business cycle. Table 8.3 illustrates the performance of these three asset classes according to the business cycle.

TABLE 8.3 Average Returns of Commodities by Business Cycles (1959–2004) (%)

	Fixed Income	Equity	Commodity Futures
Expansion	6.74	13.29	11.84
Early	9.98	16.30	6.76
Late	3.63	10.40	16.71
Recession	12.59	0.51	1.05
Early	−3.88	−18.64	3.74
Late	29.07	19.69	−1.63

Source: Gorton and Rouwenhorst (2006).

These results indicate that, on average, commodity futures and equity behave similarly during recessions and expansions, but far differently according to the stage of recessions and expansions. Commodity futures outperformed in the late stage of an expansion and the early stage of a recession, while they underperformed in the early stage of an expansion and the late stage of a recession. Part of the justification for this pattern is that commodity prices are much more sensitive to the current economic environment, while stocks are driven more significantly (than commodities) by longer-term prospects. If this relative pattern was persistent, commodity futures would indeed prove to be a powerful diversifier, especially if these diversification benefits were exploited efficiently. Based on this research, many would conclude that commodity futures offer a significant risk premium and are a powerful diversifier in a balanced portfolio of equity and fixed income. Is it that simple? Unfortunately it's not.

Erb and Harvey analyzed the same data as Gorton and Rouwenhorst but arrived at very different conclusions. For example, Gorton and Rouwenhorst concluded that the excess return of their 36-component equal-weight index was about 5%, and that the volatility of returns was about 12%. Erb and Harvey determined that the average excess return of each of the 36 individual commodity futures was −0.5%. They also determined that the average volatility of each commodity was about 30%. Thus, in the first case (Gorton and Rouwenhorst), the excess return is based on a rebalanced portfolio of equal-weight commodity futures, and in the second case (Erb and Harvey), it is based on the average excess return of each commodity's futures. What explains those differences in performance? We already answered this question in Chapter 4.

To understand the dynamic of this apparent contradiction, let's remember that, according to Equation 4.1d, the GEO mean is equal to the ARI mean less half the variance. Let's assume the ARI mean of a single commodity is 8.75%. Since the volatility of the typical commodity can be as high as 30%, the most likely GEO mean would be 4.25%, as shown in the following equation:

$$4.25\% = 8.75\% - 0.5 \times 0.30^2$$

Assuming a riskless rate of interest of 4.75%, the excess return would be −0.5%, the approximate value that Erb and Harvey calculated. However, what happens if we do not consider a single commodity, but an equal-weight portfolio of 36 commodity futures? Assuming the typical correlation between any two commodities is 15%, the volatility of the portfolio would only be 12.5%, as in the Gorton and Rouwenhorst study. Since the volatility is much lower, the drain on the ARI mean would only be about 0.75% instead of 4.5%, and the index would have a 3.25% excess return instead of a −0.5% excess return.

We do not achieve the 5% excess return measured by Gorton and Rouwenhorst. But, we had made the implicit assumption that the distribution of return of commodity futures was normal (Gaussian). If we had taken into account the possibility that commodity futures may have positive skew, the expected excess return might have been greater. Furthermore, the authors did not complete the study using the entire set of futures over the entire period, since the index initially had only nine commodities and grew to 36. Finally, the spot price of commodities may, in some cases, have increased by far more than could have been expected because of changes in demand and supply dynamics. Nevertheless, a significant portion of the excess return that Gorton and Rouwenhorst measured may not really be a risk premium, but simply the result of powerful diversification benefits that would not have been achieved with existing products.

This is significant because if we no longer assume the presence of a risk premium for single-commodity futures, and assume much of the gains result from powerful diversification benefits, we must pay much more attention to the efficiency of the index being used to invest in commodity futures. For example, although the excess returns measured by Gorton and Rouwenhorst were significant, very few investors would have actually invested in this sector in the past using an equal-weight protocol of 36 commodities. The investment policy of a popular commodity futures product was even adjusted a few years ago because of a lack of liquidity in some commodities.

Therefore, what if investors were not using an equal-weight index, but rather another index like the GSCI? In this particular case, since the GSCI is dominated by energy components, we would have to wonder whether or not the outperformance of such an index could be explained by futures market participants systematically underestimating increases in the price of oil. Considering the interest in commodities in recent years, could we make the same assumption in the future? Is it even possible that the design of the index was influenced by the knowledge that the back-tested benchmark would have performed very well because the index was created in 1991, but retroactively valued back to 1970? Furthermore, the structure of the GSCI was far from stable because it started in 1970 with only four components.

Equity indices or fixed-income indices are usually built on the principle of market capitalization, and offer a representative economic footprint despite their design flaws. In the case of commodities, we really do not know what a representative footprint is. Should we even be concerned about having a commodity portfolio structure that offers a representative footprint. Furthermore, there is no obvious methodology to create a commodity index, since commodity futures sum to zero.

Over the years, many commodity indices have been launched using different assembly methodologies. And since many of these indices have been introduced in recent decades, their performance is usually backfilled for the purpose of creating a track record. As indicated previously, it is likely that the methodology used to create the commodity index was influenced in some way by the performance of the back-filled index. Table 8.4 presents descriptive information about a few indices.

With the exception of CRB/Reuters and MLM, others have generally backfilled their performance prior to the launched date on the index. The methodologies for selecting and weighting commodities also vary. Therefore, the relative performance of all indices is driven by the construction methodologies (see Table 8.5). However, unlike equities, where a market capitalization approach dominates the usual portfolio assembly process, in this case, there is no consensus. Furthermore, if we agree with the principle that even investors in equities do not have to be bound by a cap-weight

TABLE 8.4 Commodity Futures Indices (1991–2004)

	Start Date	Backfilled	Number of Components	Selection Criteria	Weighting
CRB/Reuters	1957	1957	17	Diversification	Equal weight
DJ-UBS	1999	1991	19	Liquidity and diversification	Four-year average of liquidity and production
RICI	1998	1984	36	Worldwide demand	Production
GSCI	1991	1970	24	Economically important	Five-year average of production
DBLCI-OY	2006	1988	6	Six commodities, one per sector	Trading volume
MLM	1988	2000	Approx. 25	Volume, open interest and momentum	Equal weight

Source: Fuss, Hoppe and Kaiser (2008) [20].

TABLE 8.5 Performance Commodity Futures Indices (September 2001 to September 2011) (%)

	GEO Mean	Standard Deviation
DJ-UBS	7.5	18.2
RICI	11.3	20.0
S&P GSCI	6.7	25.1
DBLCI-OY	14.4	20.3

Source: Data from Bloomberg.

approach, what is stopping us from relying on a portfolio assembly process that is simply rational and risk efficient? Finally, commodities rarely account for a significant allocation when compared to equity or fixed income. Therefore, as investors, it is the diversification properties of commodities that we should seek, not some abstract economic representation that no one can fully support.

Attempting to Understand Commodities

Kat and Oomen (2006a, 2006b) published in-depth research about commodities. Much of their criticisms of prior research were based on their observation that commodities are heterogeneous assets and therefore it is a mistake to build our understanding using indices as if there were such a thing as an average commodity. Their objective was to identify the stylized facts about individual commodities, about portfolios of commodities and about commodities within a multi-asset class portfolio context. Their analyses were based on 142 futures contracts trading in 26 different exchanges in 8 countries from January 1965 to February 2005. Their first paper (2006a) addresses questions relative to the risk/return characteristics of single commodities, while the other (2006b) addresses issues related to commodities in a portfolio context.

As we discussed before, whether or not commodities do offer a risk premium depends on whether or not futures prices deviate from expected future spot prices. Since these variables are unobservable, the potential existence of a risk premium can only be inferred empirically. Kat and Oomen could not statistically support the existence of significant risk premiums for most commodity futures, with the exception of energy. Agricultural commodities in particular did not do well. Thus, an index that overweights agricultural commodities would probably not have performed as well as one that overweights energy commodities.

As Gorton and Rouwenhorst did, Kat and Oomen looked at the performance of commodity futures according to the business cycles and monetary regime. As we mentioned before, Gorton and Rouwenhorst had found that equity was at its best in late recession and at its worst in early recession, while commodities were performing better during the expansion cycle and worse during recession cycles. However, Kat and Oomen found that the behavioral pattern of commodities could not be generalized. For example, oats, cocoa, orange juice, and azuki beans followed a pattern similar to equity, but live cattle, hogs, lumber, rapeseed and especially energy followed a different pattern. Furthermore, they also found that most commodities shift between contango and backwardation, and that the relative frequency of these two states does not seem to depend on the economic cycle. Two exceptions, gold and silver, appear to be almost always in contango. Again, we can conclude that it might be a mistake to invest in an index of commodity futures without consideration for how they are bundled.

There is also further evidence of the complexity of commodity futures. For example, earlier, when discussing Equation 8.2, we mentioned that futures prices should incorporate information about the expected spot price.

$$F_{t,T} = E_t(S_T) - \mathrm{RP}_{t,T} \tag{8.2}$$

If we wanted to express the risk premium in terms of percentage return, we could rewrite Equation 8.2 as:

$$[E_t(S_T) - F_{t,T}] / F_{t,T} = \%RP_{t,T} \tag{8.4}$$

Therefore, a risk premium can only exist if the futures price is not equal to the expected spot price. The observed return on commodities is also often expressed as in Equation 8.5, where the futures return (which is also defined as an excess return, since the equation ignores the return on the cash collateral) is equal to the spot return plus a term called the roll return.

$$(F_T - F_{t,T}) / F_{t,T} = (S_T - S_t) / F_{t,T} + (S_t - F_{t,T}) / F_{t,T} \tag{8.5}$$

Since F_T will be necessarily equal to S_T, Equation 8.5 can be rewritten as

$$(S_T - F_{t,T}) / F_{t,T} = (S_T - S_t) / F_{t,T} + (S_t - F_{t,T}) / F_{t,T} \tag{8.6}$$

For example, let's assume the current spot price of oil is $80, while the futures price is $78 because investors expect the price of oil to decline. Let's also assume the spot price at maturity of the futures contract is $82—much higher than the expected spot return when the futures contract was acquired. In this case, the futures returns are explained in Table 8.6.

The roll return is basically the return an investor earns on the futures contract if the spot price remains the same. The roll return is also the measure that indicates if commodity futures are in contango or in backwardation. In the prior example, the futures price is less than the initial spot price. Thus, the roll return is positive and, therefore, the commodity future is in backwardation.

However, Kat and Oomen observed, as many other authors have, that although the roll returns of the 28 commodities they studied were not very significant on average, the spot returns were very positive when the roll returns were positive, and very negative when the roll returns were negative. Herb and Harvey (2006) observed that, between December 1992 and May 2004, more than 91.6% of the annualized excess performance of commodity futures was explained by the compounded annualized roll return. Thus, commodities with positive roll returns generated positive excess performance, while those with negative roll returns did not. This explains the number of indices and strategies that have been launched in the recent decade that attempt

TABLE 8.6 Sources of Returns of Commodity Futures

Futures	Spot	Roll
(82 – 78) / 78	(82 – 80) / 78	(80 – 78) / 78
5.12%	2.56%	2.56%

to emphasize an assembly process based on the degree of contango or backwardation observed in each commodity contract at any moment in time.

This observation could be consistent with the hedging pressure theory. This theory stipulates that if hedgers are net short, commodity futures should be in backwardation in order to incite investors to go net long. Conversely, if hedgers are net long, commodity futures should be in contango in order to incite investors to go net short. In the end, this would imply a form of time-varying risk premium since we must remember that, although an average nil return on single commodities is consistent with the absence of a risk premium, it does not prove the absence of a time-varying risk premium.

However, this explanation almost appears too rational in an investment world where all the investors are suddenly interested in commodities. For example, are commodity futures in contango or backwardation because of the demand and supply pressure of hedgers? Or is it because of the demand and supply pressure of hedgers and investors alike? Even if we were to assume that investors provide liquidity to the futures markets, and thus to hedgers, and should theoretically be compensated with a risk premium, the investors' group has become the dominant force of this market (there are far more investors than hedgers). Investors trading with other investors are potentially driving the risk premium down to zero (if such a risk premium ever existed). Therefore, the changes to the structure of commodity futures markets that are being observed may invalidate the conclusions of almost all prior studies on commodities ever done, and put into question the reliability of some strategies that may have been successful historically. By now, at the very least, we should be convinced that commodities are certainly not a low-hanging fruit. Table 8.7 summarizes most of the findings in the two Kat and Oomen papers.

Are Commodities a Good Inflation Hedge?

We would normally expect inflation to be negatively correlated with fixed income and equity. First, the inflation premium is a component of interest rates, and its direct impact on the pricing of nominal bonds is undeniable. In the case of equity, even if corporations are or were eventually able to maintain their real profit margins by increasing the price of their goods and services sold, investors have shown themselves to be myopic about this aspect in the past, and a negative correlation is also expected, at least over short to medium horizons.

However, commodities are real assets. They are part of our real economy, and, thus, they can directly impact inflation. Commodity futures could hedge against inflation caused by rising commodity prices, but not necessarily against the inflation caused by other factors. For example, significant increases in taxes (such as sales taxes), wage settlements and rising health care commitments can contribute to a higher level of inflation, while commodity prices decline or remain stable. Furthermore, if rising commodity prices trigger higher inflation, it could lead to a restrictive monetary

TABLE 8.7 Main Findings from Kat and Oomen Research on Commodities

Single Commodity Futures	Portfolio of Commodity Futures
With the possible exception of energy futures, there is no consistent evidence of a risk premium.	Correlations among commodity futures groupings such as grains and seeds, softs, meat and livestock, energy and metals are insignificant.
The volatility of commodity futures is similar to large-cap stocks.	Correlations with stocks and bonds are small, but vary with the cycle. Commodity futures are not always a good diversifier.
Evidence of positive skewness, contrary to popular belief, is insignificant.	There is no evidence that commodity futures lose their diversification properties in a tail risk environment.
The level of kurtosis on commodity futures is similar to large-cap stocks.	Commodity futures are positively correlated with unexpected inflation, but some commodities, such as energy and metals, are more efficient hedges.
Returns on commodity futures vary considerably with the business cycle and monetary conditions, and depending on whether or not they are in contango or backwardation.	There is still no evidence of a risk premium. The added diversification comes at the expense of a lesser return. Although energy-related commodity futures might offer a risk premium, the volatility in this particular sector is significant.
Commodities are very heterogeneous. Commodities do not react similarly to economic circumstances. Energy-related commodities appear to be a more homogeneous group.	
The vast interest in commodities from the financial community may invalidate the principles behind the hedging pressure theory and reduce the risk premium that may have existed related to this aspect.	

policy that would slow down real economic growth and cause the correlation of commodities to equity to change significantly (time-varying correlation).

Gorton and Rouwenhorst calculated the correlations of equity, fixed income and commodities to inflation, while Kat and Oomen evaluated the correlations to unexpected inflation. Hafner and Heiden (2007) [21] evaluated the correlations to both expected and unexpected inflation. Unexpected inflation was measured by the change in inflation. A summary of all results is presented in Table 8.8.

Using annual data increases the correlations of equity and fixed income with inflation, although Hafner and Heiden still reported a positive correlation of 0.28 with unexpected inflation using monthly data. Finally, Erb and Harvey reported an R-square of 43% for the regression of the GSCI excess return on unexpected inflation using yearly data. We have to remember, however, that the GSCI is dominated by an

TABLE 8.8 Correlations of Assets to Inflation

Source	Holding Period	Correlations		
		Stocks	Bonds	Commodities
Gorton & Rouwenhorst (July 1959 to December 2004)	Monthly	−0.15	−0.12	0.01
	Annual	−0.19	−0.32	0.29
	Five years	−0.25	−0.22	0.45
Hafner & Heiden (January 1991 to July 2006)	Monthly expected	−0.10	−0.06	0.14
	Monthly unexpected	−0.05	0.04	0.28
Kat & Oomen (1973 to 2004)	Annual	−0.33	−0.53	0.25

energy component. In fact, Erb, Harvey and Kempe (2007) [22] reported that not all commodities have been good inflation hedges, but energy-related commodities have provided the strongest hedge against unexpected inflation. It may be that rising or declining energy prices have contributed significantly to movements in unexpected inflation simply because of its economic significance, a link that would be unwise to generalize.

There is little doubt that some commodities can be a better hedge against inflation (at least in the short term) than either fixed income or equity. However, as we have discussed, the hedging qualities of commodities are not unrelated to the sources of inflation. We already know that equities and bonds react negatively to unexpected inflation. Thus, is our objective to find an asset class that acts as a good hedge against unexpected inflation? Or is our objective simply to find an asset class that has negative correlation to equity when equity is declining, and positive correlation to equity when equity is rising? In other words, if the allocation to commodity in a portfolio is static, the inflation-hedging efficiency of commodities is the most important factor. However, if the allocation process is dynamic, and takes into account the evolution of the diversification efficiency of commodities against equities (its correlation at specific periods in time), then it may be more important to focus on this aspect, since it would indirectly capture the hedging qualities of commodities against inflation when it is needed most. For example, Figure 8.1 illustrates the evolution of the correlation between the GSCI and the S&P 500 using two-year rolling data on the left axis, and the two-year cumulative excess return against the GSCI on the right axis. As we can easily observe, the scale of the cumulative return differential over two years can be significant.

The correlation between the GSCI and the S&P 500 is volatile but shows some persistence. Furthermore, positive excess performances for the GSCI are often associated with periods of lower correlation to equity. Thus, focusing on the evolution of the diversification efficiency of commodities with equity may in fact be a more significant concern than the inflation-hedging efficiency of commodities.

FIGURE 8.1   Correlation of GSCI to Equity (1970–2010).

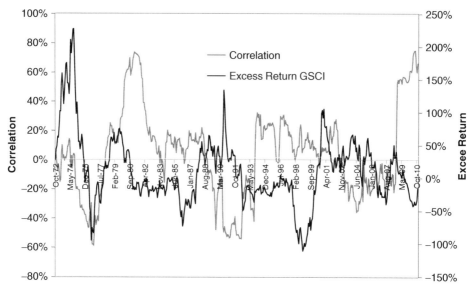

Source: Data from Bloomberg.

Persistence of Volatility and Dependence

In Chapter 5, we illustrated the persistence of volatility for fixed income and equity and the persistence of dependence between both assets by looking at the autocorrelation of the first to hundredth order using daily data. In Figures 8.2a and 8.2b, we provide the same information for a commodity index (even though commodities are very

FIGURE 8.2a   Autocorrelations of Returns and Volatilities (1988–2010).

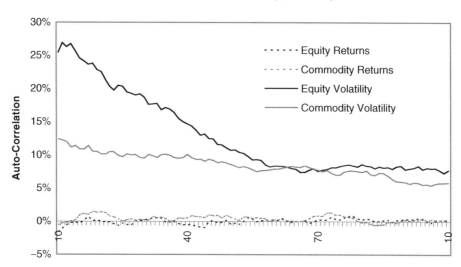

FIGURE 8.2b   Autocorrelation of Covariance (1988–2010).

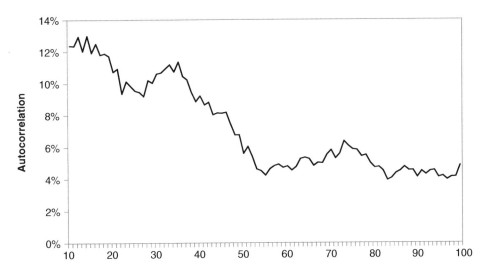

Source: Data from Datastream.

heterogeneous, which should reduce the autocorrelation) and again for equity. As with equity and fixed income, there is information about future volatility and correlation in the historical returns of commodities. However, better results could be obtained with specific clusters of commodities.

Implications of the Evidence on Commodities

The commodity futures market is complex, but the following are a few aspects we should agree on:

- Either there is no risk premium on commodity futures or there is a time-varying risk premium.
- Commodities are a very heterogeneous asset class and, thus, can offer significant diversification benefits.
- The structure of the commodity futures market has changed significantly in the last decade.
- There is information about future volatility and correlation in historical returns.

What are the implications? If the existence of a risk premium remains in question, investors can only rely on the diversification benefits that commodities offer to justify investing, mainly their impact on the GEO mean of a rebalanced portfolio. If this is the case, two other aspects are extremely relevant. First, because of the heterogeneity of the asset class, much attention must be paid to how commodities are bundled or whether baskets of commodities, such as energy, nonenergy and precious metals, should be created. For example, although we have not specifically addressed precious metals, Hillier, Draper and Faff (2006) [23] found that precious metals, gold in particular, were especially efficient at hedging portfolios during periods of abnormally high equity volatility. Despite the standard argument that gold is a great hedge against inflation, the evidence shows that gold has historically been a better hedge against volatility, and has very little correlation to inflation [24]. Second, since volatility and correlation are unstable but often show persistence, the process and structure used to integrate commodities within a portfolio may impact the decision to invest or not to invest in commodities.

Let's compare two scenarios. In the first scenario, a fixed allocation to a commodity index is used, and the portfolio is rebalanced monthly. In the second scenario, the average allocation to commodity is similar over time, but the allocation is segmented between energy, nonenergy and precious metals, and the portfolio is managed to maintain a constant volatility. We could come to the conclusion that commodities are not interesting in the first case because the diversification benefits are insufficient to compensate for the absence of a risk premium, but that commodities are interesting in the second case because the diversification benefits that commodities can bring are optimized more efficiently. We will now demonstrate some of these aspects.

A Case Study of Commodities

In light of the heterogeneity of commodities and commodity index structures, Fuss, Hoppe and Kaiser (2008) proposed that a more representative and stable benchmark be built. Their idea was to combine the common inherent information in competing indices. They renounced the use of a simple equal-weight index of indices because of the possibility that one or a few indices may perform significantly differently from the majority. To avoid this concern, they proposed to use factor analysis in order to create a composite index, which explains most of the variance in the underlying data set.

However, the result would still be based on different indices whose assembly processes are based on information about production, liquidity, open interests, etc. None of these approaches seek to exploit the heterogeneity of commodities characteristics. If we accept the argument that investors are not bound by the principle of market capitalization to build efficient equity portfolios, and that a market-cap process incorporates more significantly the effects of creation and destruction of security and sector bubbles, why would we want to base a commodity portfolio assembly process on criteria such as production or open interests? First, the theoretical argument for doing so is nonexistent, and, second, we are again more likely to participate fully in the creation and destruction of bubbles related to specific commodities.

For example, if the allocation within the GSCI index is based on a weighting average of five-year production volume, the weights attributed to commodities that saw their production increase significantly would grow and expose the portfolio more markedly to those commodities. If the allocation is based on open interest, it is likely that the most popular commodities have seen their open interest rise considerably. This will contribute to a poor diversification of pricing noise.

A statistically efficient solution (but certainly not the only one, nor necessarily the best one) may be to create an index of equally weighted liquid commodity futures while balancing commodity groups to benefit from their heterogeneous characteristics (i.e., not allowing one commodity or one category of commodities to dominate the risk of the entire index—the same principle we seek to implement within our equity protocols). A cluster analysis could help to identify commodity groups. Furthermore, although we rejected an equal-risk approach for equities (because it is unlikely to be any more efficient than equal weight in portfolios that contain dozens of securities), it may be appropriate for commodities since there are far fewer components to consider and also because commodities can have significantly different volatilities. Nevertheless, in this case study, I will rely on a simple index of seven equally weighted commodity futures. If a simple structure can be shown to be efficient, it can certainly be improved upon.

I chose the seven commodity futures primarily for their liquidity and relative economic importance. However, the first criterion was to have one or two commodities in each of the most important sectors: energy (crude oil and natural gas), grains and seeds (wheat and corn), industrial metals (copper), precious metals (gold) and softs (sugar). I did not attempt to optimize the portfolio structure. This was the only attempt at building a better index. I used the GSCI as a reference, and the period under analysis was June 1992 to September 2011. Table 8.9 presents the statistics for equity (S&P 500), fixed income (10-year Treasury), the GSCI and our equal-weight commodity index.

The equal-weight commodity index outperformed the GSCI by more than 3 percentage points yearly. More interesting is the fact that the average commodity within the equal-weight index had an average absolute return of only 2.45% (4.2 percentage points less than the index) and an average volatility of nearly 32%. Since the volatility of the index is only 17.67%, there are strong diversification benefits. Table 8.10 presents the correlation matrix of all seven commodity futures. The average cross-correlation is only 0.165, and such diversification is enough to increase the GEO mean by 3.6 percentage points. Although I will not present the information, I achieved even better returns when I used a protocol of 25 commodities grouped into five clusters.

TABLE 8.9 Statistics of Portfolio and Portfolio Components (01/06/1992 to 09/08/2011)

	GEO Mean (%)	Volatility (%)	GEO Mean to Volatility	Skewness	Kurtosis
Equity	5.46	16.13	0.34	−0.53	12.50
Fixed Income	6.80	9.32	0.73	−0.34	9.54
GSCI	3.70	22.26	0.17	−0.22	6.25
Equal-Weight Index	6.76	17.67	0.38	−0.09	5.96

Source: Data from Bloomberg.

TABLE 8.10   Correlation Matrix (01/06/1992 to 09/08/2011)

	Crude Oil	Natural Gas	Copper	Gold	Sugar	Wheat
Crude Oil						
Natural Gas	0.26					
Copper	0.22	0.08				
Gold	0.24	0.07	0.26			
Sugar	0.11	0.06	0.15	0.12		
Wheat	0.15	0.07	0.18	0.15	0.16	
Corn	0.17	0.09	0.20	0.17	0.17	0.60

Source: Data from Bloomberg.

The next step was to consider the impact of adding a commodity component to a 60/40 portfolio. The methodology consisted of adding a 5% allocation of either the GSCI or the equal-weight index, and reallocating the fixed income and equity component in order to maintain the same volatility as the original 60/40 portfolio. An equal-weight "adjusted" index was also created. This index was built from the same components as the basic equal-weight index, but the historical track record of each commodity was adjusted to remove any excess risk premium. This allowed us to concentrate on the diversification benefits of commodities. Thus, the average return of each commodity was set to be equal to the one-month London Interbank Offered Rate (LIBOR), which was only 2.52% over the period—a return far below that of either fixed income or equity. A 57.2% allocation to equity and 37.8% to fixed income allowed for maintaining approximately the same portfolio volatility in all cases. Those results are presented in Table 8.11.

The allocation to the equal-weight index improved the annualized performance by 0.19 percentage points while the GSCI deteriorated the performance by 0.09 percentage

TABLE 8.11   Statistics of Portfolio and Portfolio Components (01/09/1992 to 09/08/2011)

	GEO Mean (%)	Volatility (%)	GEO Mean to Volatility	Skewness	Kurtosis
60/40 Base Portfolio	6.80	9.32	0.73	−0.34	9.54
With GSCI	6.71	9.32	0.72	−0.36	11.08
With Equal-Weight Index	6.99	9.32	0.75	−0.33	10.90
With Equal-Weight Adjusted Index	6.82	9.32	0.73	−0.34	10.94

Source: Data from Bloomberg.

points. If we analyze the data further, we can observe that the equal-weight index is far more efficient than the GSCI at diversifying the entire portfolio. First, the equal-weight "adjusted" index outperformed the 60/40 portfolio, despite the much lower GEO mean of each commodity component. Furthermore, if we consider the allocation changes that resulted from adding a commodity component (−2.8% equity, −2.2% fixed income and +5% commodity), and consider the absolute GEO return of each component, the weighted average performance without considering any diversification impact would be −0.12% with the GSCI and +0.04% with the equal-weight index.

Thus, in the first case (GSCI), the weighted average performance impact of −0.12% was turned into a −0.09% impact on the portfolio (a 0.03% diversification gain) while the weighted average performance of +0.04% in the second case (equal-weight index) was turned into a 0.19 percentage point gain. This illustrates that an equal-weight index of seven commodities futures that is rebalanced monthly is far more efficient at diversifying a portfolio than the GSCI, whose allocation process is based on production data and subject to momentum biases. Again, if we can benefit from statistically efficient diversification we should ignore unsubstantiated index methodologies. Also, as indicated previously, I made no effort to statistically optimize the commodity futures index. Significantly better indices can be built.

Considering the heterogeneous characteristics of commodities, it is not surprising that the folks at TOBAM, which launched the maximum diversification concept, would take a look at how their approach (discussed in Chapter 6) could be applied to commodities. They too started with the assumption that the existence of a risk premium in long-only commodities is in doubt, and that the true benefit of commodities is diversification in a long/short setting. They recognized that commodities grow through cycles and display a momentum that can be captured. Their approach is based on a universe of about 24 commodities, using a momentum signal and a maximum exposure to any single commodity of 10%. The portfolio construction method is again the concept of maximum diversification, with the exception that if a commodity has a negative (positive) signal, it will be constrained to have a negative (positive) weight in the optimization. There is no explicit leverage since the sum of the absolute value of all notional positions is constrained at no more than one.

TOBAM incorporated a momentum factor within the investment protocol because of an interesting observation that they made. When the excess return of commodity futures is plotted across time, no consistent return can be observed, which argues in favor of the absence of a true risk premium. However, when the same data are plotted using momentum as a factor, significant excess return can be observed on almost all commodity futures. Therefore, it may be that in the market for commodity futures, where all futures positions necessarily sum to zero, using a momentum-based strategy may be one approach that allows the capture of a time-varying risk premium.

TOBAM evaluated their approach since 1987 and compared it to the GSCI. This led to a far more stable and significantly lower index volatility, and a much higher GEO mean. Table 8.12 presents their results. If anything, the TOBAM product and our case study illustrate that the most important concern in designing an index should be its statistical efficiency.

TABLE 8.12 TOBAM versus GSCI (01/01/1987 to 08/31/2009)

	GEO Mean (%)	Volatility (%)	Sharpe Ratio	Maximum Drawdown (%)	Time to Recovery (Months)
TOBAM	12.54	7.48	1.01	−9.55	11
GSCI	7.65	20.91	0.24	−67.65	65

Source: TOBAM. Performances prior to September 30, 2008, are simulated.

Curencies as a Diversifier

Currency futures are being used in the real economy to hedge the currency risk that is related to the global trade of goods and services and portfolio investments. Financial investors may be interested in maintaining strategic exposure to foreign currencies to improve the diversification of their portfolios. This exposure can be created through futures contracts and/or through the direct purchase of financial assets denominated in a foreign currency (such as foreign equity or foreign bonds).

Currency exposure has broader implications in portfolio management than does commodities. The currency market is also significantly larger. Since investors buy foreign currency denominated assets as a way to diversify their portfolio risk, this process automatically creates a currency exposure that may or may not be desirable. Just because an investor wants 20% of exposure to foreign currency denominated assets to achieve a more balanced sector exposure, a less concentrated security exposure and a more diversified economic exposure, we cannot assume that said investor necessarily wants 20% of exposure to the currencies of those assets. Therefore, the real issue with currencies in the context of portfolio management is not the hedging of existing currency risk, but how much and which currency exposure is desirable. Fully or even partially hedging currency exposure does not necessarily reduce risk. It can actually increase it.

Not all concerned parties understand this aspect. For example, some financial firms in Canada are required to take a regulatory capital charge on the currency exposure related to foreign equity. However, even assuming that hedging made sense, which particular currency exposure are we trying to hedge? When investing in corporations that are listed in European, US or Asian markets, how do we know the currency source of their profits? It is well known that a significant portion of the profits of large-cap US and European companies are sourced overseas. Also, does hedging even make sense? Does the exchange rate mechanism act as an economic buffer? For example, the Canadian dollar is usually procyclical. This means that investors who are based in Canada usually benefit from a weakening domestic currency in difficult economic times.

From the end of July to the end of October 2008, in the midst of the liquidity crisis, the Canadian dollar lost more than 21%. This indicates that the drop in the value of foreign equity to a Canadian investor that occurred during this period was shielded by 21%. If there is a natural hedge, why remove it by hedging? Furthermore, many

Canadian firms operate in the resource sector, where the price of resources is set in US dollars. A hedging policy should consider the link between the price movements of commodities and the strength of the Canadian dollar. Even a Canadian investor who is investing in a Canadian-based company has currency exposure. The same is true of all investors in all countries. Simply saying that a firm should hedge its exposure to the currency of the country where a company happens to be listed shows that currency risk is not well understood. Furthermore, imposing regulatory capital charges for not eliminating an exposure that offers a natural economic hedge against other exposures is irresponsible. Unfortunately, in general, there seems to be little consensus among experts. The following is a summary of some experts' findings:

- According to Perold and Shulman (1988) [25], hedging currency exposure reduces risk without affecting returns. Since currency return is a zero-sum game (your gain/loss is someone else's loss/gain) hedging can reduce risk without impacting performance. Thus, hedging offers a free lunch, and the authors recommend a full hedge.
- Fisher and Statman (2003) [26] argue that hedged and unhedged portfolios have been similarly efficient. Therefore, hedging would not necessarily be supported. Furthermore they indicate that investors who hedge their currency risk are often looking for a sure win, and their so-called hedges are really an active view on foreign currencies.
- Froot (1993) [27] agrees with Perold and Shulman, but only for short investment horizons of less than about two years. For investors with long investment horizons, he argues against hedging. According to Froot, exchange rates tend toward purchasing power parity over time, and hedging will not be efficient against risks affecting long-term exchange rates, such as inflation surprise.
- Many others argue for a partial hedge. Black (1990) [28] developed a universal hedge ratio, which leads to an approximate hedging level of 75%. He intuitively attributes the less-than-100% hedge ratio to the Siegel's paradox—mainly, the fact that the rate of appreciation of a currency against another is always greater than the reverse. For example, if currency A depreciates by 20% against currency B, currency B has, in fact, appreciated by 25% against currency A.
- Solnik (1988) [29] believes that the decision to hedge is not independent of the percentage of assets allocated in foreign currencies. At low levels of foreign exposure (less than 20%), hedging is not advisable because the currency exposure would reduce the total risk of the portfolio. At higher levels of foreign exposure, some hedging may be advisable. This argument is in line with the idea that diversification becomes less statistically efficient if a specific source of risk dominates the total risk of the portfolio.
- Solnik (1998) [30] believes that some currency exposure can help hedge local inflation and interest rate risk. Thus, he is more in line with the view of Gastineau (1995) [31] of a 50% hedge ratio.
- Walker (2006) [32] argues that currency hedging is not a free lunch, and that one cannot assume that it will reduce risk in a portfolio. As Walker (2006) and Campbell, Serfaty-de Medeiros and Viceira (2010) [33] indicate, some currencies are more

attractive than others to risk-minimizing investors. Thus, an efficient hedge may not have to be denominated in the currencies of the foreign exposure, and the amount of currency interventions required to create the proper currency exposure will differ depending on the currency of the investor.

These divergences in opinion certainly explain why the 50% hedge ratio is often so popular. To resolve this puzzle, we will initially discuss the existence of currency-related risk premiums in futures contracts and in financial assets.

Is There Evidence of a Risk Premium in Currency Futures?

Let's start with the basic notions. According to the principle of covered interest rate parity, the forward exchange rate between two currencies is equal to the spot rate adjusted for the differential in interest rate between the two countries. This relation, which is shown in Equation 8.7, is constantly arbitraged and is almost never violated in the data.

$$F_{t,T} = S_t + \text{rd}_t - \text{rf}_t \tag{8.7}$$

If we were to assume that the forward rate ($F_{t,T}$) incorporates all the information that is relevant to forecasting interest rates by replacing the forward rate in Equation 8.7 by the expected spot rate ($E(S_T)$), we get the theory of uncovered interest rate parity, which implies that the forward rate is the best (most unbiased) predictor of the future spot rate. As we can see from the equation, uncovered interest rate parity does not allow for the existence of a risk premium.

$$E(S_T) = S_t + \text{rd}_t - \text{rf}_t \tag{8.8}$$

Tests of the theory of uncovered interest rate parity are based on the following equations:

$$S_T - S_t = \alpha + \beta(\text{rd}_t - \text{rf}_t) + \mu, \text{ or:} \tag{8.9a}$$

$$S_T - S_t = \alpha + \beta(F_{t,T} - S_t) + \mu \tag{8.9b}$$

where α and β should respectively have values of 0 and 1 for uncovered interest parity to hold. It is well known that although covered interest rate parity does hold, uncovered interest rate parity does not (Froot and Thaler (1990), Engel (1996), Jurek (2009)) [34]. In most tests, the value of β was much closer to minus one, indicating that higher yield currencies tend to appreciate, not depreciate. This observation has led to the well-known carry trade (such as investing in high-yield currencies while borrowing in low-yield currencies without hedging). Such a strategy has often been profitable in the past, but it is obviously exposed to the risk that the higher-yield currencies may depreciate quickly. For example, although the carry trade has often been a profitable strategy in the long run, in the last two quarters of 2008, the carry trade produced significantly negative returns as investors around the world moved their assets to the relative safety of the US dollar.

Under uncovered interest rate parity, the payoff of the carry trade should be nil. However, when Jurek (2009) tested the carry trade on nine currencies against the US dollar from 1990 to 2007, he also found the carry trade to be profitable for all currency pairs. Why is the carry trade often profitable? First, the current consensus in the empirical literature (Landon and Smith (1999), Carlson and Osler (2003)) [35] is that exchange rates also incorporate a time-varying risk premium (rp).

$$E(S_T) - S_t = rd_t - rf_t - rp_t \tag{8.10}$$

Using Equation 8.7 we get:

$$F_{t,T} - S_t = rp_t + E(S_T) - S_t \tag{8.11}$$

The forward premium ($F_{t,T} - S_t$) is equal to the expected variation in the exchange rate adjusted for a risk premium (rp_t). Therefore, the forward rate in Equation 8.11 is no longer assumed to be an unbiased predictor of the future expected spot rate, although Bekaert, Wei and Xing (2007) [36] showed that deviations from uncovered interest rate parity are less severe over longer horizons. Carlson and Osler also concluded that the currency time-varying risk premium is strongly related to interest rate differentials, and thus may be of relevance to the carry trade. Furthermore, Bekaert, Wei and Xing presented results that were consistent with a "volatile" time-varying risk premium, where the volatility and persistence of the risk premium is different across countries. Thus, currencies, like commodities, are showing heterogeneous characteristics.

Jurek postulated that the risk premium extracted from the carry trade strategy is insurance against the possibility of major currency shocks, such as the one observed in 2008 when the US dollar appreciated strongly against most currencies (including those that had higher interest rates than in the United States). However, he found that an excess return remained after hedging the crash risk using options, indicating that the crash risk premium alone cannot account for the deviation from uncovered interest rate parity. He also found that currencies that have high interest rates and that have recently appreciated are more likely to experience strong decline. Finally, he observed that losses stemming from carry trades in 2008 did not occur because of a single crash, but because of a sequence of downward moves. This information by itself will be very useful later on.

What factors other than crash risk could account for the presence of a risk premium? Jurek indicated that if the carry trade portfolio was forced to remain dollar neutral, he could no longer identify statistically significant excess gains. This may suggest that a risk premium on currencies would be compensation for crash risk, but also compensation for investors who are short US dollars, which remain the world's main reserve currency. We actually find support for this view from other areas of the literature. It is all very interesting, but how useful is this information from an invest-ment point of view? We still need to cover other areas of interest about currencies before we can answer this question.

Is There Any Empirical Evidence of a Risk Premium in Foreign Assets?

The evidence seems to strongly support the presence of risk premiums that are related to currencies in international equity. Carrieri, Errunza and Majerbi (2004) [37] found evidence of a risk premium in emerging and developed equity markets that can be accounted for by emerging-market currency risk. They also found that this risk pre-mium is priced differently from emerging markets' specific risks. Thus, we may con-clude that even investors who are not invested in emerging markets are exposed to risk premiums that are related to emerging markets. There are spillover effects. Even though the relative economic significance of emerging and developed economies has changed significantly since this study, we can probably assume that the principle of the authors' observation remains valid. Thus, currency risk is a component of equity risk.

Walker (2008) studied the issue of currency hedging, but from the point of view of emerging-market investors. He argued that currency hedging is not a zero-sum game because hard (reserve) currencies can act as a natural hedge against port-folio losses. Hard currencies tend to appreciate when returns in the world markets turn negative. In this case, an emerging-market investor hedging the currency risk of investments located in hard-currency countries would see the volatility of his or her portfolio increasing. Furthermore, he or she would find that currency Betas with respect to global equities have increased, indicating a stronger link between equity markets and currencies. There are two possible explanations. First, stock market fluc-tuations may reflect relative growth expectations among countries, thus affecting cur-rency valuation. Second, currency values may be affected by the flow of funds. When the environment is uncertain, investors may seek to invest in safer currencies, while they seek riskier markets when it is stable.

Roache and Merritt (2006) [38] looked specifically at whether or not the stock markets of industrialized countries incorporated a currency risk premium and whether or not specific market shocks caused investors to change their pricing of risk. They analyzed as many as 33 industries in the traditional set of seven industrialized coun-tries. Here are their main findings:

- The risk premium is usually positive. Investors do require a risk premium on assets that perform poorly when the domestic currency is depreciating.
- Consequently, investors should also be willing to accept a lower rate of return (lower risk premium) on domestic assets that do well when the currency is depreciating. For example, the risk premium in Japan on export-intensive industries turned nega-tive during periods of strong yen depreciation.

We could conclude from the existing literature that currency risk does matter to almost all investors. Campbell, Serfaty-de Meideros and Viceira (2010) considered the currency issue from the point of view of a risk-minimizing investor allocating to the equity markets of the seven industrialized countries. The analysis covered the period of 1975 to 2005. As would be expected, the Canadian and Australian dollars were positively correlated to global equity markets, including their own markets. The yen and the British pound sterling were also positively correlated. The United States dollar, the euro and the Swiss franc were in the opposite group. Thus, a risk-minimizing equity investor may find it efficient to hedge his or her global equity exposure by maintaining a long position in US dollar, Swiss franc and euro, and a short position in the other currencies. A long position in the US dollar against the Canadian dollar is particularly efficient at hedging global equity. Finally, if we move from an equity investor to a bond investor, they do find that a risk-minimizing investor would want to hedge all of the currency risk.

The recent credit crisis may have changed part of this dynamic. Some currencies that were considered hard currencies (such as the euro) may not keep their status, and others may eventually emerge. Considering the current and projected competitive and fiscal environment, even the US dollar could lose some of its current status, becoming a less efficient safe haven over time. However, the principle that some currencies act as a safe haven against equity risk is sound. The main issue is how to most efficiently apply this principle in the long term.

Currency Exposure and Portfolio Volatility

There is one aspect that the literature agrees on. Highly rated fixed-income investments denominated in foreign currencies should be fully or close to fully hedged for the following reasons:

- The cash flows and the timing of the cash flows of these assets are usually known, and the cash flows themselves are highly probable. It also implicitly means that the cash flows of nominal bonds, unlike equity, are not subject to any change related to currency fluctuations. Therefore, the currency risk of such assets can be hedged very efficiently using futures, forwards or swaps.
- The volatility of exchange rates is usually greater than the price volatility of quality fixed-income assets. Since the risk premium of a quality fixed-income asset is relatively small, not hedging would expose the small expected excess return to substantial losses. If the objective of international bond diversification is to achieve a greater diversification of credit risk premiums, currency risk cannot be allowed to overwhelm the benefits targeted in this effort. The argument is even stronger when the investor is subject to local currency liability constraints, such as a pension fund.

Another way to reach a similar conclusion is to consider the basic general formula for the volatility of return on a foreign currency denominated asset (R_{FC}).

$$\sigma(R_{FC}) = [\sigma^2(R_{LC}) + \sigma^2(ER) + 2 \times Cov\ (R_{LC}, ER)]^{1/2} \qquad (8.12)$$

where $\sigma^2(R_{LC})$ and $\sigma^2(ER)$ are, respectively, the variance of the foreign asset in local currency terms and the variance of the exchange rate (local currency per unit of the foreign currency). The third term is the covariance between the local return and the exchange rate. Even if we assume that the correlation between the local return on the asset and the exchange rate were zero, the volatility of the return of the unhedged foreign asset, from the investor's point of view, would still be greater than the volatility of the local currency return. In this case, fully hedging the foreign asset would reduce the volatility of returns to approximately the level of the volatility of the local currency return, and the expected yield to maturity on the hedged asset would simply be equal to the expected yield to maturity of the local asset (adjusted for the forward premium).

However, what happens if, as we have mentioned previously, correlations between currency returns and returns on other assets (such as equity) were not nil, but positive or negative. As we have discussed, some currencies have a tendency to appreciate when global equity markets are strongly up (and confidence is rising), while others tend to appreciate when equity markets are strongly down (and confidence is declining). In the first scenario, an investor who has exposure to assets in that currency would want to hedge some of his or her equity exposure with a short currency position, even if the assets were in his or her own country. In the second scenario, an investor would want to build exposure to that currency, even if he or she did not have assets invested in that currency, since it offers a natural hedge against equity risk. Intuitively, this reasoning would lead us to conclude that two investors in two different countries who have the same globally diversified portfolio structure would want to have similar global currency exposure. Thus, currencies should be seen as an asset class, not solely as an existing risk to hedge.

Let's illustrate with an example built around two scenarios. A Canadian and a US investor both have the following portfolio structure: 60% highly rated fixed-income assets and 40% equity (i.e., 40/60). In the case of fixed-income assets, we have concluded from our past arguments that no matter what percentage of this asset class is invested internationally, it would probably be in the best interest of each investor to fully hedge the foreign currency exposure. A full hedge of high-quality fixed-income assets is likely to reduce the volatility of the fixed income from the point of view of any investor in any country. This specific aspect will be discussed again later on.

Therefore, since our two investors have fully hedged their fixed-income assets, we will concentrate on the equity component. In the first scenario, the investors remain fully invested in their own market (a home bias). However, we assume that each investor understands that the Canadian dollar tends to appreciate when equity is rising strongly and depreciate when equity is declining. The Canadian dollar has a positive correlation to the global equity market, and thus to both the Canadian and US equity markets. Therefore, even though the US investor is fully invested in his own market, he may have an incentive to sell the Canadian dollar forward, since it would hedge his own equity market risk. Furthermore, even though the Canadian investor is fully invested in Canada, he understands that he could also reduce the risk of investing in his own equity market by selling short his own currency, and thus buying the US dollar forward. If the two equity markets have similar volatilities and similar correlation to the USD/CAD exchange rate, the optimal solution for both investors would be

TABLE 8.13 Optimal Currency Position: Scenario 1 (%)

	US Investor	Canadian Investor
Hedge Fixed Income	60	60
US Equity	40	0
Canadian Equity	0	40
USD/CAD Currency Position	−20	−20
Market Exposure	40/60	40/60
Currency Exposure	120 USD / −20 CAD	80 CAD / 20 USD

to short the same allocation of Canadian dollars. In this scenario, US and Canadian investors want to short the Canadian dollar because it has a positive correlation to equity markets in both countries.

Table 8.13 shows the positions of each investor after hedging, assuming that the volatility of each equity market is 20%, the volatility of the exchange rate is 10% and the correlations between the two equity markets with the USD/CAD exchange rates are both 25%. A simple Markowitz-type minimum variance optimization would indicate that each investor should have a 20% short position in the Canadian dollar (50% of their 40% equity position). Thus, in terms of asset class exposure, both investors have a 60% fixed-income exposure and a 40% equity exposure. After hedging, the US investor is long his currency by 120% and short Canadian dollars by 20%, while the Canadian investor is long his currency and the US dollar by 80% and 20% respectively.

Someone could argue that the volatility of equity markets in Canada and the United States may differ, and that the correlations of each equity market to exchange rates may also differ. However, if investors around the world held fairly diversified global portfolios (not concentrated domestic portfolios), the volatilities of these global portfolios measured in a common currency will be similar from the point of view of any investor in any country, and the correlations of these global portfolios to specific exchange rates would also be similar. Thus, theoretically, once investors own globally diversified portfolios, they would want to implement fairly similar currency exposures.

To illustrate this aspect, we consider in Table 8.14 a second scenario, where the global market is represented by the United States and Canada (to simplify). Both investors hold 60% of their equity in the US market and 40% in the Canadian market, and correlation between the two markets is 50%. Under those circumstances, the optimal currency position that minimizes global risk is again a net 20% short position on the Canadian dollar (50% of the global equity exposure). However, since both investors have international exposure, the two investors will need different levels of

TABLE 8.14 Optimal Currency Position: Scenario 2 (%)

	US Investor	Canadian Investor
Hedge Fixed Income	60	60
US Equity	24	24
Canadian Equity	16	16
USD/CAD Currency Position	−36	−4
Market Exposure	40/60	40/60
Currency Exposure	120 USD / −20 CAD	80 CAD / 20 USD

currency positions in the forward market to achieve the 20% short exposure to the Canadian dollar that they seek. Although the net position in currency exposure is similar, the level of intervention required to achieve this net position depends on the home country of the investor.

This all fine in theory, but in the real world it would not be so easy to implement this approach, even if we believed in this basic principle. First, the level of currency intervention can be significant from the point of view of investors who are located in a reserve currency country. For example, if an advisor to a Canadian investor recommended a 4% currency hedge, the investor might agree. However, imagine an advisor recommending to the investment committee of a US institutional investor that their portfolio should have a currency hedge position more than 200% the size of their international equity exposure (36% versus 16%).

Second, it may be difficult to determine which portfolio of currencies should be designated safe haven currencies. The world is changing fast, and even if we agreed that the US dollar will remain a safe haven for many more years, could we still say the same about the euro? Correlations between global equity markets and exchange rates may be changing. Furthermore, the exposure/hedging levels that resulted from the analysis of Campbell, Serfaty-de Medeiros and Viceira were done in sample over a very long historical period.

However, before we address these problems, the astute reader might have realized that it is possible to derive from Equation 8.12 (adjusted for the possibility of hedging) the formula that determines the optimal level of currency hedging (or currency exposure). For example, the optimal level of hedging (that minimizes portfolio volatility) for an investment in an equity market is the following:

$$1 + \rho(ER_{DC/FC}, R_M) \ [\sigma^2(R_M) \ / \ \sigma^2(ER)] \tag{8.13a}$$

where $ER_{DC/FC}$ represents the exchange rate of the domestic currency of the investor per unit of the foreign currency, and R_M represents the return in local currency of the equity market. For example, if we assume that the correlation between the US equity market and the US dollar for a Canadian investor is −0.25, and the ratio of US equity market volatility to the CAD/USD exchange rate is 2, a Canadian investor in the US market should hedge (short) the US dollar by 50% of his or her equity investment, or, in other words, the investor should tolerate a 50% exposure to the US dollar. Similarly, a US investor investing in Canada facing a +0.25 correlation between the Canadian equity market and the Canadian dollar should hedge (short) the Canadian dollar by 150%, or, in other words, tolerate a +50% exposure to the US dollar.

Similarly, Equation 8.13b shows the optimal level of hedging for an investor who is attempting to reduce the volatility of an equity investment in his or her own market.

$$-\rho(\text{ER}_{DC/FC}, R_M) \times [\sigma^2(R_M) / \sigma^2(\text{ER})] \tag{8.13b}$$

For example, a Canadian investor in the Canadian market facing a −0.25 correlation between his or her own market and the US dollar should go long the US dollar by 50%. Similarly, a US investor in the US market facing a +0.25 correlation between his or her own market and the Canadian dollar should go short the Canadian dollar by 50% (i.e., go long the US dollar by another 50%). These equations are entirely consistent with the level of currency positions recommended in Tables 8.13 and 8.14. Table 8.15 illustrates the level of currency intervention required for different levels of correlations and ratio of equity to currency volatility as per Equation 8.13a.

The conclusions are fairly clear. Investors in the equity market of a safe haven currency country should more than likely hedge the currency exposure by less than 50%. Investors facing opposite circumstances would normally want to hedge more than 100% of their currency exposure. Finally, as the correlation of the return on the local currency asset to exchange rate approaches zero, or if the volatility of the asset declines in relation to the exchange rate, the hedge ratio approaches 100%. This explains why high-quality foreign currency fixed-income assets are usually fully hedged.

TABLE 8.15 Optimal Currency Hedging (%)

Ratio σ_E/σ_{ER}	Correlation				
	−0.50	−0.25	0	0.25	0.50
0.50	75	87.5	100	112.5	125
1.00	50	75	100	125	150
1.25	37.5	68.8	100	131.3	162.5
1.50	25	62.5	100	137.5	175
2.00	0	50	100	150	200
2.50	−25	37.50	100	162.5	225
3.33	−66.7	16.67	100	183.3	266.7

Persistence of Volatility and Dependence

Figures 8.3a and 8.3b show the autocorrelation of returns and volatility for currencies, as well as the autocorrelation of covariance with equity. However, the evidence for autocorrelation in these particular examples is much weaker than for equity or commodities. However, as we will see, the approach I recommend is different than that for commodities.

FIGURE 8.3a   Autocorrelations of Returns and Volatilities (1988–2010).

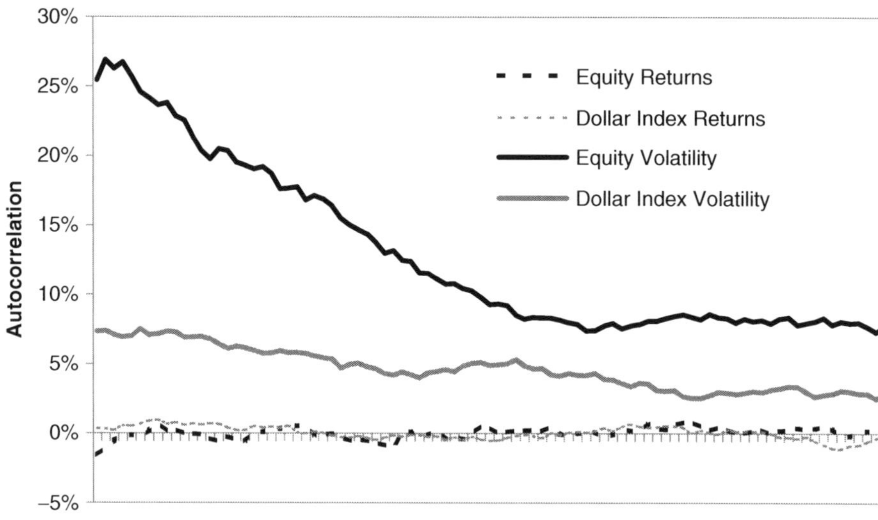

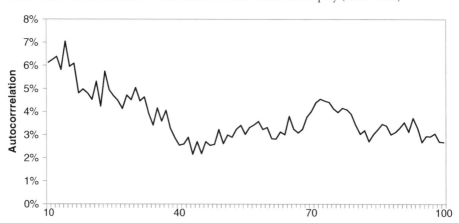

Source: Data from Datastream.

FIGURE 8.3b   Autocorrelation of Covariance of Dollar Index with Equity (1988–2010)

Source: Data from Datastream.

Implications of the Evidence on Currencies

The following are a few aspects on which we should easily agree:

- The main issue with currency risk is not how much of an existing foreign currency exposure in a global portfolio should be hedged, but rather how much currency exposure is appropriate, taking into account that we may or may not already have exposure to some currencies.
- There is some evidence that assets with values that are vulnerable to currency fluctuations may incorporate a currency-related risk premium.
- In some countries (for example, Canada and Australia), the value of the currency is more likely to be positively correlated with global growth, while the currency of other countries (for example, the United States) is more likely to act as a safe haven in difficult times.
- In the case of high-quality foreign fixed-income assets, it makes sense to hedge most of the currency risk.

What are the implications? First, blindly hedging currency risk may remove a natural hedge and increase risk. However, the size of the allocation recommendations to specific currencies that may appear optimal from a risk-management point of view may be unpalatable to many investors, depending on the country of residence of the investor. We need to think of how to integrate currency-risk management into a portfolio management process using a rationale that is acceptable to investors.

How to Use Currency Exposure in a Portfolio

Much like commodities, there are many arguments that support the use of currencies as tradable assets within a dynamically managed portfolio or strategy. Currencies are volatile, and their volatility and correlations among themselves and with other assets show some persistence, although it is much weaker than for other asset classes. Furthermore, the fact that huge losses in late 2008, which stemmed from carry trades, occurred because of a sequence of downward moves, and not a single large move, also supports the idea of using currencies within a dynamic process.

A dynamic approach may be an efficient way to indirectly capture the potential gains from the carry trade (since the objective of a dynamic volatility-based approach is not necessarily to directly exploit the carry trade). It may also allow investors to exit the strategy before they experience substantial losses related to the reversals in currency trends. The carry trade is a strategy, not a strategic position. However, there are two significant differences between currency risk and commodity risk. First, with commodities, we can choose to create an exposure to this asset class. In the case of currencies, a currency exposure is automatically created whenever we decide to trade foreign assets, even if the objective is not currency exposure, but portfolio diversification on many other levels. Second, the size of this exposure can be significant. Thus, whenever we diversify a portfolio internationally, we are forced to deal with the issue of currency exposure.

Furthermore, there are three issues that complicate the setup of a strategic policy on currency exposure. First, we know not only that hedging currency risk on quality fixed-income assets will reduce risk significantly, but also that some currencies offer a natural hedge against global equity risks. Second, we have mentioned the significant differences of opinions among researchers and even practitioners on this issue, and we know from experience that if investors and their portfolio managers adopt extreme policies on currency exposure, such as fully hedging, over-hedging or even increasing already existing currency exposure, these investors run the risk of feeling the pressure to change the currency policy at the very worst time. Investors are concerned about currency risk, but they behave as if they prefer a scenario where the foreign asset suffers currency losses and the hedge provides currency gains to the opposite scenario. The latter would require justifying to investors or managers why the currency risk was hedged. Since exchange-rate cycles are usually extremely long, an investor can be right or wrong on his or her currency strategy for a very long time, and most investors and organizations are not that patient.

The third issue is related to the difficulty of identifying the actual currency of exposure. For example, a company listed in Europe may originate a substantial portion of its cash flows from other markets. If a US investor buys securities in the Eurozone and is hedging the currency risk, he or she may be inaccurately hedging US denominated cash flows that are reported in euros. Furthermore, this company may have implemented its own hedging policy. Since the true structure of currency exposure that results from investing in international assets is probably impossible to measure accurately, and is probably time varying, only an ongoing analysis of statistical dependence between equity and currency performances could provide a relative sensitivity estimate of both series.

Nevertheless, we have to be realistic and realize that we will probably never have a precise understanding of currency risk, but that this risk is unavoidable to any global investor. So, from a strategic exposure point of view, what should the investor do? Considering the lack of a strong conviction on this issue, and the fact that the most logical approach may actually be very difficult to implement, and may require a long investment horizon to be validated, I would recommend the following two-step process, which remains consistent with the general recommendations of several authors.

Step 1: Specify a Long-Term Currency Hedging/Exposure Level

I have often mentioned that I believe in an investment process that favors strong cash flows, because cash flows reinforce the alignment of interest between investors and issuers. They are also indicative of the issuers' confidence in their ability to generate future cash flows. Thus, the basic argument is to maintain a currency hedge ratio that is based on the "certainty equivalent" return on foreign assets. At this step of the process, I will ignore the possibility that the investor might operate from a safe haven or soft currency country.

Let's first consider the issue of currency risk related to high-quality foreign fixed-income assets. Most experts on this issue will agree that fully hedging currency risk on such assets is a free lunch, since hedging will considerably reduce the volatility and will allow the investor to diversify the exposure and concentration of his or her fixed-income portfolio. The main logic behind this reasoning is the fact that the size and timing of cash flows on such assets are highly predictable, and usually not influenced by currency risk. They also account for 100%, or nearly 100%, of the entire investment expected performance. In this case, currency hedging will be very efficient at reducing risk, especially in the context of hedging local liabilities.

However, what happens if the assets are not highly rated nominal bonds, but more uncertain high-yield nominal bonds? In this situation, the investor has a much higher probability of sustaining losses related to defaults. Once cash flows become uncertain, we can no longer assume that full hedging will reduce the risk of the asset more efficiently than a partial hedging. When hedging a risky asset, we run the risk of over-hedging or under-hedging. If we fully hedge, we run the risk that portfolio losses will occur when the foreign currency is appreciating. Without hedging, we run the risk that portfolio losses may occur when the foreign currency is depreciating, accentuating losses. As Solnik (1988) indicated, some currency exposure will help to diversify the portfolio, but too much currency exposure may dominate the portfolio risk, especially since there are few currency groups, and price trends between currency groups can last for a very long time. Thus, the diversification that can be achieved within a portfolio of currencies is limited.

To retain some diversification benefit and to allow the portfolio to benefit from the rebalancing process between currencies and other assets, we would want to retain some currency exposure on the foreign assets in the portfolio. However, the more uncertain the returns on the assets are, the greater the exposure to foreign currencies that should be tolerated. At the lower end of the risk spectrum, high-quality foreign income assets would be fully hedged, while at the upper end of the risk spectrum, small-capitalization global stocks should not be hedged, or, should not be hedged significantly. The approximate ratio of the total expected return of the asset class accounted by the cash flow certainty equivalent determines the level of hedging. Figure 8.4 provides an example of what a currency-hedging policy could be, assuming that we make no assumption, for now, about the correlation between the local currency of the investor and global portfolio risk.

FIGURE 8.4 Strategic Currency Hedging According to the Asset Class.

For example, some high-payout global equity portfolios can generate current yields of more than 5%. An investor could assume that such a payout represents at least 60% of his or her total expected return. Based on this information, the investor could apply a hedge ratio of approximately 50% to 70%. These general hedging levels would represent the base case for investors, no matter their country of origin.

Step 2 – (Dynamically) Adjust the Exposure Level According to the Status of the Currency of the Investor and the Volatility of Financial Markets

If we consider currencies as an asset class, and not simply as a risk to be hedged, then the objective of currency exposure is to calibrate the exposure to currencies that is required to hedge a portfolio of assets against major market disruptions. For example, as we have mentioned, a Canadian investor may find shorting the Canadian dollar against the US dollar an efficient hedge against global equity exposure, or even his or her own domestic Canadian equity exposure. A US investor would come to the same conclusion (increasing his or her exposure to US dollars when investing internationally). However, we also know that the hedging efficiency of a currency will change over time, just as its status as a hard (reserve) currency may also evolve.

However, such changes are likely to occur slowly, and may be detected in the data. Reserve currencies cannot be substituted overnight. The size of the adjustment should be based on a sensitivity analysis of world equity markets to our currency portfolio and the level of protection desired by the investor. I will now illustrate the sensitivity of currencies to equity return and equity risk. Table 8.16a shows the correlation of 12-month trailing equity returns to currency returns for four equity markets and six exchange rates against the US dollar. Table 8.16b presents the same information, but the correlation is against equity market volatility.

The results in both tables are as expected. First, the US dollar has a tendency to depreciate (appreciate) against the Canadian and Australian dollars in a strong (weak) equity environment. It appears to be also true of the British pound. The same conclusion is observed with volatility. The US dollar appreciates against the Canadian and Australian dollars in a volatile equity environment. Unsurprisingly, the Swiss franc

TABLE 8.16a Correlation of Equity Market Returns to Currency Returns (October 1989 to October 2011)

	CAD	AUD	EUR	GPB	JPY	CHF
S&P 500	−0.40	−0.30	0.05	−0.34	0.11	0.19
S&P/TSX	−0.50	−0.34	0.18	−0.24	0.04	0.29
MSCI EAFE	−0.57	−0.54	−0.10	−0.40	−0.10	0.00
MSCI Emerging	−0.62	−0.64	−0.10	−0.32	−0.22	0.02

Source: Data from Datastream.

TABLE 8.16b Correlation of Equity Volatility to Currency Returns (October 1989 to October 2011)

	CAD	AUD	EUR	GPB	JPY	CHF
S&P500	0.23	0.23	0.07	0.18	−0.16	−0.03
S&PTSX	0.44	0.46	0.24	0.34	−0.00	0.11
MSCI EAFE	0.27	0.19	0.08	0.30	−0.39	−0.13
MSCI Emerging	0.35	0.34	0.02	0.25	−0.20	−0.11

Source: Data from Datastream.

is much less sensitive than either the Canadian or Australian dollars in the same circumstances. Furthermore, the strength of the correlation is significantly linked to the level of equity performance or volatility. For example, the correlation of the Canadian dollar to US equity returns is −77% (not shown in table), when the trailing 12-month return is negative and only −16% when it is positive. Thus, shorting the Canadian or US dollar would be an effective defensive strategy from the point of view of any equity investor in any country.

Let's now consider two investors, one based in the US, the other in Canada. Both investors have a home bias. The US investor owns 60% S&P 500, 20% MSCI EAFE, 10% S&P/TSX and 10% MSCI Emerging. The Canadian investor owns 60% S&P/TSX, 15% MSCI EAFE, 15% S&P 500 and 10% MSCI Emerging. Two currency scenarios are considered: full exposure or a 10% short position to the Canadian dollar. Table 8.17 presents the results.

TABLE 8.17 Impact of a Currency Strategy on the Portfolios of a US- and a Canadian-Based Investor (October 1989 to October 2011)

	US Investor		
	GEO Mean (%)	Volatility (%)	Correlation
No Short CAD	8.12	4.51	
Short CAD	8.10	4.38	
Spread	−0.02	−0.13	−0.58
	Canadian Investor		
	GEO Mean (%)	Volatility (%)	Correlation
No Short CAD	7.66	3.94	
Short CAD	7.60	3.86	
Spread	−0.06	−0.08	−0.37

Source: Data from Datastream.

The short Canadian dollar position was successful in reducing volatility in both cases, but it also reduced performance by 2 to 6 bps. Considering that we were short a currency that appreciated by more than 17% over the period, we could have expected a much worse performance.

We could obviously try to determine the level of short exposure that would maximize the return/risk efficiency of the portfolio. However, the level of short exposure that would maximize portfolio efficiency over time is far above what many investment committees would tolerate, especially for US investors. The Canadian investor benefits from a natural hedge when investing overseas (he or she is implicitly shorting a soft currency when investing abroad), the US investor does not. Therefore, while it is important to design a sensible currency policy, we may have more success concentrating our efforts on portfolio management aspects that are less likely to be challenged. For example, although we should implement a strategic long-term currency position based on the factors we have discussed, we could still allow a separate limited dynamic tactical position (with an upper limit) within a managed volatility program.

I recently advised a pension fund on the issue of currency hedging implementation. A service provider was offering a managed currency mandate around a neutral position of 50% for each currency to which they were exposed. I simply proposed that the neutral position of each currency be less or more than 50%, depending on whether or not the foreign currency exposure was in a procyclical or countercyclical currency. This service provider adopted my suggestion.

Private Market Assets as a Diversifier

Private market assets are real estate, mortgages, private equity, private bonds, hedge funds, etc. This is obviously more of an issue for institutional investors than retail investors. How should an institutional investor incorporate private market assets without introducing too much complexity in the allocation process?

A main issue with private market assets is the lack of widely accepted and representative benchmarks, which clouds the understanding of the risk and dependence characteristics of these asset classes. Causes of this issue are generally the illiquidity of the assets and the less-than-ideal diversification that can sometimes be achieved within the asset class. The inability to determine a "true" value for illiquid assets often forces investors to rely on appraisal prices that will typically lead to a smoothing of prices and, thus, will cause these assets to appear far less volatile and correlated than they really are.

Cao and Teiletche (2007) [39] provide an interesting example. Let's assume that an investor was offered two potential products. The two products delivered the same cumulative returns during 1995 and 2004, but the first had 18% volatility and a 100% correlation to the S&P 500 (it is, in fact, the S&P 500), while the other had 3% volatility and a 20% correlation. Should the investor be willing to pay more for the second investment, since it offers such interesting statistical properties? After all, even though the two investments delivered the same return, combining these two products should significantly improve the GEO mean as long as these characteristics could be expected to hold in the future.

In this case, the answer is no, since both investments are, in fact, the S&P 500. These statistical properties were observed simply because the performance on the second product was reported as a moving average of the daily return over the previous month. Therefore, failing to consider the impact of smoothed returns on volatility and correlation could lead to inappropriately high allocations to illiquid assets. For example, let's assume the following relation from Cao and Teiletche:

$$R_t^0 = \Sigma \; \theta_i R_{t-i} \qquad\qquad (8.14)$$

In this equation, the return on an illiquid asset R_t^0 is defined by a weighted average of current and past true returns, which are unobservable. Observed returns are determined through a smoothing process. If $\theta_0 = 1$, there is no smoothing of returns, and the return on the asset is equal to the true return. However, if $0 <= \theta_i <= 1$ and $\Sigma \; \theta_i = 1$, the asset return will be determined by a smoothing of past returns. Although the returns on the assets are expected to be equal to the true unobservable returns in the long run, this will not be the case in the short run. The consequences may be an understatement of volatility and correlation, and an overstatement of the Sharpe ratios and autocorrelation of returns. All of these factors would skew the allocation process away from a proper allocation if illiquid asset components were considered in the allocation process without any corrective measures.

Using data on venture capital returns from 1986 Q3 to 2003 Q4, and on real estate from 1978 Q1 to 2004 Q3, Cao and Teiletche demonstrated that real estate returns and venture capital show positive autocorrelations up to the twelfth lag and third lag respectively. One could expect that the solution would require the use of an autoregressive process to de-smooth the data.

Furthermore, even if we de-smooth the data, they still have to be reliable and representative of the structure of the allocation to these sectors. For example, in the case of private equity, Thomas Idzorek (2007) [40] of Ibbotson Associates mentioned that there is no widely agreed-upon time series of data representing the Beta of the asset class. Therefore, investors may be prevented from understanding the risk, return and dependence characteristics required to determine the contribution of private equity to a diversified portfolio.

The same problem exists for most illiquid asset classes, and de-smoothing will not resolve this issue. Idzorek raised the idea that investors in private equity could use publicly traded equities whose activities are consistent with the activities of private equity firms, much like using REITs as a proxy for commercial real estate.

There are, of course, significant issues with using this approach. First, unlike the equity or bond market, there is no way to invest in a representative or balanced market portfolio of private equity. As a result, most private equity portfolios would have significantly higher idiosyncratic risks than a theoretical market portfolio that no real investor can acquire. Second, it may be a mistake to assume that the private and public asset markets have similar long-term characteristics. For example, Weber (2011) [41] believes that the public and private markets for infrastructure investments can be significantly different on many levels, including the way the transactions are structured. The same observations could certainly be made of other sectors.

It has also been my experience that some investors buy public deals without proper information and the proper expertise to analyze those deals, simply because they are sometimes included in the fixed-income benchmark. For example, in Canada, there have been cases where the road shows that function to explain specific public infrastructure deals were canceled because the demand for the issue was so strong. Furthermore, the delay allowed between a deal announcement and its pricing and distribution is much too short to allow investors to do a proper analysis.

Third, as was the case with commodities, academicians and specialists do not agree on the performance of private assets. For example, according to Schmidt (2006) [42], private equity outperformed large-cap equity. However, according to Kaplan and Schoar (2005) [43] and Phalippou and Gottschlag (2009), [44] returns were at most similar and even lower. What is the truth? Not surprisingly, it appears that part of the reason for this confusion could again be related to how private equity portfolio indices are built.

Bilo, Christophers, Degosciu and Zimmermann (2005) [45] measured the performance of listed private equity from 1986 and 2003 using different weighting processes: value-weighted buy and hold, equally weighted buy and hold and, finally, equally weighted rebalanced. Table 8.18 illustrates that the performance and volatility can vary greatly according to the weighting mechanism.

Thus, what is true for equity in general is also true for listed private equity. This is yet another example of how rebalancing matters. However, in this case, investors could be using public data to justify investing in private markets on the basis of assumptions about rebalancing, which are totally inappropriate. Using public data without the proper asset allocation assumption can lead to the wrong conclusions.

This observation is reinforced by some data provided by Idzorek, who analyzed the performance of two indices of listed private equity companies, the LPE Index (a collection of private equity companies listed on NYSE, AMEX and/or NASDAQ), launched in September 2006, and its sister index, the International LPE Index (for non-US domiciled companies). Both indices were backfilled to September 1995 using a weighting mechanism selected by the Index Committee. Although the justification for the weighting mechanism used to backfill the data will probably appear reasonable

TABLE 8.18 Performance Measures of Listed Private Equity (1986–2003) (%)

	GEO Mean	Volatility
Buy and hold Value Weighted	5.4	43.2
Buy and Hold Equal Weight	5.9	37.1
Rebalanced Equal Weight	16.0	33.7
S&P 500	11.1	18.0

Source: Bilo, Christophers, Degosciu and Zimmermann (2005).

TABLE 8.19 Backfilled Performance Measures of US and Non-US Private Equity Indices (%)

Indices	Weighting Mechanisms	GEO Mean	Volatility
US	Index Committee	24.85	40.73
	Equal Weight	23.10	70.19
	Market Weight	4.49	129.91
Non-US	Index Committee	21.46	32.37
	Equal Weight	18.48	26.31
	Market Weight	10.81	46.25

Source: Idzorek (2007).

to any investor, a reasonable investor should also expect that an Index Committee may be biased toward using a weighting mechanism that will make the performance of the index look attractive. Table 8.19 presents the performance of both indices as reported, and also using two alternative weighting mechanisms, equal weight and market weight. Unsurprisingly, the performances using the weighting process chosen by the Index Committee are the most favorable and are significantly greater than those resulting from a market-weight scheme.

Therefore, a backfilled manufactured index of listed public equity companies is unreliable as a decision tool. It could lead to flawed conclusions in a Markowitz-type allocation process. Furthermore, as Phalippou and Gottschlag reported, data from listed vehicles are inappropriate to large investors, since these investors tend to invest directly in private partnerships. Investors in listed vehicles are typically small and lack the understanding of the intricacies of this asset class. This view is in line with my own observations of the public infrastructure market in Canada.

Closing Remarks on the Private Asset Market

There are five lessons to be learned about the private asset market.

1. There is no reliable data set available for evaluating the performance of many private asset markets, and no methodology can correct for the absence of appropriate and representative data. Public and private deals may be structurally different, and private portfolios cannot be easily rebalanced. Why are performances presented by private industry associations (such as NVCA and EVCA for private equity) significantly greater than performances calculated by third parties using different data sources or even the same data? It is easy to design indices that will lead to a different perception of performance. Phalippou mentions the fact that a major database reported the same quarterly performances for the same funds every quarter for many years, sometimes for as much as six years!

2. For most investors, illiquid assets do not allow for the same level of diversification that can be achieved in the public market. The level of idiosyncratic risks is higher, and, thus, a totally different level of depth of expertise is required to invest in illiquid asset classes. And a different process altogether is required to determine the proper allocation.

   I have mentioned previously how public bond issues related to public private partnerships (PPPs) were incorporated into the Canadian fixed-income index. Many fixed-income investors feel the pressure to buy these bonds because the bonds will be in the index, even though they do not usually have the expertise to evaluate these transactions, and also are not given enough time to make a truly informed decision. This last comment is tempered by the fact that, apparently, some large investors are being shown bond deals ahead of other investors, and are even being given the opportunity to request a few adjustments to the terms of the transactions. Furthermore, more knowledgeable investors will often refuse to participate in public deals since they believe it takes more than a few days to analyze documents that can be hundreds or thousands of pages long. They will ignore publicly done PPP deals in favor of private deals where they are given the opportunity to analyze and discuss the transaction for several weeks and even months.

3. Considering how important the allocation process between and within asset classes is to long-term performance, the allocation to illiquid assets should not be set at a level that can potentially constrain the allocation process. Furthermore, Ang, Papanikolaou and Westerfield (2010) [46] show that illiquidity will cause an investor to behave in a more risk-averse way with respect to both liquid and illiquid risky holdings. Basically, as the trading frequency is reduced and becomes more uncertain, the total level of risk aversion increases with the level of exposure to illiquid assets. Ang, Papanikolaou and Westerfield's conclusion is also coherent with the behavior that has been observed in so many institutions during the liquidity crisis. Therefore, it seems perfectly logical to cap the exposure to illiquid assets according to two criteria: the level of exposure to sister assets in the public markets and the degree of interference that private assets may cause to the dynamic portfolio allocation strategy.

4. Although an investor can derive a range of possible allocations to illiquid assets, the investor must first ask himself if he has access to the proper expertise that would allow him to be comfortable with an allocation. The expertise, style and philosophy of managers, as well as the investor's own needs, should help determine the proper size and nature of allocation. If investors are unfamiliar with an illiquid asset class, they should start small, deal with advisors who are willing and capable to bring them to the next level, and then revaluate after 12 to 24 months.

   There is one caveat to this recommendation. A smaller investor may face a different fee structure than larger investors, and may not have access to funds and quality of co-investment opportunities. The public asset market is an equal-opportunity market for almost all investors. The private market is not.

5. Fees still matter. Although returns are difficult to forecast in most cases, the investor should be aware of the significance of fees in the markets for private assets. It has been reported that total fees in private equity can be as high as 4% to 6% annually. Therefore, although investors investing in markets for private assets may seek to capture the illiquidity premium related to these markets, they might end up paying as much in fees. Phalippou (2008) reported the following comments on private equity from David Swensen of Yale, one of the most knowledgeable private equity investors:

> While the value added by operationally oriented buyout partnerships may, in certain instances, overcome the burden imposed by the typical buyout fund's fee structure, in aggregate, buyout investments fail to match public alternatives . . . In the absence of truly superior fund selection skills (or extraordinary luck), investors should stay away, far, far away from private equity investments . . . Some part of the failure of buyout managers to produce risk adjusted returns stems from the inappropriate fee structure.

Fraser-Sampson (2007) [47] made the argument that only top-quartile funds should be invested. This would be good advice, except for three issues. First, Philippou found that there is no long-term persistence in returns between new funds and older funds. A private equity manager may have a few good years, but once you find out about this manager, there is no evidence that the next fund will be as productive. Second, the performance of private equity funds, excluding first quartile, is extremely disappointing. Third, performance appears to be cyclical. Investors who allocate on the basis of prior performance usually do so during a period when significant capital is committed to the sector (because so many investors follow the same logic), which translates into lower performance in the future.

A disturbing study on the performance of private market assets is that of Mulcahy, Weeks and Bradley of the Kauffman Foundation (2012) [48] concerning venture capital funds. The paper evaluates 100+ funds (both mature and non-mature) over the period of 1985 to 2011. The following are its main conclusions:

- Only 20% of venture funds generated returns that beat a public-market equivalent by more than 3% annually and more than 50% underperformed the public market equivalent after fees.
- Only four of thirty venture capital funds with committed capital of more than $400 million delivered returns better than those of a publicly traded small-cap stock index.
- 75% of venture funds failed to deliver the expected return in the first 27 months. Eventually, 78% did not achieve returns sufficient to reward for long-term investing.
- Since 1997, less cash has been returned to investors than has been invested in venture capital.

According to the authors, the investment model is broken. The most significant misalignment occurs because venture capitalists are not paid to generate returns that exceed the public market. Managers are typically paid a 2% management fee on committed capital, and a 20% profit sharing. This encourages the creation of bigger funds and allows managers to lock high levels of fee-based personal income, even when no capital is returned to investors. The fact that large investors establish target allocations, which requires investing even when opportunities are lacking, is only aggravating this situation.

A recent experience of mine also highlights the importance to investors of not cavalierly giving up liquidity. In the spring of 2012, I met with a hedge fund manager in the credit space, and had one of the shortest meetings of my life. This manager had a decent performance from the late 1990s to 2005, but the manager rightly decided then to short credit related to subprime. His main fund recorded a performance of more than 100% in a single year. A 100% growth in assets highlights three issues. First, you suddenly have twice the amount of assets to manage. Second, many investors will suddenly want to invest with you. Third, if your assets increase by a factor of five or more, it does not mean that you know where to invest those assets. This manager was not disciplined. He accepted all inflows that were offered and did not know where to invest those inflows. When performances in 2008 were dismal, many of these investors withdrew their contributions very quickly. To avoid these issues, the manager now wants much longer commitments from investors. He had significant assets, but I was still wondering what the business model was, or if there was one beyond generating fees. I left after 25 minutes.

My purpose is certainly not to fully discourage investors from investing in the private asset market. However, investors must remain skeptical of any information used to sell them the opportunity to invest in the private asset market. Investors should not be obsessed with the idea of identifying an appropriate benchmark. These markets are much too heterogeneous to allow for the use of an appropriate benchmark. Investors should simply specify the goals they want to achieve (such as outperforming the yield of a tradable security of similar maturity by "X" bps in the long term) and benchmark and structure their program against those specific goals.

Finally, the fact that volatility is misrepresented (too low) can sometimes be an advantage. Marked-to-market is a theoretically sound concept, but in crisis time investor sentiment can destroy the value of many assets indiscriminately. If the private assets are of good quality, and if the valuation process leads to a smoothing of price volatility, the portfolio managers may be subject to less pressure from investors to act rashly during a crisis situation. This may not be rational, but it is a hard fact.

Closing Remarks

In a low-interest-rate environment, investors seek new products and asset classes that can provide higher excess returns. Many investors believe that they need to multiply the number of asset classes and products in their portfolio to improve their returns. It is likely that many of them already have enough diversity of risk premiums, but that the risk weight allocated to those risk premiums is inefficient. Furthermore, the search for diversity may end up adding significantly higher fees, which could cancel out the before-fee benefits of some new products or asset classes. This does not mean that investors should totally shy away from private market assets such as real estate, private equity and hedge funds, but it certainly means that they should try to exploit more efficiently the benefits that public market assets can offer before expanding toward other options. Therefore, the allocation to illiquid assets should not be set at a level that can interfere with the allocation process. Finally, because idiosyncratic risks are much more difficult to diversify away, high confidence in the expertise of managers of private market assets is even more paramount than in public markets.

In contrast, most public market assets offer the qualities required to build efficient portfolios, but there are two caveats to this statement. First, even if some asset classes have the required characteristics, it does not mean that the assets could not be assembled more efficiently. Second, in the case of commodities, the presence of a risk premium remains in doubt and we must rely on creating an efficient index (maybe even more than one) and using an efficient asset allocation among asset classes.

Currencies present a special challenge. The exposure to currency risk automatically derives from international diversification, and the level of currency intervention that would theoretically be required to create a more efficient portfolio is well beyond what many investors would be willing to tolerate. Thus, we may still implement a more efficient currency exposure strategy, but we should mostly rely on other aspects of the portfolio management process to substantially improve the overall efficiency of the portfolio.

Notes

1. Kat, Harry M. (2006), "How to evaluate a new diversifier with 10 simple questions," Cass Business School.
2. Xu, Xiaoquing Eleanor, Liu Jiong, and Anthony L. Loviscek (2010), "Hedge fund attrition, survivorship bias, and performance—Perspectives from the global financial crisis," Seton Hall University, TIAA-CREF.
3. Lack, Simon (2012), *The Hedge Fund Mirage: The Illusion of Big Money and Why It's Too Good to Be True*, John Wiley & Sons, Inc.
4. Heaney, Vince (2006), "From trading to owning commodities," *Financial Times*, March 20, http://www.ft.com/cms/s/0/516ee596-85bf-11dc-8170-0000779fd2ac.html#axzz24aM8Uskx.
5. Keynes, John M. (1930), *A Treatise on Money* Vol. 2, London: Macmillan.
6. Cootner, P. (1960), "Returns to speculators: Telser versus Keynes," *Journal of Political Economy* 68(4), 396–404.
7. Hirshleifer, D. (1990), "Hedging pressure and future price movements in a general equilibrium model," *Econometrica* 58, 411–428.

8. Kaldor, Nicholas (1939), "Speculation and economic stability," *Review of Economic Studies* 7, 1–27.

9. Brennan, Michael (1959), "The supply of storage," *American Economic Review* 48(1), 50–72.

10. Gorton, Gary B., Fumio Hayashi, and K. Geert Rouwenhorst (2007), "The fundamentals of commodity futures return," Yale ICF Working Paper No. 07–08.

11. Basu, Devraj and Joelle Miffre (2010), "Capturing the risk premium of commodity Futures: The role of Hedging Pressure," SKEMA Business School and EDHEC Business School.

12. Grauer, Frederick L.A. and Robert H. Litzenberger (1979), "The pricing of commodity futures contracts, nominal bonds and other risky assets under commodity price uncertainty," *Journal of Finance* 34(1), 69–83.

13. Dusak, Katherine (1973), "Futures trading and investor returns: An investigation of commodity market risk premiums," *Journal of Political Economy* 81(6), 1387–1406.

14. Bodie, Zvi and Victor I. Rosansky (1980), "The risk and return in commodity futures," *Financial Analysts Journal* 36(3), 27–39.

15. Kolb, R.W. (1992), "Is normal backwardation normal?" *Journal of Futures Market* 12(1), 75–91.

16. Deaves, Richard and Itzhak Krinsky (1995), "Do futures prices for commodities embody risk premiums?," *The Journal of Futures Markets* 15(6), 637–648.

17. Kat, Harry M. and Roel C.A. Oomen (2006a), "What every investor should know about commodities—Part I: Univariate return analysis," Cass Business School—City University; Kat, Harry M. and Roel C.A. Oomen (2006b), "What every investor should know about commodities—Part II: Multivariate return analysis," Cass Business School—City University.

18. Gorton, Gary and Geert Rouwenhorst (2006), "Facts and fantasies about commodity futures," *Financial Analysts Journal* 62(2), 47–68.

19. Erb, Claude B. and Campbell R. Harvey (2006), "The strategic and tactical value of commodity futures," *Financial Analysts Journal* 62(2), 69–97.

20. Fuss, Roland, Christian Hoppe, and Dieter G. Kaiser (2007), "Review of commodity futures performance benchmarks," *The Handbook of Commodity Investing*, Chapter 7, John Wiley & Sons, Inc.

21. Hafner, Reinhold and Maria Heiden (2007), "Statistical analysis of commodity futures returns," *The Handbook of Commodity Investing*, Chapter 9, John Wiley & Sons, Inc.

22. Erb, Claude, Campbell R. Harvey, and Christian Kempe (2007), "Performance characteristics of commodity futures," *The Handbook of Commodity Investing*, Chapter 8, John Wiley & Sons, Inc.

23. Hillier, David, Paul Draper, and Robert Faff (2006), "Do precious metals shine? An investment perspective," *Financial Analysts Journal* 62(2), 98–106.

24. Christian, Jeffrey M. (2007), "Some thoughts on risk management for commodity portfolios," *The Handbook of Commodity Investing*, Chapter 12, John Wiley & Sons, Inc.

25. Perold, André F. and Evan C. Schulman (1988), "The free lunch in currency hedging: Implications for investment policy and performance standards," *Financial Analysts Journal* 44(3), 45–50.

26. Fisher, Kenneth L. and Meir Statman (2003), "Hedging currencies with hindsight and regret," Fisher Investments Inc., Santa Clara University.

27. Froot, Kenneth (1993), "Currency hedging over long horizons," National Bureau of Economic Research, Working Paper No. 4355.

28. Black, Fisher (1990), "Equilibrium exchange rate hedging," *Journal of Finance* 45(3), 899–908.

29. Solnik, Bruno (1988), "Global asset management," *Journal of Portfolio Management* 35(2), 43–51.

30. Solnik, Bruno (1998), "Why not diversify internationally rather than domestically?" *Financial Analysts Journal* 30(4), 48–54.

31. Gastineau, Gary L. (1995), "The currency hedging decision: A search for synthesis in asset allocation," *Financial Analysts Journal* 51(3), 8–17.

32. Walker, Eduardo (2008), "Strategic currency hedging and global portfolio investments upside down," *Journal of Business Research*, 61, 657–668.

33. Campbell, John Y., Karine Serfaty-de Medeiros, and Luis M. Viceira (2010), "Global currency hedging," *Journal of Finance* 65(1), 87–121.

34. Jurek, Jakub W. (2009), "Crash-neutral currency carry trades," Princeton University; Engel, Charles (1996), "The forward discount anomaly and the risk premium: A survey of recent evidence," *Journal of Empirical Finance* 3, 123–192; Froot, Kenneth. A. and Richard Thaler (1990), "Anomalies: Foreign exchange," *Journal of Economic Perspectives* 4, 179–192.

35. Landon, Stuart and Constance Smith (1999), "The risk premium, exchange rate expectations, and the forward exchange rate: Estimates for the Yen-Dollar rate," MPRA Paper 9775, University Library of Munich, Germany; Carlson, John A. and Carol L. Osler (2003), "Currency risk premiums: Theory and evidence," Purdue University and Brandeis University.

36. Bekaert, Geert, Min Wei, and Yuhang Xing (2002), "Uncovered interest rate parity and the term structure," *Journal of International Money and Finance* 26 1038–1069.

37. Carrieri, Francesca, Vihang Errunza and Basma Majerbi (2004), " Does emerging market exchange risk affect global equity prices?," McGill University, University of Virginia and University of British Columbia.

38. Roache, Shaun K. and Matthews D. Merritt (2006), "Currency risk premia in global stock markets," International Monetary Fund.

39. Cao, Dan and Jérôme Teiletche (2007), "Reconsidering asset allocation involving illiquid assets," *Journal of Asset Management* 8(4), 267–282.

40. Idzorek, Thomas (2007), "Private equity and strategic asset allocation," Ibbotson Associates.

41. Weber, Barbara (2011), "Infrastructure as an asset class," CFA Conference Montreal,

42. Schmidt, Daniel M. (2006), "Private equity versus stocks – Do the alternative Asset's risk and return characteristics add value to the portfolio?," *The Journal of Alternative Investments* 9(1), 28–47.

43. Kaplan, S. and A. Schoar (2005), "Private Equity Performance: Returns, persistence and capital flows," *Journal of Finance* 60, 1791–1823.

44. Phalippou, Ludovic and Oliver Gottschalg (2009), "The performance of private equity," *The Review of Financial Studies* 22(4), 1747–1776.

45. Bilo, Stéphanie, Hans Christophers, Michel Degosciu, and Heinz Zimmermann (2005), "Risk, returns, and biases of listed private equity portfolios," Morgan Stanley—London, University of Basel.

46. Ang, Andrew, Dimitris Papanikolaou, and Mark M. Westerfield (2011), "Portfolio choice with illiquid assets," Columbia Business School, Northwestern University, University of Southern California.

47. Fraser-Sampson, Guy (2007), "Private equity as an asset class," Wiley Finance.

48. Mulcahy, Diane, Bill Weeks, and Harold S. Bradley (2012), "We have met the enemy . . . and he is us—Lessons from twenty years of the Kauffman Foundation's investment in venture capital funds and the triumph of hope over experience," The Ewing Marion Kauffman Foundation.

CHAPTER 9

Allocation Process and Efficient Tax Management

"In this world, nothing is certain but death and taxes" (Benjamin Franklin 1789). However, private investors face four certainties, death, taxes, fees and risks, while some institutional investors can benefit from a tax-exempt status and/or assume an infinite—or, at least, a very long—horizon. In this chapter we will discuss how taxation and the eventuality of death influence the investment and risk-management process for individual investors.

According to a survey by Horan and Adler (2009) [1], although 76% of clients expect their advisors to incorporate tax considerations into the portfolio management process, only 11% report tax-adjusted performance. Until the late 1990s, much of the literature on asset allocation ignored the impact of taxation. But there are exceptions. Asset managers such as First Quadrant have been writing about the importance of efficient tax management for investment portfolios for at least two decades. Furthermore, tax-adjusted asset management has been made more relevant by the instability and complexity of the tax code, especially in the United States. For example, although most Americans pay lower taxes than Canadians, an analysis of the principles of the two tax codes in application in 2010 and in prior years leads to interesting observations. The Canadian tax code is much less likely to distort the investment process. It presents a more integrated approach, and its underlying principles have been more coherent and stable. Comparing the two systems will improve our understanding of the impact and distortion caused by taxation, even for investors located in other countries.

When investors consider taxes, they often limit their concerns to the impact of taxes on returns. However, taxation will also impact risk. Therefore, the asset allocation and risk-management process cannot be appropriately conducted without considering taxation. Taxation complicates the investment process. A portfolio that is deemed to be efficient before taxes may not be efficient on an after-tax basis. The investment process of taxable investors must be completed on an after-tax basis because the objective of most investors is to maximize the utility of lifetime consumption, and because goods and services are purchased with after-tax income.

However, every investor is unique, and the tax code is complex and evolving. Therefore, our goal is not to consider all the specificities of the tax code (since these can change at any time), but to concentrate on the main principles underlying the philosophy of tax policies in order to make a more time-invariant argument and present an analytical process than can be adapted to specific situations.

This chapter is only relevant in supporting the development of asset management platforms dedicated to individual investors (although the principles of some findings could be extended to taxable institutional investors). It does challenge some of the views on issues such as tax-loss harvesting and other strategies designed to delay taxation. However, we are not going to attempt to capture all of the details and nuances of taxation and estate planning. This chapter should only be used as a basic reference, and investors should still seek their own tax advice.

Taxation Issues for Individual Investors

The asset allocation process for private investors is more complex than for institutions. Private investors have various life expectancies, a wider range of risk aversion and life goals. They are subject to different levels of tax rates, which vary according to the type of investment income, and the trigger for taxes on capital gains is at the discretion of the investor when assets are sold. Private investors are more prone to irrational behavior than corporate and institutional investors, since they usually do not benefit from the same level of advisory expertise (although institutions are represented by managers who, in many cases, have been shown to behave irrationally) and are more stressed by the short-term fluctuations of their personal wealth. Furthermore, individual investors are allowed to locate some of their financial assets in tax-deferred and tax-exempt accounts. Although this opportunity is worth relatively less to extremely wealthy individuals, it can remain very relevant even to investors and households who own several million dollars in assets—especially if they have the benefit of a work plan with employer contributions. Furthermore, the impact of a work plan in the overall allocation process will obviously differ depending on whether it is a defined contribution or defined benefit plan. Finally, estate taxes are very relevant in the United States, because the US tax code offers better tax relief on assets after an investor has died than it did while the investor was alive! Therefore, to truly understand taxation and its impact on asset allocation and risk management, we must understand the following concepts:

- How different components of investment returns are taxed.
- How the location of financial assets in specific portfolios (tax exempt and tax deferred) changes tax liabilities and risk.
- How after-tax returns can be optimized in the context of capital gains, capital losses and eventual death, and how over-optimization of tax liabilities can hinder the long-term after-tax performance.

We will conclude this chapter with two case studies.

Components of Investment Returns, Asset Location, Death and Taxes

Tax policy for assets that are located within a taxable account will differ depending on the source of investment returns (such as interest, dividends and capital gains). For example, foreign dividends will usually be taxed at a higher rate than domestic eligible dividends, and interest income will usually be taxed at a higher rate than capital gains. However, if those same return components are located in a tax-exempt or tax-deferred account (such as Roth IRA (Individual Retirement Arrangement) and traditional IRA in the United States), the tax treatment will be determined by the rules that apply specifically to those accounts, no matter the source of investment income. For example, returns on assets invested in a traditional or Roth IRA will accumulate tax-free whether the source of income is interest, foreign dividends or capital gains. Thus, when tax policy is considered, the asset allocation decision (i.e., the allocation among asset classes) cannot be dissociated from the asset location decision (the portfolio in which these assets classes are located), since it may be more efficient overall to locate specific assets in specific portfolios. Furthermore, death can trigger specific tax events that wealthy investors may want to consider.

Tables 9.1a and 9.1b summarize the most important elements of the tax policy that apply to taxable portfolios in Canada and in the United States as of 2011. The first table covers the tax treatment of components of investment returns, while the second discusses the tax events that are triggered at death. The following are common elements of tax policy in both countries:

- Interest income is taxed at the ordinary tax rates.
- Foreign dividends are taxed at the ordinary tax rates.
- Capital gains are usually taxed at a much lower level than interest income to reward risk taking by investors.
- Capital losses can be used against capital gains.
- Taxes on net capital gains can only be levied if these gains have been realized (i.e., when assets have been sold). If investors have the option to decide when to realize net capital gains, they will implicitly have to determine the appropriate trade-off between postponing taxation and maintaining a balanced portfolio through periodic rebalancing.

However, there are differences between the two tax regimes. First, some sources of interest income in the United States are exempt from federal and or state taxation. Investors usually recognize the tax benefit of such securities by requiring lower returns than on taxable securities of similar risk, although the implicit tax rate (calculated by comparing the required returns on taxable and tax-exempt securities of similar characteristics) is usually less than the ordinary tax rate. This will incite investors to locate tax-exempt securities in taxable accounts. There is no equivalent in Canada.

TABLE 9.1a Taxes and Sources of Investment Returns

Source of Income	United States	Canada
Interest	Fully taxed at ordinary income tax rate. There are exceptions such as municipal bonds, which are untaxed at the federal level and at the state level if investors are residing in the state of issuance.	Fully taxed at ordinary income tax rate. No exceptions.
Dividend from domestic eligible corporation	Lower tax rate than non-eligible and foreign dividends, but long-term tax policy is unclear.	A tax credit is provided that seeks primarily to bring the effective tax rate of individual investors in line with the differential tax rate between individuals and corporations.
Non-eligible and foreign dividend	Fully taxed at ordinary tax rate.	Fully taxed at ordinary tax rate.
Capital gains (principal)	Taxed when realized. Some capital losses can be reported against regular income.	Taxed when realized.
Short-term capital gains (< 12 months)	Fully taxed at ordinary tax rate. Some capital losses can be reported against regular income.	50% of capital gain taxed at the marginal tax rate.
Long-term capital gains (> 12 months)	Taxed at less than ordinary tax rate.	
Capital loss	Can be used against current or forward capital gains.	Can be used against capital gains three years back, in the current year and forward.
Capital loss (restriction)	Loss is no longer deductible if same investment is repurchased within 30 days.	Loss is no longer deductible if same investment is repurchased within 30 days.

In the United States, capital gains are taxed at a lower level than the ordinary tax rate, but only if the security has been held for more than 12 months. Investors may have an incentive to keep individual securities for at least a year to avoid the higher tax rate. There is no such issue in Canada, because Canada applies the ordinary tax rate on half the capital gains whether the security has been held for more or less than 12 months. Furthermore, both countries only allow the use of capital losses against capital gains (a small amount can be used to offset personal income in the United States), but in Canada, capital losses can be reported against gains realized during the previous three years (in the United States, only corporations are allowed this characteristic).

TABLE 9.1b Taxes and Death

	United States	Canada
Capital gains and estate taxes	No capital gains taxes. The tax basis of assets is reset to the current market value. There is a significant tax rate applied to estates (35%), but there is a $5 million exclusion per individual, $10 million per couple.	Estates are treated as deemed disposition of assets upon death unless estates are inherited by spouse or common-law partner. Capital gains are taxed at capital gains rates and retirement savings plan at applicable ordinary tax rate. There is no estate tax otherwise since 1972.

This allows for a less asymmetric distribution of after-tax returns and a more consistent allocation process, since Canadian investors will be able to use capital losses against capital gains more quickly and consistently than a US investor, at least on average.

The policies of the two countries concerning the taxation of dividends for domestic eligible corporations also differ. In the United States, there has been a long debate as to whether or not taxing dividends constitutes double taxation. Although the top current tax rate on dividends from domestic eligible corporations in 2011 was less than the ordinary tax rate, the dividend tax rate in the United States has been modified frequently. However, Canada has, for a very long time, applied a stable and systematic policy to tax dividends from eligible domestic corporations at a rate close to the differential tax rate between individuals and corporations. This is implicitly done through the use of a tax credit, which is adjusted whenever tax rates are changed. For example, if the Canadian government lowers the tax rate on corporations, the dividend tax credit will likely be reduced, thus increasing the effective tax rate for individuals on dividends. If the tax rate were increased, the same process would apply in reverse. Thus, under such a principle, Canadian investors can assume that dividends received from an eligible domestic corporation will most likely remain taxed at a much lower level than the ordinary tax rate. In some provinces, this approach can lead to negative tax rates on dividends for investors in specific tax brackets. The approach is coherent with the principle of avoiding double taxation.

Finally, tax events at death are also very different in both countries. Since 1972, estates in Canada have been treated as sales (deemed disposition of assets) upon death, except where the estate is inherited by a surviving spouse or common-law partner. Taxes owed are paid by the estate, and not by the beneficiaries. Under US law, an estate tax (above a certain asset value, which has been often adjusted) applies (except among spouses), but there are no capital gains taxes since there is an automatic reset of the tax basis of assets to market value at death. This implies that a US investor may have an incentive as she ages to avoid rebalancing her portfolio, since her beneficiaries will not have to pay any capital gains tax after her death.

Although one must hope that tax policy always seeks to achieve some rational economic objectives, principles underlying the US tax code and its greater instability are more likely to complicate and distort the investment process than in Canada.

Furthermore, in Canada, provinces have a highly harmonized tax code with the federal government. In the United States, tax policies differ significantly from state to state.

Another important fiscal aspect is the existence of tax-exempt or tax-deferred accounts. A tax-exempt account, such as a Roth IRA in the United States and the Tax-Free Savings Account (TFSA) in Canada, is simply a plan that authorizes tax-exempt investments. The contributions are not tax deductible and the returns on investments and withdrawals are tax-free.

Traditional IRA and 401(k) plans in the United States as well as Registered Retirement Savings Plans (RRSPs) in Canada are tax-deferred plans. Income from investments will also accumulate tax-free with these plans, but the contributions to the plan are tax deductible at the ordinary tax rate, while the withdrawals are fully taxable (not just the return on investments). Furthermore, employers can also contribute to these plans. Again, the tax framework that applies to these accounts (and others) is more complex in the United States than in Canada. The Canadian plan also allows greater flexibility, since unused contributions can be carried forward indefinitely, and the same plan is used for individual and employer-sponsored contributions. This information is summarized in Tables 9.2a and 9.2b.

Tax-Exempt, Tax-Deferred, Taxable Accounts and Asset Allocation

The fact that different sources of investment income are taxed at different rates, that income within a Roth IRA or traditional IRA accumulates tax-free and that IRA contributions and withdrawals may be deducted and taxed at different rates implies that the asset allocation decision will not be independent of the asset location decision. Therefore, we need to explain how taxation specifically influences the investment process for individual investors. There are at least four taxation principles that investors should remember.

First Principle: Taxation Impacts Return and Risk

Let's assume that a tax-exempt investment has an equal probability of realizing a −7.5% or +20% capital gain over one year. The average of these two expected returns is +6.25%. If the tax rate on capital gains is 20%, the after-tax return of each scenario would be −6% (i.e., higher than the untaxed return) and +16% (i.e., less than the untaxed return). The average of the two returns is smaller, at +5%. Although taxes have reduced the average return that the investor can expect, they have also reduced the risk, since the government not only participates in sharing the investors' gains, but it also participates in sharing losses (assuming the investor has realized gains that can be used to offset realized losses).

Table 9.3 from Reichenstein (2006) [2] shows how taxation impacts the cumulative return of fixed income and equity over "n" periods under different assumptions of asset location and trading frequency. In the case of equity, the before-tax return on

TABLE 9.2a Tax-Exempt Account and Taxes (2010)

	United States	Canada
Name	Roth IRA (Individual Retirement Arrangement).	TFSA (Tax-Free Savings Account).
Maximum Contribution	$5,000 yearly, $6,000 if above 50 years old. Contribution is phased out depending on income.	$5,000 yearly plus any unused contribution from prior years. No phasing out.
Taxation	Investment is not tax deductible, but will accumulate and will be withdrawn tax-free.	Investment is not tax deductible, but will accumulate and will be withdrawn tax-free.
Other Aspects	Contributions are not cumulative. Unused contributions are lost. Contributions are indexed to inflation in fixed increments.	Contributions are cumulative. Unused contributions can be made later. Contributions are indexed to inflation in fixed increments.

TABLE 9.2b Tax-Deferred Account and Taxes (2010)

	United States	Canada
Name	Traditional IRA (Individual Retirement Arrangement) and 401(k) (employer plan).	RRSP (Registered Retirement Savings Plan). Plan can be set as employer sponsored and/or set by individual.
Maximum Employee Contribution	$5,000 yearly (IRA), $6,000 above 50 years old. $16,500 yearly (401(k)), $22,000 if above 50 years old. Contribution to IRA phased out depending on income.	Lowest of 18% of previous year's earned income or $22,000 plus any unused contribution from prior years. No phasing out.
Taxation	Contributions are tax deductible. Capital will accumulate tax-free, but withdrawal will be taxed as regular income.	Contributions are tax deductible. Capital will accumulate tax-free but withdrawals will be taxed as regular income.
Other Aspects	Contributions are not cumulative. Unused contributions are lost. Contributions are indexed to inflation in fixed increments.	Contributions are cumulative. Unused contributions can be made later. Contributions are indexed to average salary increases in fixed increments.

investment (r) does not take into account dividends, only capital gains. Incorporating dividends would not change the results.

Within a Roth IRA, taxation does not impact the relative importance of fixed income and equity returns, since they both accumulate tax-free. The same is true of a traditional IRA if the ordinary tax rate is identical during the contribution and withdrawal periods. Consequently, in a traditional IRA, taxation does not target the return on investment, but rather any amount (regardless of whether the source is investment income or capital) that is withdrawn from the IRA account. For example, if an investor is in a 35% tax bracket and owns $1,000 in an IRA, the after-tax value of this investment is currently $650, since he or she would pay $350 of taxes if he or she were to take the $1,000 out of the IRA. This principle remains valid with the passage of time and the accumulation of tax-free return.

Let's assume the investor can generate a 5% annual return before taxes, and plans to withdraw the money from his or her IRA in 10 years. The final value of the investment before tax would be $1,628.90. If "tr" is the expected ordinary tax rate in 10 years, and assuming it remains at 35%, the after-tax value of the IRA will be $1,058.78, which still corresponds to an annual return of 5% on the initial after-tax value of $650. Thus, the true long-term benefit of an IRA is the tax-free compounded return, not the initial reduction in taxable income. The tax benefit received when the contribution was made will be reversed by the future tax liabilities that have to be paid when the money is withdrawn. Thus, lower expected returns (such as lower interest rates on bonds) reduce the incentive to allocate to an IRA.

Thus, money invested in a Roth IRA is untaxed, while money invested in a traditional IRA will eventually be fully taxed at the ordinary tax rate when withdrawn. However, only the return on securities held in a taxable account is taxed. The capital remains tax exempt. If it is a bond, the coupon will be taxed annually. If it is a capital gain and if the investment is traded actively (i.e., sold within 12 months of the date of purchase), the gain will be taxed at the short-term capital gains rate (in the United States). If the investment is traded passively (i.e., sold after 12 months), the gain will be taxed at the long-term capital gains rate, but only when realized. As indicated, in Canada, both gains (short term and long term) would be taxed at the single capital gains tax rate.

As we have seen, taxation influences returns, but it also influences risk and the purchasing power of the capital invested. Table 9.4 illustrates more specifically the relative influence of taxation on these three factors, depending on the types of accounts and

TABLE 9.3 Final After-tax Investment Value

Fiscal Status of Investment	Fixed Income	Equity
Roth IRA	$(1 + r)^n$	$(1 + r)^n$
Traditional IRA	$(1 + r)^n (1 - \text{tr})$	$(1 + r)^n (1 - \text{tr})$
Taxable Bonds	$[1 + r(1 - t)]^n$	
Taxable Equity (Active Investor)		$[1 + r(1 - t)]^n$
Taxable Equity (Passive Investor)		$(1 + r)^n (1 - \text{tc}) + \text{tc}$

Source: Reichenstein (2006).

TABLE 9.4 Final After-Tax Investment Value

Fiscal Status of Investment	Principal	Return	Risk
Roth IRA	100%	100%	100%
Traditional IRA	$(1 - tr)$	100%	100%
Taxable Bonds	100%	$(1 - t)$	$> (1 - tc)$
Taxable Equity (Active Investor)	100%	$(1 - t)$	$(1 - t)$
Taxable Equity (Passive Investor)	100%	$> (1 - tc)$	$> (1 - tc)$

Source: Reichenstein (2006) and Chen (2009).

sources of returns. The information is from Reichenstein (2006) and Chen (2009) [3]. The results are intuitive. First, since a Roth IRA is a tax-exempt account, the investor owns 100% of the capital, 100% of the return and 100% of the risk. However, in a traditional IRA, the investor only own $(1 - tr)$ of the capital since any amount withdrawn from the account will be taxed at the ordinary tax rate. Thus, in this case, the investor still owns 100% of the return and 100% of the risk but on a lesser capital base determined by the after-tax value of the investment.

Taxable assets are different. The investor always owns 100% of the capital. However, he or she only owns a portion of the return. In the case of a passive equity investor, the portion of before-tax return owned by the investor is usually greater than $(1 - tc)$ simply because capital gains may not be realized for many years. Thus, the investor implicitly benefits from an interest-free loan, which reduces the effective tax rate on the eventual realization of capital gains.

However, the tax rate used to calculate the after-tax return is not necessarily the appropriate rate that must be used to determine the after-tax risk. For example, although the main source of return on a bond is the coupon, price fluctuations and, thus, capital gains and losses are often the main sources of risk. Therefore, it is the tax rate that applies to capital gains that most influences the risk of bonds (unless the trading is very active and/or the expected losses on current income are significant), not the ordinary tax rate.

What Table 9.4 has illustrated, in general, is that taxation can have asymmetric effects on capital, returns and risks, depending on the source of income and the type of accounts. If these effects are asymmetric, they should impact the decision allocation process and the determination of what is a properly efficient portfolio on an after-tax basis.

Second Principle: Taxation Impacts the Rebalancing Strategy

The principle of realizing capital losses as early as possible is almost always valid, since the reduction in tax liabilities allows for a greater investment base. However, the principle of postponing capital gains as long as possible is only valid if we assume that the present value of financial gains that is achieved by postponing taxes becomes less valuable than the potential gains that result from a more balanced and/or more efficient and less costly portfolio. This particular aspect is extremely important for all investors, and I will address it specifically later on. Thus, assuming we ignore for the time being the portfolio efficiency aspect related to rebalancing, we will use several examples to illustrate the relevance of timing capital gains and losses.

Let's assume three horizons (10, 20 and 30 years), two return scenarios (4% and 7% annually, solely from capital gains), three taxation scenarios and three portfolio turnover scenarios. The three portfolio turnover scenarios are as follows:

1. Capital gains remain fully untaxed, even at horizon end.
2. All capital gains are short term and, thus, fully realized each year within 12 months.
3. Capital gains are only realized if securities have been held for more than 12 months. However, the annual portfolio turnover can be 100%, 50% and 10%. Turnovers of 50% to 100% a year are common among active managers (Unified Trust Company estimated that the average turnover for mutual funds was above 90%), while turnovers of 5% to 20% are more consistent with index funds and some low-turnover investment protocols such as RAFI. Furthermore, the residual unrealized capital gains will be fully taxed at horizon end. The potential consequences of the reset of the tax basis to market value at death will be discussed later on.

Long-term and short-term realized capital gains are taxed respectively at 15% and 35%. The objective is to calculate the effective compounded return and, implicitly, the effective tax rate. Results are presented in Table 9.5. The first scenario (untaxed) is either that of a tax-exempt account or that of an investor who never realized any capital gains until death, whose heirs benefit from a grossed-up tax basis of assets to market value (in the United States only). Although this scenario may be somewhat unrealistic, this return is the target we wish to be the closest to. The second scenario (fully taxed) is our worst case. It reflects a situation where the asset manager has a style with extremely high turnover and no concern for tax efficiencies. Under this scenario, capital gains are subject to the highest tax rate in the United States.

The next three scenarios assume turnovers of 100%, 50% and 10%, but the manager is very careful in each case about waiting at least 12 months to trade any security, even in the 100% turnover case. Any remaining capital gain is fully taxed at horizon end. There are two conclusions we can reach from these results. First, once the manager of a fund avoids realizing capital gains on assets held less than 12 months, the gains obtained from reducing the turnover only become more significant at very low turnover, and only if this approach is maintained for a very long time and the average yearly capital gain is fairly high. The benefits of a lower turnover are not linear, and thus there is simply not that much tax efficiency gained by reducing turnover from 100% to 50%. The real significant gains are obtained when the asset managers avoid selling securities that were held for less than 12 months and/or if turnover is kept very low, such as 20%. This raises another challenge for actively managed funds in the United States.

TABLE 9.5 Compounded Returns and Portfolio Strategy (%)

Return	Horizon	Untaxed	Fully Taxed	Turnover with Taxes at Death		
				100%	50%	10%
	10 years	4.0	2.6	3.4	3.42	3.46
4%	20 years	4.0	2.6	3.4	3.42	3.49
	30 years	4.0	2.6	3.4	3.42	3.50
	10 years	7.0	4.55	5.95	6.00	6.12
7%	20 years	7.0	4.55	5.95	6.00	6.19
	30 years	7.0	4.55	5.95	6.00	6.23

Actively managed funds not only realize capital gains much more frequently than indexed funds and many lower-turnover investment protocols, but they are also much more likely to generate short-term capital gains that are taxed at the highest rate. Thus, strangely enough, greater taxes are being generated by the very activity that is intended to enhance returns, but often fails. This issue is more problematic for US investors, since Canadian investors pay the same capital gains tax whether the security was held for more or less than 12 months. To illustrate this aspect, Figure 9.1 displays the differential return between active mandates of varying turnover (from 100% to 10% yearly) and an indexed mandate (with an assumed turnover of 5%) for a US and Canadian investor, assuming the gross return before is identical in all cases. The yearly average capital gain is either 4% or 7% before tax, and we assume half the turnover for US investors is realized as short-term capital gains (less than 12 months). For Canadian investors, we use a 20% tax rate on capital gains, whether it is short term or long term. We use a 20-year horizon in all cases and ignore, for the time being, transaction costs, to isolate solely the tax aspect of higher turnover.

FIGURE 9.1 Active Management, Indexed Management and Taxes.

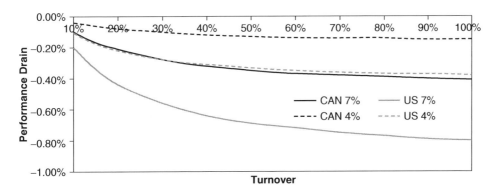

As expected, the tax cost related to turnover is much more of an issue for US investors than for Canadian investors, since Canada does not differentiate between short-term and long-term gains. A low turnover index outperforms an active mandate by no more than about 40 bps yearly in Canada on average, and only if we assume a fairly high yearly average capital gain. Under a more normal return scenario, the tax drag may be no more than 15 bps. However, as indicated, this differential return does not account for higher management fees and transaction costs in the case of an active mandate. Although it is always useful to limit unnecessary turnover, higher taxes is not the only unfortunate consequence of turnover. There are also other considerations related to transaction costs and market impact (for very large investors). We will leave the specific consequences of these aspects aside for the moment.

In the United States, the conclusion is different. The average active equity fund could generate as much as 40 to 80 bps of excess tax cost compared to an indexed fund if the investors or asset managers are not careful about the timing of capital gains. Considering transaction cost and excess management fees, the confidence in an active manager to outperform an index or low-turnover product has to be extremely high. Overall, if an indexed product has a 5% turnover, Figure 9.1 illustrates how important it is to invest in either products that maintain a turnover of less than 20%, or products that mostly generate long-term capital gains. A 15% turnover will reduce the tax drag by about two-thirds compared to the traditional mutual funds. This is without considering the much lower transaction costs of low-turnover protocols versus most active funds.

Jeffrey and Arnott analyzed this issue in 1993 [4]. Looking at 71 large-capitalization US equity funds from 1982 to 1991, they observed that actively managed mutual funds are even less likely to outperform index funds on an after-tax basis. Furthermore, we have already covered the literature on active management extensively. If (excessively) active management is a negative-sum game excluding the effect of taxes, it becomes an even more negative-sum game after taxes. More recent studies, such as Wotherspoon and Longmeier (2006) [5], have shown that 1% of pre-tax Alpha may be required to outperform a low-turnover plain-vanilla index after taxes (excluding the impact of higher fees on actively managed funds). Their analysis of 866 US mutual funds (between June 1995 and June 2005) showed that 53% underperformed their indices before tax, while 63% underperformed the same indices when both the performance of the funds and that of the indices are measured on an after-tax basis. Thus, taxable investors should seek low-cost, low-turnover tax-efficient funds.

There is, of course, one event that could change this recommendation. If investors expect the tax rate on long-term capital gains to be raised significantly, it may be entirely logical to realize as much capital gains as possible as quickly as possible. This eventuality should not be ignored, especially in the United States. There were 12 revisions of the capital gains tax rate in the United States from 1970 to 2010. The long-term top rate of 15%, which was set in 2003, is the lowest ever. Considering the current US budget deficit, it may be strategically optimal to consider realizing some of the existing capital gains not by choosing asset managers who have high turnovers (this would also generate significantly higher transaction costs), but through a strategic, one-time portfolio decision. This is one of the reasons why an unstable fiscal policy unnecessarily complicates the portfolio management process. There is enough uncertainty in the financial world. Investors do not need fiscal instability.

To illustrate, let's assume a US investor whose investment horizon is either 10, 20 or 30 years. The investor holds a tax-efficient fund with an annual turnover of 10%. The current capital gains tax rate is 15%, but what if it were to rise to 20%, 25% or even higher? Would it be preferable for this investor to generate all or part of his or her unrealized capital gains and then return to his or her previous tax-efficient low-turnover policy? Or should the investor maintain the status quo? The answer depends on five factors:

1. The ratio of the tax basis of assets to their current market value
2. The expected return on the portfolio
3. The investment horizon
4. The level of increase in the capital gains tax rate
5. The expected timing of the tax increase

Figures 9.2a and 9.2b illustrate the impact on performance of realizing the full capital gains now, assuming an increase in the capital gains tax rate from 15% to 20%, 25%, 30% or 35%, adjusted for different ratios of tax basis to current market value (from 100% to 30%). There are six figures in order to analyze the impact of different investment horizons (10, 20 or 30 years from top to bottom) and yearly average capital gains (4% or 7% from left to right). Figure 9.2a assumes that all unrealized capital gains are taxed at maturity.

Investors who expect the capital gains tax rate to increase should almost always realize these gains now, whatever the horizon and the tax basis. There are a few exceptions, such as if we expect the increase in tax rate to be very small, or if the expected yearly capital gains are extremely significant, but even in these cases, the cost of being wrong about the size and timing of a tax increase is not so important. However, we know that US investors can benefit from the reset of their asset basis at death. Does this eventuality change our conclusions? Figure 9.2b answers this question.

In this situation, the consequences are obviously more significant if the horizon is short and the tax basis of assets is very small in relation to the market value. Considering life expectancies in the United States at age 60 (approximately 81 for men and 84 for women) and at age 70 (approximately 84 for men and 86 for women), this is potentially more of an issue for individuals in their 70s, assuming health is not currently an issue. The bottom line is that if investors expect the capital gains tax rate to be raised, only very narrow circumstances would justify not realizing those gains before the tax rate is increased. The exception may be investors with an expected life span of approximately 15 years or less who own a portfolio with a very low tax basis.

Realizing capital losses as quickly as possible seems like a no-brainer. If we can achieve a lower tax liability by selling an asset, why wait? There is one caveat. An asset sold at a loss, in the United States or Canada, cannot be repurchased within 30 days or the capital loss will not be recognized. This is known as the "wash sale rule" in the

FIGURE 9.2a Increase in Capital Gains Tax Rate and Portfolio Policy (All Capital Gains Realized at Horizon).

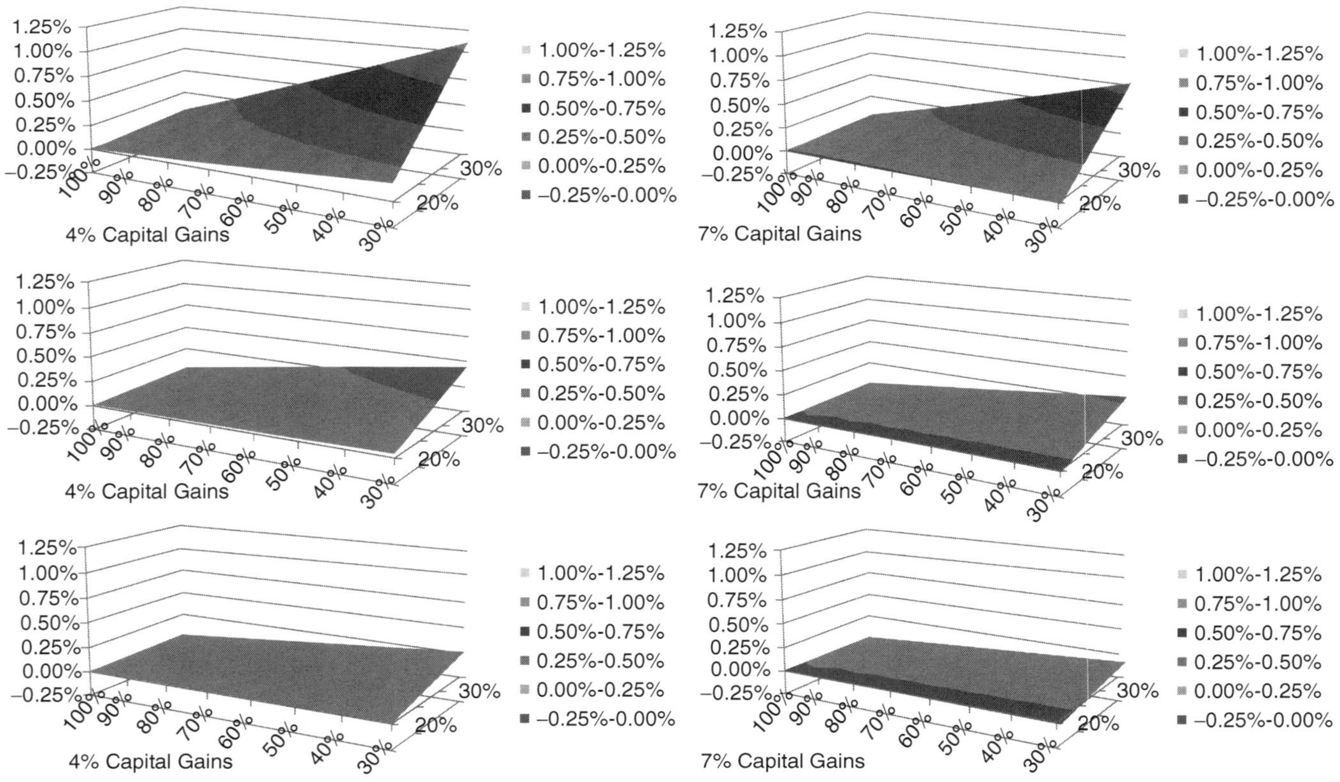

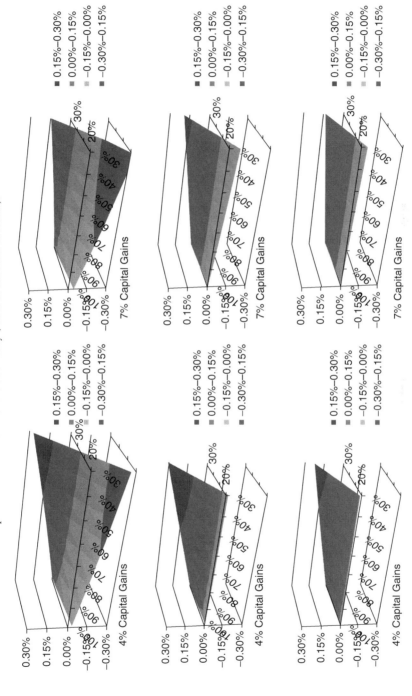

FIGURE 9.2b Increase in Capital Gains Tax Rate and Portfolio Policy (Reset of Tax Basis at Death).

269

United States and the "superficial loss rule" in Canada. The investor will have to wait 30 days or find a similar replacement asset. In many investment plans, this issue can be managed, especially if a portfolio is well diversified and single asset concentration is not an issue.

An example can easily illustrate the logic of selling assets that have a market value lower than their tax basis. Let's assume an asset that trades at $100 with a tax basis of $100 as well. The asset declines in value to $80 (−20%) and then regains its prior value of $100 (+25%). For example, the asset may be an exchange-traded fund that could be replaced by another exchange-traded fund, similar in risk and return characteristics. We could also assume that the poor performance of the asset is attributed to its sector and, thus, that it could be replaced easily with another similar security.

If the investor is passive, there are no tax consequences because the end price is equal to the initial price, and the potential tax liabilities remain nil. However, if the investor sold the asset when its value was $80, and was able to pair the capital loss of $20 with a capital gain, then the investor would have reduced his or her tax bill by $3, assuming that the capital gains tax rate is 15%. The investor could then use that $3 to buy more of the security. As the asset value increased back to $100, the investor would own $103.75 of that asset:

$$(\$80 + \$3) \times 125\% = \$103.75$$

However, the investor would not have necessarily gained the entire $3.75. He or she would now have a lower tax basis (since the investor would have realized the capital loss) and a potential tax liability of $3.1125 for a net current gain of $0.6375:

$$(\$103.75 - (\$103.75 - \$83) \times 15\%) - \$100 = \$0.6375$$

This gain would be achieved because the investor would have bought a rising asset using an interest-free loan from his or her government.

Third Principle: Tax-Deferred Investments Are Usually as Efficient as Tax-Exempt Investments, and Both Are Significantly More Efficient than Taxable Investments

The following example illustrates the relative benefits of an investment in a Roth IRA, a traditional IRA and a taxable account. We will assume a 35% ordinary tax rate, and an investment in a portfolio that yields either a 4% return (such as a high-grade bond portfolio) or a 7% return (such as a high-yield portfolio). The investment period is 10 years, after which the investor will liquidate the same amount of assets (for consumption) in each of the following 10 years until the account is depleted. Our initial objective will be to determine the relative initial investment that would yield the same after-tax income in all three cases. Table 9.6 illustrates this example, but only for the 7% investment return scenario.

The analysis is based on a contribution of $1,000 to a traditional IRA. Since the ordinary tax rate of the investor is 35%, the after-tax cost of this contribution is

$650. Therefore, the investor is indifferent in terms of cash outflow between making a $1,000 contribution to a traditional IRA and a $650 contribution to a Roth IRA. The investment in both accounts will accumulate tax-free, but since the amount invested in the traditional IRA is greater, the value accumulated in the traditional IRA account at Year 10 will also be greater ($1,967.15 versus $1,278.65). However, the investor is no better off with the traditional IRA account. Assuming the investment still generates a 7% return during the withdrawal period, the investor will be able to cash a yearly income with his or her IRA of $280.08 before tax for 10 years, or $182.05 after tax. By comparison, the amount accumulated in the Roth IRA

TABLE 9.6 The Efficiency of Tax Deferral or Tax Exemption

	Year	Traditional IRA	Roth IRA	Taxable Account	After-Tax Withdrawal	Before-Tax Withdrawal
Investment Period		1,000.00	650	920.90		
	1	1,070.00	695.50	962.80		
	2	1,144.90	744.19	1,006.60		
	3	1,225.04	796.28	1,052.40		
	4	1,310.80	852.02	1,100.29		
	5	1,402.55	911.66	1,150.35		
	6	1,500.73	975.47	1,202.69		
	7	1,605.78	1,043.76	1,257.42		
	8	1,718.19	1,116.82	1,314.63		
	9	1,838.46	1,195.00	1,374.44		
	10	1,967.15	1,278.65	1,436.98		
Withdrawal Period	11	1,824.77	1,186.10	1,320.31	182.05	280.08
	12	1,672.43	1,087.08	1,198.34	182.05	280.08
	13	1,509.42	981.12	1,070.81	182.05	280.08
	14	1,335.00	867.75	937.48	182.05	280.08
	15	1,148.38	746.44	798.09	182.05	280.08
	16	948.68	616.64	652.35	182.05	280.08
	17	735.01	477.76	499.98	182.05	280.08
	18	506.39	329.15	340.68	182.05	280.08
	19	261.76	170.14	174.13	182.05	280.08
	20	0.00	0.00	0.00	182.05	280.08

TABLE 9.7 Efficiency of a Tax-Deferred and Tax-Exempt Contribution (%)

Return on Asset	10-Year Investment Period and 10-Year Withdrawal Period	30-Year Investment Period and 30-Year Withdrawal Period
4	+23	+79
7	+42	+161

will be able to generate a $182.05 tax-free income. There is no economic difference between the two plans.

However, to generate the same after-tax cash flow from a taxable account would require a significantly higher after-tax initial contribution. Although the withdrawals from a taxable account are tax-free, the return on investment does not accumulate tax-free. The example shows that a $920.90 initial investment would be required. This is nearly 42% more than the after-tax contribution required from the traditional IRA or Roth IRA, and it illustrates the power of tax-free return compounding. This effect will obviously be greater for higher yielding assets and over longer investment and withdrawal periods. Table 9.7 illustrates the excess after-tax contribution in a taxable account that is required in order to achieve the same efficiency as an after-tax contribution in tax-deferred and tax-exempt accounts under different scenarios.

These results are based on the assumption that the ordinary tax rates of the investor during the contribution year and during the withdrawal period are the same. For example, an investor taxed at a lower rate during retirement would need less before-tax income to generate the same after-tax income. In this case, a traditional IRA would yield a superior after-tax income compared to a Roth IRA. Many investors assume that they will be taxed at a lower rate during retirement. However, considering the substantial fiscal deficits of many governments, these investors should also ponder the possibility that tax brackets on ordinary income may change. That said, this is only an issue for investors who cannot contribute the full contribution amounts to traditional IRA and to Roth IRA, since investments in both plans are far more efficient than investment in a taxable account. Thus, if investors can afford to make the maximum contribution, they should do so.

This example also illustrates another aspect. Although an investor should be indifferent between investing in a Roth IRA or in a traditional IRA, once the investments have been made, $1 of assets in a Roth IRA does not have the same value as the same $1 of assets in a traditional IRA. Looking at Table 9.6, we can conclude that $1 of assets in an IRA has

$$(1 - \text{ordinary tax rate}) \times \text{the efficiency of \$1 of assets in a Roth IRA.}$$

The same general conclusion applies to a $1 investment in a taxable account. If $1 of assets in each of the three accounts does not offer the same purchasing power to the investor, it probably does not have the same risk. If it does not have same risk, the assets invested should not be considered as having the same tax-adjusted risk-weighted allocation depending on the location of these assets. This explains why Reichenstein (2006) argued that most investors improperly measure their asset allocation weights.

Fourth Principle: In Most Circumstances, Investors Should Locate the Most Tax Inefficient, Highest-Yielding Securities in a Tax-Exempt or Tax-Deferred Portfolio, and the Most Tax Efficient, Lowest-Yielding Securities in a Taxable Portfolio

Let's start with a simple example. Two securities have a 6% expected return before tax. Investment income from security A is taxed at the ordinary tax rate of 35%, while investment income from security B is taxed at a lower dividend tax rate of 15%. If the investor has the same amount invested in both securities, and locates security A in a tax-exempt account and security B in a taxable account, the expected after-tax return is 5.55%. Doing the reverse allocation would reduce the performance to 4.95% yearly. However, this is an incomplete comparison, since it does not take into account how taxation modifies the risk of each component. For example, the risk under the first scenario is greater than that under the second scenario. Thus, it may be more appropriate to evaluate the efficiency of the after-tax asset location decision using a risk-neutral framework.

Dammon, Spatt and Zhang (2004) [6] developed such a framework. They considered two assets, a riskless taxable bond and a risky asset—presumably equity. Their stated objective was to determine the marginal impact of shifting one after-tax dollar of risky asset to the riskless asset in the tax-exempt account against an x-dollar shift from the riskless asset to the risky asset in the taxable account. However, since Dammon, Spatt and Zhang assumed a similar tax rate for dividends and interest income, and a lower tax rate for capital gains, I modified their model to allow the tax rate on dividends to be different from the tax rate on investment income. Equation 9.1 measures to net after-tax change in wealth over one period resulting from the shift in allocation. The first term measures the impact on wealth of shifting $1 of risky asset for $1 of riskless asset in the tax-exempt portfolio, while the second term measures the impact of shifting x dollars of riskless assets to the risky assets in the taxable portfolio.

$$W = [r - (1 + g)(1 + d) - 1] - x[(1 + g)(1 + d(1 - t_d) - g t_g - 1) - r(1 - t)] \quad (9.1)$$

where r, d, and g are the yield on a riskless asset, the dividend yield and the capital gains return and t, t_d and t_g are the tax rates that apply to each source of return. It can be shown that if x is equal to the value given from Equation 9.2, that the impact of the asset shift remains insensitive to g (the capital gain return). Thus, the shift would have no impact on the overall risk of the portfolio, assuming that g is the only source of risk.

$$x = (1 + d) / [1 + d(1 - t_d) - t_g] \quad (9.2)$$

Furthermore, this interpretation is only valid if we assume that taxes on capital gains are paid on a yearly basis, since this is a single-period model. It also implicitly assumes that capital losses can be reported against capital gains in the same year. If not, the time value of money would have to be taken into account.

Table 9.8 shows how shifting the allocation between a tax-exempt portfolio and a taxable portfolio under those assumptions impacts the change in wealth. Results are also presented for tax-deferred portfolios. Twenty-four scenarios are presented. The annual yield on the riskless asset remains the same under all scenarios (4%), but the dividend yield varies from 3% to 5%, while the capital gain can be either 4% or 6%. For example, if we assume that tax rates were identical for all sources of returns (as in the first set of scenarios), the net gain would be nil under all scenarios but the tax-exempt multiple would be 1.538 implying that $1.538 of assets would have to be shifted in the taxable portfolio to remain risk neutral if $1 of asset was shifted in the tax-exempt portfolio.

The second set of scenarios assumes that the tax rates on dividends and interest income are the same, while the tax rate on capital gains is lower. This is the situation that prevails when the investment is in foreign equity. This is also the situation that would prevail if the risky asset were not equity but high-yield bonds. According to this scenario, it is preferable to hold the riskless asset in the tax-exempt account only if it offers a greater income yield. This means that in the case of foreign equity, it may be preferable to put high-dividend-yield foreign securities in the tax-exempt account if their dividend yield is higher than the yield on the riskless asset. Years ago, this eventuality would have been unlikely, but we have seen in recent years that some equity portfolios can be structured to produce dividend yields greater than investment-grade bond yields.

I will also use the case of high-yield bonds to provide a different perspective on the same issue. Long-term yields on securities are made of four components, an inflation component, a real return component, a risk premium component and a liquidity component. Tax principles do not differentiate between the four sources of yield. Governments will, unfortunately, tax all four indiscriminately. Two securities of similar duration will have the same inflation and real return component, but not necessarily the same risk and liquidity premiums. Assuming these premiums are set at appropriate levels that properly account for expected losses and lower liquidity, the investor should avoid having the assets with the highest premiums taxed, since it will reduce their return-to-risk ratio considerably. Thus, high-yield bonds are among the first asset class to be located in tax-exempt and tax-deferred portfolios. Finally, the third and fourth sets of scenarios assume a tax rate on dividends, which is less than on interest income. In this situation, the decision to locate fixed-income securities in tax-deferred accounts is strongly supported.

In all scenarios, the objective of remaining risk neutral imposes a shift of a greater amount of risky assets to riskless assets in the taxable portfolio. This result is entirely consistent with Reichenstein (2006), who argued that an investor in a tax-exempt account owns 100% of the capital and of the risk, while he or she owns 100% of the capital and less than 100% of the before-tax risk in a taxable account. Thus, if we reduce the level of risky assets in the tax-exempt account, it becomes necessary to increase the amount of risky assets proportionally in the taxable account to keep the overall risk of all portfolios constant. However, this adjustment would be less if capital gains were only realized over time. In this case, it may be useful to use the average

TABLE 9.8 Net Wealth Gain Resulting from Asset Location (%)

r (%)	d (%)	g (%)	t_d (%)	t_r (%)	t_g (%)	Tax-Exempt Multiple	Tax-Deferred Multiple	Net Gain Tax-Exempt	Net Gain Tax-Deferred
4	3	4	35	35	35	1.538	1.000	0.00	0.00
4	4	4	35	35	35	1.538	1.000	0.00	0.00
4	5	4	35	35	35	1.538	1.000	0.00	0.00
4	3	6	35	35	35	1.538	1.000	0.00	0.00
4	4	6	35	35	35	1.538	1.000	0.00	0.00
4	5	6	35	35	35	1.538	1.000	0.00	0.00
4	3	4	35	35	15	1.185	0.770	0.23	0.15
4	4	4	35	35	15	1.187	0.772	0.00	0.00
4	5	4	35	35	15	1.190	0.773	−0.23	−0.15
4	3	6	35	35	15	1.185	0.770	0.23	0.15
4	4	6	35	35	15	1.187	0.772	0.00	0.00
4	5	6	35	35	15	1.190	0.773	−0.23	−0.15
4	3	4	15	35	15	1.176	0.765	0.94	0.61
4	4	4	15	35	15	1.176	0.765	0.94	0.61
4	5	4	15	35	15	1.176	0.765	0.94	0.61
4	3	6	15	35	15	1.176	0.765	0.94	0.61
4	4	6	15	35	15	1.176	0.765	0.94	0.61
4	5	6	15	35	15	1.176	0.765	0.94	0.61
4	3	4	20	35	15	1.178	0.766	0.76	0.50
4	4	4	20	35	15	1.179	0.766	0.71	0.46
4	5	4	20	35	15	1.180	0.767	0.65	0.42
4	3	6	20	35	15	1.178	0.766	0.76	0.50
4	4	6	20	35	15	1.179	0.766	0.71	0.46
4	5	6	20	35	15	1.180	0.767	0.65	0.42

effective tax rate to determine the proper allocation adjustment that keeps risk constant, or to use scenario and/or simulation analyses.

US investors also have access to tax-exempt municipal bonds. Although these securities are exempt from federal taxation, and usually from state taxation if held by an investor residing in the state of issuance, these securities do trade at a lower yield than other non-tax-exempt securities of similar risk. Therefore, although they are tax exempt, the after-tax yields do reflect an implicit tax rate. For example, if a state-issued bond trades at 4%, and a non-tax-exempt bond of similar risk trades at 5%, we could conclude that the state-issued bond has an implicit 20% tax rate (*tm*). Dammon, Spatt and Zhang used the same type of risk-neutral framework to analyze the efficiency of owning municipal bonds. More specifically, they asked:

> Is it preferable to own equity in the taxable account and a taxable bond in the tax-exempt account [option A] or to own a tax-exempt bond in the taxable account and an equity fund in the tax-exempt account [option B]?

They showed that in order for option B to be preferable, we must meet the following condition:

$$t_g > t_d - [r(t_d - t_m)(1 + d)] / (r - d) \qquad (9.3)$$

where *tm* is the implicit tax rate on municipal bonds. When the authors published their article, interest rates were much higher than they are today, and they used a 36% tax rate on dividends. At the time, they concluded that option B would be advisable only if the effective tax rate on capital gains was fairly high (above about 20%), and, thus, if the equity portfolio was not managed tax efficiently. If their example had been completed using a much lower tax rate on dividends (such as 15%) and much lower interest rates, the case for option B would look even weaker. The only potential exception would be investors who hold an equity portfolio that pays a dividend yield greater than the bond yield. Thus, in most cases, tax-exempt bonds should only be considered if the investor has already saturated his or her tax-deferred and tax-exempt accounts with taxable bonds, and if the target allocation requires an even greater allocation to fixed income.

Capital Gains Management and Tax-Loss Harvesting

We have, thus far, illustrated the importance of asset location within the portfolio allocation process when taxes are considered. However, we have yet to discuss a significant issue: the trade-off between postponing capital gains and the benefits of maintaining a balanced and/or more efficient and/or less costly portfolio.

The management of realized capital gains timing presents itself in two ways, first through rebalancing within asset classes (especially equities) and second through rebalancing among asset classes and investment products. In both cases, we must determine if avoiding/postponing portfolio rebalancing for the purpose of reducing short-term tax payments is a worthwhile trade-off. The challenges in both cases are somewhat different.

For example, in the case of investment products, the best approach to minimizing tax liabilities is simply to avoid high turnover strategies. However, even if several investment protocols (such as RAFI) can generate lower turnover, it is still usually higher than the turnover of traditional index funds. Is it worth using more efficient investment protocols at the expense of a slightly higher turnover than a market-cap indexed product? How significant is the excess cost related to portfolio turnover? Can we neutralize the capital gains that would normally be generated in portfolios that have slightly higher turnovers using a proactive capital loss harvesting policy? How do we deal with portfolios that have existing concentrated positions and a low tax basis?

Rebalancing among asset classes raises different challenges. We could ignore the rebalancing and let the allocation drift to avoid realizing capital gains. We could use a rebalancing methodology based on specific allocation triggers that would minimize the required rebalancing (for example, by rebalancing to a tolerance band and not to the target). However, if we use a volatility-based portfolio management process, the turnover may be substantially higher, and may trigger more substantial capital gains, although a volatility management protocol can also incorporate guidelines designed to reduce turnover. If investors have a large portion of their capital invested in tax-deferred or tax-exempt accounts, they may also be able to use the assets within these accounts to rebalance their entire portfolio. However, for investors who have substantially more assets, this is probably not a realistic alternative. Eventually, we will have to weigh the benefits of rebalancing and managing risk on the long-term GEO mean against the benefits of postponing tax payments. Should postponing taxes trump a process that is designed to improve performance through risk management?

Developing a comprehensive approach that maximizes long-term after-tax GEO mean requires that we incorporate the effects of capital loss tax harvesting and the process by which it can be implemented. Capital loss harvesting is a process that seeks to purposely sell assets that are trading at a loss in order to generate capital losses that can be used to offset realized capital gains. However, not all investors can have full control over this process. For example, investors in a mutual fund or an ETF cannot control the realization of capital gains and capital losses within these instruments. The investor may decide to liquidate his or her holdings of mutual funds or ETFs to generate capital losses when needed, but he or she cannot control how capital gains and losses are generated at the single-security level within those products. This complicates the objective of creating a global tax-efficient portfolio. And then there is the issue of the grossed-up tax basis in the United States at death. How can we take this factor into account? We will address these issues one by one starting with the issue of tax-loss harvesting.

The basic principle of successful tax management is simple: avoid and/or defer taxes that can be avoided and/or deferred, and use tax deductions that are available as long as it does not adversely impact the after-tax efficiency of the portfolio. The purpose of tax-loss harvesting is to increase the amount of capital that is invested at all times. However, the problem with efficient tax management is implementation.

Firms such as First Quadrant and Parametric Portfolio Associates have completed several simulations of the value of tax-loss harvesting. The work done by First Quadrant was completed in 2001 [7], when capital gains tax rates were higher than in 2011. First Quadrant generated 500 simulations of returns on a portfolio of 500 assets (a simulated S&P 500) over 25 years. They assumed long-term average returns for dividends and capital gains, a market volatility and a stock-specific volatility in line with historical experience. Their simulations covered scenarios ranging from the type of environment observed during the Great Depression era to spectacular cumulative returns. They also assumed a natural turnover, such as having one company substituted from the index every month. Finally, their baseline case relied on an assumption of a 35% capital gains tax rate. This assumption will be generalized later on.

Their objectives were to measure the effect of using a proactive tax-loss harvesting strategy compared to a passive index on a yearly basis as well as cumulatively. They ignored the "wash sale rule," since they indicated that the differences with other simulations that incorporated the wash rules were marginal. They reported their results for the median portfolio as well as for the 25th and 75th percentile portfolios. Finally, the results were presented with the assumption of no realization of the unrealized capital gains/losses at the end of the 25th year (a reasonable assumption if we assume a grossed-up tax basis at death), or assuming full realization of all unrealized capital gains/losses. The following are their general conclusions:

- If we ignore the tax liability at the end of the 25-year period, the final value of the portfolio would have been raised between 22.5% (25th percentile scenario) and 30% (75th percentile scenario). This represents excess returns of, respectively, 87 bps and 112 bps annually, assuming a 7% annualized return for the passive index. Ignoring the potential tax liability at horizon end may be acceptable in the case of a gross-up of the tax basis at death.
- Performance gains are much more significant in the first five years of the process. Obviously, as the market value of the portfolio climbs over time, fewer loss-harvesting opportunities arise. However, gains of 0.50% a year are still likely after many years.
- If we consider the tax liability at the end of the 25-year period, the gains over a passive approach are reduced. The net gains range from approximately 12% (25th percentile) to 17.5% (75th percentile) on a full after-tax basis. This represents excess returns of, respectively, 49 bps and 69 bps annually assuming a 7% annualized return for the passive index. We should have expected the net gain to decline. If we proactively seek to realize capital losses, the tax basis will be lower than it would have been otherwise, and the potential tax liabilities at horizon end will be higher.

As indicated, these results were obtained under the assumption of a 35% capital gains tax rate. Lower tax rates would reduce the benefits of tax-loss harvesting. For example, if the net gain for a median scenario is 14%, assuming a 35% capital gains tax rate, it becomes 8% if we assume a 20% tax rate. The net gain is fairly proportional to the tax rate. Therefore, it would be approximately 6%, assuming a 15% rate. Even at this low level, it represents an additional 25 bps a year after tax, or 31 bps before tax.

A more recent study by Parametric (2010) [8] provides similar results. Assuming a 10-year horizon, 8% average market return, 15% market volatility, 35% single-stock volatility and 35% and 15% tax rates respectively on short-term and long-term realized capital gains, they evaluated the gains from tax harvesting at 13% cumulatively, although this ignores the potential tax liabilities at the end of the 10-year horizon. These results are in line with their own experience across hundreds of accounts (1.4 % average over 7 years).

As would be expected, potential gains from tax-loss harvesting are independent of neither the market conditions (volatility and performance) nor the tolerance of the investor for tracking error. For example, when technology stocks declined in the early 2000s, the performance of the average stock in the S&P 500 was actually positive. Thus, there were many opportunities to sell securities at a loss and to offset these losses with other securities that could be sold at a gain. Tax-loss harvesting is more profitable in an environment with greater volatility and greater dispersion in stock returns. Furthermore, although the benefits of tax-loss harvesting are usually greater in the initial years of implementation, a new crisis, such as in 2008, creates new opportunities. Table 9.9 from Parametric (2010) presents the average annual gain depending on single-stock volatility and average yearly returns.

Tax-loss harvesting is a defensive strategy because it is likely to be the most profitable in a bearish and volatile environment. This is to be expected since, in a bull market, there are fewer and fewer opportunities to sell securities at a loss. Furthermore, tax harvesting is obviously more profitable in a higher-tax-rate environment. It is not that we wish for higher taxes, but that it becomes even more important to be tax efficient as taxation increases. Finally, tax-loss harvesting can cause a greater tracking error against a benchmark. Parametric has shown how the Alpha that can be extracted for tax harvesting will create some tracking error since the wash sale rule will prohibit buying back the same securities. However, this is only an issue for investors who use standard cap-weight indices as their benchmark. This would not necessarily be an issue for investors who use nonmarket-cap investment protocols. Therefore, what can we conclude on tax harvesting?

TABLE 9.9 Tax Benefits and Market Conditions

Volatility	Return Scenario		
	Bearish (4%)	Normal (8%)	Bullish (14%)
55% High	2.4%	2.2%	2.0%
35% Normal	1.5%	1.3%	1.0%
25% Low	1.3%	1.0%	0.8%

Source: Parametric (2010).

- There is an advantage to generating capital losses as soon as possible, assuming that the constraints caused by the wash sale rule can be neutralized through the purchase of other assets of similar characteristics.
- Tax harvesting capital losses is a proactive issue. We cannot assume that all managers pursue an active tax-loss harvesting approach, or that all investment vehicles are as efficient at managing those opportunities. For example, we cannot assume that a mutual fund would be managed in order to maximize capital-loss harvesting. In fact, most are not.
- Many ETFs are indexed products; they are not usually built specifically for this purpose, although they usually generate little turnover and are therefore fairly tax efficient.
- Nonmarket-cap investment protocols can be efficient at managing the realization of capital losses, since securities that are being sold can be easily replaced by other securities that meet the general criteria of the protocols. Furthermore, since many of these protocols can have relatively low turnovers (but certainly not all, such as minimum variance), a tax-loss-harvesting policy could be efficient at neutralizing the capital gains generated during rebalancing. The lower the turnover, the easier it should be in the long run to find enough assets that could be sold at a loss.
- In principle, tax-loss harvesting would be more efficient in Canada than in the United States because of investors' ability to carry realized capital losses against the realized capital gains of the previous three years.

Despite all the evidence that has been presented so far, we have to remain cautious about the real benefits of tax-loss harvesting. For one, some of the evidence is based on simulations. The true benefits of tax-loss harvesting would also be impacted by the autocorrelation of returns in the market, and the authors of the different simulations on the issue make no mention of how this aspect was considered. Furthermore, although tax-loss harvesting can have a meaningful short-term impact on a portfolio that has significant unused capital losses, in the long term it is difficult to determine if the obsession with reducing taxes occurs at the expense of greater portfolio efficiency. For example, in the case of investment protocols, would we also limit the trading in order to avoid capital gains if the portfolio lacked sufficient capital losses? At some point, this is not only an issue about harvesting losses, but about balancing realized gains and losses. A case study of tax efficiency, including a tax-loss-harvesting strategy in a real portfolio environment, will be presented at the end of this chapter.

Is It Optimal to Postpone Net Capital Gains?

We will start this section by reiterating one important observation: the most efficient way to minimize tax impacts related to capital gains is to avoid high-turnover portfolios that generate significant short-term capital gains, and concentrate on low-turnover investment protocols that generate mostly long-term capital gains and are return-risk efficient.

Several authors have attempted to model how the taxation of capital gains and the reset provision of the tax basis at death (in the United States) influence the consumption and investment decisions of investors over their lifetime. Although these models are not designed to help determine how taxation should impact the investment process of a very specific individual, they do help to understand basic allocation principles that should be considered.

Dammon, Spatt and Zhang (2001)[9] investigated the effects of taxation on consumption and investment in the presence of capital gains taxes and short sale restrictions. Previously, Constantinides (1983) [10] had shown that it is optimal to realize losses and defer gains indefinitely, and that the investment and rebalancing decisions can remain independent of the consumption decision. This hypothesis requires that investors use derivatives and/or short selling to postpone the realization of capital gains. Such an approach would require a substantial short selling activity, and considering the fact that tax laws in the United States have limited the ability to postpone capital gains by offsetting long and short positions, the consumption and investment decisions can no longer be separate.

Dammon, Spatt and Zhang simulated the consumption investment process of investors from age 20 to 100. They used a two-asset portfolio made of a riskless bond and risky equity, incorporated US mortality tables and assumed that investors have a power utility function. They made specific assumptions about the level of interest rates, dividends, tax rates, expected capital gains and volatility. Since the specific results of any optimization process are extremely sensitive to these assumptions, we will concentrate on their general conclusions only. We will also complete these observations with the authors' 2003 work [11].

As we would expect, they found the optimal consumption and investment decisions to be a function of age, relative portfolio holdings (is the portfolio underweight or overweight equities?) and tax basis.

- The optimal consumption wealth level is related to the tax basis. As we already know, a larger embedded capital gain implies a higher embedded tax liability, which reduces the after-tax wealth of the investor. Thus, by deferring capital gains, the investor increases his or her wealth, which allows the investor to increase his or her consumption. However, we should remember that this argument does not ponder the possibility that not realizing a capital gain and not rebalancing a portfolio may hinder the geometric return of the portfolio. We will address this aspect later.
- The consumption decision of elderly investors is driven by their bequest motive. The stronger the desire to leave more assets to their heirs, the more likely it is that the investor will want to postpone the realization of capital gains. This aspect is not so important for younger investors.
- Taxes incite a shift toward equity because of better tax treatment on capital gains versus interest income, and because of the ability to defer taxes on capital gains.
- In the absence of embedded unrealized capital gains, the optimal equity holding and the desire to rebalance is mostly age dependent. Thus, investors who have access to significant tax losses are much more likely to rebalance their portfolio toward the optimal debt equity level.

- Even in the presence of potential tax liabilities related to unrealized capital gains, the size of a capital gain that an investor is willing to realize will increase with the degree to which the portfolio is overweight to equity, and will decrease with age. Dammon, Spatt and Zhang found that a young investor with a capital gain of even 100% would still find it reasonable to rebalance his or her portfolio. However, an elderly investor may have an incentive to tolerate a higher and increasing allocation to equity because of the reset provision. This conclusion would not apply to a Canadian investor who does not benefit from the reset clause. It also means the behavior of a Canadian investor would be more consistent through time.
- If the tax rate on capital gains goes up (assuming this was not anticipated by the investor), the incentive not to realize capital gains increases. A higher tax basis is required before investors of any age will be willing to realize capital gains to rebalance their portfolio.
- Investors of all ages will reduce their allocation to equity if equity volatility increases. However, elderly investors will remain much more sensitive to the tax basis. Young investors will reduce their allocation even if the tax basis is low. Elderly investors will require a higher tax basis (close to the market value) to significantly adjust their portfolio.

Although these observations are informative and intuitive, we still need to develop a framework that can be more easily implemented—an argumentation that is powerful enough without the need for utility functions. To do so, we will start with a simple environment where the initial tax basis and the possibility of a capital gain reset at death are ignored. We will then move on to more complex scenarios.

Let's first consider the possibility of using low-turnover investment protocols instead of a market index. Such protocols will usually have a higher turnover (ranging from 10% to 30% for many) than an index whose turnover may be as low as 5%. Figure 9.1 showed that a Canadian investor might incur a loss of approximately 5 bps to 20 bps, depending on the actual turnover (10% to 20%) and average size of the yearly capital gains (4% to 7%), while a US investor might incur a loss of 11 bps to 45 bps. Although this is much less than the cost incurred by the average active managers, it should not be ignored. We could argue that several nonmarket-cap investment protocols should easily outperform this excess cost, but, for now, we will approach this issue from a different angle.

Figure 9.1 was built around the assumption that a 10% turnover automatically translates into 10% of the embedded capital gains being realized. We also assumed that 50% of the capital gains in the case of the United States are short term. Thus, these results did not consider the possibility that the net capital gain may be lower than the turnover implies, because of a proactive tax-loss-harvesting policy and the fact that many investment protocols do not require that short-term capital gains (less than 12 months) be realized. For example, in Figure 9.1 a portfolio with a 20% turnover trails the performance of a portfolio with a 5% turnover (a more index-like portfolio) by 44 bps annually, if we assume that the average yearly capital gain is 7%, and that half the realized capital gains are short term. However, if we assume that no short-term capital gains were realized in either case, the outperformance would merely be 17 bps. Thus, much can be accomplished if asset managers created tax-efficient investment protocols. Furthermore, as indicated previously we ignored the possibility of improving the portfolio efficiency through a tax-loss-harvesting protocol.

Birge and Yang (2007) [12] indirectly looked at this issue. Their argument is as follows. An investor who holds an extremely well-diversified portfolio of assets, and who avoids capital gains unless required by his or her consumption needs, could avoid taxes on net positive capital gains for many years, assuming that he or she is very efficient at harvesting capital losses for tax purposes. Under different scenarios of liquidation (required for consumption) ranging from 3% to 7% annually, the authors found that investors could postpone their initial taxable capital gains by more than 10 to 15 years. The argument is simple. If the portfolio is extremely well diversified, and the underlying assets have significant idiosyncratic (specific) risks, there are almost always securities that can be sold at a loss to offset the realized capital gains required to finance consumption.

This aspect is important. Traditional indexed investments cannot be used efficiently to harvest losses because the wash sale rule would prohibit the managers of these indices from buying back the same security within 30 days. Only quasi-indexed products could harvest losses. Furthermore, once a retired investor is liquidating part of his or her holdings yearly, he or she will not be able to avoid capital gains on an index product unless, of course, the tax basis is negative. However, low-turnover investment protocols could be inherently more efficient at harvesting losses. Although several low-turnover investment protocols are offered right now, and although trading rules are often incorporated into these protocols to minimize turnover, the management process may not be designed with the purpose of aggressively harvesting capital losses. But it can be done. In fact, there is no reason why a tax-loss-harvesting program could not be integrated within a global portfolio solution that incorporates several asset classes, although the full benefit of such an approach could only be achieved if a central manager administers the investment program.

For example, capital losses within an asset class could be used to offset capital gains generated by the rebalancing of asset classes to their targets. Thus, the excess cost linked to higher turnover can be made more irrelevant if investors used low-turnover protocols (less than 20%), avoided short-term capital gains and harvested capital losses efficiently. In the absence of a low-tax-basis issue on existing investments, the decision to move from index products to investment protocols with slightly higher turnover may not be a significant matter. Until now, we have not even raised the issue that rebalancing can be after-tax efficient if it increases the return-to-risk efficiency of the portfolio. This is our next topic.

Let's consider the following example taken from Stein, Siegel and Narasimhan (2000) [13]. An investor holds $1 million in equity assets with a tax basis of $0. The expected price appreciation is 7% yearly, while the dividend yield is 3%. Dividends are taxed at 39.6%, and capital gains at 20%. We will consider the impact of different tax rates later on. The investment horizon is 20 years, and the investors liquidate all assets at horizon end. Assuming all after-tax dividends are reinvested yearly, what

TABLE 9.10   After-Tax Liquidation Values (in $ Million)

Final Wealth	Poorly Diversified Portfolio	Well-Diversified Portfolio
Expected	4.5	3.8
Standard Deviation	13	2.4
Most Likely	0.5	2.5
Probability < $1 Million	43%	2%
Probability < $2 Million	60%	21%

Source: Stein, Siegel and Narasimhan (2000).

would the final wealth be if the investor either keeps the current asset or if he or she sells this asset now, incurs the $200,000 tax on capital gains and buys another investment offering similar dividend yields and expected price appreciation? We could easily show that the after-tax wealth at maturity is $4.51 million in the first case and $3.77 million in the second case. The situation appears simple.

However, let's assume the asset currently held is a single-security or a poorly diversified portfolio. Such portfolios would have much higher idiosyncratic risks than a well-designed and well-diversified portfolio. Thus, although the poorly diversified portfolio has a greater expected after-tax value at maturity, the distribution of final wealth might be significantly different. Assuming the poorly diversified portfolio has 40% volatility, while the well-diversified portfolio has 15% volatility, the outcome distribution of each option would be significantly different. Results in Table 9.10 are from Monte Carlo simulations conducted by Stein, Siegel and Narasimhan.

The example illustrates that investors with highly concentrated portfolios should consider the entire distribution of potential wealth. Well-diversified portfolios have volatilities ranging from 15% to 20%, while the volatility of securities can be as low as 15% for some, but as high as 30% to 60% for most. Dammon, Spatt and Zhang (2000) [14] have also specifically addressed the issue of rebalancing a portfolio when the investor holds a highly concentrated and volatile position. They find that, unless an investor is very old, and the tax basis of the concentrated position is extremely low, there would still be a strong incentive from a risk/return point of view to rebalance the portfolio. However, although every investor would prefer to postpone taxes on capital gains, the situation of investors who own volatile and highly concentrated positions with a low tax basis is different from investors who own an already diversified portfolio with a low tax basis. Thus, we will consider two possibilities:

1. An investor who owns a diversified but high-turnover portfolio is considering a change to a low-turnover diversified investment protocol.
2. An investor who owns a concentrated portfolio is considering replacing or diversifying his or her holdings with a diversified investment protocol.

From a Diversified High-Turnover Portfolio to a Diversified Low-Turnover Investment Protocol

In this scenario, we are solely interested in the impact of turnover on taxes and on other costs, not in the return-to-risk efficiency of low-turnover investment protocols. The impact of turnover on performance is difficult to measure accurately. There is the bid-ask spread, the possible impact of trading on pricing (market impact) for large investors and there may be other operational costs. Estimates related to the cost of turnover vary greatly.

Carhart (1997) regressed the residual returns (based on the four-factor model) of mutual funds on variables such as fees and turnover. He found that a 100% turnover turned into a 95 bps excess cost to the fund. Bogle (2001) estimated an even higher cost. However, Peterson, Pietranico, Riepe and Xu (2002) [15] could not find a statistically significant relation between portfolio turnover and before- or after-tax returns. However, if we assume that the average manager does not outperform the market, that the average manager has a high turnover and that a high turnover is not necessarily required to achieve a more efficient portfolio, it would be hard to accept that turnover does not contribute to a lower expected return on average. The question is not really if, but by how much? For example, Blanchett (2007) [16] evaluated the relation between the portfolio turnovers of funds grouped by deciles against excess return using data on 2,151 to 2,722 funds between 2001 and 2006. Subsets of large-cap, mid-cap, small-cap and foreign funds were created. Results are presented in Table 9.11 and are entirely consistent with expectations. The cost of turnover is far more significant for foreign and small-cap stocks than for large- and mid-cap stocks.

Tables 9.12a and 9.12b evaluate the relative performance of moving an allocation from an existing fund under different scenarios of tax basis and turnover to an investment protocol with a 15% turnover. We consider two growth scenarios (4% and 7%), a 3% dividend yield and a 60/40 split between long-term and short-term capital gains. The tax rate is 15% on dividends and long-term capital gains and 35% for short-term capital gains. Finally, the cost related to turnover is fairly conservative, at 20 bps per 100% of turnover. There is no tax-loss-harvesting effort. Table 9.12a assumes no reset of capital gains at maturity, while Table 9.12b does.

TABLE 9.11 Impact of Turnover on Performance

Category	Impact per 100% of Turnover
Large-Cap	−19 bps
Mid-Cap	−45 bps
Small-Cap	−80 bps
Foreign	−98 bps
All Combined	−48 bps

Source: Blanchett (2007).

Not that all of the scenarios are realistic. For example, a very low initial tax basis is unlikely if the turnover of the active portfolio is very high. Furthermore, a tax basis of 25% is also unlikely if the manager maintained a turnover of 25% or higher, unless the manager was extremely efficient at tax harvesting capital losses. A basis of 35% to 50% would be more coherent with a turnover of 25%. Assuming there is no reset of asset value to market value at maturity, there are few circumstances that may prevent an investor from switching to a low-turnover investment protocol from an active protocol if he wanted to, especially if the management fee of this active protocol were greater—an aspect we have not considered.

Furthermore, if the investor truly believes that a low-turnover investment protocol can be even more efficient in the long run, there is no obvious reason why a transfer of assets could not be done, unless the investment horizon is very short, much shorter than 10 years. If we consider the possibility of a reset of the tax basis, the decision is still justified if the horizon is greater than 10 years and the initial tax basis and turnover are both greater than about 50%.

From a Concentrated Portfolio to a Diversified Low-Turnover Investment Protocol

In the previous example, we did not consider the impact of the return distribution on the decision process because we assumed that we were dealing with diversified

TABLE 9.12a   Impact of Turnover on Performance (No Reset of Tax Basis) (%)

| | | $g = 4\%$ | | | | | $g = 7\%$ | | | |
| | | Turnover | | | | | Turnover | | | |
	Basis	25%	50%	75%	100%	Basis	25%	50%	75%	100%
10 Years	25%	−0.66	−0.39	−0.12	0.15	25%	−0.84	−0.44	−0.04	0.37
	50%	−0.41	−0.22	−0.03	0.15	50%	−0.51	−0.22	0.07	0.37
	75%	−0.18	−0.07	0.04	0.15	75%	−0.22	−0.02	0.17	0.37
	100%	0.02	0.06	0.11	0.15	100%	0.04	0.15	0.26	0.37
20 Years	25%	−0.50	−0.24	0.02	0.28	25%	−0.17	0.23	0.63	−0.56
	50%	−0.30	−0.11	0.09	0.28	50%	−0.01	0.31	0.63	−0.33
	75%	−0.13	0.01	0.15	0.28	75%	0.14	0.39	0.63	−0.12
	100%	0.03	0.12	0.20	0.28	100%	0.26	0.45	0.63	0.08
30 Years	25%	−0.38	−0.13	0.12	0.37	25%	−0.39	0.01	0.41	0.80
	50%	−0.23	−0.03	0.17	0.37	50%	−0.21	0.13	0.47	0.80
	75%	−0.08	0.07	0.22	0.37	75%	−0.05	0.24	0.52	0.80
	100%	0.04	0.15	0.26	0.37	100%	0.10	0.34	0.57	0.80

TABLE 9.12b   Impact of Turnover on Performance (Reset of Tax Basis)

		g = 4%					*g* = 7%			
		Turnover					Turnover			
	Basis	25%	50%	75%	100%	Basis	25%	50%	75%	100%
10 Years	25%	−1.47	−0.75	−0.01	0.74	25%	−1.44	−0.53	0.39	1.33
	50%	−0.90	−0.36	0.19	0.74	50%	−0.86	−0.14	0.59	1.33
	75%	−0.39	−0.01	0.36	0.74	75%	−0.33	0.22	0.77	1.33
	100%	0.09	0.31	0.52	0.74	100%	0.16	0.55	0.94	1.33
20 Years	25%	−0.69	−0.22	0.26	0.74	25%	−0.64	0.01	0.66	1.33
	50%	−0.41	−0.03	0.36	0.74	50%	−0.35	0.21	0.77	1.33
	75%	−0.15	0.15	0.44	0.74	75%	−0.09	0.38	0.86	1.33
	100%	0.09	0.31	0.52	0.74	100%	0.16	0.55	0.94	1.33
30 Years	25%	−0.43	−0.04	0.35	0.74	25%	−0.37	0.19	0.76	1.33
	50%	−0.24	0.08	0.41	0.74	50%	−0.18	0.32	0.82	1.33
	75%	−0.07	0.20	0.47	0.74	75%	−0.01	0.44	0.88	1.33
	100%	0.09	0.31	0.52	0.74	100%	0.16	0.55	0.94	1.33

portfolios in both cases (active management and investment protocols). However, a concentrated equity position is likely to be more volatile than a diversified investment protocol. Therefore, in this case, we cannot only consider the expected after-tax return of the current concentrated position and of the diversified passive protocols. We must also consider the entire distribution of returns of both alternatives. For example, single securities or concentrated portfolios can easily have volatility of returns above 40%, while a diversified index or passive protocol may have a volatility ranging from 15% to 20%. This aspect will not only influence the risk distribution but also the GEO mean.

Let's start with a simple example. We will assume all securities have volatilities of 40% and an ARI mean of 15%. If an investor owns a single security, his or her expected GEO mean would be 7% if the distribution of returns was normal, since:

$$15\% - 0.5 \times 0.40^2 = 7\%$$

But, if the investor were to own 100 of these securities (with equal weights to simplify), the volatility of that portfolio would be approximately 22.16% if the average of pairwise correlations was about 30%. The fact that we now have a portfolio of securities, and not a single security, does not change the average expected ARI mean. It is still 15%. However, since the volatility of the portfolio is now 22.16%, the expected long-term GEO mean has increased to 12.54%, an increase of 5.54 percentage points!

If the investor has a portfolio invested in a few securities with a very low tax basis, avoiding and/or postponing the realization of capital gains may not be financially optimal. The investor might be exposed to more extreme and negative outcomes, and, if the horizon is sufficiently long, this postponement might hurt his or her expected long-term return. This does not mean that the entire concentrated investment has to be sold (because the concentrated portfolio may contribute to the diversity of the passive or index portfolios), but rather that the investor should consider diversifying a significant portion of his or her holdings.

To illustrate this aspect, we will compare the expected return distribution after taxes of two possible scenarios using a Monte Carlo simulation. In the first scenario, the investor maintains a concentrated and volatile portfolio with a tax basis of 25% and a standard deviation of 30%. In the second scenario, the investor realizes his or her capital gain fully in order to invest in a more diversified portfolio with a volatility of 20%. Except for the initial restructuring of the portfolio under the second scenario, the yearly turnover is identical in both cases, at 15%. The ARI mean of all securities in both portfolios was set at only 10%, but the two portfolios also generate identical dividend yields of 3%. The tax rate on dividends is 15%, while the average tax rate on capital gains is 23%. We consider four horizons: 5, 10, 20 and 30 years. Is it preferable to avoid the initial taxes on capital gains and maintain a volatile portfolio? Or would it be better to realize those gains and invest in a more diversified portfolio? Table 9.13 answers this question.

Even if the investment horizon is five years, there is a strong incentive to realize the capital gains immediately and invest in more efficient portfolios. This incentive increases further with the lengthening of the investment horizon. Thus, there is a possibility that investors obsessed with short-term tax minimization may be hurting their long-term performance. Managing risk can improve expected returns. The previous example was limited to equities, and yet we illustrated that switching an existing concentrated equity allocation to a more diversified equity protocol may be worthwhile, even at the expense of higher taxes in the short term.

TABLE 9.13   Tax Basis, Diversification and Performance (%)

	Scenario 1: High Volatility: Avoid Initial Capital Gains			
	5 Years	10 Years	20 Years	30 Years
Expected Return	5.9	5.3	5.2	5.2
Standard Deviation	10.7	7.8	5.8	4.9
	Scenario 2: Low Volatility: Realize Capital Gains			
	5 Years	10 Years	20 Years	30 Years
Expected Return	7.2	7.0	7.0	7.2
Standard Deviation	7.1	5.2	4.0	3.4

Case Study 1: The Impact of Tax-Efficient Investment Planning

This case study illustrates the importance of asset location and management of capital gains. We will consider the situation of a young professional, Bob, who intends to retire at age 55. Our objective is to determine the present value of a 30-year before-tax annuity that Bob could purchase, depending on different investment plans and strategies. We use a 30-year annuity for comparison simply because it is easier to visualize the impact of an investment plan on financial well-being in terms of yearly income in current dollars. We are not necessarily advising the purchase of such product. These products are usually expensive.

We will compare five investment plans. No matter what plan Bob uses, he will commit the same after-tax income every year, and his contributions will grow with his income. The investment plans are the following:

- The investor only invests in taxable investments. He has no IRA.
- The investor commits the maximum amount possible to a 401(k)\ plan (first), and there is no employer contribution. The investor does not optimize his asset location (he allocates similarly all assets in all accounts).
- The investor follows the same plan as above, but he does optimize his asset location.
- The two previous scenarios are repeated, except that for each, Bob's employer will match Bob's contribution to the 401(k) dollar for dollar up to a maximum of 6% of Bob's pre-tax compensation.

Finally, each investment plan can be implemented using one of two types of products: high-turnover active mandates and low-turnover investment protocols. The turnover of the active equity mandate is 75%, while that of the low-turnover protocol is 15%. We also assume the management expense ratios (MERs) of both approaches are identical (60 bps for equity and 30 bps for fixed income), although, in most cases, we should expect active mandates to be more costly than an investment protocol. However, we have to remember that our objective is solely to illustrate the impact of proper tax management. The investor maintains an asset allocation of 60/40, risk adjusted for taxes. The portfolio is rebalanced once a year. The equity and fixed-income portfolio have the following characteristics:

- Equity: The ARI mean is 8.5% (of which 3% are dividends) and the volatility is 15%.
- Fixed Income: The ARI mean is 5.5% and the volatility is 7%.
- The average correlation between fixed income and equity is 30%.

The inflation rate is 2.5% annually on average. An inflation assumption is required to compute the allowed contribution limits to the 401(k) and Roth IRA, and to calculate the value of the annuity in real terms. Finally, Bob is a fairly successful individual. While his current salary is $100,000, it will increase by 6% annually, or 3.5 percentage points above the inflation rate. This means that in present value terms, his salary in 30 years would be close to $273,817. He will invest 7.5% of his salary for the first 10 years, 15% for the following 10 years and then 25% in the last 10 years. Finally, we will make the following assumptions: a 35% tax rate for interest income and short-term capital gains, and a 20% tax rate for dividend income and long-term capital gains. Whether or not Bob's situation is representative of many individuals is not the question. The real issue is the relative significance of the investment decisions that Bob makes today in terms of asset location and management of capital. I have not incorporated the issue of tax harvesting into this example. Table 9.14 presents the most likely annuity income, as well as the 10th, 25th, 75th and 90th percentile after running 1,000 scenarios. I also present the average annuity value and its standard deviation.

The upper and lower segments of Table 9.14 present the same information for low or high portfolio turnover conditions. Even if we ignore the potential impact of higher MER on active mandates, the greater turnover of the active mandate reduces

TABLE 9.14 Value of an Annuity

	Low Turnover				
	All Private	401(k)	401(k) Tax Efficient	401(k) + Employer	401(k) + Employer Tax Efficient
Bottom Decile	59,020	67,393	69,441	85,348	87,270
Bottom Quartile	68,112	78,580	80,470	100,384	102,302
Median	80,969	95,345	96,759	122,449	124,194
Top Quartile	94,744	112,751	113,648	146,450	147,254
Top Decile	110,481	113,129	134,188	174,666	175,814
Average	83,380	98,621	99,791	127,367	128,634
Standard Deviation	20,960	27,368	26,523	36,982	36,175
	High Turnover				
Bottom Decile	58,380	67,113	68,838	84,970	86,444
Bottom Quartile	65,994	77,820	78,979	99,706	101,227
Median	76,815	93,109	93,109	120,663	120,794
Top Quartile	87,636	109,477	109,477	143,097	141,721
Top Decile	100,458	128,789	125,045	170,046	165,312
Average	78,409	96,303	95,645	125,048	124,400
Standard Deviation	16,832	25,446	22,998	35,080	32,593

the average annuity of a fully taxable portfolio from $83,380 to $78,409, a decline of about 5%. However, fully using the tax benefits of a 401(k) plan, but without any asset location optimization, increases the total annuity by almost 20% in both cases (high and low turnover). Furthermore, optimizing asset location does not have a significant impact (on average) on the high-turnover scenario, but it does improve the performance of the low-turnover scenario. It appears that a high-turnover approach nullifies many of the benefits that asset location optimization should provide on average, but it does slightly improve the annuity distribution. The benefit of a 401(k) plan, even without the contribution of an employer, is obvious.

The impact of higher MER on many investment products was not considered in the simulation because the objective was to specifically isolate the impact of the asset location decision. However, further simulations indicated that standard MER could reduce the value of the expected annuity by as much as 15%.

Case Study 2: Efficient Investment Protocols and Tax Efficiency

The objective of this case study is to evaluate the tax efficiency of a nonmarket-cap investment protocol, and the usefulness of a tax-loss-harvesting strategy. To illustrate our case, we will use the protocol discussed in Tables 6.9a and 6.9b. This protocol is applied to a global portfolio of large-capitalization stocks. The protocol contains 150 securities, equally weighted and rebalanced annually. The weight of the US market against the rest of the world is determined by a moving average of its weight over five years. The same process is used for sector weights. The 150 securities are selected according to the payout rate (dividend and share buyback). Securities whose dividend rates are above a threshold are excluded to avoid investing in firms that can potentially no longer afford their dividends. The portfolio is rebalanced during the last two weeks of March. However, some external factors, such as mergers and acquisitions, can trigger the replacement of specific securities prior to the official rebalancing date. The period being studied is March 2000 to March 2011.

The annualized performance and volatility of this portfolio was respectively 11.03% and 29.26% (fairly high because of the 2007 to 2009 liquidity crisis). The protocol significantly outperformed the S&P 1200. The nature of this protocol leads to a fairly high turnover (55%), still less than many active managers, but significantly higher than many other investment protocols. The payout rule and the fact that the protocol is based on 150 stocks out of a possible pool of 1200 securities is responsible for increasing the turnover. However, a live portfolio would have a lesser turnover, such as 30% to 40%. Investment protocols such as minimum variance, maximum diversification and many others, including the one used for this test, usually integrate mechanisms that are designed to reduce turnover without materially impeding portfolio efficiency. For example, even a minimum variance protocol may incorporate a tolerance band designed to minimize turnover as long as the maximum efficiency of the portfolio is only slightly compromised. In our case, the same principle could be applied by maintaining existing positions in the

TABLE 9.15 After-tax Simulation of an Investment Protocol (March 2000–March 2011) (%)

| Scenario | No Capital Gain at Maturity | | Capital Gain at Maturity | | Percentage of Taxes Attributed to . . . | | |
	Return	Effective Tax Rate	Return	Effective Tax Rate	Dividend	Short-Term Capital Gains	Long-Term Capital Gains
#1	9.45	14.34	9.25	16.17	48	6	46
#2	9.00	18.48	8.80	20.26	47	6	47
#3	9.06	17.92	8.83	19.99	47	6	47

portfolio as long as these securities remain among the top 200 in terms of ranking. However, in this test, the integral protocol is applied.

Three scenarios are considered. In the first scenario, investors would have a right to get full deductions on net capital losses in the same year these losses occur. This is an even more favorable scheme than the Canadian rule that allows carrying losses against gains that were realized over the last three years. In the second scenario, net capital losses can only be carried against future capital gains. In the third scenario, we added the possibility of tax loss harvesting to the second scenario. Since there is an unrealized capital gain remaining in March 2011, we will assume that this gain is fully taxed at maturity. The tax rates are 15% for US dividends, 35% for foreign dividends, 35% for short-term capital gains and 15% for long-term capital gains. All results are presented in Table 9.15.

These results bring a few aspects to light. First, the fact that investors cannot automatically receive a tax credit for incurred capital losses has a significant impact on returns. This is particularly costly because most significant declines in stock markets are followed by a rise. Thus, investors do not have the benefit of a higher investment basis when they need it the most. Surprisingly, the impact of tax loss harvesting was not significant. There are many reasons for this. First, the investment protocol produced a significant return over the period, despite the crisis of 2007 to 2008. A high return obviously reduces the opportunity for tax loss harvesting. Second, the protocol generates mostly long-term capital gains, which are taxed at the lowest rate. The right hand side of Table 9.15 indicates that almost 90% of capital gains taxes (long and short term) can be attributed to long-term capital gains. Thus, even though the turnover of this protocol is fairly high at 55%, the protocol is efficient at generating mostly long-term capital gains.

I also computed the theoretical impact of being able, somehow, to postpone taxation on long-term capital gains by a full 11 years. It would have added another 0.26% to the performance. Although it is not insignificant, it pales in comparison to the benefit that an efficient investment protocol can bring in the long term. Thus, it make sense to impose some rules that can reduce portfolio turnover, but not at the expense of portfolio efficiency.

Closing Remarks

The principles of after-tax allocation are simple, but proper implementation can be complicated. The following are among the most important aspects:

- Pay attention to asset location, not only asset allocation.
- Manage risk on an after-tax basis.
- Avoid investment products with high asset turnover and/or high short-term capital gains (in the United States) *unless* they significantly contribute to overall diversification.
- Defer realization of capital gains *only if* it does not hinder portfolio efficiency.
- Harvest losses *only if* it does not hinder portfolio efficiency.
- Consider the possibility that tax rates may increase.
- Consider the potential impact of the reset of the tax basis for elderly investors, but do not allow the reset of the tax basis at death to hinder proper risk management if the investor is relatively young.

The tax code is complex, and we have only raised some of the more important considerations. However, the material we have covered so far implicitly illustrates that the impact of taxation on the portfolio management process is not independent of wealth. For example, an investor who has most of his or her portfolio invested in a traditional and/or a Roth IRA account faces a fairly simple situation. At the other extreme, investors who are extremely wealthy will be mostly concerned with the proper management of capital gains and losses, and the potential effect of a reset of the tax basis at death. If these investors hold high-turnover portfolios, it may be profitable to move assets to low-turnover portfolios if we assume that the low-turnover portfolios are more efficient, even at the expense of triggering capital gains taxes. Furthermore, if these investors own extremely concentrated investment positions, then a transition program toward a more balanced portfolio, which even incorporates the use of derivatives on a temporary basis, may be required. The greatest conceptual complexity may be that of investors with wealth ranging from a few million dollars up to $5 or $10 million. These investors may have traditional IRA and Roth IRA accounts that contain a relevant portion of their assets, and they may still face issues related to the tax basis of their portfolio. Furthermore, the potential effect of a reset of the tax basis at death is still relevant to these investors, even though their spouses may be able to avoid estate taxes.

However, one of the most important aspects is the possibility that the benefits of tax-loss harvesting may be exaggerated for many reasons. First, the managers of some portfolios may have neglected tax efficiency in the past but, after they have taken initial corrective measures, it is far from obvious that short-term tax efficiency should dominate the allocation process. There is an opportunity cost that is difficult to measure. Furthermore, simulations may exaggerate the tax benefits because they do not properly incorporate the autocorrelation of returns.

Thus, overall, most investors should concentrate on building efficient portfolios and incorporating the impact of taxes on risk. In most cases, they should not allow taxation concerns related to capital gain taxes and tax-loss harvesting to overtake portfolio efficiency.

Notes

1. Horan, Steven and David Adler (2009), "Tax-aware investment management practice," *Journal of Wealth Management* 12(2), 71–88.
2. William Reichenstein (2006), "After-tax asset allocation," *Financial Analysts Journal* 62(4), 14–19.
3. Chen, Jerry (2009), "After-tax asset allocation," Simon Fraser University.
4. Jeffrey, Robert H. and Robert D. Arnott (1993), "Is your alpha big enough to cover its taxes?" First Quadrant Corporation.
5. Wotherspoon, Gordon and Geoff Longmeier (2006), "The value of tax efficient investments—An analysis of after-tax mutual fund and index returns," *Journal of Wealth Management* 9(2), 46–53.
6. Dammon, Robert M., Chester S. Spatt, and Harold H. Zhang (2004), "Optimal asset location and allocation with taxable and tax-deferred investing," *Journal of Finance* 59(3), 999–1037.
7. Arnott, Robert D., Andrew L. Berkin, and Jia Ye (2001), "Loss harvesting—What's it worth to the taxable investor?" First Quadrant.
8. Bouchey, Paul (2010), "Tax-Efficient Investing in theory and practice," Parametric.
9. Dammon, Robert M., Chester S. Spatt, and Harold H. Zhang (2001), "Optimal consumption with capital gains taxes," *Review of Financial Studies* 14, 583–616.
10. Constantinides, G. (1983), "Capital market equilibrium with personal tax," *Econometrica* 51, 611-636.
11. Dammon, Robert M., Chester S. Spatt, and Harold H. Zhang (2003), "Capital gains taxes and portfolio rebalancing," TIAA-CREF Institute.
12. Birge, John R. and Song Yang (2007), "A model for tax advantages of portfolios with many assets," *Journal of Banking and Finance* 31(11), 3269–3290.
13. Stein, David M., Andrew F. Siegel, Premkumar Narasimhan, and Charles E. Appeadu (2000), "Diversification in the presence of taxes," *Journal of Portfolio Management*, 27(1) 61–71.
14. Dammon, Robert M., Chester S. Spatt, and Harold H. Zhang (2000), "Diversification and capital gains taxes with multiple risky assets," Carnegie Mellon University.
15. Peterson, James D., Paul A. Pietranico, Mark W. Riepe, and Fran Xu (2002), "Explaining after-tax mutual fund performance," *Financial Analysts Journal* 58(1), 75–86.
16. Blanchett, David (2007), "The pre-tax costs of portfolio turnover," *Journal of Indexing* 9(3), 34–39.

PART IV

Creating an Integrated Portfolio Management Process

CHAPTER 10

Understanding Liability-Driven Investing

Liability-driven investment (LDI) is not a financial product nor is it an investment strategy. It is a portfolio process designed to meet an investor's objectives and liabilities. LDI implicitly means that the structure of a portfolio of assets should be consistent with the structure of the investor's liabilities. In the case of pension funds with defined benefits, for example, the primary objectives of LDI are usually to limit the volatility of the funding status and help maintain a more stable level of contribution over time. The trade-off is assumed to be a lower expected return and, thus, a higher level of financial contribution, although this conclusion may be based on a narrow understanding of LDI. LDI should be perceived as a mandate, not to be managed simply by imposing constraints on the portfolio management process (such as maximum equity weight and cash flow matching), but rather by integrating it into the fabric of our portfolio management process. Furthermore, LDI can only be successful (by design and not by chance) if applied within a dynamic portfolio management process. It will most likely fail or lead to significant regret if applied within a static process, especially if a pension plan is significantly underfunded.

It seems that LDI has been in fashion since the early 2000s, and has become even more so in recent years with the growing problem of pension fund deficits. However, the concept is certainly not new. The basic requirement of any investment program, whether it is for an individual, a pension fund, a foundation or a life insurance company, has always been that it must be guided by the objectives and constraints of the investor. Furthermore, if liabilities are simply an indirect representation of future consumption needs, there is already significant literature that deals with the issue of portfolio choices in the context of life cycle and consumption [1]. Thus, it is peculiar that this new buzzword—LDI—and an area of research surrounding it have been created by the advisory industry (somewhat too late again) to express a mandate that already existed (managing assets with a concern for the liability structure and future consumption needs), but that was not properly implemented, at the very least, in pension funds.

A neglected objective has been inaccurately portrayed as a new strategic approach, and we are all to blame for this negligence. A survey conducted by CREATE (a UK-based think tank) in 2006 showed that when pension funds were asked which asset class would best meet funding needs over the next five years, LDI finished 12th as a priority. LDI is obviously not an asset class, but there was a lack of interest for the potential consequences of asset liability mismatches at the time. Investors believed that alternative investments and the Yale model (for all) would save the day. They did not [2].

The challenges of LDI are usually not well explained, nor are they well understood. As Muralidhar (2011) [3] describes, the improper management of assets and liabilities can lead to less-than-desirable investing because pension plans could be implementing a narrow interpretation of LDI (matching cash flows or durations) at potentially the very worst time (when interest rates are extremely low). Therefore, our objective in this chapter is to better understand LDI and its challenges, and to determine how the portfolio management concepts discussed thus far, including nonmarket-cap invest-ment protocols and management of volatility, and other concepts yet to be discussed, fit within an LDI concern. Such an understanding will allow us to design a more coherent liability-driven portfolio management process (LDPMP).

Understanding Duration Risk

Assets have duration. So do liabilities. Interest rate duration is defined as the sensitiv-ity of the present value of a set of cash flows to a change in the discount rate. However, a change in the discount rate can occur for many reasons. It could be explained by a change in inflation, a change in the real rate of return, a change in the risk premium or even a change in the liquidity premium. One of the reasons (but certainly not the only one) for the pension fund debacle was a substantial duration mismatch between assets and liabilities. However, which durations are we talking about? Is it inflation? Real rate? Credit premium?

Since we usually invest in order to meet some liability requirement, the nature of this liability will determine the type of duration hedge we are seeking. Let's consider two types of liability structures: nominal and real. A nominal liability structure requires that a series of nominal (inflation indifferent) cash flows be met at specific dates in the future, such as $100 a year for 20 years. The present value of such a liability structure will be impacted by all sources of interest rate fluctuations. If the discount rate used to value the liability cash flow declines from 7% to 6%, the present value will rise from $1,059 to $1,146, whether the decline is attributed to a change in inflation, real rate or liquidity premium. A nominal cash flow has both real rate and inflation durations.

By comparison, the present value of an indexed liability structure, one whose cash flows are fully adjusted to inflation (such as $100 a year for 20 years in real terms), will not be affected similarly if the decline in interest rate is attributed to lower inflation or a higher real rate of return. For example, assuming that the inflation assumptions used to index the liabilities are identical to the inflation premium that is embed-ded in the discount rate, and that the real rate is a constant, the present value of the liability stream would remain at $1,146 if the decline (or even a rise) in interest rates was attributed to a change in inflation expectations. However, if it were attributed to another factor (a change of the real rate, the credit risk premium or even of the inflation premium), the present value would rise or decline. A fully indexed liability structure has real rate duration but no inflation duration.

Liability structures are either fully nominal, fully indexed or partially nominal and indexed. For example, a life insurance policy usually guarantees a nominal payment to the beneficiary at death. The greater uncertainty in this case is not the amount of the nominal payment, but its timing. An individual who is planning his or her retirement should probably aim to generate a fully indexed periodic income to maintain his or her standard of living. Some pension funds face an intermediate situation, since liabilities can be partially indexed or fully indexed, usually with a yearly cap. For example, let's consider a worker whose pension compensation is a function of the number of years of service at retirement, such as a 2% payout per year of service. At retirement, the plan may incorporate, or not, a cost-of-living adjustment (COLA) clause. If the plan does not incorporate a COLA, it will still be sensitive to wage inflation until the worker retires. If it does incorporate a COLA, it will also be sensitive to whatever measure is used to determine the cost-of-living adjustment after retirement. Many public plans incorporate a COLA, while corporate plans often do not.

In principle, the combination of nominal and real return bonds could have been a solution to the issue of indexation (full or partial). Siegel and Waring (2004) [4] explain how a combination of these two components can meet a mix of duration needs. This is illustrated in Figure 10.1, inspired by Siegel and Waring. The two axes express inflation and real rate durations. Nominal bonds are shown as a 45-degree line because they have similar sensitivity to an identical change in interest rates triggered by real rate fluctuations or inflation premium fluctuations. However, Treasury inflation-protected securities (TIPS) sensitivity is displayed as a horizontal line because they have sensitivity to real rate fluctuations but none to inflation fluctuations. In reality, the empirical slope for TIPS related to inflation duration has not quite been zero because investors have been increasing their demand for the asset in recent years, thus impacting the real rate.

In theory, the cash flows of a fully indexed liability stream would be fully sensitive to inflation and could be met with a 100% TIPS portfolio (ignoring for now expected return requirements and availability of financial instruments that have appropriate durations), while a fully nominal liability (whose cash flows are totally insensitive to inflation) could be met with a 100% nominal bond portfolio. Therefore, it is easy to conceptualize that investors confronted with liabilities that are not fully indexed could potentially satisfy those requirements with a combination of both instruments. Furthermore, as Figure 10.1 illustrates, there are infinite ways to achieve specific inflation and real interest rate durations by combining nominal bonds and TIPS, although only two potential combinations are illustrated in the graph. Furthermore, The Vanguard Group (2008) [5] has shown that the least volatile portfolio structures are not necessarily those that lead to the lowest volatility of the funding ratio. For example, portfolios that seek to minimize the volatility of the funding ratio will usually incorporate a significantly greater allocation to strip bonds.

FIGURE 10.1   Matching Liability Requirements with Nominal Bonds and TIPS.

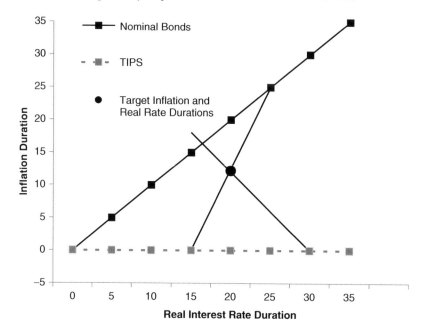

To better understand the complexity of managing and hedging a defined benefit pension liability, let's consider three hypothetical situations for a pension plan: a new plan, an ongoing plan and a fully mature plan (where all the employees within the plan are already retired). In each case, the plan either incorporates a COLA or does not. In all, we have six scenarios. Initially, we consider only two investing/hedging instruments: nominal bonds (coupons and strips) and TIPS. We will ignore risks other than those related to inflation and investment returns, such as mortality, marriage (a partial transfer of benefits to the spouse at the death of the beneficiary), natural employee turnover, etc. This discussion will illustrate that even if we were to assume that a plan sponsor could afford (because of the low expected return) to limit his or her investments to standard nominal bonds and TIPS, there are formidable hedging challenges.

The easiest case to analyze is that of the fully mature plan—a plan that no longer receives any new contributions from employees and employers (assuming it is fully funded). If the plan does not incorporate a COLA, all liability cash flows are known with certainty and can be fully met with standard coupon and strip bonds. Even if there are significant changes in interest rates attributed to changes in expected inflation, real return, risk premiums or liquidity premiums, the liabilities can be efficiently met by the bond portfolio as long as it has been appropriately configured in duration space, and credit losses are within expected parameters.

If the plan incorporates a COLA and is fully indexed, the nominal liabilities will increase with inflation. However, if the discount rate used to calculate the present value of future liabilities (PVoFL) is inflation sensitive, the PVoFL would remain unchanged and the inflation duration would be nil. There is only one instrument that can be said, with a high level of certainty, to have no duration to inflation, and that is inflation-linked bonds (ILBs) such as TIPS. Thus, assuming that the appropriate ILBs of desired maturities are available in the market, and that ILBs and liabilities are indexed according to the same inflation measure, those liabilities could be fully hedged. Finally, if the plan only incorporates a partial COLA, a combination of nominal bonds and ILBs could match the liabilities.

In this first example, an efficient hedge can only be achieved if the instruments have the appropriate maturities (i.e., if there is no reinvestment rate risk). Although bonds do incorporate an expected inflation premium, standard coupon bonds or strips cannot be used to hedge unexpected inflation, even though standard bonds may incorporate an inflation risk premium to compensate for the uncertainty related to inflation (a return buffer of sorts). If investors use ILBs to hedge unexpected inflation, they may be foregoing the inflation risk premium. The inflation risk premium on these instruments may even be negative if the demand for ILBs exceeds what is available in the market.

The previous scenarios become more complex if we assume that the funding status of the pension plan is at the opposite spectrum, such as a pension fund with almost no existing assets. In this case, most of the required funding will have to come from future contributions. Even assuming the plan has no COLA, the payment at maturity will still be impacted by salary inflation (including changes in salary scales related to promotions, which must be estimated and integrated to calculate future liabilities). Although the yearly contributions will increase with compensation, the portfolio of assets must still track inflation and there may be discrepancies between inflation related to the cost of living and salary inflation. Nevertheless, conceptually, ILBs are the most efficient instrument (if cost is not an issue) to hedge inflation risk during this accumulation period.

However, there is an added risk, which is very substantial. When a plan is in an accumulation phase, it is very difficult to protect it against a decline in real return. For example, let's assume that the return assumption on assets is 2% in excess of inflation. Let's also assume that the economy slows down significantly, and the real return on standard nominal bonds has declined to 1% and remains at that level for a very long time. Thus, the discount rate used to value liabilities also decline by 1%. In this case the PVoFL will increase substantially, while there will be no commensurate increase in the value of assets because there are simply very few assets in the portfolio, and future contributions will only be invested on the basis of a 1% real return. In order to protect the portfolio against a significant decline in real return, the plan sponsors would have had to use derivatives of significant size (buying coupon bonds and TIPS forward)—an unlikely scenario for most plan sponsors. Even a dynamic allocation process could not hedge this risk efficiently.

The last two scenarios are those of plans that have current assets but that will still require future contributions to meet future liabilities. In this case, the assets currently held can be invested to meet benefits already earned, but since these benefits will be paid well into the future, longer-duration assets are required. Furthermore, if the existing assets are relatively significant in reference to the present value of future contributions, the plan sponsors could invest the portfolio in even longer-duration assets to hedge part of the real return on investments related to future contributions. Using assets with longer duration than is currently required is equivalent to buying bonds forward.

Let's consider for example a pension fund with one beneficiary who has been participating in the plan for 10 years and will retire in 11 years, and who is expected to draw benefits for another 15 years during retirement. The individual will receive a pension equivalent of 42% of his or her salary at retirement, and there is no COLA. The interest rate and inflation durations of this plan are approximately 17.6 and 9.8 years respectively. The inflation duration is significantly less than the interest rate duration because of the absence of a COLA. Thus, it is entirely attributed to the increase in salary over the next 11 years. The current assets of the plan (fully invested in 15-year strip bonds) are 29.4% of the PVoFL, and the annual contributions to the plan as a percentage of salary are set to allow a fully funded pension plan. The inflation rate is assumed to be 2.5% and the discount rate is 5.0% for a real rate of return of about 2.5% (precisely 2.44% if we account for the geometric effect).

Let's assume the discount rate declines to 4% and that it is entirely attributed to a decline in the real rate of return. The final value of existing assets will not be impacted by this decline (the cash flow of the strip bonds at maturity remains the same), but new contributions will be invested at a much lower return than was expected. The decline will lead to an actuarial deficit of 13.4% of the initial PVoFL unless annual contributions are increased. If the real rate had risen instead of declined, the actuarial surplus would have been 11.0% of the initial PVoFL.

However, what if the maturity of the strip bonds had been 20 years instead of 15 years? In this case, a decline or a rise of 1% of the discount rate would have led to an actuarial deficit or surplus of −11.7% or +9.8% respectively. Longer-duration assets have reduced the real return risk related to future contributions. Thus, depending on the ratio of existing assets to the total PVoFL, it may be possible to hedge more or less of the investment return uncertainty of future contributions by adjusting the duration of existing assets.

This discussion illustrates that LDI is a complex problem. We have to evaluate the appropriate interest rate and inflation duration, and the appropriate portfolio mix to hedge these risks. This is actually the simplest task. How do we structure our recommendations, knowing that both nominal bonds and TIPS have low expected returns? The real yield on US TIPS reached a maximum level of 4.36% in January 2000, but has been far below that level ever since, although it is likely that much of this yield may have been a liquidity premium (at the time). Hedging current pension liabilities at low levels of nominal and real yields would have a considerable impact on contribution requirements at a time when there is already a substantial shortfall in assets. Furthermore, increasing the duration of standard coupon or strip bonds, in order to benefit from a higher yield, exposes investors to unexpected inflation. The ILB market has grown, but is still of insufficient size and diversity to answer the needs of pension funds. Finally, we have not even addressed the possibility that changes in inflation may be linked to changes in other premiums (real rate, credit, liquidity and the inflation premium itself). The challenges of defined benefit plans are substantial, and it is not surprising that most plan sponsors seek to terminate their current defined contribution plans. However, this does not remove the challenges of managing existing plans, nor does it change the fact that the objective of most investors is to generate inflation-adjusted payout. Thus, much material must still be covered before we can propose a coherent LDPMP (liability-driven portfolio management process).

Equity Duration

Since many investors use equity to compensate for the low expected return of fixed income (although most investors have not been rewarded by this approach in the last decade), the question of equity duration has been raised by many. When sensitivity of equity to interest rate fluctuations is measured empirically, its duration appears very short. The Brandes Institute (2008) [6] measured the average one-year rolling empirical duration of the S&P 500 as being 3.3 years. They also observed some variations depending on the nature of the underlying equities. For example, All Cap indices (whether growth or value) had empirical durations of less than two years. The strength of the relation was also weak, with R-squared in the 20% range, compared to more than 80% for bond aggregate indices that incorporated a significant corporate component. Equities have a low and uncertain sensitivity to interest rates.

These results are derived from Leibowitz's (1986) [7] approach to equity duration. More specifically:

$$RE - Rf = \alpha + DE \times \Delta + \varepsilon \qquad (10.1)$$

where $(RE - Rf)$ is the return differential between equity and the yield on a riskless asset, Δ is the yield change on a long-term fixed-income instrument and DE is the equity duration. DE is implicitly equal to DB (bond duration) multiplied by Beta. However, both The Brandes Institute and Blitzer and Srikant of Standard and Poor's (2005) [8] made the argument that equity duration could be much higher and that "equity duration could be of significant importance in immunization, risk management, and asset allocation" (Blitzer and Srikant). Two approaches that lead to significantly higher equity duration are presented, although none are particularly useful in the allocation process. However, it is just as important to discuss what not to do, as it can help us understand what we should do.

Casabona, Fabozzi and Francis (1984) [9] derived the following equity duration from the dividend discount model. Basically:

$$DE = 1 / (k - g) \qquad (10.2)$$

This is an intuitive solution that shows that duration is an increasing function of the growth rate (g) and a decreasing function of the discount rate (k). This approach would conceptually lead to very high duration, but it has been criticized for not taking into account the potential sensitivity of g to k. Therefore Blitzer and Srikant incorporated a sensitivity factor.

$$DE = [1 / (k - g)] \times (1 - \partial g / \partial k) \qquad (10.3)$$

This basically says that the duration of equity is also determined by the sensitivity of the growth rate to a change in the discount rate. If the growth rate had no sensitivity to the discount rate, duration would be as in Equation 10.2, but it would be less if growth had some positive sensitivity to the discount rate. For example, if higher inflation contributed to a higher discount rate but also higher profit growth, duration would be less. Blitzer and Srikant estimated the duration of the S&P 500 from 1973 to 2003 according to Equation 10.3 using the historical growth rate of quarterly dividends for g, the Moody's Baa Yield series for k and the correlation of changes of g to k for the sensitivity factor. They found that equity duration declined significantly from a range of 20 to 35 years in the 1970s and early 1980s to about 15 years, except for the late 1990s where duration peaked at 20 to 25 years. Using similar methodology, The Brandes Institute estimated equity duration as of June 2007 at 28.6 years for the S&P 500 index, and at 21.3 and 46.4 years for the value and growth versions of the index. Both The Brandes Institute and Blitzer and Srikant believed that a realistic LDI approach should take into account equity duration.

The Brandes Institute and Blitzer and Srikant had issues with the fact that the empirical duration of equity is low when the traditional empirical measure of duration is used. Thus, they proposed an approach that requires estimating the sensitivity of long-term growth in dividends to changes in interest rates. However, although this approach leads to significantly higher duration estimates, there are three issues:

1. There is tremendous noise around the estimate of the sensitivity of g to k.
2. This sensitivity is time varying and may depend on specific circumstances.
3. There are probably strong lead-lag effects.

If we go back to Equation 5.6, which is reproduced below, the sensitivity of g to k may depend on the source of the fluctuation in k (inflation, real rate and risk premium) and on crossover effects. Let's now consider several scenarios.

$$[k - g] = [I - I_g] + [RR - RG_g] + ERP$$

The Impact of Inflation

The value of equity may initially decline significantly when interest rates rise (and thus will have a high empirical duration) if the increase is attributed to expectations of higher inflation, and if investors are either unconvinced of the ability of corporations to maintain their profitability margins when inflation increases (basically, assuming that cost would increase faster than revenues) and/or are myopic about the impact of inflation on nominal growth and nominal liabilities. The latter explanation is the Modigliani and Cohn hypothesis (1979) [10]. In this particular case, the short-term sensitivity of g to *k* would be small, and equity duration would be high. However, if corporations are in fact able to pass on further price increases to their customers over time, their profitability margins will be maintained in real terms, and the previous decline in equity value will be reversed. Therefore, in the long term, inflation-related duration could be small.

However, it is not even that simple. For example, an external shock (such as a financial crisis that triggers a deleveraging in the entire economy) can impact expected growth and consequently expected inflation. Thus, the issue in this case is not the sensitivity of *g* to *k*, but the sensitivity of *k* to *g*. Furthermore, these two scenarios may be asymmetric. For example, if higher expected inflation is triggering a change in interest rates, the impact on corporate margins may be less apparent if management is able to react promptly to new information. Furthermore, even if a change in inflation eventually impacted real economic growth, this effect may only occur gradually. However, in the case of an external shock, the shock itself could impact revenues and, thus, corporate margins extremely quickly. If this leads to a decline in interest rates and inflation, not only could the duration measure be significant, but it would also have the wrong sign. It will appear as if lower interest rates and lower inflation led to a decline in equity value, instead of an increase in equity value.

The Impact of Real Return and Real Growth

The issue with real return and real growth is also one of synchronization. If we were to assume that real growth and real return were linked and perfectly synchronized, the sensitivity of *g* to *k* would be small, and fluctuations in either may have little impact on duration. However, investors may react differently to specific circumstances. For example, a decline in real expected growth will usually cause a decline in equity value, even if this decline is accompanied by or will eventually cause a decline in the real rate of return. Furthermore, an increase in real growth rate expectations may cause equity prices to improve, even if this eventually causes an increase in the real rate of return. However, as we already indicated in Chapter 5, there are certainly strong lead-lag effects on performance related to the real rate of return and to real growth that contribute to a low short-term sensitivity of *g* to *k*. This is why a patient and disciplined investor could use this information as a trading strategy. However, our purpose in this section is only to illustrate that measures of equity duration derived from Equation 10.3 would be unreliable as an allocation tool. Investors and investment committees are not likely to take comfort in being told that equity may have a high duration, while losing 30% of the value of their equity investments in a crisis, and seeing their liabilities increase because of lower interest rates.

The Impact of the Risk Premium

Ferson and Harvey (1991) [11] showed that the primary source of predictability in portfolio returns is the time variation in the expected risk premium. Equity would have strong duration sensitivity to a change in the risk premium. In this case, if there were differences between short-term and long-term durations, it would not be attributed to lead-lag effects or to myopic behavior by investors who fail to understand the effect of inflation on nominal growth rates [12], but to time-varying risk aversion. Furthermore, it is even possible that changes in inflation expectations can impact the risk premium, since investors may assume it will impact monetary policy and negatively impact real growth.

The Franchise Factor Model

The Franchise Factor model, developed by Leibowitz and Kogelman (2004) [13], seeks to solve the paradox of low empirical equity duration and high duration using dividend discount models. The "Franchise Factor" (FF) model segregates earnings from existing business operations from future business, called, respectively, earnings from "tangible value" (TV) and earnings from "franchise value" (FV). According to the FF model, TV is more bond-like and would result in lower duration, such as 6 to 10 years, while FV duration would be much higher, such as 30+ years. TV duration is lower because it represents the present value of future earnings from current businesses, while FV is much more complicated. It depends on the profitability and growth of new businesses. Bruce Grantier of InvestorLit (2012) [14] reported the following statement by Leibowitz:

> The TV is largely based on existing investments where the product pricing and cost structure may be pretty sticky and not very responsive to new inflation regimes. In contrast, the FV represents new investment opportunities that are elective and would presumably be shaped to reflect both the accumulated inflation as well as the future inflation prospects.

Thus, the ability of firms to "flow-through" inflation into earnings and dividends would differ according to TV and FV. Grantier also raises the possibility that there may be a relation between equity duration and style. For example, what if value stocks were more likely to have TV assets? It is likely that the level and certainty of the duration measure would be different for value and growth stocks. We will see later on that Amenc, Martellini, Goltz and Milhau (2010) [15] also made the argument that the way we structure equity portfolios can influence the degree of liability hedging efficiency, although their argument was not specifically linked to style. This is an area of research that deserves more interest.

Closing Remarks on Equity Duration

Although this discussion is interesting, it is not always helpful to the allocation process. The Brandes Institute and Blitzer and Srikant's approach to equity duration is meant to justify allocating more to equity in the context of long-term liabilities, but these approaches do very little to help manage investors and plan sponsors' fears of significant equity decline. Furthermore, these analyses are done solely from the point of view of equity, and do not incorporate the interactions between equity and other asset classes, and the time-varying changes in those interactions. These analyses also fail to consider how these interactions can be affected by the choice of a rebalancing process. Thus, even if we were to agree that equity duration is high in the long run (an aspect that could be disputed, depending on the source of interest rate changes), the recent decade has shown that investors are simply unable to maintain such a long-term static perspective.

The Leibowitz and Kogelman and the Grantier interpretation that duration could be related to style (and to other factors, as we will discuss later on) does open the possibility that equity portfolios could be structured to offer more desirable duration characteristics, at least to some degree.

Hedging Inflation

Inflation hedging is an important issue for many pension plans. The empirical efficiency of many assets' ability to hedge inflation and unexpected inflation has been addressed in recent research. Several assets will be considered, such as Treasury bills (cash), bonds and foreign bonds, inflation-linked bonds, equity, real estate and commodities. Before we present some empirical evidence, let's consider the characteristics of each asset class (with the exception of equity and TIPS, which have already been discussed in this chapter, and commodities, which were discussed in Chapter 8).

- Cash: According to Irving Fisher (1930) [16], the nominal rate (i) is equal to the real rate (RR) + expected inflation (E(I)). If we add to this relation that the nominal rate also incorporates a risk premium related to inflation uncertainty RP(σ_I), we get:

$$i = \text{RR} + \text{E}(I) + \text{RP}(\sigma_I) \tag{10.4}$$

  However, making the assumption that any changes in inflation automatically translate into a one-to-one change in interest rates is probably too simplistic. The risk premium related to unexpected inflation may change with inflation itself, and the real return may not be independent of the other two variables, because inflation may be, among other things, the symptom of other factors.

- Bonds: The same issues that apply to cash certainly apply to bonds. Furthermore, the complexity increases with as the bonds mature. Longer-maturity bonds are likely to have greater inflation uncertainty, and the presence of a naturally upward sloping yield curve may reflect causes other than an inflation risk premium, such as market segmentation and preferred investor habitats.
- Foreign Bonds: Although some research looks at foreign bonds as a hedge, the efficiency of this hedge is mostly explained by the long-term purchasing power parity theorem. However, as we already explained in Chapter 8, currency risk is usually significant in relation to interest rate risk, and therefore most currency risk related to foreign high-grade quality bonds should be hedged. Furthermore, purchasing

power parity is a concept that can only be validated over extremely long periods. Thus, we should separate the issue of foreign currencies as an inflation hedge or as an asset class from that of instruments in which we invest in foreign currencies.

- Real Estate: Real estate has had a reputation as a hedge against inflation, and since real estate is a real asset, its inflation hedging qualities should be stronger than those of financial assets. Several studies concluded that residential and commercial real estate offered a good inflation hedge (see Attié and Roache (2009) [17] for a review), although we also know, by now, that even if we accept those findings, a real asset can only be an efficient inflation hedge in the presence of a fairly balanced market for this asset class.

Tables 10.1a and 10.1b present the main results from the analysis of Bekaert and Wang (2010) [18] concerning the efficiency of fixed income and equity as an inflation hedge. Although there are other studies, such as Attié and Roache and Amenc, Martellini, Goltz and Milhau of EDHEC-Risk Institute (2010), they all reached similar conclusions. The Bekaert and Wang study covers as many as 45 countries over the period of January 1970 to January 2005. To derive unexpected inflation, it is assumed that the expected inflation is defined as the current-year one-year inflation at (t) and thus unexpected inflation is the difference between observed inflation at ($t + 1$) and at t. A precise inflation hedge would require an inflation Beta of about 1. However, the argument could be made, under certain circumstances, that a Beta of 0 could also provide a good hedge in the very long term. For example, if two assets have similar expected returns and volatilities but display no correlation, the cumulative returns of these two assets will get closer with the passage of time. I will come back to this aspect later on. The inflation Beta is determined from:

$$\text{Nominal Return} = \alpha + \beta \,\text{inflation} + \varepsilon \tag{10.5}$$

TABLE 10.1a   Inflation Beta: Bonds

	Inflation			Unexpected Inflation		
	1 Year	3 Years	5 Years	1 Year	3 Years	5 Years
Developed	0.28	0.84	1.12	−0.58	−0.22	0.36
Emerging	0.98	2.02	2.11	0.92	1.93	2.09

TABLE 10.1b   Inflation Beta: Stocks

	Inflation			Unexpected Inflation		
	1 Year	3 Years	5 Years	1 Year	3 Years	5 Years
Developed	−0.25	−0.05	0.12	−0.44	−0.59	−0.58
Emerging	1.01	1.03	1.00	0.97	1.03	1.03

Source: Bekaert and Wang (2010).

Let's start with one-year horizon inflation Betas. Both are well below 1 for bonds and equities in developed markets. They are much lower and fairly negative for unexpected inflation. In emerging markets, Betas remain fairly high and close to 1, but this result is entirely attributed to Latin American countries and cannot be generalized. The Betas of Asia and Africa are well below 1. In fact, more than half the countries in the study have negative Betas for bonds and equities.

As we move from a one-year horizon to multiyear horizons, the inflation and unexpected inflation Betas of equity remain low in developed markets. The inflation Betas of bonds improve, but probably reflect the effect of previous inflation being well priced into bonds (if even by chance), especially in the long term. Let's also remember that much of the difficulties of pension funds in recent years have not been related to extremely wrong inflation assumptions, but simply to much-shorter-than-required bond durations, and to aggressive exposure to variable assets. Nevertheless the unexpected inflation Betas remain fairly low. Finally, Latin America still drives the coefficient for emerging market durations at longer horizons.

We can conclude from these results that equity is not a good inflation hedge, at least at horizons of less than five years, and that bonds (especially in developed markets) have actually been accurate hedges over longer horizons. This indicates that perhaps long-term inflation expectations were fairly accurate on average, and/or that an inflation-related risk premium has adequately compensated investors. We should not assume that this observation will prevail in the future.

Bekaert and Wang did the same analysis for other asset classes such as treasury bills, real estate and gold futures. Real estate is defined as publicly traded real estate companies, and the data were only available for 25 countries. Surprisingly, treasury bills did not provide the inflation-hedging efficiency we would have expected. This obviously indicates that the real return is not constant, but it also indicates that it tends to decline in higher-inflation environments. Real estate, defined as publicly traded companies, has not been a good hedge, although gold futures had a strong positive inflation Beta.

If anything, these results and those of other studies show how difficult it is to hedge a portfolio against unexpected inflation. There are a few instruments that can provide a reliable hedge, and among these are ILBs and potentially some commodities.

In Equation 10.4, we added an inflation risk premium ($RP(\sigma_I)$) to the basic Fisher equation. Estimating the inflation risk premium is not an easy task. Even if we were to use TIPS to isolate the real return, TIPS are relatively recent instruments and may have incorporated a liquidity premium for many years. Furthermore, even if we knew with relative certainty the size of the real return, how do we differentiate between inflation expectations (which are unobservable but sometimes approximated with information from surveys) and the inflation risk premium? Nevertheless, the consensus appears to be that:

- there is, on average, a positive inflation risk premium;
- this premium is (as most risk premiums are) time varying;

- this premium is more significant when inflation is higher, and can even be negative when inflation is extremely low and stable (i.e., the premium is regime dependent); and
- it can be significant and it increases with maturity.

Building a Liability-Driven Portfolio Management Process

We have learned in this book that the risk characteristics of most assets are time varying (volatilities, cross-correlations, risk premiums, duration sensitivity to real return or inflation, etc.). Therefore, it should be no surprise that the design of a more efficient LDI methodology should rest on an adaptive dynamic allocation process that takes into account changes in volatility and cross-correlations. A passive approach, except for full and costly matching of interest-rate and inflation-duration needs (assuming it is even possible), will most likely not meet the investor's requirements.

To develop our LDPMP, I will start with a review of a Vanguard Monte Carlo simulation (2008). This example is useful in helping to stage the global problematic. It is based on a fully funded plan that has a liability duration of 15 years. The reference duration-matched portfolio is made of 45% nominal bonds and 55% strip bonds. The simulation compares this portfolio to three riskier portfolios. Returns are generated from the Vanguard Capital Markets Model, a model that relates returns to numerous risk factors. Table 10.2 presents the structure of all four portfolios, as well as performance characteristics, as measured according to 10th, 50th and 90th percentiles. For example, the median scenario for Portfolio A produced an average asset-to-liability ratio of 96% over the 10-year period.

We will ignore for now the fact that this example does not appear to integrate any inflation consideration related to liabilities. Portfolios A and B have approximately the same duration, despite a 35% equity allocation in Portfolio B. Since The Vanguard Group has assumed that the duration of equity is zero, the only durations for domestic and strip bonds that are consistent with the durations reported for all portfolios are respectively 4.75 and 24.

It is obvious from the results that the simulation parameters assume that risky assets are likely to outperform less risky assets over a 10-year horizon, even at the 10th percentile level. Based on this simulation, a plan sponsor would be tempted to take more risk, since the 10th percentile scenario shows a higher average and terminal value. However, we obviously lived through a decade when performance was within the 10th percentile scenario with disastrous consequences. Thus, we must design a process by which the distribution of possible events is not only tighter, but also centered on a higher expected return. A static allocation process based on long-term and stable allocations to asset classes cannot be the solution.

Most advisors (Watson Wyatt, Russell Investments, Goldman Sachs, EDHEC-Risk Institute, etc.) recommend a building-block approach that integrates two components: a liability-hedging portfolio (LHP) and a performance-seeking portfolio (PSP) that is often divided into Beta and Alpha components. As Muralidhar explained, the strategy is usually to increase the allocation to the LHP as the funding status declines

TABLE 10.2 Portfolio Structures and Performance Characteristics (%)

Assets	Portfolio A	Portfolio B	Portfolio C	Portfolio D
US Equity	0	20	40	40
International Equity	0	15	20	20
Domestic Bonds	45	0	0	40
Strip Bonds	55	65	40	0
Duration	15.3	15.6	9.6	1.9
Asset/Liability Ratio				
-10th	90	95	101	100
-50th	96	110	121	120
-90th	102	128	144	145

Source: Vanguard Investment Counseling & Research (2008).

or risk aversion increases in order to protect capital. However, as they also indicated, it would have been preferable to implement this approach when the environment was more favorable. Furthermore, except for insisting on a better match of duration needs between the LHP and the liabilities, this is hardly a new approach (a portfolio of Beta risks with an Alpha overlay). Finally, what are the appropriate Alpha and Beta portfolios? Is there such a thing as a reliable Alpha? By now we should doubt the cost benefit efficiency of what is often proposed to investors, and concentrate on implementing efficient portfolio management processes. We need asset components that are efficient (low cost, less sensitive to market bubbles and more likely to produce higher absolute returns) and a dynamic allocation process that improves the risk/return profile of the portfolio against projected liabilities.

Amenc, Martellini, Goltz and Milhau addressed several of these points. Their recommendations were also based on the two building blocks (LHP + PSP) and a dynamic approach. They started with the principle that LDI involves two types of asset-management decisions: the design of better building blocks, and an improved allocation process between those building blocks. For example, they supported the argument that cap-weight portfolios are not good benchmarks because they are poorly diversified. They also believed that portfolio structures with better hedging properties against inflation can be built. Equation 10.6 summarizes their approach.

$$W = \lambda \, / \, \gamma\sigma \, \text{PSP} + (1 - 1/\gamma) \, \beta \, \text{LHP} \tag{10.6}$$

This equation essentially indicates that the allocation to PSP, LHP and cash (not specified) is a function of the efficiency of the PSP portfolio (defined by its Sharpe ratio, λ), the investor risk aversion (γ), the volatility of the PSP portfolio (σ) and the Beta (β) of the liability portfolio to the LHP. If risk aversion was extremely high, most of the allocation would be channeled to the LHP.

Since parameters related to interest and inflation rates, as well as volatility and correlations, are time varying, the allocation process should be dynamic. Amenc, Martellini, Goltz and Milhau proposed linking the allocation to equity to proxies of asset pricing attractiveness (such as dividend yields or P/E ratios) and to potentially incorporate risk control processes, such as constant proportion portfolio insurance (CPPI), that can help protect a risk budget. Although the implementation proposed in this book is different, we are in agreement with the general principles of using better building blocks and managing the allocation dynamically. However, we would also prefer an approach that integrates, implicitly or explicitly, liabilities within the process.

Why Does Tracking Error Increase in Stressed Markets?

Many pension funds with defined benefit obligations are having difficulties because of declining interest rates (because their assets had shorter duration than liabilities). They are also experiencing trouble due to poorly performing variable assets (after they had significantly increased their exposure to these assets in the 1980s and 1990s). Pension fund assets had significant tracking errors against liabilities. Thus, it is useful to understand why tracking error increases in stressed markets.

Morgan Stanley (2011) [19] published a fairly simple, but useful, research paper that illustrates the impact of diversification on portfolio volatility, correlation to equity and sensitivity to market risk (Beta). The analysis is based on a Monte Carlo simulation of a hypothetical portfolio of two assets. The first asset is equity. The second asset is a "diversifying portfolio" of one to ten diversifiers that have identical correlations to equity and no correlation to each other (to simplify). The weight of equity is 40%, and the remaining 60% is equally weighted among the one to ten diversifiers. All diversifiers have the same volatility as equity. We could think of these diversifiers in terms of a portfolio of alternative risk premiums.

The paper analyzed four scenarios. In the first two scenarios, the correlation of each diversifier to equity is either 20% or 40%. The impact of the correlation assumption on volatility, correlation to equity and Beta, as the number of diversifiers increases from one to ten, is presented in the first two graphs of Figure 10.2. The volatility of the portfolio is expressed as the ratio of portfolio volatility to equity volatility.

Unsurprisingly, when the correlation is 20% and the number of diversifiers increases from one to ten, the ratio of portfolio volatility to equity volatility declines from about 0.78 to 0.55. Most of the diversification benefits are achieved after four or five diversifiers are included. However, as we increase the number of diversifiers, the correlation of portfolio returns to equity returns actually increases from about 0.67 to 0.94. It reaches levels as high as 90% with only five asset diversifiers. This may seem odd, but we have already explained the reason for this observation. As we increase the number of diversifiers, the volatility of the sub-portfolio declines, and the 40% equity allocation accounts for an increasing proportion of the total volatility. The portfolio automatically becomes more correlated with equity.

FIGURE 10.2 Impact of Diversification on Volatility, Correlation and Beta.

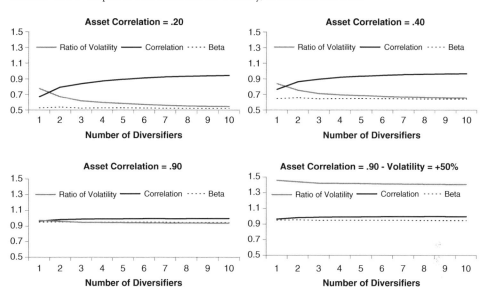

The Beta of the portfolio, or its average sensitivity to equity fluctuations, remains fairly stable at around 0.52, but the volatility of the excess return of the portfolio (not illustrated) against the market (Beta adjusted) will decline from about 0.58 to about 0.18. Thus, Beta becomes a more effective sensitivity measure of portfolio return to equity return as the number of asset diversifiers increases. Again, this is not unexpected because equity accounts for an increasing proportion of total portfolio risk as we diversify the sub-portfolio. These observations would logically bring us to conclude that the weight of equity should be reduced as we increase the efficiency of the portfolio of diversifiers.

As the correlation of the diversifiers to equity increases, several changes occur. The ratio of portfolio volatility to equity volatility increases fairly significantly, as does Beta. However, although the correlation of portfolio returns to equity returns also increases, the change is not significantly different because this correlation was already very high at a very low level of correlation of asset diversifiers.

Our interest is mostly in understanding the consequences of a financial crisis on portfolio characteristics. Usually two circumstances occur during such a crisis. Correlations between asset classes, as well as with investment strategies, will go up, and volatility will also increase substantially. However, we want to distinguish between the relative effects of increasing correlation and volatility. The third and fourth graphs in Figure 10.2 show the impact of an increase in asset diversifiers' correlation to equity (to 0.90) and of an increase in both correlation and volatility (50% greater volatility).

In each of these two scenarios, the correlation of the portfolio to equity and the Beta are close to 1. However, although the ratio of portfolio volatility to equity volatility has increased to almost 1 in the third scenario, it has increased to more than 1.4 times the previous equity volatility in the fourth scenario. Thus, the message is clear. We often make the argument that correlations between most assets increase substantially during a crisis (i.e., that diversification efficiency decreases). However, we should be even more concerned with the rise in volatilities. Again, this supports the necessity of designing asset components that are less sensitive to substantial increases in volatility, and of developing a dynamic asset allocation process that considers the time-varying nature of volatility and correlation.

Impact of Managing Volatility in Different Economic Regimes

In Chapter 7, we discussed the benefits of a managed-volatility portfolio. However, as we move from a two-component portfolio to a multicomponent portfolio, a simple volatility target or constraint is insufficient, and it becomes necessary to design an objective function or impose another constraint (without which there would be infinite solutions). It may also be necessary to impose allocation constraints, since the solution may be either unacceptable or unstable (generating unacceptable turnover). Nevertheless, the initial example we will use is that of a target volatility portfolio of two assets (fixed income and equity). Why?

As volatility increases, a managed-volatility process would force the asset manager to transfer allocation from equity to fixed income, more so if the volatility of both assets had increased. This allocation transfer would be reinforced if the rise in volatility was accompanied by an increase in correlation between the two assets. If the correlation declined, the allocation adjustment would be less. The transfer would probably still be of the same sign, since we have just seen that the rise in volatility of the components (fixed income and equity) is likely to have a stronger impact on portfolio volatility than the decline in the correlation. The allocation adjustment is also likely to impact the empirical duration of the portfolio (i.e., the value sensitivity of the entire portfolio to changes in interest rates). The same reasoning applies in reverse. Intuitively, a managed-volatility portfolio would seem consistent with LDI concerns (although other concepts could be used, such as CVaR or the spread between nominal interest rate and nominal growth as an allocation signal (see Chapter 5)). Therefore, it is also relevant to understand how volatilities and correlations behave according to different regimes.

The approach is similar to that of Bridgewater discussed in Chapter 7, since we assume four potential economic regimes that are defined solely by growth and inflation. Our initial objective is to discuss how the volatility of equity, the correlation between equity and fixed income and the relative performance of the two assets should behave under each regime. This is illustrated in Table 10.3.

Although the implicit assumptions made in Table 10.3 about performance, volatility and correlation are certainly not absolute (this is not our goal at this point), they are, to a certain degree, intuitive. Since 2008, and at least until 2012, we have been in a regime of declining inflation and growth, at least in the industrialized world. The

TABLE 10.3 Economic Regimes and Asset Behavior

Inflation	Growth	Performance	Volatility	Correlation	When
Declining	Declining	FI > E	+++	Negative	Early and late 2000s
Rising	Declining	FI > E	+++	Positive	Much of the 1970s and early 1980s
Declining	Rising	E >> FI	+	Positive	Much of the 1980s and 1990s
Rising	Rising	E > FI	++	~	Mid-2000s

extreme case of this regime is a deflationary environment such as the situation that has existed in Japan for two decades now. In such a regime, fixed income will significantly outperform equity, at least until interest rates are unable to go further down, correlation will be negative and volatility will not only increase because of lower growth expectations but also because of a rising equity risk premium. However, the one scenario that could lead to a positive correlation is that of a crisis of confidence in sovereign credit. Some countries have already experienced this situation. Furthermore, the lower the yield on fixed income, the less likely it is that a negative correlation can be sustained.

The 1970s and early 1980s were a case of rising inflation and lower growth. Correlations were positive as inflation drove returns down on both equity and fixed income. Equity was volatile because of rising risk premiums as well. Nevertheless, this is an even worse scenario for equities than for bonds. This is a very difficult regime in which to manage assets, since both asset classes are performing poorly. This is a case where asset components other than equity and fixed income (such as cash, commodities, real return bonds, etc.) and possibly some hedging strategies designed to manage tail risk may be useful.

The scenario of declining inflation and rising growth has dominated the last 40 years. In this case, both assets should do well, but equity should outperform fixed income because risk premiums are likely to decline significantly. Correlation will be positive and volatility should be low, on average.

The one regime we have not observed significantly over this period is that of rising growth and inflation. In the mid-2000s, we had a slight increase in inflation as the economy was being boosted by low interest rates, lower taxes and deregulation (with catastrophic consequences, however). Although we may expect equity to outperform fixed income, this is a more difficult environment to rationalize in terms of volatility and correlations. Correlations are likely to be less definite, since growth will favor equity but inflation will harm fixed income.

Baele, Bekaert and Inghelbrecht (2010) [20] have done significant work on the determinant of stock and bond co-movements. They considered 10 state variables divided between macro variables (such as output gap, inflation and interest rates) and non-macro variables (such as stock and bond market illiquidity and variance premiums). They found that non-macro variables, especially stock and bond market liquidity factors, are much more significant at explaining the correlation between equity and bonds. However, this should not surprise us. Measures of liquidity are much more timely and powerful at expressing market sentiments at a specific point in time than macro variables could ever be. However, let's not forget that our main argument should remain that if volatilities and correlations show persistence, such information should be integrated into our portfolio management process, whether the cause is lower expected inflation or a flight to safety effect. We can and should always attempt to rationalize why correlations and volatilities are changing over time, but, from a portfolio management point of view, we must concentrate on the fact that the correlations and volatilities we observe today are likely to persist, and we cannot ignore this information.

It may be useful in completing this discussion to visualize how asset weights would evolve as an investor attempts to manage portfolio volatility when equity volatility and equity/fixed-income correlation fluctuates over time. We can then discuss if the evolution in portfolio allocation is consistent with expectations. We will consider a scenario where the average fixed-income and equity volatilities are 7% and 18%, and correlation about 0% (not far below the average values observed over the last 40 years). Figure 10.3a illustrates the evolution of fixed income, equity and commodity volatilities since the early 1970s using three-year rolling daily data. Commodities will be used in another example later on. Figure 10.3b presents the correlation data for those three assets. The figures show that equity volatility can be as low as 10% and as high as 30% (or even higher), and that the correlation between equity and fixed income can be as low as –60% to as high as +60%. The average correlation of about 0% is the result of very different correlation regimes from the 1970s to the mid-1990s, and then from the mid-1990s to 2011. The range of correlations is consistent with Baele, Bekaert and Inghelbrecht.

Tables 10.4a and 10.4b present the allocation weights that would allow portfolio volatility to remain constant using the range of values for equity volatility and correlation discussed above. Two levels of constant average volatilities are used, those of 60/40 and 40/60 portfolios. The values in bold show the solutions where the equity allocation remains within ±15% of the long-term targeted allocation in the 40/60 case, and within +15% and −20% in the 60/40 case. Such constraints may be required either to limit excessive potential risk (resulting from a rapid regime change) or to limit portfolio turnover. Nevertheless, the data illustrate two types of allocation issues: those resulting from very low equity volatility and those resulting from high equity volatility with high equity fixed-income correlations. High equity volatility can usually be managed when correlations are negative.

The first issue is not as problematic as the second because it involves maintaining a portfolio whose risk is below the long-term targeted risk. However, an inflationary environment that would lead to a strong and positive correlation is definitively the most challenging environment. However, we have seen in Chapter 7 that weight constraints can improve the performance of a volatility managed portfolio.

To further illustrate the consequence of strong positive or negative correlation, Tables 10.5a and 10.5b compare the portfolio volatility of a 40/60 portfolio under different equity volatility and correlation assumptions with the portfolio volatility of a portfolio that attempts to maintain the same volatility as a 40/60 portfolio under normal equity volatility and correlation assumptions, but is subject to the ±15% equity allocation constraint.

FIGURE 10.3a Volatilities of Equity, Fixed Income and Commodities.

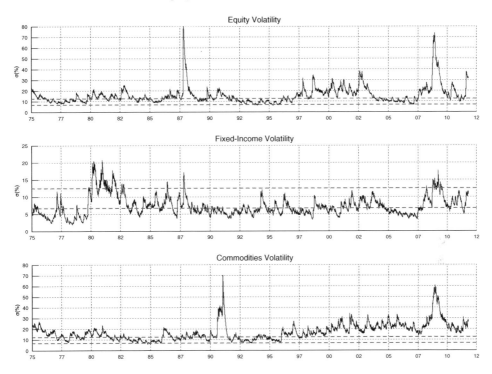

FIGURE 10.3b Correlations Among Equity, Fixed Income and Commodities.

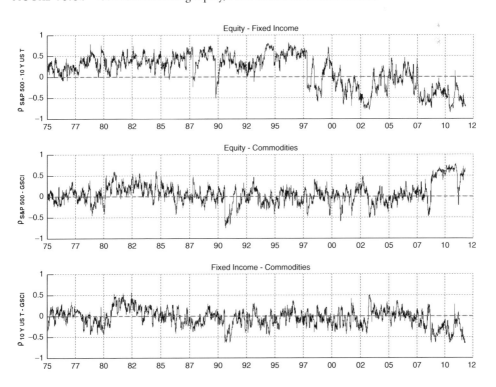

TABLE 10.4a   Equity Weights (40/60 Average Risk Level) (%)

	Correlation						
Volatility	−60%	−40%	−20%	0%	20%	40%	60%
10%	88	87	85	83	79	75	68
12%	77	74	71	67	62	**55**	**46**
14%	68	65	60	**55**	**50**	**42**	**34**
16%	61	**57**	**52**	**47**	**40**	**33**	**26**
18%	**55**	**51**	**46**	**40**	**34**	**28**	22
20%	**50**	**46**	**41**	**35**	**30**	23	17
22%	**46**	**41**	**36**	**32**	**25**	20	15
24%	**42**	**38**	**33**	**28**	22	17	13
26%	**39**	**35**	**30**	**25**	20	15	12
28%	**37**	**32**	**28**	23	18	14	10
30%	**34**	**30**	**26**	21	16	13	9

TABLE 10.4b   Equity Weights (60/40 Average Risk Level) (%)

	Correlation						
Volatility	−60%	−40%	−20%	0%	20%	40%	60%
10%	100	100	100	100	100	100	100%
12%	95	95	94	93	92	**91**	**89**
14%	84	83	81	**79**	77	**74**	**70**
16%	75	**74**	**71**	**68**	**65**	**61**	57
18%	**69**	**66**	**63**	**60**	57	**52**	47
20%	**63**	**60**	**57**	**53**	**50**	45	41
22%	**58**	**55**	**52**	**48**	**44**	40	36
24%	**53**	**50**	**47**	**44**	40	36	32
26%	**50**	**47**	**43**	**40**	36	32	29
28%	**47**	**43**	**40**	37	33	30	26
30%	**44**	**41**	**37**	34	31	27	24

The average volatility of a 40/60 portfolio was 8.3%. This volatility can climb to 11.9% if equity volatility increases to 30% while correlation declines to −20%. However, if the portfolio equity allocation had been reduced to 26%, as proposed in Table 10.4a, the volatility of the portfolio would have remained at 8.3%. We can also see from the data that an increase in equity volatility to 30% and correlation to +60% would contribute to raising portfolio volatility to 14.9%, but this volatility could have

TABLE 10.5a Portfolio Volatility (Stable 40/60 Allocation) (%)

	Correlation						
Volatility	−60%	−40%	−20%	0%	20%	40%	60%
10%	3.7	4.5	5.2	5.8	6.4	6.9	7.3
12%	4.1	5.0	5.7	6.4	7.0	**7.5**	**8.1**
14%	4.6	5.5	6.3	**7.0**	7.6	**8.2**	**8.8**
16%	5.1	**6.1**	**6.9**	7.7	8.3	**9.0**	9.5
18%	**5.8**	**6.7**	7.6	**8.3**	**9.0**	**9.7**	10.3
20%	**6.4**	**7.4**	**8.3**	**9.0**	**9.8**	10.4	11.0
22%	**7.1**	**8.1**	**9.0**	**9.8**	**10.5**	11.2	11.8
24%	**7.8**	**8.8**	**9.7**	**10.5**	11.2	11.9	12.6
26%	**8.6**	**9.5**	**10.4**	**11.2**	12.0	12.7	13.3
28%	**9.3**	**10.3**	**11.1**	12.0	12.7	13.4	14.1
30%	**10.1**	**11.0**	**11.9**	12.7	13.5	14.2	14.9

TABLE 10.5b Portfolio Volatility (Stable Average Risk with Equity Allocation Constraints) (%)

	Correlation						
Volatility	−60%	−40%	−20%	0%	20%	40%	60%
10%	4.4	5.1	5.8	6.3	6.9	7.4%	7.8%
12%	5.3	6.1	6.7	7.3	7.9	**8.4**	**8.4**
14%	6.3	**8.4**	**8.3**	**8.4**	**8.4**	**8.4**	**8.4**
16%	7.4	**8.4**	**8.3**	**8.3**	**8.4**	**8.4**	**8.4**
18%	**8.4**	**8.3**	**8.3**	**8.3**	**8.4**	**8.4**	8.7
20%	**8.3**	**8.4**	**8.3**	**8.4**	**8.4**	8.6	9.2
22%	**8.4**	**8.3**	**8.4**	**8.4**	**8.3**	9.0	9.6
24%	**8.3**	**8.4**	**8.4**	**8.3**	8.7	9.4	10.1
26%	**8.3**	**8.4**	**8.4**	**8.4**	9.1	9.9	10.5
28%	**8.4**	**8.4**	**8.4**	8.8	9.6	10.3	11.0
30%	**8.4**	**8.4**	**8.4**	9.2	10.0	10.7	11.4

been kept at 11.4% if the equity allocation had been reduced to 25% (−15%). Thus, as we would expect, the constrained managed-volatility portfolio maintains a higher level of portfolio risk when equity volatility and correlations are lower. The reverse is observed if volatility and correlations are high. Furthermore, we may take comfort in the fact that the very highest levels of volatilities in the past 40 years usually occurred in concert with lower correlations. However, the future could be different.

A managed-volatility approach increases the allocation to fixed income in uncertain times (and thus increases the allocation to assets with less noisy duration sensitivity—an aspect we will measure empirically later on). Limiting portfolio volatility is a more difficult issue in a rising-correlation environment, but the managed-volatility approach is still an improvement over the base case. Furthermore, we have only allowed two asset classes in this example. A more realistic allocation process would incorporate other asset classes, such as commodities and a portfolio of well-balanced alternative risk premiums, and more efficient asset components than standard market-cap-weight products, which may help mitigate and better control the increased portfolio volatility that results from rising equity volatility and equity fixed-income correlation. For example, we should consider incorporating lower-volatility equity components along with normal equity volatility components since it is likely that the managed-volatility process would unload more of the higher-volatility components first. I will also illustrate some of these principles in a simple but real setting in the last segment of this chapter.

Incorporating More Efficient Asset Components

Pension funds and other investors have been hit with the perfect storm, a situation in which long-term interest rates and real rates declined significantly while most variable-rate assets have performed poorly over the previous decade or more. There is little that can be done at this point concerning lower long-term real rates. Investors will have to rely on superior dynamic allocation processes and well-designed variable asset components to improve their performance.

As I indicated, Amenc, Martellini, Goltz and Milhau (2010), believe that asset components with better hedging properties can be built. They believe that market-cap protocols lead to poorly diversified portfolios. As we have seen, many equity indices, but also commodity indices, are poorly built, and hedge funds are expensive. There are three objectives that we would hope to achieve with more efficient structured investment protocols: superior long-term performance, lower drawdowns during difficult times and more appropriate correlations of returns, or, at least, of excess returns with fixed income or inflation.

Two of these issues have already been addressed. Most of the content of Chapters 6 and 8 were to demonstrate that traditional benchmarks underperform more efficiently structured protocols because of the inherent flaws in those benchmarks. Figure 6.3 illustrated that the excess return of a blend of nonmarket-cap equity protocols has a negative correlation to market returns. In fact, the late 1990s represented the greatest concentration of underperformance of these protocols against traditional benchmarks, but it occurred in a very favorable equity environment. This is not surprising since the weighting of securities within these protocols is usually fairly insensitive to security or sector momentum. Table 6.17 also showed this correlation remained low to fairly negative in most periods, except in the 1970s, although the minimum variance protocol maintained a negative correlation during this period. Furthermore, a blend of protocols still usually maintained a positive excess performance over this period, despite the stronger positive correlation.

Thus, combining different protocols within the same investment program is important to increasing the probability of excess performance. Table 10.6 shows the correlation of excess performance of the same four investment protocols that we studied in Chapter 6 against one another: equal weight, Smoothed Cap 60, RAFI and minimum variance (MinVar).

TABLE 10.6 Correlations among Nonmarket-Cap Investment Protocols

	Smoothed 60	RAFI	MinVar	Average Correlations
1973–2009				
Equal Weight	38	0.47	0.51	0.46
Smoothed 60		0.86	0.31	0.52
RAFI			0.41	0.58
MinVar				0.41
1973–1979				
Equal Weight	−0.02	0.22	0.31	0.17
Smoothed 60		0.76	−0.29	0.15
RAFI			0.41	0.46
MinVar				0.14
1980–1989				
Equal Weight	−0.10	−0.10	0.40	0.07
Smoothed 60		0.85	0.34	0.36
RAFI			0.41	0.39
MinVar				0.38
1990–1999				
Equal Weight	0.43	0.48	0.67	0.53
Smoothed 60		0.90	0.50	0.61
RAFI			0.41	0.60
MinVar				0.52
2000–2009				
Equal Weight	0.60	0.51	0.10	0.40
Smoothed 60		0.91	0.27	0.59
RAFI			0.41	0.61
MinVar				0.26

Perhaps unsurprisingly, the Smoothed 60 protocol is highly correlated to RAFI, but all other protocols appear to have distinctive characteristics. They mostly have positive correlations to one another, but this is to be expected since all protocols have low to negative correlations to market returns. The last column in Table 10.6 shows the average correlation of each of the four protocols to the other three. With a few exceptions, MinVar appears to differentiate itself the most. We could conclude that an investor should rely on more than one type of protocol, perhaps at least two or three, to achieve the most stable excess performance under most regimes, and a low-volatility protocol (such as MinVar, TOBAM Maximum Diversification or another low-volatility alternative) should also be incorporated. Chapter 11 will illustrate how a combination of protocols performs within a managed-volatility program.

Few studies on the impact of using nonmarket-cap protocols on the correlation to fixed income were ever done. Djehiche and Rinné (2006) [21] evaluated the interest rate sensitivity and empirical duration of the RAFI protocol. They found that in the United States, RAFI displayed a higher correlation to bonds than the S&P 500 (0.36 versus 0.23) and a higher empirical duration (3.6 versus 2.5 years). The result is partly attributed to the observation that nonmarket-cap protocols tend to outperform market-cap protocols more significantly during recessions than during expansions. Since interest rates usually decline during recessions, the correlation to fixed income should improve, at least on average.

In Chapter 6, we compared the performance of several protocols including equal risk, Smoothed 60, RAFI and MinVar. However, we could not support the conclusions of Djehiche and Rinné using our own data. Correlations of these four protocols to fixed income were not significantly higher. Nonmarket-cap protocols should be invested not because they offer better correlation to fixed income, but because they help to avoid the pitfalls that result from market-cap protocols. Furthermore, even if the correlation of excess returns of these protocols to liabilities was nil, this is still a very desirable characteristic as long as we are confident that nonmarket-cap protocols are efficient at delivering excess returns against market-cap indices in the long term.

Incorporating Illiquid Components

We invest in illiquid assets either because we wish to capture a liquidity premium or because these assets offer a distinctive risk premium that is simply not available in the market for liquid assets. This is less of an issue for retail investors, since they often have no access to such assets and usually no desire for such exposure. However, having illiquid assets is not an obstacle to a managed-volatility program as long as we do not allow the allocation of illiquid assets to restrict the rebalancing process. Illiquid assets often incorporate the same type of risk premiums (credit, inflation, market risk, etc.) as liquid assets (other than liquidity). Therefore, if the objective of a managed-volatility program is to control total portfolio risk caused by specific market risks, illiquid assets will not interfere with the portfolio management process as long as these risk premiums are fairly well represented in both liquid and illiquid assets, and the size of the allocation to illiquid assets does not interfere with the management of the portfolio. For example, institutional investors who have a relatively significant allocation to commercial mortgages and real estate could use their fixed-income and traditional equity components to manage their total risk exposure, which would buy them the time they would require should they ever desire to rebalance the allocation of these components.

Role of Investment-Grade Fixed-Income Assets

Most of our discussions in this book have centered on how to build more efficient investment protocols for variable assets (equity and commodities), and more efficient asset allocation strategies. Investment-grade fixed income is a relatively low volatility asset class. The main risks are related to changes in yield curve level, slope and credit risk premium.

However, let's consider investment-grade fixed income in the context of all we have discussed thus far. First, the investor must determine which duration is appropriate to his or her portfolio. As many pension plan sponsors have discovered, simply because a fixed-income benchmark has a specific duration does not mean that it is appropriate to most investors. Benchmarks reflect the specific duration needs of borrowers, not lenders. We may also want the risk of our fixed-income component to better balance the risk of our equity component. Second, the asset allocation and rebalancing strategy should already capture interest rate risk in a global setting. Therefore, if we hire a fixed-income manager who takes strong duration views, these views may interfere with the global strategic plan of the investor. Third, why do we hire a fixed-income manager? Is it for his credit expertise or her interest rate forecasting expertise? These are two very different skills. Fourth, we have also shown evidence that most fixed-income managers are not really any better at outperforming their benchmark than equity managers.

Finally, we have seen that much value creation can occur with proper investment protocols applied to variable assets and an allocation/rebalancing strategy. We have repeatedly indicated that volatility is required in order to profit significantly from statistically reliable strategies. Much of the volatility of quality fixed income is attributed to a risk factor (interest rate), which should be dealt with within the allocation process among asset classes, and not within a fixed-income mandate. For example, if a portfolio had only three components, equity and long-term and short-term (or cash) fixed-income assets, interest rate risk would be implicitly managed within the allocation process between those three components.

Therefore, an integrated management process that incorporates appropriate asset components and an efficient allocation and rebalancing process requires that its fixed-income portfolio delivers the appropriate duration characteristics (that its structure be coherent with the duration characteristics of liabilities) and credit risk, and mostly that it keeps the investor out of trouble. There is enough volatility in equities, commodities, alternative risk premiums and asset allocation without adding an unnecessary risk factor and creating added confusion. Finally, there are much greater opportunities to exploit idiosyncratic risks in equities, commodities and other alternative risk premiums than in fixed income. Assets with larger and more distinctive idiosyncratic risks have much greater excess return potential.

This does not mean that a better fixed-income portfolio structure could not be designed. For example, Arnott (2010) [22] has already indicated that the smoothing of price noise is not limited to equity, but can also be applied to fixed income. That said, as we've seen, the expected benefits are not as important as with equity and commodities. However, in the context of a global fixed income portfolio, the gains could be more significant and this process could be implemented using GDP weights (or other market-indifferent factors) to allocate between different countries. However, other asset classes offer greater statistical potential and thus, improving the efficiency of investment grade fixed income is not the top priority.

Incorporating Liabilities

What is the difference between managing a portfolio of assets with and without liabilities? Most allocation models are built around a utility function that seeks to maximize returns for a given level of risk. Let's solely concentrate on the risk aspect. The following set of equations specifies the requirements for a constant volatility portfolio that allows no short positions.

$$(x' \, W \, x)^{0.5} = \sigma_p \qquad\qquad (10.7)$$

$$\sum x_i = 1$$

$$x_i \geq 0$$

Where x is a vector of weights, W is the covariance matrix and σ_p the targeted portfolio volatility. Since there are infinite ways to achieve a fixed volatility with more than two assets, an objective function would also be required to find a single solution. However, how does this set of equations really change if we incorporate liabilities?

We know that most liabilities could be represented by a combination of fixed-income securities. The main issue for investors is that those assets have a low expected return, while other asset classes have high tracking error. However, if we wanted to design a portfolio with a concern for the liability structure, Equation 10.7 would be replaced by the following:

$$(\mathbf{x'} \, \mathbf{W} \, \mathbf{x})^{0.5} = \sigma_{TE} \qquad\qquad (10.8)$$

$$\sum x_{Ai} = 1$$

$$\sum x_{Li} = -1$$

$$x_{Ai} \geq 0$$

$$x_{Li} \leq 0$$

The targeted volatility for the asset portfolio has been replaced by a targeted tracking error (σ_{TE}). The vector of weights incorporates weights that are related to invested assets as well as weights that are related to non-invested assets, which are meant to mimic liabilities. Invested asset weights must sum to 1, while weights related to non-invested assets, meant to replicate liabilities, must sum to −1 (assuming the replication is fairly accurate). Thus, the traditional case of managing a constant volatility portfolio is simply a special case of Equation 10.8 without liabilities. It is also obvious from Equation 10.8 that in order to minimize the tracking error, some invested asset components should have the same characteristics as those non-invested assets required to mimic the liabilities. However, as bizarre as it may seem, this approach (reducing tracking error against liabilities) may potentially not be the most efficient one to implement in the context of a pension fund with defined benefit liabilities. Here is why.

We have shown that a pension fund could theoretically achieve a near perfect match against liabilities by acquiring a proper mix of nominal and inflation-linked bonds. In this case, the hedging would be efficient at all times, but this approach would also be very costly. As we allow the portfolio to deviate from this fully hedged allocation in order to increase expected returns, a tracking error is created. I also mentioned earlier that even if our portfolio of assets had significant tracking error to liabilities, such a portfolio could be desirable in the long run if we could design it to minimize correlation to liabilities. As I indicated earlier, two assets of similar volatility and expected return will eventually produce similar compounded gains if their returns are not correlated. It may be difficult to create a fully uncorrelated portfolio, but if we were to combine all of the processes discussed in this book and improve on some of them, we could go a long way in achieving this goal.

Therefore, we face two options. Either we design dynamic portfolios that have a greater correlation to liabilities (as in Equation 10.8), or we design dynamic portfolios that have near-zero correlation to liabilities. However, the second portfolio would have to be very efficient. The first approach could have lower tracking error, but it would likely lead to more concentrated portfolios on average and limit the diversification of assets and strategies that can be maintained at all times. The second approach would allow a more balanced set of investment possibilities, but the tracking error would likely be more significant. We must also make sure that we have designed a very efficient portfolio structure. However, we have the tools to design efficient components in equity, commodity, alternative risk premiums and fixed income. We can also efficiently manage the overall risk of a portfolio that incorporates all of these components.

Incorporating an Objective Function

In order to allocate to a portfolio in a more-than-two-asset-class setting, an objective function is required to avoid an infinite number of allocation possibilities. Thus far in this book, we have attempted to avoid using expected return as part of the process. We've done this for two main reasons. First, there is much more persistence in short-term volatility and dependence than in returns. Second, risk factors that load more heavily on performance usually require a long horizon.

I mentioned previously that one objective function that can be used within a managed-volatility program is the maximization of returns, where returns are defined as historical performance over a long period. Therefore, this is akin to allowing the covariance matrix to dictate the allocation, since long-term expected return components would not vary. We will use this approach in the case study of this chapter and in Chapter 11, along with another approach that can be more efficient at promoting portfolio diversification (especially if we increase the number of asset classes beyond two or three), but that does not require any expected return inputs. However, the structure of the second objective function will not be disclosed. One of our goals is to determine if a conceptually more efficient objective function does, in fact, improve portfolio efficiency.

Case Study

The goal of this case study is to illustrate the usefulness of a managed-volatility approach in the context of liabilities. The analysis is applied to four static portfolio structures, specified in columns two to four of Table 10.7, over the period January 31, 1975, to September 9, 2011.

We will ignore the presence of liabilities for the moment. Our initial aim is to compare the efficiency of four static allocations to managed-volatility portfolios. However, contrary to the approach used in Chapter 7, where the volatility target was determined by the historical volatility over the entire horizon, we are opting to use the previous three-year rolling volatility of each of the four static portfolios as a monthly target. This approach is interesting for three reasons. First, since volatility is unstable, the approach allows the portfolio to adapt to long-term changes in volatility regime while still smoothing huge spikes in short-term volatility. Second, for investors who are used to thinking in terms of target weight allocation, the process is more likely to ensure that the average risk of the portfolio is consistent with the average risk of specific target weight portfolios as perceived by the investor (which may increase his or her comfort with the approach). Third,

TABLE 10.7 Parameters of Simulated Portfolios (%)

Portfolio	Fixed Income	Equity	Commodities	Min/Max Fixed Income	Min/Max Equity	Min/Max Commodities
A1	60	40			25–55	
A2	40	60			40–75	
A3	60	35	5	40–80	20–50	0–10
A4	40	50	10	25–60	30–65	0–15

the monthly allocations are derived with and without allocation constraints on asset classes.

Although the min/max allocation range for specific assets within the constrained portfolios may still appear wide to some investors, narrower ranges could be imposed if we increase the number of asset components and incorporate more efficient components to create a realistic operational environment. For example, we saw in Chapters 6 and 8 that some nonmarket-cap protocols can lead to lower-volatility portfolios (because of a better structure), and that the excess performance of most approaches can have low cross-correlations. If the volatility of an entire portfolio can be reduced through a more efficient assembly process without compromising long-term performance, and if we have access to components that offer a diverse set of volatility characteristics, it will be possible to impose more restrictive weights on allocation and still improve efficiency. Furthermore, not all components have to be adjusted at all times to target a specific level of volatility, and new contributions (for a portfolio in an accumulation phase) can also ease the allocation process. Finally, specific trading rules can be implemented to limit unnecessary turnover. All of these aspects can help limit the dynamic changes in allocations if properly implemented.

Since two of our reference portfolios have more than two assets, an objective function or another type of constraint is required to ensure that we have a single allocation solution. As indicated earlier, two objective functions are used. Objective function 1 (OF1) is simply based on the maximization of a Sharpe ratio where the expected returns are specified as long-term static returns. I have used a stable 3% risk premium for equity against bonds and a 0% risk premium for commodities (since we are not using an efficient index in this case study, but the standard GSCI). Objective function 2 (OF2) does not require any expected return and it is designed to become more efficient as the number of assets increases. Thus, OF2 is solely concerned with the efficiency of the portfolio structure, while OF1 considers the return to risk trade-off.

Table 10.8 specifies the basic financial characteristics of our three asset classes. It shows that commodities provided a return similar to fixed income, while the volatility was twice as high.

TABLE 10.8 Basic Financial Statistics of Portfolio Components (January 1975 to September 2011)

	Equity	Commodities	Fixed Income
GEO Mean	10.59	6.69	6.56
Standard Deviation	17.67	19.36	8.02
Skewness	−1.17	0.15	−0.59
Kurtosis	30.30	7.78	12.38

TABLE 10.9   Basic Financial Statistics of Structured Portfolios (January 1975 to September 2011)

		40/60	60/40	35–5–60	50–10–40
Static Portfolios	GEO Mean to Volatility	0.95	0.81	1.00	0.88
	Skewness	(0.37)	(0.81)	(0.33)	(0.79)
	Kurtosis	13.85	22.76	12.55	20.72
OF1 Unconstrained	GEO Mean to Volatility	0.97	0.92	1.03	0.96
	Skewness	0.13	0.15	0.03	(0.01)
	Kurtosis	8.33	7.92	7.14	6.51
OF2 Unconstrained	GEO Mean to Volatility	1.04	1.06	1.13	1.10
	Skewness	(0.25)	(0.18)	(0.18)	(0.19)
	Kurtosis	10.15	8.10	5.68	5.51
OF1 Constrained	GEO Mean to Volatility	1.03	0.95	1.07	1.03
	Skewness	(0.01)	(0.26)	(0.02)	(0.21)
	Kurtosis	7.60	9.82	7.47	8.37
OF2 Constrained	GEO Mean to Volatility	1.03	0.99	1.15	1.07
	Skewness	(0.19)	(0.23)	(0.10)	(0.20)
	Kurtosis	9.48	9.69	7.28	7.82

Table 10.9 provides similar information for all portfolios (static and volatility managed) according to each objective function. Both functions lead to more efficient portfolios than a static portfolio (greater information ratio, lower skewness and kurtosis). As we would expect, the improvement is much more significant for riskier portfolios. OF2 appears more risk/return efficient. On average, the information ratios of OF2 are nearly 15% to 20% greater than those of the static portfolios.

Figures 10.4a and 10.4b present the changes in asset allocation for all four portfolios and for each objective function. Although the graphs appear to indicate that there were numerous allocation changes, we also have to remember that the period covered by this analysis is nearly 37 years. Furthermore, the changes in allocation profile are

FIGURE 10.4a OF1: Allocation of Constrained Portfolios.

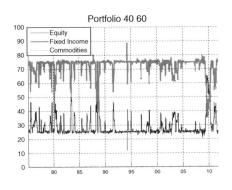
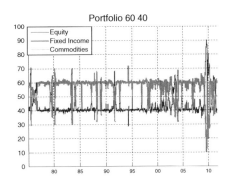

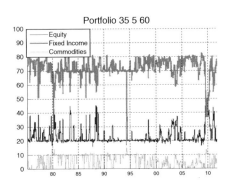
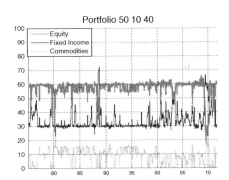

FIGURE 10.4b OF2: Allocation of Constrained Portfolios.

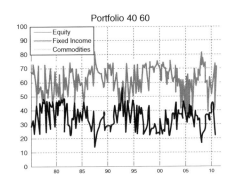
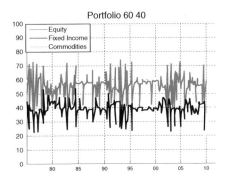

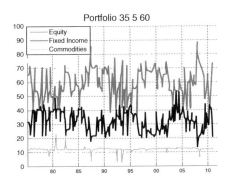
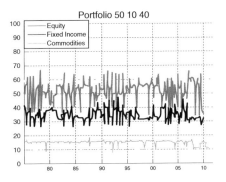

very different for the two objective functions. For example, OF1 is more likely to create corner allocation solutions (where the allocations for fixed income and equity often hit their respective upper and lower limits). This is to be expected since OF1 uses long-term static expected returns. In the three-asset case, the allocation to commodities is much more volatile if OF1 is used. If anything, these two examples illustrate again that many different objective functions could be considered. In Chapter 11, we will pay more attention to the portfolio turnovers that result from applying OF2.

One of our concerns is whether the use of a managed-volatility approach leads not only to more stable returns, but, more specifically, to more stable returns when they are needed the most. When answering this question, we will only consider the three-asset case in order to reduce the number of graphs presented. Figures 10.5a and 10.5b show the three-year moving average of returns for the 35–5–60 and the 50–10–40 portfolios for each objective function. Both approaches were efficient at improving performance when it was needed most: in the aftermaths of the technology crisis and the recent credit crisis. In essence, the dynamic allocation process that resulted from applying OF1 and OF2 produced excess returns on average, which were negatively correlated to equity returns.

I also measured the level of empirical duration of all portfolios. This is presented in Figures 10.6a and 10.6b. The empirical duration is the price sensitivity of each managed-volatility portfolio to changes in interest rates using three-year rolling data.

FIGURE 10.5a   OF1: Three-Year Moving Average Return.

FIGURE 10.5b   OF2: Three-Year Moving Average Return.

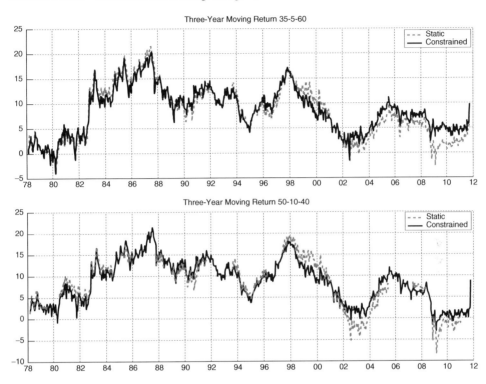

Based on our prior discussions, we would normally expect the duration sensitivity to increase when it is needed most. Although the level of empirical duration was higher on average for both objective functions, OF1 was more likely to lead to a higher level of empirical duration. Thus, we may conclude that the increased performances that were observed in both Figures 10.5a and 10.5b were not explained by similar structural causes. OF1 is more likely to contribute to a higher level of empirical duration, while OF2 simply improves the efficiency of the portfolio, but without the same impact on duration. Thus, the choice of an objective function is obviously not independent of the investment objectives.

Allocating in the Context of Liabilities

I have incorporated liabilities using the methodology specified in Equation 10.8. They are treated as an asset with a negative weight of 100%. Only the constrained case is considered. The target volatility is the tracking error measured over the previous three years. In Table 10.10, the information ratio is specified as the ratio of excess returns (against liabilities) to the tracking error.

In the context of a two-asset portfolio, OF1 and OF2 are similarly efficient, and both are slightly more efficient than the static portfolios. However, as we incorporate

FIGURE 10.6a: OF1: Empirical Duration.

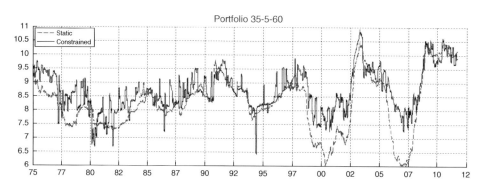

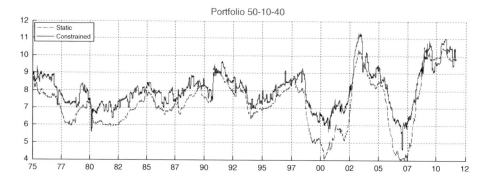

FIGURE 10.6b: OF2: Empirical Duration.

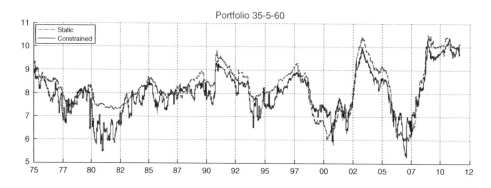

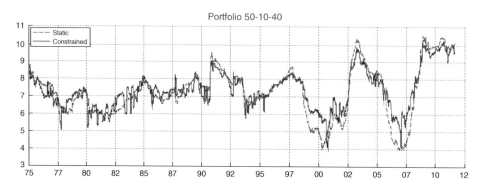

TABLE 10.10 Basic Financial Statistics of Structured Portfolios (January 1975 to September 2011)

		40/60	60/40	35–5–60	50–10–40
Static Portfolios	Information Ratio	0.21	0.21	0.20	0.19
	Skewness	(1.24)	(1.24)	(1.25)	(1.24)
	Kurtosis	28.47	28.47	26.99	26.10
OF1 Constrained	Information Ratio	0.25	0.25	0.22	0.21
	Skewness	(0.78)	(0.84)	(0.77)	(0.83)
	Kurtosis	16.01	17.49	14.68	15.61
OF2 Constrainned	Information Ratio	0.25	0.28	0.27	0.24
	Skewness	(1.01)	(0.77)	(0.71)	(0.66)
	Kurtosis	20.58	16.31	12.50	12.01

a third asset, OF2 is more efficient, with 20% less tracking error than the static port-folios (not shown). OF2 is a more efficient objective function.

Figures 10.7a and 10.7b illustrate the allocations for OF1 and OF2. In the two-asset case, the allocations are not so different. That should not surprise us. However, the pattern of allocation is significantly different in the three-asset case. For example, with OF1, it is common for the equity allocation to be closer to the upper bound-ary, and it declines when market volatility is higher. With OF2, it is common for the equity allocation to be closer to the lower boundary, and it increases when the diver-sification potential is improving. Furthermore, the allocation pattern of commodities is exactly reversed between OF1 and OF2, which further illustrates that OF2 is more concerned with diversification efficiency.

However, are we better off managing gross asset volatility or net asset volatility (i.e., incorporating liabilities in the objective function)? There is one aspect that sig-nificantly differentiates the two approaches: how each function reacts to changes in correlation between equity and fixed income. When volatility increases, the portfolio will move into a safer mode whether we are managing gross asset volatility or net asset volatility. However, if correlation increases (decreases) and we are managing gross asset volatility, the portfolio will move into an even safer mode (a relatively riskier mode). However, the reverse will occur if we are managing net asset volatility, since the fixed-income component has an implicit short position. This means that equity allocations will be increased (decreased) when correlations are higher (lower).

If we are managing the allocation dynamically, and if a greater correlation of assets to liabilities is targeted, such allocation patterns would be rational, although counter-intuitive, since it conceptually leads to a less efficient diversification of assets. However, OF2 appears to have avoided this issue because the objective function itself imposes

FIGURE 10.7a   OF1: Allocation of Constrained Portfolios.

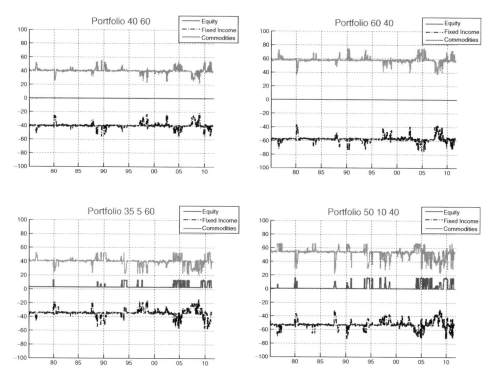

FIGURE 10.7b   OF2: Allocation of Constrained Portfolios.

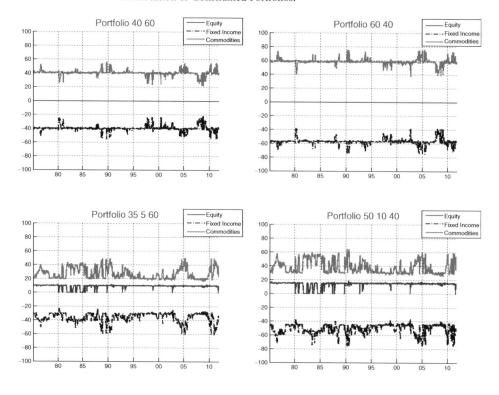

the greatest possible diversification. Therefore, the decision to manage volatility on a net-asset basis is very dependent on the choice and efficiency of the objective function.

Closing Remarks

LDI is a very complex issue, but, considering the instability in asset performance, volatility and cross-correlations, it is unlikely that a static allocation process would be advisable. Managing assets against liabilities is a compromise between expected excess return and tracking error. However, tracking error is not necessarily a problematic issue if we can be fairly certain that the excess returns are relatively uncorrelated with the returns on liabilities in the long term. Managing volatility at the portfolio level is an approach that can be part of the solution. It can produce more stable excess returns, especially during those periods when they are most needed. However, managing volatility may not be enough. As we have illustrated in Chapters 6 and 8, we must also build more efficient portfolio components whose excess returns are either uncorrelated or negatively correlated with gross returns.

This view is consistent with Barrett, Pierce, Perry and Muralidhar (2011) [23] who made the argument that a smart rebalancing process must be based on systematic, well-defined and documented rules. The rules must be based on peer-reviewed journal articles and thus on the best evidence. The purpose is to improve performance through risk management, not simply risk measurement. Many risk officers don't understand the nuance between the two concepts. In this book we have managed risk directly using dynamic measures of volatility. However, risk could also be managed using other indicators, such as relative value indicators. However, the main purpose of this book is to demonstrate how much we can improve the management process simply by exploiting information about prices and other simple statistical properties. It does not mean that further improvements cannot be implemented. In the next and final chapter, we will integrate many of the features that have been identified in this book, and demonstrate how we can significantly improve the return/risk profile of any portfolio, not only for large institutions but also for retail investors.

Notes

1. Cocco, Joao F., Francisco J. Gomes, and Pascal J. Maenhout (2005), "Consumption and portfolio choice over life cycle," *Review of Financial Studies* 18(2), 491–533.
2. Research Affiliates (2008), "The perfect storm: Part 2," RAFI Fundamentals (December).
3. Muralidhar, Arun (2011), "LDI—Less than desirable investing?" *aiCIO Magazine*, November 15.
4. Siegel, Laurence B. and M. Barton Waring (2004), "TIPS, the dual duration, and the pension plan," *Financial Analysts Journal* 60(5), 52–64.
5. Stockton, Kimberly A., Scott J. Donaldson and Anatoly Shtekhman (2008), "Liability-driven investing: A tool for managing pension plan funding volatility," Vanguard Investment Counseling & Research.

6. Brandes Institute (2008), "Liability-driven investing and equity duration," Brandes Institute Research Paper No. 2008-01, January 2008.

7. Leibowitz, Martin L. (1986), "Total portfolio duration: A new perspective on asset allocation," *Financial Analysts Journal* 42(5), 19–29.

8. Blitzer, David M. and Srikant Dash (2005), "Equity duration—Updated duration of the S&P 500," Standard and Poor's.

9. Patrick, Casabona, Frank J. Fabozzi, and Jack C. Francis (1984), "How to apply duration to equity analysis," *Journal of Portfolio Management* (Winter).

10. Modigliani, Franco and Richard A. Cohn (1979), "Inflation, rational valuation and the market," *Financial Analysts Journal* 35(2), 24–44.

11. Ferson, Wayne E. and Campbell R. Harvey (1991), "The variation of economic risk premiums," *Journal of Political Economy* 99(2), 385–415.

12. Campbell, John Y. and Tuomo Vuolteenaho (2008), "Inflation illusion and stock prices," *American Economic Review* 94(2), 20–23.

13. Leibowitz, Martin L. and Stanley Kogelman (2004), *Franchise Value: A Modern Approach to Securities Analysis*, John Wiley & Sons, Inc.

14. Grantier, Bruce (2012), "Equity duration—Sensitivity to discount rates and the Franchise Factor model," InvestorLit Review #1.

15. Amenc, Noel, Lionel Martellini, Felix Goltz, and Vincent Milhau (2010), "New frontiers in benchmarking and liability-driven investing," EDHEC-Risk Institute.

16. Irving Fisher (1930), "The theory of interest as determined by impatience to spend income and opportunity to invest it," MacMillan Company.

17. Roache, Shaun K. and Alexander P. Attié (2009), "Inflation hedging for long-term investors," International Monetary Fund, Working paper no. 09/90.

18. Bekaert, Geert and Xiaozheng Wang (2010), "Inflation risk and the inflation risk premium," *Economic Policy* 25(64), 755–806.

19. Leibowitz, Martin and Anthony Bova (2011), "Portfolio strategy - The correlation paradox", Morgan Stanley Research North America.

20. Baele, Lieven, Geert Bekaert, and Koen Inghelbrecht (2010), "The determinants of stock and bond comovements," *Review of Financial Studies* 23(6), 2374–2428.

21. Djehiche, Boualem and Jonas Rinné (2006), "Can stocks help mend the asset and liability mismatch?" Working Paper, Informed Portfolio Management, AB Stockholm.

22. Arnott, Robert D., Jason C. Hsu, Feifei Li and Shane D. Shepherd (2010), "Valuation-indifferent weighting for bonds," *The Journal of Portfolio Management* 36(3), 117–130.

23. Barrett, Timothy B., Donald Pierce, James Perry, and Arun Muralidhar (2011), "Dynamic Beta—Getting paid to manage risks," *Investment Management Consultants Association* 12(2), 67–78.

CHAPTER 11

Conclusion and Case Studies

Institutional investors and retail investors are paying significant fees for management expertise and portfolio structuring advice. All investors want the highest possible level of return for the least amount of risk, but the first principle of investing is do not overpay for expertise that is unsubstantiated, for processes that are disguised as expertise, for similar or identical exposure that can be achieved substantially less expensively through other product channels and for guarantees that are unnecessary and expensive. Although I will not address this issue specifically, I have analyzed over the last two years numerous products being offered whose fees are so high that investors are statistically very unlikely to outperform the minimum guarantees being offered. Furthermore, the investors' expected payoff distribution is sometimes hidden in a web of complexity.

In one particular meeting, I illustrated to an individual that in almost *all* market circumstances, a simple portfolio of one equity ETF and three government bonds of specific maturities could outperform a complex product that a very large institution had offered to him. In another case, I calculated that a structured product would not provide a 55-year-old investor with a positive compounded return unless he lived past 80 years old. If he lived to be 90, well past his current life expectancy, his realized annualized return would be about 2.5%. These conclusions were not based on return forecasts, but on structural certainty. Furthermore, although I have been in the financial industry for 18 years, I often have to read documents that explain these products several times to get a proper understanding of their fee structure. A disclosure document does not protect investors if its complexity is beyond the comprehension of most, or its unnecessary length a challenge to their patience (and mine). Until a few years ago, we could have been blind to these issues, but the evidence against paying excessive fees for financial services is now substantial.

We can believe institutional investors are better informed than private investors, but the large sums of money being invested in investment products that charge significant fixed and variables fees show that they may also be paying too much.

Some institutional products impose annual fees beyond 3%. The industry is very efficient at marketing its new concepts and ideas. Furthermore, it is as much of a challenge (maybe even more) to convince institutional investors to pay less attention to cap-weight benchmarks than to convince them to invest in hedge funds or private equity.

Can an investor be successful relying solely on systematic processes/protocols? The evidence thus far says yes. The expertise that investors truly need is an understanding of the structural portfolio qualities required to outperform inefficient traditional benchmarks. However, I am not aware of any program that offers a fully integrated approach that incorporates most of the components discussed in this book. Therefore, this chapter will answer two questions:

1. How can we build a fully integrated process that lead to a portfolio that has the relevant structural qualities?
2. How well can it perform?

As I am starting to write this chapter, I still do not know the answer to the second question, although I have implemented several of the components that we have discussed in the portfolios of institutional investors (mostly insurers). Considering what we have covered thus far, we know that the performance will be favorable, but the combination of many efficient components within an efficient rebalancing process has not been fully tested. This is what makes this last chapter particularly interesting. Answering the first question simply requires that we pay attention to the important elements that we have introduced in this book. Among them are the following:

- A sufficient number of asset blocks and asset components within those blocks. We must allow an efficient diversification of the most important market risks.
- A portfolio structure that does not allow an asset to dominate the entire risk, and/or a portfolio management process that manages and limits the risk contribution of any asset to the entire portfolio over time.
- A sufficient variety of efficient portfolio components built to exploit the different structural qualities required to outperform traditional benchmarks.
- Not allowing the management policy of an asset class to pollute the dynamic allocation process. For example, interest rate risk cannot simultaneously be managed within the overall allocation process and within the fixed-income portfolio.
- An appropriate objective function for allocating.
- Not allowing the process to recommend allocations that cannot possibly be implemented. We must also have reasonable turnover.
- Avoiding complexity initially and use processes that can easily be implemented and then refined over time.
- Having scalability (for large institutional investors).

Furthermore, there is also the issue of implementation—perhaps the biggest challenge. We may have good intentions, but there are significant obstacles to the implementation of asset protocols and of efficient asset-management and risk-management processes. For example, I have been exposed to situations where regulatory requirements imposed on institutional investors were so ill-conceived that regulatory capital could have been reduced had the level of risk been substantially increased! Also, some accounting rules paralyze the portfolio management process. When you combine both the accounting and regulatory impediments that corporate entities are subject to, asset managers often wonder if they are actually managing or simply navigating obstacles. I have been asking myself this question for at least five years. Thus, the most efficient portfolio management processes can only be partially implemented for those investors.

Finally, maintaining any process is a challenge. Either the investor will pressure the advisor to make changes in difficult times, or a new advisor will be hired and will change the existing processes to show off his or her own expertise. Convincing an investor, even an institutional one, that he or she should maintain the same strategy for a long period is almost an impossible challenge. This is why the benefits of owning portfolios that have the appropriate structural qualities we have discussed are likely to persist.

In the retail sector, the challenge is also formidable, as most advisors and consultants would probably want to see a three- to five-year track record before recommending anything. As we indicated before, a track record is required for an active manager to properly understand his or her style and consistency of process (although for some, it is just about investing in managers who have performed well recently). However, in the case of investment and allocation processes/protocols, the obstacle to implementation and distribution is the lack of confidence that comes from having advisors/consultants who do not have a deep enough understanding of investment issues. We have the evidence but not the confidence. This is a very frustrating aspect of our industry, but an opportunity for disciplined investors.

Once I completed the first 10 chapters of this book, I asked seven people with a variety of professional backgrounds (among them, hedge fund and equity managers, a head of research, academics, a financial software developer and institutional advisors) to give me feedback. Five of them had each written several financial books and had published in academic journals. Among many very useful comments, one reader indicated that I had not considered one aspect: how does an investor, whether a person or an institution, determine the portfolio structure that is appropriate?

To be honest, my intention was never to fully cover this topic. This entire effort is an exercise in efficient processes, and I truly believe that the issue of cohesion between portfolio structure and investor needs can be more easily covered once we understand the main drivers of efficient portfolio management. However, one of the secondary benefits of implementing risk-management processes is a more reliable understanding of "how much can be lost over what time horizon." This knowledge is one of the most important parameters of any asset allocation decision.

Case Studies: Portfolio Components, Methodology and Performance

In order to simulate a more realistic investment environment over a period of more than 30 years, we must consider the following portfolio components:

- Fixed Income: A 50/50 portfolio of 10- and 30-year bonds rebalanced monthly. A longer duration than traditional benchmarks is used to more efficiently balance the risk contribution of all components.
- Equity: Two indices (S&P 500 and MSCI EAFE) and a portfolio of three US protocols combined into a single portfolio (one-third Fundamental, one-third MinVar and one-third MaxDiv) rebalanced monthly. The MaxDiv data were provided by TOBAM. I also used a second portfolio of optimized protocols where the allocation was determined by a momentum methodology like the one illustrated in Chapter 6. However, although it is useful to simulate a strategy over a long period, we must remain aware that the IT infrastructure required to manage MinVar and MaxDiv protocols probably was not available prior to the early 1990s, at least to most investors.
- Commodities: One index (GSCI) and a single protocol of equally weighted commodities rebalanced monthly, following the simple design presented in Chapter 8.

The number of assets that can be incorporated within the portfolio is constrained by the length of the test period (1980 to September 2011). It seems essential to illustrate the effect of portfolio management processes over several investment cycles, even at the expense of lesser diversification. For example, it would have been interesting to incorporate global (instead of solely US) equity protocols, and it would also have been interesting to incorporate a portfolio of specialized risk premiums as a form of alternative asset component. Finally, a currency exposure strategy could also have been added.

Data availability and time constraints have limited the scope of the simulation. We could also have allowed the three US equity protocols to be allocated individually, instead of being blended into a single portfolio. However, the objective is also to simplify the rebalancing process and limit the adjustments to the most important asset groups. Furthermore, any process can be improved upon. Finally, although we could have incorporated a cash component, the presence of an asset class that has almost no volatility and no correlation to any other asset is very disturbing to an optimization process. Table 11.1 presents the performance characteristics of each component in the portfolio during five periods.

We initially consider six portfolio allocation structures (see Table 11.2). Two of these portfolios are fully indexed. (40/60 I and 60/40 I). We also consider four other portfolios where a portion of the US equity indexed exposure is replaced by either a portfolio of three equal-weight US equity protocols (40/60 P1 and 60/40 P1) or by an optimized portfolio of these same three protocols (40/60 P2 and 60/40 P2). In both cases, the GSCI is replaced by a commodity protocol.

TABLE 11.1 Total Annualized Returns of Portfolio Components (%)

Portfolio Components	Periods				
	1980–2011	1980–1990	1990–2000	2000–2005	2005–2011
10-Year Bond	9.07	12.38	7.97	8.33	6.53
30-Year Bond	9.91	12.14	8.77	10.07	8.26
S&P 500	11.29	18.14	18.80	(2.26)	2.07
Blend of Nonmarket-Cap Equity Protocols	13.30	20.01	14.03	12.92	3.55
MSCI EAFE	8.13	20.14	5.50	(1.25)	2.76
GSCI	6.42	10.92	4.01	14.13	(1.54)
Commodity Protocol	9.78	8.35	9.23	15.74	8.43

TABLE 11.2 Parameters of Simulated Portfolios (%)

Assets	40/60 I	40/60 P1 P2	60/40 I	60/40 P1 P2
Fixed Income	60	60	40	40
Equity	35	35	50	50
S&P 500	25	10	25	15
US Equity Protocols		15		20
MSCI EAFE	10	10	15	15
GSCI	5		10	
Commodity Protocol		5		10

Table 11.3 presents the performance data for all six portfolios. A monthly calendar rebalancing is used for all portfolios. Portfolios 40/60 I and 60/40 I are the two basic portfolio structures against which all future comparisons will be made. Other aspects such as turnover, tracking error and performance patterns such as drawdowns will only be discussed once we have compared the performance of all methodologies.

As I indicated previously, the fixed-income component incorporates 50% of long-term bonds in order to reduce the volatility differential between fixed income and equity, and to improve the diversification bonus. Although this information is not presented, I evaluated the impact specifically related to the diversification bonus that

TABLE 11.3 Performance with Monthly Rebalancing

	Portfolios	1980–2011	1980–1990	1990–2000	2000–2005	2005–2011
GEO Mean (%)	40/60 – I	10.20	14.94	10.67	5.98	6.00
	40/60 – P1	10.59	15.07	10.21	8.21	6.59
	40/60 – P2	10.81	15.13	10.35	8.64	6.98
	60/40 – I	10.14	16.08	10.82	4.68	4.99
	60/40 – P1	10.92	16.07	11.01	7.64	6.05
	60/40 – P2	11.22	16.16	11.19	8.22	6.57
Volatility (%)	40/60 – I	8.01	9.45	6.95	6.93	7.87
	40/60 – P1	7.51	8.86	6.51	6.37	7.49
	40/60 – P2	7.49	8.77	6.58	6.35	7.47
	60/40 – I	8.66	9.00	7.09	8.26	10.32
	60/40 – P1	8.00	8.52	6.60	7.32	9.41
	60/40 – P2	7.97	8.38	6.70	7.28	9.38
GEO Mean to Volatility	40/60 – I	1.27	1.58	1.54	0.86	0.76
	40/60 – P1	1.41	1.70	1.57	1.29	0.88
	40/60 – P2	1.44	1.73	1.57	1.36	0.93
	60/40 – I	1.17	1.79	1.53	0.57	0.48
	60/40 – P1	1.37	1.89	1.67	1.04	0.64
	60/40 – P2	1.41	1.93	1.67	1.13	0.70
Skewness	40/60 – I	(0.14)	(0.18)	(0.27)	(0.09)	0.01
	40/60 – P1	(0.11)	(0.13)	(0.35)	(0.12)	0.11
	40/60 – P2	(0.09)	(0.09)	(0.35)	(0.11)	0.10
	60/40 – I	(0.39)	(0.65)	(0.18)	(0.13)	(0.28)
	60/40 – P1	(0.36)	(0.66)	(0.29)	(0.15)	(0.11)
	60/40 – P2	(0.31)	(0.53)	(0.29)	(0.14)	(0.11)
Kurtosis	40/60 – I	7.37	7.33	4.83	3.86	8.49
	40/60 – P1	6.91	6.54	5.26	3.94	7.92
	40/60 – P2	6.51	6.12	5.29	3.90	7.45
	60/40 – I	11.27	13.92	4.59	3.87	11.52
	60/40 – P1	11.51	13.88	5.05	3.89	11.52
	60/40 – P2	10.10	11.67	5.20	3.79	10.61

results from using a portfolio of higher duration than a standard index. I estimated it to be in the range of 7 to 10 bps. The impact could have been more significant had we incorporated a credit component.

Over 31 years, the investment protocols (P1 and P2) significantly increased portfolio performance, even though we limited the substitution of indexed positions by protocols to only 50% of the combined exposure of equity and commodity. The impact is proportionally more significant for the 60/40 portfolios (+0.78% and +1.08%) than for the 40/60 portfolios (+0.39% and +0.61%). The volatility is also lower in both cases, leading to substantially higher GEO mean to volatility ratios. The same conclusions apply to all subperiods, even though the investment protocols (P1 and P2) underperformed the 40/60 I and 60/40 I portfolios in the 1990s. I completed an identical analysis using yearly rebalancing instead of monthly. Although I will not present those results, they are consistent with those of Chapter 7. Yearly rebalancing is found to be more efficient than monthly rebalancing, and the impact is also more significant for the riskier portfolio.

We now turn to the analyses in the context of risk-based allocation using three methodologies: RiskMetrics, GARCH and CVaR. The objective function is OF2 (Chapter 10). However, I will only present the results for the RiskMetrics methodology, since the GARCH results were marginally different on all measures (GEO mean to volatility, skewness and kurtosis) and not superior overall. The CVaR results were also not convincingly superior, except in specific circumstances. However, we will still consider these other methodologies later on when we evaluate tracking error, turnover and drawdowns to determine if other factors could justify using a more complex methodology.

Table 11.4 compares the statistics for five portfolio structures: the standard monthly calendar rebalancing using indexed components, equal weight protocols or optimized protocols (as in the previous table), and a RiskMetrics volatility-based allocation strategy with optimized protocols and either a monthly or yearly rebalancing interval. Using different rebalancing intervals for the RiskMetrics approach may imply that we are targeting different portfolio objectives. A longer rebalancing interval assumes we are interested in the effect of improving the GEO mean through a more stable long-term volatility while still allowing the benefits of short-term relative momentum in asset classes. However, a portfolio with a shorter rebalancing interval will not benefit significantly from relative asset momentum, but it may, theoretically, offer better protection against significant shocks if drawdowns are indeed preceded by volatility shocks. We also tested a sixth scenario where the rebalancing interval is annual but earlier rebalancing could be triggered by a volatility shock. I will not present those results because this scenario did not improve portfolio efficiency.

The results are fairly impressive because the last approach improved returns by 1.25% and 1.88% annually, even though only 20% to 30% of the entire portfolio allocations have been substituted. We also observed a progressive improvement in GEO mean from the first to last approach, with the exception of the monthly rebalancing of the 60/40 portfolio using the RiskMetrics methodology. However, even

TABLE 11.4 Comparison of Five Portfolio Structures/Rebalancing Processes

	Excess Return		GEO Mean to Volatility	
Methodology	40/60	60/40	40/60	60/40
Base Portfolio	—	—	1.27	1.17
With Equal-Weight Protocols	+0.39%	+ 0.78%	1.41	1.37
With Optimized Protocols	+0.61%	+ 1.08%	1.44	1.41
+ Monthly Managed Volatility	+0.93%	+1.02%	1.49	1.47
Or + Yearly Managed Volatility	+1.25%	+1.88%	1.52	1.57
	Skewness		Kurtosis	
Base Portfolio	(0.14)	(0.39)	7.37	11.27
With Equal-Weight Protocols	(0.11)	(0.36)	6.91	11.51
With Optimized Protocols	(0.09)	(0.31)	6.51	10.10
+ Monthly Managed Volatility	(0.05)	(0.21)	5.86	6.92
Or + Yearly Managed Volatility	(0.06)	(0.18)	6.31	6.48

in this case, the GEO mean to volatility ratio improves because the realized volatility of the risk-managed portfolios is less than that of the base portfolios. It is also very informative that a managed-volatility program with a yearly rebalancing interval improves performance and the GEO mean to volatility so significantly when compared to a monthly rebalancing interval. This indicates that, although it is important to structurally control for the impact of changes in volatility and dependence across time, we should not ignore the benefits of exploiting the persistence of relative cycles between asset classes. In fact, the impact of persistence in relative cycles seems to be captured even more efficiently when portfolios are rebalanced toward a risk target than toward fixed allocation weights (Chapter 7). There are certainly improvements that could be made to this process. Finally, especially for the 60/40 allocation, managing volatility has improved the kurtosis. We will have a more informative view of the impact of managing volatility when we analyze the drawdowns later on.

There are several conclusions that we can draw. First, it obviously pays to rebalance using a risk target, but the benefits are greater for riskier portfolios. This is not unexpected. This is also reflected in the fact that the improvement in kurtosis is far more significant for riskier portfolios.

The CVaR test was done by targeting the 95% 21-day CVaR derived from the historical three-year rolling data. We did not test the yearly rebalancing interval in this case, since it seemed somewhat incoherent to do so. We initially compared the efficiency of this approach with that of a managed-volatility program with a monthly rebalancing interval. In terms of GEO mean to volatility ratio, the results were similar in the case of a 40/60 portfolio, but actually better in the case of 60/40 portfolio because of both better returns and lower volatility. However, the efficiency is similar to what was achieved with a yearly volatility rebalancing.

We will now analyze the turnover, tracking error and drawdowns of several of the different methodologies that we have looked at: monthly calendar rebalancing, managed-volatility programs with monthly or yearly rebalancing using either Risk Metrics or GARCH, and CVaR with monthly rebalancing. Two rolling horizons are used: quarterly and annually. Tracking error and volatility measures are annualized. All tests assume the use of optimized protocols with the exception of the base case (monthly calendar rebalancing). Results are presented in Tables 11.5a to 11.5d.

TABLE 11.5a Statistics for Quarterly Rolling Horizon (40/60) (%)

	Calendar Monthly	RiskMetrics Monthly	GARCH Monthly	RiskMetrics Annual	GARCH Annual	CVaR
ARI Mean	2.48	2.70	2.74	2.77	2.73	2.74
Volatility	8.43	8.56	8.57	8.56	8.51	8.50
Worst Loss	9.35	11.36	10.35	10.15	10.15	11.48
Tracking	—	2.41	2.48	2.39	2.48	2.42

TABLE 11.5b Statistics for Quarterly Rolling Horizon (60/40) (%)

	Calendar Monthly	RiskMetrics Monthly	GARCH Monthly	RiskMetrics Annual	GARCH Annual	CVaR
ARI Mean	2.49	2.72	2.75	2.91	2.86	2.86
Volatility	9.38	8.85	8.83	8.71	8.71	8.67
Worst Loss	18.67	11.73	11.26	10.63	10.31	10.88
Tracking	—	3.88	3.92	4.13	4.28	4.26

TABLE 11.5c Statistics for Annual Rolling Horizon (40/60) (%)

	Calendar Monthly	RiskMetrics Monthly	GARCH Monthly	RiskMetrics Annual	GARCH Annual	CVaR
ARI Mean	10.39	11.32	11.48	11.65	11.49	11.46
Volatility	9.98	9.92	9.92	10.14	10.00	9.86
Worst Loss	15.59	13.01	13.42	13.65	11.96	13.85
Tracking	—	2.96	3.05	2.55	2.62	2.96

TABLE 11.5d Statistics for Annual Rolling Horizon (60/40) (%)

	Calendar Monthly	Risk Metrics Monthly	GARCH Monthly	RiskMetrics Annual	GARCH Annual	CVaR
ARIMean	10.54	11.56	11.63	12.34	12.14	11.98
Volatility	11.27	10.53	10.55	10.37	10.16	10.23
Worst Loss	28.92	15.27	16.42	15.05	14.19	12.42
Tracking	—	4.18	4.18	4.12	4.22	4.63

As indicated before, the simple RiskMetrics methodology with annual rebalancing performed fairly well according to the ARI mean. The volatility of all rebalancing methodologies for 40/60 portfolios is similar, but in the case of the 60/40 portfolios, all risk-based rebalancing methodologies have a slightly lower volatility than the monthly calendar rebalancing. The worst loss is also much smaller for risk-based rebalancing than calendar rebalancing for 60/40 portfolios. For example, the worst loss in the case of a yearly horizon has been reduced from 28.92% (a 3.5 standard deviation event) to about 15% (a more acceptable 2.5 standard deviation event). Risk-based rebalancing leads to more reliable worst-case forecasts (based on the expected volatility), and would help the investor decide the appropriate level of risk. For 40/60 portfolio risks, the worst loss is only slightly improved, which illustrates, as we would have expected, that risk-based rebalancing is obviously more efficient at controlling the losses of riskier portfolios. Of course, we should not base our conclusions solely on the worst loss over a more than 30-year horizon, and I will come back to this aspect later on.

Tracking error is in the range of 2.5% to 3.0% for 40/60 portfolios and 4.0% to 4.5% for 60/40 portfolios. However, 55% to 60% of the tracking error can be attributed to the equity and commodity protocols. The balance of the tracking error is attributed to the risk-based allocation process.

A good way of visualizing the impact of risk management on the return distribution is to rank the yearly rolling returns of different methodologies in increasing order. For example, Figures 11.1a and 11.1b compare the monthly calendar rebalancing to RiskMetrics with annual rebalancing. Figure 11.1a does this for the 40/60 portfolio risk level while Figure 11.1b does this for the 60/40 portfolio risk level. The average performance spread is 1.26% for the 40/60 portfolio, while it is 1.78% for the 60/40.

As we already expected, the impact of risk management is much stronger in the 60/40 case. However, the impact is not only felt at low levels of returns. Even when returns are stronger, the risk-management methodology usually outperforms on average. The same analysis was done for the GARCH approach, but the difference with RiskMetrics was hardly noticeable.

However, although the risk-based methodology seems to dominate the calendar-based methodology, this obviously does not mean that the first methodology outperforms the second for each rolling one-year horizon. In fact, in both cases, the risk-based methodology combined with optimized equity protocols outperforms the calendar-based methodology with indexed instruments about two times out of three over 12-month horizons. It is important to remember that data points on each curve are not representative of a plot against time, but simply of observations that are ranked in increasing order regardless of time.

Figures 11.2a and 11.2b do represent a plot against time. Figure 11.2a illustrates the two-year annualized absolute rolling return for the 40/60 based portfolio with monthly calendar rebalancing and the two-year annualized relative rolling returns of the portfolio with investment protocols and RiskMetrics annual rebalancing (against the based portfolio). Figure 11.2b illustrates the same data but for the 60/40 portfolios.

FIGURE 11.1a Annualized Return Calendar versus RiskMetrics (40/60).

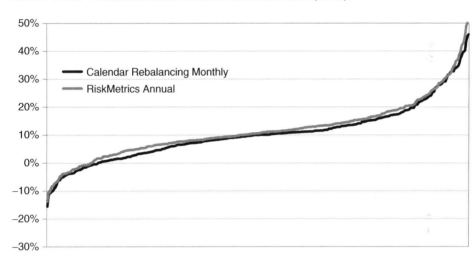

FIGURE 11.1b Annualized Return Calendar versus RiskMetrics (60/40).

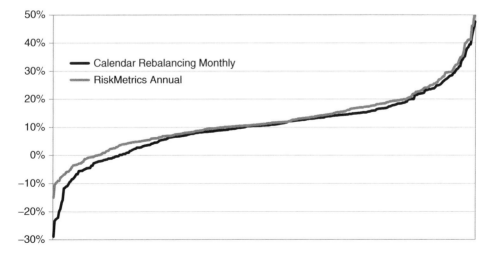

FIGURE 11.2a   40/60 Portfolios—Two Year Annualized Rolling Returns.

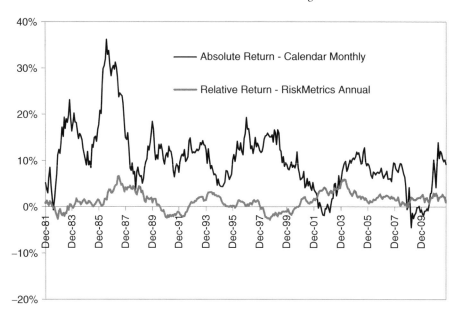

FIGURE 11.2b   60/40 Portfolios—Two Year Annualized Rolling Returns.

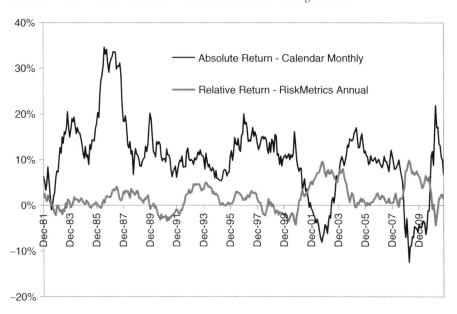

Thus, we may conclude that substantial improvements in Sharpe ratios are possible if we combine optimized equity protocols, commodity protocols and risk-based allocation, even using a simple RiskMetrics approach with yearly rebalancing intervals. Even better results could be achieved if we incorporated other asset components and more efficient processes. However, what about turnover? This information is in Table 11.6.

TABLE 11.6 Turnover

Methodology	Turnover (%)	
	40/60	60/40
Monthly Calendar Rebalancing (Annualized)—Indices	25.0	29.1
Monthly Calendar Rebalancing (Annualized)—Protocols	23.7	27.2
Yearly Calendar Rebalancing—Indices	8.8	10.3
Yearly Calendar Rebalancing—Protocols	8.3	9.2
Risk-Based Rebalancing—RiskMetrics	18.4	28.7
Risk-Based Rebalancing—GARCH	16.0	27.6

A monthly rebalancing would have a fairly significant annualized turnover, but very few investors are likely to implement such a strict process. The yearly rebalancing is much lower and may be more representative of the level of rebalancing required or tolerated for such a simple approach. It is interesting that turnover is lower when efficient investment protocols are included in the portfolio. This is probably a result of their greater performance stability, especially during difficult periods. Although we do not present all of our results, this is a characteristic that is observed in all our comparisons.

Risk-based rebalancing increases turnover, although the relative increase is much greater for a riskier portfolio (three times as much) than for a less risky portfolio (nearly twice as much). This is certainly not surprising. Turnover is slightly lower when GARCH models are used—a consequence of the mean reversion process implicit to GARCH. The turnover level is also not independent of the number of asset components in the portfolio. Other tests indicate that it initially increases as the number of components increase, but it eventually stabilizes and even declines as a portfolio becomes more risk balanced. Also, using a risk tolerance band against the target can reduce turnover.

Conclusion

I have been told that when Eugene Fama was asked, "What do you think about Alpha transport?" he replied, "It is pretty easy to transport since there is no Alpha."

This brings me to another question. What is Alpha? I assume that investors who believe in the Alpha concept would define it as an excess return that cannot be explained by standard risk premiums. They would probably attribute this Alpha to managers' specific expertise and to their ability to extract value from neglected components of the market. Does this book have anything to do with the Alpha concept and whether or not it exists? Let's start by remembering what our core principles are.

Investor discipline is one of the primary ingredients of a successful investing process. However, there are two other essential considerations. First, we need a core approach on which we can base this discipline. Second, we must have great confidence in this core approach, or it is unlikely that we can remain disciplined. Confidence comes from personal character, experience and education.

What is our core message? First, that we have not yet fully exploited diversification; second, that risk premiums are not well balanced; and third, that we must not allow the market to dictate the risk and structural characteristics of our portfolio. Thus, investors must realize that improved portfolio efficiency in a low-interest-rate environment does not necessarily require more complex and illiquid products, but rather smarter assembly and allocation processes.

A fascinating aspect of all that we have discussed is that there are so many ways to achieve the goal of more efficient portfolio solutions. As I was writing this book, I kept thinking of different concepts and methodologies upon which a portfolio platform could be built, some very simple and some more complex. If you think about asset management as a way of expressing required structural core qualities, and if you understand what these core qualities are, you may think of an efficient way in which to design an emerging-market product, a commodity product, an alternative product or an asset allocation product that will have the characteristics you seek and are comfortable with. Furthermore, you do not have to compromise some of your requirements, such as transparency or liquidity. In fact, transparency does not need to be an issue at all, and liquidity is actually a quality that we use to improve portfolio efficiency.

Thus, does this book have anything to do with the Alpha concept? I have mentioned in the Preface that our objective is not to outperform the market, but to allow the market to underperform. This book is not about short-term wins but about long-term processes. It is not about pretending we know what will happen in the next three months. It is not about closet indexing but about building efficient portfolios. Therefore, market indices are simply benchmarks for those who are interested in a comparison, not a starting point for building portfolios. Is this Alpha as most investors understand it? Maybe it is, maybe it is not, but I don't care.

What is important is whether or not applying such principles will still lead to better performance than the market in the long run. I have had many discussions with portfolio managers and CIOs about the concepts raised in this book. Very few of them have a global understanding of the structural deficiencies of traditional portfolios. Furthermore, they are hesitant to implement changes that will differentiate them too much from their peers. Whenever an idea is proposed to an investor, inevitably the investor asks, "Who else is doing this?" It may be a relevant question, but often it becomes a major impediment to innovation. Therefore, I remain convinced that our collective behavior is unlikely to change. Consequently, the door remains open to develop better and more efficient product concepts and achieve superior risk-adjusted returns.

Bibliography

Adkisson, J.A. and Don R. Fraser (2003), "Realigning the stars," Working Paper No. 2003a.

Amenc, Noel and Véronique Le Sourd (2007), "Rating the ratings—A critical analysis of fund rating systems," EDHEC-Risk Institute.

Amenc, Noel, Lionel Martellini, Felix Goltz, and Vincent Milhau (2010), "New frontiers in benchmarking and liability-driven investing," EDHEC-Risk Institute.

Amihud, Yakov, and Ruslan Goyenko (2009), "Mutual fund's R2 as predictor of performance," Stern School of Business, McGill University.

Ang, Andrew, Dimitris Papanikolaou, and Mark M. Westerfield (2011), "Portfolio choice with illiquid assets," Columbia Business School, Northwestern University, University of Southern California.

Arnott, Robert D., and Peter L. Bernstein (2002), "What risk premium is normal?," *Financial Analyst Journal* 58(2), 64–85.

Arnott, Robert D., Andrew L. Berkin, and Jia Ye (2001), "Loss harvesting—What's it worth to the taxable investor?" First Quadrant.

Arnott, Robert D. and Clifford S. Asness (2003), "Surprise! Higher dividends = Higher earnings growth," *Financial Analysts Journal* 55(1), 70–87.

Arnott, Robert (2008), "Where does finance theory lead us astray?" EDHEC Symposium, Nice.

Arnott, Robert D., Jason C. Hsu, and John C. West (2008), *The Fundamental Index: A Better Way to Invest*, John Wiley & Sons, Inc.

Arnott, Robert D., Jason C. Hsu, Feifei Li, and Shane Shepherd (2010), "Valuation-indifferent weighting for bonds," *Journal of Portfolio Management* 36(3), 117–130.

Arnott, Robert, Jason C. Hsu, Jun Liu, and Harry Markowitz (2010), "Does noise create the size and value effects?" University of California at San Diego and Research Affiliates.

Asness, Clifford S., Tobias J. Moskowitz, and Lasse H. Pedersen (2009), "Value and momentum everywhere," AQR Capital Management, Graduate School of Business—University of Chicago and NBER, Stern School of Business—New York University, CEPR, and NBER.

Avramov, Doron, Tarun Chordia, and Amit Goyal (2006), "The impact of trades on daily volatility," *Review of Financial Studies* 19(4), 1241–1277.

Baele, Lieven, Geert Bekaert, and Koen Inghelbrecht (2010), "The determinants of stock and bond comovements," *Review of Financial Studies* 23(6), 2374–2428.

Baker, Malcolm, Brandon Bradley, and Jeffrey Wurgler (2011), "Benchmarks as limits to arbitrage—Understanding the low-volatility anomaly," *Financial Analysts Journal* 67(1), 40–54.

Bank, Steven A. (2004), "The dividend divide in Anglo-American corporate taxation," University of California Los Angeles—Law & Economics Research Paper Series, Research Paper No. 04–3.

Barras, Laurent, O. Scaillet, and Russell Wermers (2010), "False discoveries in mutual fund performance: Measuring luck in estimated alphas," *Journal of Finance* 65(1), 179–216.

Barrett, Timothy B., Donald Pierce, James Perry, and Arun Muralidhar (2011), "Dynamic Beta—Getting paid to manage risks," Investment Management Consultants Association 12(2), 67–78.

Basu, Devraj and Joelle Miffre (2010), "Capturing the risk premium of commodity Futures: The role of Hedging Pressure," SKEMA Business School and EDHEC Business School.

351

Bekaert, Geert, Min Wei, and Yuhang Xing (2002), "Uncovered interest rate parity and the term structure," *Journal of International Money and Finance* 26,1038–1069.

Bekaert, Geert and Xiaozheng, Wang (2010), "Inflation risk and the inflation risk premium," *Economic Policy* 25(64), 755–806.

Bernstein, William J. (2002), "How much pie can you buy?," Efficient Frontier.

Bernstein, William J. and David Wilkinson (1997), "Diversification, rebalancing, and the geometric mean frontier."

Bertrand, Philippe and Jean-Luc Prigent (2002), "Portfolio insurance strategies: OBPI versus CPPI," GREQAM, Université Montpellier.

Bilo, Stéphanie, Christophers Hans, Michel Degosciu, and Heinz Zimmermann (2005), "Risk, returns, and biases of listed private equity portfolios," Morgan Stanley—London, University of Basel.

Birge, John R. and Song Yang (2007), "A model for tax advantages of portfolios with many assets," *Journal of Banking and Finance* 31(11), 3269–3290.

Black, Fisher (1990), "Equilibrium exchange rate hedging," *Journal of Finance* 45(3), 899–908.

Blanchett, David (2007), "The pre-tax costs of portfolio turnover," *Journal of Indexing* 9(3), 34–39.

Blitzer, David M. and Srikant Dash (2005), "Equity duration—Updated duration of the S&P 500," Standard and Poor's.

Bluebook on Integration (2003), Report of the Department of Treasury.

Bodie, Zvi and Victor I. Rosansky (1980), "The risk and return in commodity futures," *Financial Analysts Journal* 36(3), 27–39.

Bogle, John C. (2000), *Common Sense on Mutual Funds: New Imperatives for the Intelligent Investor*, John Wiley & Sons, Inc., 99–100.

Bogle, John C. (2005), "The mutual fund industry 60 years later: For better or worse" in "Bold thinking on investment management," *The Financial Analysts Journal 60th Anniversary Anthology*, CFA Institute, 37–49.

Bogle, John C. (2005), "The relentless rules of humble arithmetic" in "Bold thinking on investment management," *The Financial Analysts Journal 60th Anniversary Anthology*, CFA Institute, 127–144.

Bouchey, Paul (2010), "Tax-Efficient Investing in theory and practice," Parametric.

Boudoukh, Jacob, Roni Michaely, Matthew Richardson, and Michael R. Roberts (2007), "On the importance of measuring payout yield: Implications for empirical asset pricing," *Journal of Finance* 62(2), 877–915.

Brancato, Carolyn Kay and Stephan Rabimov (2007), "The 2007 Institutional Investment Report", The Conference Board of Canada.

Brandes Institute (2008), "Liability-driven investing and equity duration," Brandes Institute Working Paper No. 2008-01.

Brandt, Michael W and Qiang Kang (2002), "On the relationship between the conditional mean and volatility of stock returns: A latent VAR approach," *Journal of Financial Economics* 72(2), 217–257.

Brandt, Michael W., Pedro Santa-Clara, and Rossen Valkanov (2009), "Parametric portfolio policies: Exploiting characteristics in the cross-section of equity returns," *Review of Financial Studies* 22(1), 3411–3447.

Brennan, Michael (1959), "The supply of storage," *American Economic Review*, 48(1), 50–72.

Briand, Remy, Frank Nielsen, and Dan Stefek (2009), "Portfolio of risk premia: A new approach to diversification," Barra Research Insights.

Briner, Rob, David Denyer, and Denise M. Rousseau (2009), "Evidence-based management: Concept cleanup time?" *Academy of Management Perspectives* 23(4), 19–32.

Brock, Woody (2012), *American Gridlock: Why the Right and Left are Both Wrong—Commonsense 101 Solutions to the Economic Crisis*, John Wiley & Sons, Inc.

Brockhouse Cooper (2009), "Manager selection after the financial crisis—Lessons from the crash and how to apply them."

Brown, S.J. and W.N. Goetzmann (1995), "Performance persistence," *Journal of Finance* (50(2), 679–698.

Campbell, John Y., and John Ammer, "What moves the stock and bond market? A variance decomposition for long-term asset returns," *The Journal of Finance* 48(1), 3–37.

Campbell, J. Y., and B. Thompson (2008), "Predicting Excess stock returns out of sample: can anything beat the historical average?", *Review of Financial Studies* 29(4), 1509–1531.

Campbell, John Y. and Samuel B. Thompson (2008), "Predicting excess stock returns out of sample: Can anything beat the historical average*?" Review of Financial Studies* 21(4), 1509–1531.

Campbell, John Y. and Tuomo Vuolteenaho (2008), "Inflation illusion and stock prices," *American Economic Review* 94(2), 20–23.

Campbell, John, Karine Serfaty-de Medeiros, and Luis M. Viceira (2010), "Global currency hedging," *Journal of Finance* 65(1), 87–121.

Cao, Bolong (2008), "Testing methods and the rebalancing policies for retirement portfolios," Ohio University—Department of Economics.

Cao, Dan and Jérôme Teiletche (2007), "Reconsidering asset allocation involving illiquid assets," *Journal of Asset Management* 8(4), 267–282.

Carhart, Mark M. (1997), "On persistence in mutual fund performance," *Journal of Finance* 52(1), 57–82.

Carhart, Mark M., Jennifer N. Carpenter, Anthony W. Lynch, and David K. Musto (2002), "Mutual fund survivorship," *The Review of Financial Studies* 15(5), 1439–1463.

Carlson, John A. and Carol L. Osler (2003), "Currency risk premiums—Theory and evidence," Purdue University, Brandeis University.

Carrieri, Francesca, Vihang Errunza and Basma Majerbi (2004), "Does emerging market exchange risk affect global equity prices?," McGill University, University of Virginia and University of British Columbia.

Carver, Andrew B. (2009), "Do leveraged and inverse ETFs converge to zero?" *Institutional Investors Journal* 2009(1), 144–149.

Chan, Louis K. C., Narasimhan Jegadeesh, and Josef Lakonishok (1996), "Momentum strategies," *Journal of Finance* 51,1681–1713.

Chen, C., R. Chen, and G. Bassett (2007), "Fundamental indexation via smoothed cap weights," *Journal of Banking and Finance* 31(12), 3486–3502.

Chen, Jerry (2009), "After-tax asset allocation," Simon Fraser University.

Chen, Joseph, Harrison Hong, Ming Huang, and Jeffrey D. Kubik (2004), "Does fund size erode mutual fund performance? The role of liquidity and organization," *American Economic Review* 96(5), 1216–2302.

Choueifaty, Yves (2006), "Methods and systems for providing an anti-benchmark portfolio," USPTO No. 60/816,276 filed June 22, 2006.

Choueifaty, Yves and Yves Coignard (2008), "Toward Maximum Diversification," *The Journal of Portfolio Management* 35(1), 40–51.

Choueifaty, Yves, Tristan Froidure, and Julien Reynier (2011), "Properties of the most diversified portfolio," TOBAM.

Chow, Tzee-men, Jason Hsu, Vitali Kalesnik and Bryce Little (2011), "A survey of alternative equity index strategies," *Financial Analysts Journal* 67(5), 37–57.

Christian, Jeffrey M. (2007), "Some thoughts on risk management for commodity portfolios," *The Handbook of Commodity Investing*, Chapter 12, John Wiley & Sons, Inc.

Christoffersen, Peter, Vihang Errunza, Kris Jacobs, and Xisong Jin (2010), "Is the potential for international diversification disappearing?" McGill University, Houston University.

Clark, Truman A. (1999), "Efficient portfolio rebalancing," Dimensional Fund Advisors Inc.

Clements, Jonathan (1999), "Stock funds just don't measure up," *Wall Street Journal*, October 5.

Cocco, Joao F., Francisco J. Gomes, and Pascal J. Maenhout (2005), "Consumption and portfolio choice over life cycle," *Review of Financial Studies* 18(2), 491–533.

Connors, Richard J. (2010), *Warren Buffett on Business*, John Wiley & Sons.

Constantinides, G. (1983), "Capital market equilibrium with personal tax," *Econometrica* 51, 611–636.

Cootner, P. (1960), "Returns to speculators—Telser versus Keynes," *Journal of Political Economy* 68(4), 396–404.

Cremers, Martijn K.J. and Antti Petajisto. (2009), "How active is your fund manager? A new measure that predicts performance," Yale School of Management.

Cutler, D.M., J. M. Poterba, and L.H. Summers (1989),"What moves stock prices?" *Journal of Portfolio Management* 15(3), 4–12.

Dalio, Ray (2005), "Engineering targeted returns and risks," Bridgewater.

Dammon, Robert M., Chester S. Spatt, and Harold H. Zhang (2000), "Diversification and capital gains taxes with multiple risky assets," Carnegie Mellon University.

Dammon, Robert M., Chester S. Spatt, and Harold H. Zhang (2001), "Optimal consumption with capital gains taxes," *Review of Financial Studies* 14, pp. 583–616.

Dammon, Robert M., Chester S. Spatt, and Harold H. Zhang (2003), "Capital gains taxes and portfolio rebalancing," TIAA-CREF Institute.

Dammon, Robert M., Chester S. Spatt, and Harold H. Zhang (2004), "Optimal asset location and allocation with taxable and tax-deferred investing," *Journal of Finance* 59(3), 999–1037.

Daniel, Kent D., David Hirshleifer, and Avanidhar Subrahmanyam (2000), "Covariance risk, mispricing and the cross section of security returns," NBER, Working Paper 7615.

Daniel, Kent D., and Sheridan Titman (1999), "Market efficiency in an irrational world," *Financial Analyst Journal*, 55, 28–40.

Daryanani, Gobind (2008), "Opportunistic Rebalancing," Journal of Financial Planning 18(1), 44–54.

Deaves, Richard and Itzhak Krinsky (1995), "Do futures prices for commodities embody risk premiums?," *The Journal of Futures Markets* 15(6), 637–648.

Del, Guercio and Paula A. Tkac (2001), "Star Power—The effect of Morningstar ratings in mutual fund flows," Working Paper No. 2001–15, Federal Reserve Bank of Atlanta.

Demay, Paul, Sébastien Maillard and Thierry Roncalli (2010), "Risk-based indexation," Lyxor Asset Management.

DeMiguel, Victor, Lorenzo Garlappi, and Raman Uppal (2007), "Optimal versus naive diversification—How inefficient is the 1/N portfolio strategy?" London Business School, McCombs School of Business—University of Texas at Austin.

diBartolomeo, Dan, and Erik Witkowski (1997), "Mutual fund misclassification: Evidence based on style analysis," *Financial Analysts Journal* 53(5), 32–43.

Djehiche, Boualem and Jonas Rinné (2006), "Can stocks help mend the asset and liability mismatch?" Working Paper, Informed Portfolio Management, AB Stockholm.

Dusak, Katherine (1973), "Futures trading and investor returns—An investigation of commodity market risk premiums," *Journal of Political Economy* 81(6), 1387–1406.

Engel, Charles (1996), "The forward discount anomaly and the risk premium: A survey of recent evidence," *Journal of Empirical Finance* 3, 123–192

Engle, Robert (2001), "GARCH 101—The use of ARCH/GARCH models in applied econometrics," *Journal of Economic Perspectives* 15(4), 157–168.

Erb, Claude B. and Campbell R. Harvey (2006), "The strategic and tactical value of commodity futures," *Financial Analysts Journal* 62(2), 69–97.

Erb, Claude, Campbell R. Harvey, and Christian Kempe (2007), "Performance characteristics of commodity futures," *The Handbook of Commodity Investing*, Chapter 8, John Wiley & Sons, Inc.

Estrada, Javier (2006), "Fundamental indexing and international diversification," IESE Business School.

Estrada, Javier (2010), "Geometric mean maximization: An overlooked portfolio approach?," IESE Business School.

Fama, Eugene F. and Kenneth R. French (1988), "Dividend yields and expected stock returns," *Journal of Financial Economics* 22(1), 3–25.

Fama, Eugene F. and Kenneth R. French (1992), "The cross-section of expected stock returns," *Journal of Finance* 47(2), 427–465.

Fama, Eugene F. and Kenneth R. French (2007a), "Migration," *Financial Analysts Journal* 63(3), 48–58.

Fama, Eugene F. and Kenneth R. French (2007b), "The Anatomy of Value and Growth Stock Returns," *Financial Analysts Journal* 63(6), 44–54.

Fernholz, R., R. Garvy and J. Hannon (1998), "Diversity-weighted indexing," *Journal of Portfolio Management* 24, 74–82 .

Ferson, Wayne E. and Campbell R. Harvey (1991), "The variation of economic risk premiums," *Journal of Political Economy* 99(2), 385–415.

Fink, Jim (2012), "Burton Malkiel: Value investor?" *Investing Daily*, March 23.

Fisher, Kenneth L. and Meir Statman (2003), "Hedging currencies with hindsight and regret," Fisher Investments Inc., Santa Clara University.

Fleming, Jeff, Chris Kirby, and Barbara Ostdiek (2001), "The economic value of volatility timing," *Journal of Finance* 56(1), 329–352.

Francis, John Clark, Christopher Hessel, Jun Wang, and Ge Zhang (2009), "Portfolios weighted by repurchase and total payout," Zicklin School of Business, Long Island University.

Fraser-Sampson, Guy (2007), "Private equity as an asset class," Wiley Finance.

Froot, Kenneth (1993), "Currency hedging over long horizons," National Bureau of Economic Research, Working Paper No. 4355.

Froot, Kenneth. A. and Richard Thaler (1990), "Anomalies: Foreign exchange," *Journal of Economic Perspectives* 4, 179–192.

Fuss, Roland, Christian Hoppe, and Dieter G. Kaiser (2008), "Review of commodity futures performance benchmarks," *The Handbook of Commodity Investing*, Chapter 7, John Wiley & Sons, Inc.

Gastineau, Gary L. (1995), "The currency hedging decision: A search for synthesis in asset allocation," *Financial Analysts Journal* 51(3), 8–17.

Goetzmann, W.N., and Roger Ibbotson (1994), "Do winners repeat?" *Journal of Portfolio Management* 20(2), 9–18.

Goldman Sachs Asset Management (2012), "S&P GIVI: Active insight plus passive efficiency," Perspectives (April).

Goltz, Felix and, Guang Feng (2007), "Reactions to the EDHEC study—Assessing the quality of stock market indices," An EDHEC Risk and Asset Management Research Centre Publication.

Gorton, Gary and Geert Rouwenhorst (2006), "Facts and fantasies about commodity futures," *Financial Analysts Journal* 62(2), 47–68.

Gorton, Gary B., Fumio Hayashi, and K. Geert Rouwenhorst (2007), "The fundamentals of commodity futures return," Yale ICF Working Paper No. 07–08.

Goyal, Amit and Ivo Welch (2008), "A comprehensive look at the empirical performance of equity premium prediction," *The Review of Financial Studies* 21(4), 1455–1508.

Goyal, Amit, and Sunil Wahal (2008), "The selection and termination of investment management firms by sponsor plans," Goizueta Business School—Emory University, and WP Carey School of Business—Arizona State University.

Graham, Benjamin (1976), "A conversation with Benjamin Graham," *Financial Analysts Journal* 32(5), 20–23.

Grantier, Bruce (2012), "Equity Duration: Sensitivity to Discount Rates and the Franchise Factor Model," InvestorLit Review #1.

Grauer, Frederick L.A.W. and Robert H. Litzenberger (1979), "The pricing of commodity futures contracts, nominal bonds and other risky assets under commodity price uncertainty," *Journal of Finance* 34(1), 69–83.

Hafner, Reinhold and Maria Heiden (2007), "Statistical analysis of commodity futures returns," *The Handbook of Commodity Investing*, Chapter 9, John Wiley & Sons, Inc.

Hasanhodzic, Jasmina and Andrew W. Lo (2007), "Can hedge-fund returns be replicated? The linear case," *Journal of Investment Management* 5(2), 5–45.

Hillier, David, Paul Draper, and Robert Faff (2006), "Do precious metals shine? An investment perspective," *Financial Analysts Journal* 62(2), 98–106.

Hirshleifer, D. (1990), "Hedging pressure and future price movements in a general equilibrium model," *Econometrica*. 58, 411–428.

Hocquard, Aleaxandre, Nicolas Papageorgiou and Ralph Uzzan (2011–2012), "Insights corporate newsletter—Constant volatility strategy update," Brockhouse Cooper.

Hong, Harrison and Jeremy C. Stein (1999), "A unified theory of underreaction, momentum trading and overreaction in asset markets," *Journal of Finance* 54(6), 2143–2184.

Horan, Steven and David Adler (2009), "Tax-aware investment management practice," *Journal of Wealth Management* 12(2), 71–88.

Hossein, Kazemi, Thomas Schneeweis, and Dulari Pancholi (2003), "Performance persistence for mutual funds—Academic evidence," Center for International Securities and Derivatives Markets.

Hsu, Jason C. (2006), "Cap-weighted portfolios are sub-optimal portfolios," *Journal of Investment Management* 4(3), 1–10.

Ibbotson, Roger G. and Amita K. Patel (2002), "Do winners repeat with style?," Yale IFC Working Paper No. 00-70.

Ibbotson, Roger G., Chen Zhiwu, and Wendy Y. Hu (2011), "Liquidity as an investment style," Yale School of Management and Zebra Capital Management LLC.

Idzorek, Thomas (2007), "Private equity and strategic asset allocation," Ibbotson Associates.

Idzorek, Thomas M., James X. Xiong, and Roger G. Ibbotson (2011), "The liquidity style of mutual funds," Morningstar Investment Management and Zebra Capital Management.

Inderst, Georg (2009), "Pension fund investment in infrastructure," OECD Working Paper on Insurance and Private Pensions, No. 32.

Ilmanen, Antti (2011), *Expected Returns: An Investor's Guide to Harvesting Market Rewards*, Wiley Finance.

Ilmanen, Antti and Jared Kizer (2012), "The death of diversification has been greatly exaggerated," *Journal of Portfolio Management* (Spring), 15–27.

Investment Company Institute, "2009 Investment Company Factbook—A review of trends and activity in the investment company industry," 49th Edition.

Irving Fisher (1930), "The theory of interest as determined by impatience to spend income and opportunity to invest it," MacMillan Company.

Jeffrey, Robert H. and Robert D. Arnott (1993), "Is your alpha big enough to cover its taxes?" First Quadrant Corporation.

Jegadeesh, Narasimhan and Sheridan Titman (1993). "Returns to buying winners and selling losers: Implications for stock market efficiency," *Journal of Finance* 48(1), 65–91.

Jegadeesh, Narasimhan and Sheridan Titman (2001), "Momentum," University of Illinois, University of Texas and NBER.

Jin, Xue-jun, and Xia-Ian Yang (2004), "Empirical study on mutual fund objective classification," *Journal of Zhejiang University Science* 5(5), 533–538.

Jondeau, Eric and Michael Rockinger (2008), "The economic value of distributional timing," Swiss Finance Institute.

Jun Tu and Guofu Zhou (2011), "Markowitz meets Talmud: A combination of sophisticated and naïve diversification strategies," *Journal of Financial Economics* 99, 204–215.

Jurek, Jakub W. (2009), "Crash-neutral currency carry trades," Princeton University.

Kaldor, Nicholas (1939), "Speculation and economic stability," *Review of Economic Studies*, 7, 1–27.

Kaplan, S. and A. Schoar (2005), "Private Equity Performance: Returns, persistence and capital flows," *Journal of Finance* 60, 1791–1823.

Kat, Harry M. (2006), "How to evaluate a new diversifier with 10 simple questions," Cass Business School.

Kat, Harry M. and Roel C.A. Oomen (2006a), "What every investor should know about commodities—Part I: Univariate return analysis," Cass Business School—City University.

Kat, Harry M. and Roel C.A. Oomen (2006b), "What every investor should know about commodities—Part II: Multivariate return analysis," Cass Business School—City University.

Kat, Harry M. and Helder P. Palaro (2006), "Replicating hedge fund returns using futures—A European perspective," Cass Business School.

Keynes, John M. (1930), *A Treatise on Money* Vol. 2, London: Macmillan.

Khorona, Ajay, Henri Servaes, and Peter Tufano (2006), "Mutual funds fees around the world," Working Paper, Georgia Institute of Technology, London Business School, Harvard Business School.

Kim, Moon, Ravi Shukla, and Michael Tomas (2000), "Mutual fund objective misclassification," *Journal of Economics and Business* 52(4), 309–323.

Kirkegaard, Jacob F. and Carmen M Reinhart (2012), "The return of financial repression in the aftermath of the great contraction," Peterson Institute Working Paper.

Kolb, R.W. (1992), "Is normal backwardation normal?" *Journal of Futures Market* 12(1), 75–91.

Kong, Aiguo, David E. Rapach, Kack K. Strauss, and Guofu Zhou (2011), "Predicting market components out of sample—asset allocation implications," *Journal of Portfolio Management* 37(4), 29–41.

Kopcke, Richard W. and Francis M. Vitagliano (2009), "Fees and trading costs of equity mutual funds in 401(k) plans and potential savings from ETFs and commingled trusts," Center for Retirement Research at Boston College.

Kritzman, Mark, Sebastien Page, and David Turkington (2010), "In defense of optimization: the fallacy of 1/N," The Financial Analysts Journal 66(2), 31–39.

Lack, Simon (2012), *The Hedge Fund Mirage: The Illusion of Big Money and Why It's Too Good to Be True*, John Wiley & Sons, Inc.

Landon, Stuart and Constance Smith (1999), "The risk premium, exchange rate expectations, and the forward exchange rate: Estimates for the Yen-Dollar rate," MPRA Paper 9775, University Library of Munich, Germany.

Langlois, Hugues and Jacques Lussier (2009), "Fundamental indexing—It's not about the fundamentals," Desjardins Global Asset Management.

Lee, Marlena I. (2008), "Rebalancing and returns," Dimensional Fund Advisors.

Leibowitz, Martin L. (1986), "Total portfolio duration: A new perspective on asset allocation," *Financial Analysts Journal* 42(5), 19–29.

Leibowitz, Martin, and Anthony Bova (2010), "Portfolio strategy—Policy portfolios and rebalancing behavior," Morgan Stanley Research North America.

Leibowitz, Martin and Anthony Bova (2011), "Portfolio strategy—The correlation paradox", Morgan Stanley Research North America.

Leibowitz, Martin L. and Stanley Kogelman (2004), *Franchise Value: A Modern Approach to Securities Analysis*, John Wiley & Sons, Inc.

Lopez, Claude and Javier Reyes (2007), "Real interest rates stationarity and per capita consumption growth rate," University of Cincinnati.

Lussier, Jacques, and Sébastien Monciaud (2007), "Developing and investment culture," Desjardins Global Asset Management.

Maginn, John L., Donald L. Tuttle and Dennis W. McLeavey (2010), Managing Investment Portfolios: A Dynamic Process, John Wiley & Sons, Inc.

Maillard, Sébastien, Thierry Roncalli and Jérôme Teiletche (209), "On the properties of equally-weighted risk contributions portfolios," SGAM Alternative Investments and Lombard Odier.

Malkiel, Burton G. (1995), "Returns from investing in equity mutual funds 1971–1991," *Journal of Finance* 50(2), 549–572.

Marcucci, Juri (2005), "Forecasting stock market volatility with regime-switching GARCH models," University of California at San Diego.

Markowitz, H. (1952), "Portfolio Selection," *Journal of Finance* 7(1), 77–91.

Martellini, L and V. Milhau (2010), "From deterministic to stochastic life-cycle investing—Implications for the design of improved forms of target-date funds," EDHEC-Risk Institute.

McCalla, Douglas B. (1997), "Enhancing the efficient frontier with portfolio rebalancing," *Journal of Pension Plan Investing* 1(4), 16–32.

Modigliani, Franco and Richard A. Cohn (1979), "Inflation, rational valuation and the market," *Financial Analysts Journal* 35(2), 24–44.

Monks, Robert A.G. and Nell Minow (2011), *Corporate Governance*, John Wiley & Sons, Inc.

Mulcahy, Diane, Bill Weeks, and Harold S. Bradley (2012). "We have met the enemy . . . and he is us—Lessons from twenty years of the Kauffman Foundation's investment in venture capital funds and the triumph of hope over experience," The Ewing Marion Kauffman Foundation.

Muralidhar, Arun (2011), "LDI: Less than desirable investing," aiCIO Magazine, November 15.

O'Neill, Jim (2012), "Monthly Insights—April 12th", Goldman Sachs Asset Management.

Papageorgiou, Nicholas, Alexandre Hocquard, and Sunny Ng (2010), "Gestion dynamique du risque: Une approche par contrôle de la volatilité," Document technique, Brockhouse Cooper.

Patrick, Casabona, Frank J. Fabozzi, and Jack C. Francis (1984), "How to apply duration to equity analysis," *Journal of Portfolio Management* (Winter).

Perold, A. (1986), "Constant portfolio insurance." Harvard Business School, unpublished manuscript.

Perold, A. and W. Sharpe (1988), "Dynamic strategies for asset allocation," *Financial Analysts Journal* (January-February), 16–27.

Perold, André F. and Evan C. Schulman (1988), "The free lunch in currency hedging: Implications for investment policy and performance standards," *Financial Analysts Journal* 44(3), 45–50.

Peterson, James D., Paul A. Pietranico, Mark W. Riepe, and Fran Xu (2002), "Explaining after-tax mutual fund performance," *Financial Analysts Journal* 58(1), 75–86.

Pfeffer, Jeffrey and Robert I. Sutton (2006), "Management half-truths and nonsense—How to practice evidence-based management," adapted from *Hard Facts, Dangerous Half-Truths, and Total Nonsense: Profiting from Evidence-Based Management*, Harvard Business School Press.

Phalippou, Ludovic and Oliver Gottschalg (2009), "The performance of private equity funds," *Review of Financial Studies* 22(4), 1747–1776.

Phelps S., and L. Detzel (1997), "The non-persistence of mutual fund performance," *Quarterly Journal of Business and Economics* 36, 55–69.

Plaxco, Lisa M. and Robert D. Arnott (2002), "Rebalancing a global policy benchmark," First Quadrant.

Pliska, Stanley and Kiyoshi Suzuki (2004), "Optimal tracking for asset allocation with fixed and proportional transaction costs," *Quantitative Finance* 4(2), 233–243.

Pollet, Joshua M. and Mungo Wilson (2006), "Average correlations and stock market returns," University of Illinois, Hong-Kong University.

Rajamony, Jayendran and Shanta Puchtler (2011), "What is minimum variance and how does it work?" Numeric Investors.

Reay, Trish, Whitney Berta, and Melanie Kazman Kohn (2009), "What's the evidence on evidence-based management?" *Academy of Management Perspectives* 23(4), 5–18.

Reinhart, Carmen M. and Vincent R. Reinhart (2010), "After the fall," Federal Reserve Bank of Kansas City, Jackson Hole Symposium.

Research & Affiliates (2008), "The perfect storm: Part 2," RAFI Fundamentals (December).

Rice, Matthew, and Geoff Strotman (2007), "The next chapter in the active vs. passive management debate," DiMeo Schneider & Associates, L.L.C.

Rice, Matthew, and Geoff Strotman (2010), "The next chapter in the active versus passive debate," DiMeo Schneider & Associates, L.L.C.

Riepe, M.V. and B. Swerbenski (2007), "Rebalancing for taxable accounts," *Journal of Financial Planning* 20(4), 40–44.

Roache, Shaun K. and Matthews D. Merritt (2006), "Currency risk premia in global stock markets," International Monetary Fund.

Rohleder, Martin, Hendrik Scholz, and Marco Wilkens (2007), "Survivorship bias and mutual fund performance: Relevance, significance, and methodological differences," Ingolstadt School of Management, Catholic University of Eichstaett-Ingolstadt.

Roncalli, Thierry and Guillaume Weisang (2008), "Tracking problems, hedge fund replication and alternative Beta," SGAM Alternative Investments and University of Evry.

Shiller, R. (1981), "Do stock prices move too much to be justified by subsequent changes in dividends?" *American Economic Review* 71(3), 421–436.

Siegel, Laurence B. and M. Barton Waring (2004), "TIPS, the dual duration, and the pension plan," *Financial Analysts Journal* 60(5), 52–64.

Schmidt, Daniel M. (2006), "Private equity versus stocks—Do the alternative Asset's risk and return characteristics add value to the portfolio?," *The Journal of Alternative Investments* 9(1), 28–47.

SmithBarney-Consulting Group (2005), "The art of rebalancing—How to tell when your portfolio needs a tune-up?"

Solnik, Bruno (1988), "Global asset management," *Journal of Portfolio Management* 35(2), 43–51.

Solnik, Bruno (1998), "Why not diversify internationally rather than domestically?" *Financial Analysts Journal* 30(4), 48–54.

Sorensen, Eric H. and Sanjoy Ghosh (2010), "Rewarding fundamentals," *Journal of Portfolio Management* 36(4), 71–76.

S&P Indices—Research & Design (2010), "Equal weight indexing—Seven Years later."

Stein, David M., Andrew F. Siegel, Premkumar Narasimhan, and Charles E. Appeadu (2000), "Diversification in the presence of taxes," *Journal of Portfolio Management* 27(1), 61–71.

Stockton, Kimberly A., Scott J. Donaldson and Anatoly Shtekhman (2008), "Liability-driven investing: A tool for managing pension plan funding volatility," Vanguard Investment Counseling & Research.

Tamura, H. and Y. Shimizu (2005), "Global fundamental indices—Do they outperform market-cap weighted indices on a global basis?" Global Quantitative Research, Nomura Securities Co Ltd, Tokyo.

The United States Department of Treasury (2003), "General explanation of the administration's fiscal year 2004 revenue proposals."

Tugwell, Rexford G. (1933), "The Industrial discipline and the governmental arts".

Turkington, David (2011), "Regime shifts and Markov-switching models: Implications for dynamic strategies," State Street Associates.

Walker, Eduardo (2008), "Strategic currency hedging and global portfolio investments upside down," *Journal of Business Research*, 61, 657–668.

Walker, Susanne (2010), "Morgan Stanley issues a mea culpa on Treasuries forecast that was 'wrong'," Bloomberg, August 20, http://www.bloomberg.com/news/2010-08-20/morgan-stanley-issues-a-mea-culpa-on-treasuries-forecast-that-was-wrong-.html.

Walkshausl, Christian and Sebastian Lobe (2009), "Fundamental indexing around the world," University of Regensburg.

Wang, Peng, Rodney N. Sullivan, and Yizhi Ge (2011), "Risk-based dynamic asset allocation with extreme tails and correlations," Georgetown University, CFA Institute.

Weber, Barbara (2011), "Infrastructure as an asset class," CFA Conference Montreal,

William Reichenstein (2006), "After-tax asset allocation," *Financial Analyst Journal* 62(4), 14–19.

Wotherspoon, Gordon and Geoff Longmeier (2006), "The value of tax efficient investments—An analysis of after-tax mutual fund and index returns," *Journal of Wealth Management* 9(2), 46–53.

Xu, Xiaoquing Eleanor, Liu Jiong, and Anthony L. Loviscek (2010), "Hedge fund attrition, survivorship bias, and performance—Perspectives from the global financial crisis," Seton Hall University, TIAA-CREF.

Zhang, Chu (2008), "Decomposed Fama-French factors for the size and book-to-market effects," Department of Finance—Hong Kong University of Science and Technology.

Index

Printed and bound by CPI Group (UK) Ltd, Croydon, CR0 4YY

17/04/2025